D0207922

The Encyclopedia of
Native American
Legal Tradition

THE ENCYCLOPEDIA OF NATIVE AMERICAN LEGAL TRADITION

Edited by
Bruce Elliott Johansen

Foreword by Charles Riley Cloud

Greenwood Press
Westport, Connecticut • London

Library of Congress Cataloging-in-Publication Data

The encyclopedia of Native American legal tradition / edited by Bruce
   Elliott Johansen ; foreword by Charles Riley Cloud.
       p.   cm.
   Includes bibliographical references and index.
   ISBN 0–313–30167–0 (alk. paper)
     1. Indians of North America—Legal status, laws, etc.
   2. Customary law—United States.   I. Johansen, Bruce E. (Bruce
   Elliott), 1950–
   KF8204.E53   1998
   346.7301'3—dc21   97–21994

British Library Cataloguing in Publication Data is available.

Library of Congress Catalog Card Number: 97–21994
ISBN: 0–313–30167–0

First published in 1998

Greenwood Press, 88 Post Road West, Westport, CT 06881
An imprint of Greenwood Publishing Group, Inc.

Printed in the United States of America

The paper used in this book complies with the
Permanent Paper Standard issued by the National
Information Standards Organization (Z39.48–1984).

10 9 8 7 6 5 4 3 2 1

Copyright Acknowledgments

The editor and the publisher are grateful to the following for granting permission to reprint
from their materials:

NATURAL MAN (AND WOMAN) copyright © 1996 by Bruce A. Burton

HAUDENOSAUNEE (IROQUOIS) WOMEN, LEGAL AND POLITICAL STATUS
copyright © 1996 by Barbara A. Mann

SEQUOYAH STATEHOOD DRIVE © 1997 by Barbara A. Mann

Contents

Foreword: To Save a Democracy

A recent television program on the History Channel purported to tell the true story of Pocahontas. The program's host, Roger Mudd, while discussing the English settlement at Jamestown, indicated with authority that it was then and there that the first representative government in America was assembled. After all, several months before the program was aired, the Commonwealth of Virginia and its public officers had celebrated and announced to the world that representative government in America began at Jamestown in the colony of Virginia. Presumably it was imported from England. In addition, visitors today to colonial Williamsburg and the Virginia museums at Jamestown and Yorktown learn little, if anything, about the representative democratic governments of the Indians who had lived beyond memory in what the newcomers called Virginia and America. Few visitors are aware that these democratic Indian nations and their representative governments were here and flourishing long before the time of Columbus. Few know that the word "caucus" is an Indian word adopted into English that describes a basic ingredient of democratic representative government. There was no word for it in the English language.

None of these visitors are told about the Iroquois representative government and how it began a confederacy uniting five independent tribal-state representative governments. Most would be amazed to discover that this Indian federal government was spread out over the present states of New York, Pennsylvania, and Ohio and extended down into what is now Virginia. They would find it hard to believe that the law of this confederacy was retained in a constitution of, by, and for its people that dealt with many areas similar to those of the U.S. Constitution. Other than for certain federal areas such as common defense (as is the case in America today), local matters remained the sole responsibility of local tribal-state governments. Sovereignty of the individual was paramount to all other considerations. Personal liberty was sacred. Freedoms of speech and religion were preserved. It was the Iroquois leaders, citing the example of their confederation, who first urged the union of the colonies for strength and protection. Benjamin Franklin was an avid listener and reporter. His Articles of Confederation bear a remarkable resemblance to the Iroquois Constitution.

Most of us who learned Indian history from movies are surprised to find out about the Iroquois Constitution, which predated the U.S. Constitution by several hundred years. It provided for a Council not unlike the U.S. Congress with checks to balance the power between the original five tribal-state governments. It promoted consensus and harmony and produced peace. Local autonomy was honored and preserved. Freedom of speech was protected, and women had the right to vote. Representative leaders could be recalled from the Council for failure to act appropriately. Power was possessed by the people and flowed to their leaders, who were required to be servants of the people. Most who examine the available documentary evidence observed and recorded by some of the Founding Fathers have no doubt that the Iroquois and other Indian nations such as the Cherokee influenced and made substantial contributions to U.S. representative democracy. In 1987 a resolution of the One Hundredth Congress, First Session, acknowledged these contributions. Despite the evidence available today, many still cling to the belief that ideas of freedom and democracy, including representative government, were only to be found in England and were exported to America by the English. For some, faith in this belief rivals a religious fervor so great that those who have spoken about Indian influence on U.S. democracy seemingly are considered to have committed acts of blasphemy.

The truth of the matter is that for most of us older citizens, Indians and their contributions were written out of our history books. During the recent bicentennial celebration of the U.S. Constitution and Bill of Rights, many prominent leaders and scholars exposed their lack of knowledge in this area. Henry F. Graff, a professor of history at Columbia University, wrote that "the Bill of Rights is a homegrown product. Americans [immigrants in America] invented the freedom it guarantees: *nowhere in the world was there a document prescribing it or an institution practicing it that the founding fathers could plagiarize or ape*" (emphasis added).[1]

Former U.S. Supreme Court Chief Justice Warren E. Burger was obviously unaware of Indian history known to many of the Founding Fathers such as Benjamin Franklin and John Adams when he assumed that the Founding Fathers invented our concept of democracy and declared that there was no other government in the world that governed with separated powers and divided powers providing checks and balances on the exercise of authority by those who governed in the period between 1775 and 1800. During that period, John Adams, in his *Defence of the Constitutions of the Governments of the United States of America*,[2] urged the Constitutional Convention to study the governments of the Indians because they have the most perfect example of separation of powers.

Another such older American is University of Virginia law professor A. E. "Dick" Howard. He enjoys a national reputation as a leading scholar on constitutional law. In the past, Howard has agreed with Yorktown museum staff in saying that there is no "scholarly" research to support the claim that Native American governments influenced the writing of the U.S. Constitution and its Bill of Rights or that they contributed to the patriots' cause during the American Revolution.[3] Apparently Professor Howard was taught the same myth as the rest of us. In the same vein, consider Rhode Island Supreme Court justice Joseph R. Weisberger. His lectures are in great demand all over the United States, and he is an eminent national authority on constitutional law. He frequently teaches judges at the National Judicial College. He wrote an article, "The First Amendment: Have We Gone too Far?" that was published in the *Judges Journal*, a magazine of the Judicial Division of the American Bar Association. In this article, Justice Weisberger proposed that the Founding Fathers in denying Congress the power to abridge freedom of speech and the press intended only to preserve that freedom that had been enforced by the English and colonial courts. He agreed with the statement that "they [the Founding Fathers] did not intend to create a new absolute concept *that had never existed on earth*" (emphasis added).[4] Contrary to this statement, historical evidence abounds to show that absolute freedom of speech was an important part of the individual sovereignty of Indians. Undoubtedly it helps explain why so many Europeans broke the laws of their governments and took up the ways of the Indians, while very few Indians left their governments and adopted those of the Europeans.

Not so long ago, I would not have questioned what has been said by these scholars. I would have agreed that representative government began at Jamestown. After all, even though I am a card-carrying member of the Cherokee Nation of Oklahoma, I had been educated in the schools of Virginia, including the Marshall-Wythe School of Law at the College of William and Mary. I was taught about the savages who were at Jamestown and Plymouth Rock. I do remember that I questioned why the patriots dressed up as savages at the Boston Tea Party, but never received a satisfactory answer. By chance a few years ago, I was proselytized by a book, *Forgotten Founders*, written by Bruce E. Johansen. I became acquainted with Professors Johansen and Donald A. Grinde, Jr., a Yamasee from the vicinity of Savannah, Georgia. They were discovering and revealing Indian influences on the evolution of U.S. democracy. They coauthored a book, *Exemplar of Liberty: Native America and the Evolution of Democracy*. I became a disciple, and their book continues to be like a bible for me. From them I learned that the Sons of Liberty dressed in Indian regalia and adopted for their organization the governing principles of the Iroquois Confederation. I learned that the symbol of an Indian as liberty was more than propaganda for the American Revolution. I realized that those colonists who became Americans drew their ideas from the American Indians as well as the English—it was evident in their manner, dress, speech, and beliefs.

The Onondaga are one of six nations in the Iroquois Confederacy. Oren Lyons is an Onondaga leader. He endeavored to teach me about the Indian roots of democracy and enabled me to understand how religion and government can support one another while remaining separate. All over the world he is called upon to explain and teach the Indian roots of democracy. Another Indian scholar is Professor Kirke Kickingbird. His published works have done much to bring into our consciousness the substantial Indian contributions to our democracy. Chief Lyons, Professors Johansen, Grinde, and Kickingbird, and I presented a program at the 1990 Annual Meeting of the American Bar Association in Chicago. Its purpose was to establish a working relationship between state and tribal courts by rediscovering the Indian roots of American democracy. The Native American Tribal Court Committee of the National Conference of Special Court Judges continues in its efforts to improve this relationship by "educating the educated" about the many contributions of Native Americans to our unique democracy.

Perhaps American constitutional law scholars, as well as historians, should first go to their dictionaries and look up the word "American." Failing to do this, they probably would define the word by describing any of those immigrants who constitute the vast majority of people who live here now. They would add "Native" to describe an Indian. By turning to page 78 in *Webster's Ninth New Collegiate Dictionary*, they would find that the first definition of this noun describes an American as an Indian of North or South America. At the time of the American Revolution, the civilized world began to call the colonists "Americans" and depicted them as Indians. At the same time, the colonists began to call themselves "Americans." They knew that they were calling themselves Indians. All of us who call ourselves Americans today have this Indian root, but few of us know it. Beyond this, a surprising number actually have a history of Indian blood in their family trees.

I have a hobby. I ask people if they are part Indian. I have been conducting this informal poll for many years. Better than 40 percent have said "yes." Most of them cannot prove it. Most often it has been passed down in the family by word of mouth. Frequently, the Indian blood has been identified as Cherokee. At a racial equality conference in Washington, D.C., each African-American speaker I asked, including Rev. Jesse Jackson, reported that there was a history of Indian blood in his or her family. My theory is that as the immigrants began to flood the frontier, there was more and more contact between them and frontier Indians. Clearly there was much intermarriage between the Cherokee and the Scotch-Irish. By the end of the eighteenth century, many Cherokee leaders had more Scotch-Irish blood than Cherokee. The famed Cherokee leader John Ross was, in fact, one-eighth Cherokee. Intermarriage with Indians was promoted. Thomas Jefferson told an Indian delegation that "your blood will mix with ours, and will spread, with ours, over this great Island [Indian word for America]."[5]

When the United States was born, the people who fueled and fought the Revolution often were more Indian than immigrant in both blood and their belief in equality, liberty, and individual sovereignty. A distinguished American legal scholar and historian, Yale professor Felix Cohen, said,

[I]t is out of a rich Indian democratic tradition that the distinctive political ideals of American life emerged. Universal suffrage for women as for men, the pattern of states that we call federalism, the habit of treating chiefs as servants of the people instead of their masters, the insistence that the community must respect the diversity of men and the diversity of their dreams—all these things were part of the American way of life before Columbus landed.[6]

Even our justice system has been influenced by Indian tradition. The modern trend toward mediation is really not new. Indian nations have practiced it beyond memory. In the General District Court of the City of Norfolk, Virginia, an experiment for several years has been the Peacemaker Council, which is based on the present Peacemaker Courts of the Navajo and Iroquois nations. It is a form of mediation intended to use peer pressure to settle disputes and restore peace and harmony. Participation is entirely voluntary. The results have been phenomenal. The parties often find solutions not available to the court. They realize that our adversary system often makes matters worse. They find that the real solution is to sit down and talk, listen, and reach a consensus for peace and harmony. Best of all, they give the court most of the credit for the results. Contrast this with surveys today that indicate that more than two-thirds of the people say that they have no faith in our judicial system.

The same people indicate that they have lost faith in our political system. An answer seems to be that we are straying from our Indian ideals and democratic tradition. Instead of striving for consensus, many political leaders seem to insult and only search for power. No longer do the people seem to have an equal opportunity to select their leaders. Campaigns are so costly and the need to raise money is so great that the rich gain what seems to be undue influence. Our leaders seem no longer to be our servants, and like masters, they often accumulate their greatest wealth while in office. As was the case in Europe, individual families and corporations seem to have become all-powerful. Inequality seems to be growing. To save our democracy, we need to return to our Indian democratic roots.

NOTES

1. Henry F. Graff, "At Liberty," *Constitution* (from the *Foundation for the U.S. Constitution*) 3:1 (Winter 1991): 17.

2. John Adams, *Defence of the Constitutions of the Governments of the United States of America* (Philadelphia: Hall & Sellers, 1787).

3. Statement made at a special meeting of the Museum Committee, Board of Trustees, Jamestown-Yorktown Foundation, Williamsburg, Virginia, April 1992. This meeting was called to air a complaint filed by Judge Cloud that programs sponsored by the museum were concentrating solely on English common law (and ignoring Native American precedents) in the formation of the U.S. Constitution and Bill of Rights.

4. Zechariah Chaffee, Book Review of *Free Speech and Its Relation to Self-Government*, by Alexander Meiklejohn (New York: Harper & Brothers, 1948), in *Harvard Law Review* 62 (1949): 891, 898.

5. Donald A. Grinde, Jr., and Bruce E. Johansen, *Exemplar of Liberty: Native America and the Evolution of Democracy* (Los Angeles: UCLA American Indian Studies Center, 1991), 156.

6. Ibid., 235.

CHARLES RILEY CLOUD

Introduction

The field of American Indian Law and Policy, historically and systematically, has had little to do conceptually with American Indian law, or methods of conflict resolution. . . . While excellent treatments of Cheyenne, Dakota, and Cherokee and other conceptions of law exist, the scholarship involved has made little impact on the evolution of Indian policy up to present times. Rather than being a branch of comparative law, the formal field of American Indian law is a very special, complex, and often contradictory and confusing branch of Anglo-American legal thinking.[1]

The Encyclopedia of Native American Legal Tradition is the first attempt in book form to inject traditional Native American political and legal systems into the study of law in the United States. It includes detailed descriptions of several major Native American nations' legal and political systems, such as the Iroquois, Cherokee, Choctaw, Cheyenne, Creek, Chickasaw, Comanche, Sioux, Pueblo, Mandan, Huron, Powhatan, and Mikmaq.

While generalization is risky because the variety of Native American peoples always presents exceptions, many traditional tribal governments were more judicial in nature than legislative, according to Vine Deloria, Jr., and Clifford Lytle in *American Indians, American Justice* (1983). Unless a private quarrel affected the general tribal welfare, it was usually settled by the family members affected. The solution usually involved a gift or some other form of restitution. In some cases, the family against whom a serious crime, such as murder, was perpetrated demanded that the murderer join their group and take the place of the person he had killed.

Traditional tribal justice usually emphasized restitution rather than retribution, although retribution, sometimes in starkly personal terms, sometimes played a role in serious crimes, especially murder. An extremely antisocial person might be exiled from the community to a near-certain death, also a form of retribution. Banishment was often viewed as worse than execution, since a person without a community often ceased to exist as a human being in the eyes of the tribe. In most cases, members of the families involved sought to arrive at mutually agreeable compensation to restore the equilibrium of social relations within the group. Social norms also were different from "majority" or "Anglo" society; people used each other's property in a manner that some whites defined as thievery, but tribal sanctions against intellectual dishonesty were often extremely strictly enforced.

In Native American domestic law (marriage, divorce, adoption, social welfare, and so on), affairs were usually handled by the immediate family or the clan; extended families were the norm. The families and clans often were dominated by women; the grandmother was often the principal figure of authority in the extended family. In the Iroquois Confederacy, the clan mothers chose the chiefs with the advice of family members who held title, as a group, to a seat on the national or confederate council.

This is not an Indian law casebook (students should consult the standard casebook in the field),[2] although it does contain outlines of many major Indian law cases, congressional acts, and treaties, mainly in an effort to provide a sense of temporal continuity and legal context. We have sought to restrict our focus to major cases that raise broad issues (often having to do with the nature of sovereignty) that have application throughout Indian Country.

American Indian law has evolved from a rich history; it is, indeed, one of the major taproots of U.S. jurisprudence. According to legal scholar Charles Wilkinson, between 1970 and 1981, the U.S. Supreme Court construed 22 laws written before 1800, 8 of them involving Indian law. Of the 29 interpretations during 1970 to 1981 of laws written between 1800 and 1850, 14 involved Indians. Between 1970 and 1981, the Supreme Court ruled on a total of 182 laws passed between 1850 and 1875, of which 32 involved Indian law. Overall, roughly one-quarter of the legal interpretations from the first century of U.S. law involved Native Americans. As a subject area of law, only the Reconstruction-era civil-rights statutes have been referenced more often by the Supreme Court, according to Wilkinson.

Treaties have been the most frequent sources of litigation in Indian law. According to Wilkinson, "These laws are unique in our jurisprudence: for they set aside territory within the United States for self-government, subject to federal supervision, by sovereigns that are both preconstitutional and extraconstitutional."[3]

This encyclopedia also includes personal profiles of individuals important to the evolution of Indian law, such as Felix Cohen and John Collier. Native American figures also are profiled, notably Deskaheh, who took the Iroquois' case for sovereignty to the League of Nations after World War I, and Canassatego, the Onondaga (Iroquois) chief who, on July 4, 1744, proposed that the thirteen colonies form a union on the Iroquois' model. This book also includes surprising historical incidences, such as a bill introduced in the Virginia Assembly by Patrick Henry about 1760 that would have provided governmental subsidies for Indian-white marriages, and the nature of laws passed by early New England settlements that forbade "Indianizing," or leaving the colony to take up life with local Indian peoples. Readers also will discover how a Cheyenne wins religious asylum from a crime, and how the Inuit (Eskimo) settle disputes with song duels.

Any study brings a temptation to systematize. This may be doubly true in American Indian law, a subject in which any serious student can be powerfully tempted to make legal, ethical, moral, and historical sense of two centuries of conflicting "Indian policy." It is also something of a challenge. I am not a lawyer, but I do know something of the intellectual history that gave rise to the Constitution, and the role of Native American confederacies in shaping our ideas and character.

As I began to compile this volume, the daily news was carrying numerous stories about the notion that Americans should have a "contract" with their government. Most of the Americans who have placed their political faith in such an instrument have not been party to any of the 371 ratified treaties between Native American peoples and the United States. These treaties are the original "contracts with America."

Let us begin with a truism from our European legal heritage—that a treaty is a contract between sovereign governments. Until late in the last century, treaties were the standard model of relations between Native American peoples and the U.S. government. When the Constitution was being debated and ratified, treaties with American Indian nations were the major preoccupation of the new nation's Department of State. Since that time, the implications of Native American sovereignty have been eroded by a number of legal decisions, speculations, and assumptions. In recent years, many Native Americans, including a growing number of attorneys and judges, have come again to examine whether the body of "Indian law" practiced today reflects the spirit of the U.S. Constitution, the supreme law of the land. The body of law that the United States applies to Native Americans has evolved far from its roots in the Constitution and the treaties.

When I foray into "Indian law," I emerge from each such expedition feeling as if I have recently looked at a wall that has been painted and repainted, over and over, by different painters, in different colors, at different times—an often chaotic river of precedent that twists and turns through our history, sometimes doubling back on itself. I am thinking of the Missouri River near Omaha, with its shoals of mud that are shaped by prevailing currents. In our history regarding "Indian affairs," the shoals are shaped by prevailing currents of greed, opportunism, ethnocentric religious morality, and ethnocentric altruism.

Our river of law begins at the headwaters of the Constitution, which was written at a time when the framers had to deal with a geopolitical contradiction: while Euro-American settlement occupied only a ribbon of seaboard along the Atlantic, the Treaty of Paris, signed with England in 1783, "gave" the new United States "title" (in the European sense) to the continent westward to the Mississippi River. At the time, most of this land was occupied by Native American nations exercising sovereignty over their own internal and external affairs. This area was not fully controlled by the U.S. military until well after the year 1800. The United States may have won a "title" to this area in Paris, but most of it still remained to be acquired through a combination of treaty making, war, and illegal immigration from the East that lasted until after the lives and deaths of Tecumseh, Little Turtle, Black Hawk, Sequoyah, and many other Native American people. The U.S. acquisition of this territory was not smooth, easy, or bloodless. General Arthur St. Clair lost nine hundred men (and some of their wives) to Little Turtle. This was the biggest of many battles waged while the United States was filling up the territory that the Treaty of Paris said it owned.

The Constitution and the treaty-making system were products of the eighteenth century, a time of slow-moving frontiers and relative equity in relations between the ambassadors of the new United States and Native American nations along its borders. The diplomatic relationship of Indian nations and the new United States provided the context in which Benjamin Franklin and other founders of the United States incorporated Iroquois ideas of federalism into their new system of government. Relations with Native American nations were defined as international business between nations functioning as diplomatic peers. Even Benjamin Franklin's fertile imagination did not conjure up the railroad, the cotton gin, or mass starvation in Europe, all of which sped the surge of humanity across the continent. Franklin thought that a thousand years would pass before immigrants filled the continent. He missed by nine hundred. Omaha and Seattle, 1,800 miles distant, were founded at the same time (shortly after 1850). That is how quickly the frontier swept across the continent.

If one studies the rhetoric of Jefferson in light of U.S. relations with

Indian nations, a change in perception becomes evident at the turn of the century. While Jefferson served as secretary of state, he most often addressed Native American representatives as "brothers." By the time he became president in 1801, the reference became "children." Settlement erupted across the Appalachian Mountains and reached the West Coast of North America within fifty years. European demographics and advances in technology (especially the railroad) caused one of the greatest human movements in recorded history. Along with this movement came the evolution of a subjugation system for the Native American peoples who stood in the path of expanding European-American immigration. Diplomacy across the frontier thus ceased to be an exercise of peer relations when power relations changed.

The Bureau of Indian Affairs (BIA), first a department of the U.S. Army, was transferred to the Interior Department about the time frontiers were closing in western North America (Canadian policy followed a course similar to that of the United States). Law evolved to justify a system in which Native Americans were defined as "wards of the state." In 1871, treaty making was ended by Congress. From that year forward, the treatment of Native Americans was defined wholly as an internal matter by the United States. The goal of all policy at the time was assimilation, which was often advanced by "reformers" as an alternative to outright extermination, as with the slogan invented by General Richard Pratt, founder of the government's Indian school system, "Kill the Indian, save the man." Without asking for it, Native American peoples who had been purposefully deprived of independent means of sustenance (such as the buffalo) became objects of a "trust" relationship with the government that extended from the cradle to (and, in the case of Native American artifacts and remains, beyond) the grave. Professor Milnar Ball observed that "trust," as it applies to American Indians, can be compared to a system of accounting in which the United States, the debtor, pays itself and calls the exchange a payment to the Indians. "In sum," Ball wrote, "the trust is an affirmative basis for claims of power and does not arise from the Constitution."[4] I cannot improve on the Indian Law Resource Center's characterization of "trust" (which I also have borrowed from Professor Ball) as "racial discrimination and unfettered United States power disguised as moral legal duty."[5] While most trusts are said to have beneficiaries, this one was designed from the beginning to produce victims.

The Constitution says nothing about "domestic dependent nations," "trust responsibility," or "wardship." The so-called plenary power that Congress is said to enjoy over Native American nations is a direct contradiction of the peer relationship implied by the signing of treaties by representatives of sovereign peoples. All of these concepts evolved in the nineteenth and twentieth centuries as part of Euro-American society's subjugation of Native American societies. Within one century, the settlement frontier erupted over the Appalachians and reached California, Washington, and Oregon.

Chief Justice John Marshall's rulings occupy a special place in the development of legal rationales for the subjugation system that evolved to deal with the Native American survivors of the "westward movement." His opinion that Indian nations comprised "domestic dependent nations" laid the foundations of "trust responsibility" and the wardship system, although these legal doctrines were not fully developed until well into the twentieth century. Justice Marshall may have intended neither "wardship" nor "trust" as legal doctrines. He was trying to salvage a degree of sovereignty for the Cherokees and other peoples who were about to be "removed" to Indian Territory (later Oklahoma) by order of President (and former Indian fighter) Andrew Jackson. Jackson's conception of law had much more to do with power relationships than with a sense of justice. When Jackson ignored Marshall's ruling, the chief justice was greatly aggrieved and thought of resigning from the Supreme Court.

According to Russel Barsh and James Henderson, Marshall "fictionalized discovery into conquest. This, he freely confessed, [was] an unjust but expedient solution." Marshall wrote:

However extravagant the pretensions of converting the discovery of an inhabited country into conquest may appear; if the principle has been asserted in the first instance, and afterwards sustained; if a country has been acquired and held under it; if the property of the great mass of the community originates in it, it becomes the law of the land, and cannot be questioned. . . . However this restriction may be opposed to natural right, and to the usages of civilized nations, yet, if it be indispensable to that system under which the country has been settled, and be adapted to the actual condition of the two peoples, it may, perhaps, be supported by reason, and certainly cannot be rejected by courts of justice.[6]

While President Jackson's repudiation of the Supreme Court was clearly an impeachable offense under the Constitution, the issue at hand (states' rights, asserted over the Cherokees by Georgia) was too incendiary in the pre–Civil War South to permit a serious debate on the issue with provocation of the type that finally compelled Georgia and other southern states to secede from the United States three decades later.

We will examine the gap between legality and reality during this century of fast-moving frontiers, as well as the differing perceptions of each party of historical events that led to specific legal actions that shaped the course of precedent. The following is only one of many examples illustrating the gap between legal form and the substance of day-to-day reality. In the early 1870s, the Poncas of Nebraska were forcibly removed from their lands along the beautiful Niobrara River by the U.S. Army and were assigned a reservation in Indian Territory. The United States did not take the land for itself, but for the Sioux Nation, following a geographical error of rather large magnitude in the Fort Laramie Treaty of 1868. In 1877, a band of Poncas, led by Standing Bear, resolved to return to their homeland so that Standing Bear could bury his recently deceased son. They arrived at the homeland of the U'mahas ("Omaha" is anglicized) with their feet bleeding in the snow, after they had eaten their horses and their moccasins.

The U'mahas sheltered Standing Bear's Poncas and told their story to lawyers in Omaha, who filed suit in the federal district court of Judge Elmer Dundy. The legal arguments revolved around the army's presumed right to "remove" Indians against their wills. Judge Dundy found that a Native American person could not be forced to move to assigned reservations without consent. Dundy was a careful man, and he confined his ruling to Standing Bear and the people in his party. His idea, interpreted and enforced broadly, could have crippled the forced relocation program that, after forty years, was still compelling unwilling Native American peoples to move to Indian Territory, which would become Oklahoma.

Within a month of Judge Dundy's ruling, Big Snake, Standing Bear's brother, not understanding the strict construction of Judge Dundy's ruling, decided to test it by leaving the Poncas' assigned reservation in Indian Territory. When he was captured, Big Snake said that he was free to travel as he pleased, and that he had done nothing wrong. The troops then accused Big Snake of making trouble and shot him dead. Big Snake had thought all along that if his brother could go where he pleased, he had the same right.

In this volume, the reader will encounter a proposal by Native American peoples in the state that was about to become Oklahoma to form a Native American state called Sequoyah. They complied with all the requirements of U.S. law and beat white settlers to Congress with a petition for statehood, which was ignored. The reader also will learn how the Dawes (Allotment) Act of 1887 functioned as a legal real-estate agency for the westward movement.

Historically, watching court decisions on American Indian law is like watching a very intricate intellectual dance in which the same fundamental issues are viewed very differently given different historical circumstances, variations in the makeup of the courts, and the idiosyncratic details of each individual case. In *Menominee Tribe v. United States*, for example, the Supreme Court held that Menominee hunting and fishing rights survived the termination of the tribe by Congress. The Court said that Congress had made no such statement in the Menominee Termination Act. Thus Wisconsin was not allowed to enforce its fishing and game laws on individual Menominees. The Court held hunting and fishing rights to be included in original treaties and stated that "the intention to abrogate or modify a treaty is not to be lightly imputed to Congress."

In other cases, however, the same court has held that Congress may abrogate Indian treaties unilaterally; this point is an area of major debate among scholars of American Indian law. One may compare this ruling, for example, to *Montana v. United States*, adjudicated by the U.S. Supreme Court in 1981, in which aboriginal Crow land was awarded to Montana without compensation. The Court held that the bed of the Bighorn River was owned by the state despite a treaty signed in 1868 that reserved the land for the tribe.

Along this trail of contradiction, one may enlist the Supreme Court's opinion in *Elk v. Wilkins* (1884). In this case, the U.S. Supreme Court held that an Indian is not made a citizen by the Fourteenth Amendment to the Constitution. This position holds even if the Indian is living apart from his or her tribe. The Court also ruled that acts of Congress do not generally apply to Indians unless they are specifically mentioned.

At issue was the constitutional status of American Indians for purposes of citizenship and voting. The Fourteenth Amendment had granted citizenship to "all persons born or naturalized in the United States, and subject to the jurisdiction of the United States." Did American Indians fall under this definition? A federal district court ruled that the Fourteenth Amendment did not apply to Indians who had not been "born subject to its jurisdiction—that is, in its power and obedience."[7] John Elk had been born outside of U.S. jurisdiction, but moved to Omaha as an adult and lived what the court described as a "civilized" life. He sought to become a citizen and exercise the right to vote in Omaha elections during 1880. The Supreme Court ruled that the Fifteenth Amendment (which grants the right to vote to all citizens regardless of race) did not apply in Elk's case, because he was not born in an area under U.S. jurisdiction. Therefore, Elk was not a citizen within the meaning of the Fourteenth Amendment.

Elk v. Wilkins posed an intriguing irony in late-eighteenth-century America, when the ideological landscape even of "friends of the Indian" promoted assimilation as an alternative to extermination. At a time when assimilation was at high tide, an individual Indian who wanted voting rights was being told that he was, in essence, a foreigner.

Looking at Indian law as a whole, one is amazed by its nature—that of an intricate dance by which the lawgiver convinces himself that the taking of the continent was justified under the assumptions of his own presumably humane law. The forcible subjugation of children in the schools of an alien culture illustrates what had become, by 1870, of the sovereignty implied by the signing of treaties. As the frontier closed on the Northern Plains, Native American people were given two options: submit to the system or die. This was most simply expressed in the late nineteenth century by the Plains Indian agent's refusal of rations to Indians who did not do as they were told. This was colonialism at its most basic level, in open-air concentration camps. On the Plains, extermination of the buffalo destroyed an entire way of life. The Bureau of Indian Affairs molded the wardship doctrine into one of the most pervasive forms of personal human oppression known to human history. This subjugation system was being invented during the years when the frontier was said to have closed, law by law and program by program, without basis in the Constitution, and with no real advice from the affected parties. The form of oppression was entirely foreign to its objects, whom it was meant to make European in every manipulatable way.

The whole potpourri of missionaries, boarding schools, government bureaucracies, and so forth evolved from non-Indian interpretations of "wardship" and "trust," as well as the demands of Anglo-American real-estate speculators and their lawyers. These laws and policies are not the logical or humane extensions of a mutually beneficial relationship between peoples, but the legal conveniences by which the bulk of North America was being transferred from one group of peoples to another.

Since the 1960s, self-determination efforts have been nibbling away at the system of dependence, but it is still legally entrenched. I thank Jewell James for the observation that it took Congress seventeen attempts (and three decades) to repudiate Termination. In hundreds of small ways, Native American people are still reminded that they live in colonial enclaves administered by the BIA. I was talking once with a Navajo woman about women's names and marriage. When I married, my wife kept her own name—Patricia Keiffer—and so I asked my friend why she didn't keep hers. Better yet, since she is Navajo, a matriarchal culture, why didn't her husband take her name? She smiled and told me matter-of-factly that keeping her own name might be a good idea, but that she could not exercise such a right without spending most of the rest of her life waging bureaucratic battle with the still-patriarchal BIA, which always demanded the husband's name.

Now let us consider this woman's situation in the context of certain legal referents. First, as a Navajo, she is a U.S. citizen by act of Congress. As a citizen, one might assume that she has rights of self-expression that include the choice of her own name.

Second, according to the opinions of many eminent judges, my friend, as a Navajo and an American Indian, is a "ward" of the United States. One might assume then that the BIA holds her name (which it defines) "in trust" and lets her use it only when she follows its rules.

Third, as a Navajo, she is party to treaties that define her as a member of a sovereign nation vis-à-vis the United States. The contradictions that are obvious here are repeated thousands of times a day on individual and collective bases throughout Indian Country.

Any attempt to deal with "Indian law" must begin with the peer relationship provided by the Constitution and the treaties. It must uproot the enforced dependency of "wardship" and "trust." What we aim to do here, perhaps, is to make legal sense out of a system that is based on legal and political assumptions that no longer apply. This will not be easy. In our time, as in Justice Marshall's, economic interests often drive interpretations of law, and there are powerful interests that have a stake in weakening Native American sovereignty. There will always be attempts to abrogate the treaties.

We need to examine the Constitution in a frame of mind that will befit a new century, a time in which people will come to understand that when Europeans came to the Americas, they encountered complex civilizations that functioned quite ably on their own, so well that their food fed the immigrants, and their concepts of governance helped shape the ideological genesis of new Euro-American nations here. We are, once again, redefining American federalism.

In the encyclopedia entries, **boldface** type highlights cross-references to other entries or to treaties discussed in the entry on Treaties, Specific Agreements and Provisions. Unsigned entries are by the editor of the encyclopedia.

NOTES

1. Joyotpaul Chauduri, "American Indian Policy: An Overview," in *American Indian Policy in the Twentieth Century*, ed. Vine Deloria, Jr. (Norman: University of Oklahoma Press, 1985), 15.

2. David H. Getches, Daniel M. Rosenfeld, and Charles F. Wilkinson, *Cases and Materials on Federal Indian Law* (St. Paul, MN: West Publishing, 1979, 1993).

3. Charles F. Wilkinson, *American Indians, Time and the Law: Native Societies in a Modern Constitutional Democracy* (New Haven: Yale University Press, 1987), 14.

4. Milnar Ball, "Constitution, Court, Indian Tribes," *American Bar Foundation Research Journal* (Winter 1987): 65.

5. Ibid., 62.

6. Russel Lawrence Barsh and James Youngblood Henderson, *The Road: Indian Tribes and Political Liberty* (Berkeley: University of California Press, 1980), 48.

7. *McKay v. Campbell*, 16 Fed. Cas. 161 (1871) (No. 8840).

A

ALASKA NATIVE CLAIMS SETTLEMENT ACT (1971) 43 U.S.C. §§
1601 *et seq*.

The Alaska Native Claims Settlement Act extinguished native title to
land in Alaska; it also included submerged land and hunting and fishing
rights. The act also cleared the way legally for a major north-south oil
pipeline. Alaska natives were given fee-simple title to more than forty
million acres of land, as well as $462.5 million over eleven years in
payments and a 2 percent royalty on mineral development, up to a total
of $500 million. Some of the native corporations were enriched in the
1970s and 1980s by discovery of oil under their lands.

The act set up thirteen regional corporations with stockholding membership comprising the 80,000 Inuit, Aleuts, and American Indians in
the area. Native stockholders were required to maintain ownership for
twenty years (until 1991), after which they were to be allowed to sell
their interests. Alaskan native leaders asserted that such a provision
resembled the discredited General **Allotment Act**; in 1988, Congress
amended the law to allow the corporations to decide as a whole whether
individual shares could be sold.

ALBANY PLAN OF UNION (1754)

Beginning nearly two generations before the American Revolution,
the circumstances of diplomacy brought opinion leaders of the English
colonies and the **Iroquois Confederacy** together to discuss the politics
of alliance. Beginning in the early 1740s, Iroquois leaders strongly urged

the colonists to form a federation similar to their own. The Iroquois' immediate practical objective was unified management of the Indian trade and prevention of fraud. The Iroquois also stressed that the colonies should unify against France.

This set of circumstances brought **Benjamin Franklin** into the diplomatic equation. He first read the Iroquois' urgings to unite when he was a printer of Indian treaties, beginning in 1736. By the early 1750s, Franklin was more directly involved in diplomacy itself, at the same time that he became an early, forceful advocate of colonial union. All of these circumstantial strings were tied together in the summer of 1754 when colonial representatives, Franklin among them, met with Iroquois sachems at Albany to address issues of mutual concern and to develop the Albany Plan of Union, a design that echoes both English and Iroquois precedents.

The Albany Congress convened on June 19, 1754. Most of the sessions took place at the Albany courthouse. On June 28, 1754, the day after the Mohawk leader **Hendrick** arrived with the Mohawks, James DeLancey, acting governor of New York, met with him. The two hundred Indians in attendance sat on ten rows of benches in front of the governor's residence, with colonial delegates facing them in a row of chairs, their backs to the building. Hendrick repeated the advice **Canassatego** had given colonial delegates a decade earlier to unite on the Iroquois model. This time, the advice came not at a treaty conference, but at a meeting devoted to drawing up a plan for the type of colonial union the Iroquois had been requesting. The same day, at the courthouse, the colonial delegates were in the early stages of debate over the plan of union.

DeLancey replied, "I hope that by this present Union, we shall grow up to a great height and be as powerful and famous as you were of old." On July 10, 1754, Franklin formally proposed his Plan of Union before the congress. Franklin wrote that the debates on the Albany Plan "went on daily, hand in hand with the Indian business."

In drawing up his final draft, Franklin was meeting several diplomatic demands: the English Crown's desire for control, the colonies' desires for autonomy in a loose confederation, and the Iroquois' stated advocacy of a colonial union similar (but not identical) to their own in form and function. For the Crown, the plan provided administration by a president-general, to be appointed by England. The individual colonies were to be allowed to retain their own constitutions, except as the plan circumscribed them. The retention of internal sovereignty within the individual colonies closely resembled the Iroquois system.

Franklin chose the name "Grand Council" for the plan's deliberative body, the same name generally applied to the Iroquois central council. The number of delegates, forty-eight, was close to the Iroquois council's fifty, and each colony had a different number of delegates, just as each

Haudenosaunee (Iroquois) nation sent a different number of sachems to Onondaga. The Albany Plan was based in rough proportion to tax revenues, however, while the Iroquois system was based on tradition.

Basically, the plan provided that Parliament was to establish a general government in America, including all the thirteen colonies, each of which was to retain its own constitution except for certain powers (mainly mutual defense) that were to be given to the general government. The king was to appoint a president-general for the government. Each colonial assembly would elect representatives to the Grand Council.

The Albany Plan was defeated by the individual colonial assemblies, but it provided a prototype for Franklin's **Articles of Confederation** twenty years later. For example, Article IX of the articles vested the Continental Congress with "the sole and exclusive right and power of . . . regulating the trade and managing all affairs of Indians not members of any of the states; provided, that the legislative right of any state within its own limits not be infringed or violated." This was similar to the provision that Benjamin Franklin wrote into the Albany Plan at the behest of the Iroquois and other Native Americans.

ALCATRAZ ISLAND, OCCUPATION (1969)

With the struggle against **Termination** as a catalyst, American Indian activism and nationalism were transformed by the occupation of the former federal penitentiary at Alcatraz Island in San Francisco Bay by roughly three hundred Native Americans beginning November 19, 1969. They were requesting title to the island under a federal law that gave Indians first refusal on federal "surplus" property. The resulting media attention provided a national platform for discussion of American Indian issues relating to **self-determination**. The objectives of the occupation included the building of an American Indian culture center and the launching of a nationalistic Native American movement called the Confederation of American Indian Nations (CAIN). On December 16, 1969, the occupants at Alcatraz issued the following statement:

We are issuing this call in an attempt to unify our Indian brothers behind a common cause. . . . We are not getting anywhere fast by working alone as individual tribes. If we can get together as brothers and come to a common agreement, we feel that we can be much more effective, doing things for ourselves, instead of having someone else doing it, telling us what is good for us. So we must start somewhere. We feel that we are going to succeed, we must hold on to the old ways. *This is the first and most important reason we went to Alcatraz Island.* (leaflet, author's files)

With their nationalistic focus, leaders at Alcatraz wanted to create a movement for national American Indian autonomy that would resolve the conflicts between unity and self-determination. In reality, the Alcatraz protesters saw some of their goals achieved even though they left the island in 1971. Although the seizure of Alcatraz did not result in gaining title to the island and building an American Indian culture center, it did focus attention, as no one had done before, on the Native American issues of American Indian identity, self-determination, and land base.

At one point, the Indians occupying Alcatraz offered a plan for an Indian republic that parodied U.S. Indian policy:

We will give to the inhabitants of this island a portion of the land for their own to be held in trust by . . . the Bureau of Caucasian Affairs to hold in perpetuity—for as long as the sun shall rise and the rivers go down to the sea. We will further guide the inhabitants in the proper way of living. We will offer them our religion, our education, our life-ways, in order to help them achieve our level of civilization and thus raise them and all their white brothers up from their savage and unhappy state. We offer this treaty in good faith and wish to be fair and honorable in our dealings with all white men. (leaflet, author's files)

FURTHER READING

Blue Cloud, Peter. *Alcatraz Is Not an Island*. Berkeley, CA: Wingbow Press, 1972.
Josephy, Alvin, Jr. *Red Power*. New York: McGraw-Hill, 1971.
O'Brien, Sharon. *American Indian Tribal Governments*. Norman: University of Oklahoma Press, 1989.

ALLOTMENT ACT, GENERAL (DAWES ACT) 25 U.S.C.A. § 331; 24 Stat. 388

The General Allotment Act, passed by Congress in 1887, provided nationwide procedures to divide Native American lands owned in common into individual or family-owned plots, opening the balance of the land (often as much as 90 percent of it) for non-Indian settlement. In many cases, Indians were paid a per capita share of these lands' sales price. As a mechanism for the transfer of land from one group of people to another, allotment worked hand in glove with the practice of "homesteading," the granting of land to immigrating European Americans. Homesteading peaked in 1884, three years before the passage of the General Allotment Act.

The General Allotment Act was passed by Congress at a time of growing non-Indian pressure to open remaining Native American lands for settlement. At the time, the **Sioux** Nation, by treaty, still owned most of western South Dakota; the Flatheads and Blackfeet held title to much of western Montana; and a coalition of local native nations, such as the Kiowa, and "removed" Indians, such as the **Cheyennes** and **Apaches**, occupied western Oklahoma. The **Crow** held a large area in southern Montana.

Reformers, calling themselves "friends of the Indian," advocated allotment as an alternative to extermination for Indians as the frontier closed around them. The theory of turning Indians into farmers in the Jeffersonian yeoman image was outdated by the late nineteenth century as the United States industrialized rapidly. The rigid allotments also failed to take into account the amount of land needed to sustain a family in the arid American West.

Allotments were fixed by the act at 160 acres (a quarter section) for the head of a family, or 80 acres (an eighth section) for a single person over eighteen years of age. The land was to be held in trust for twenty-five years, then released in fee simple to the owner. The act then held that an Indian would become an American citizen subject to the laws of the state in which he or she resided. The act indicated that allotment would extinguish Indian title to the land.

The introduction of private property was advanced ideologically as an aid in "civilizing" native peoples. In reality, it was a government-sponsored real-estate agency for transferring land from Indians to European Americans. As a result of allotment, Indian-owned landholdings shrank from 138 million acres in 1887 to about 50 million in 1934, according to **John Collier**, commissioner of Indian affairs at the end of the period. Sixty million acres were lost through the release of "surplus" lands to federal government ownership or sale to homesteaders. Twenty-six million acres of land were transferred to non-Indians after they were released from trust status by purchase, fraud, mortgage foreclosures, and tax sales. Of the 48 million acres remaining in Indian hands by 1934, 20 million were too arid for productive farming, which had been the goal of allotment to begin with. By 1933, 49 percent of Indians on allotted reservations were landless. At that time, 96 percent of all reservation Indians were earning less than $200 a year.

The law was originally written so that Indians could not sell their land for twenty-five years, as a protection against speculation, but land-hungry settlers found many ways to get around that limit. If Indians refused allotment (and many did), it could be ordered for them. Yakimas in eastern Washington pulled up surveyors' markers. In Wyoming, Arapaho horsemen destroyed surveyors' tapes.

Once the legislation was implemented, its intent fell before the ring of land speculators and Indian agents who made livings off Native Americans. The law was written so that after each Native American family had been allocated 160 acres, or each single person 80 acres, the remaining reservation lands were opened for non-Indian homesteaders. The first Native American group to be affected by allotment was the Iowas. After each family was allotted 160 acres, 90 percent of the Iowas' reservation land was thrown open to non-Indian settlement. **Cheyennes** and Arapahoes who had been forcibly moved to **Indian Territory** (now Oklahoma) lost 80 percent of the land that had been guaranteed to them "forever" just twenty years earlier.

Allotment-related frauds were especially common in Oklahoma after oil was discovered on some Indian lands. According to Peter Nabokov, "Fraudulent wills were drafted for dead Indians. Deeds were forged for people who never existed. Non-Indian opportunists were appointed as 'guardians' for Indian children soon to inherit land from their parents. Allottees were bribed or murdered to steal their property" (1991: 260).

Because allotment was based on the model of the Anglo-American nuclear family, many Indians who were subjected to its provisions were required to do more than change their property-holding customs. Indian extended families were devastated by the allotment system, in which close relatives who had lived together often were given distant parcels of land. Long-established ties between grandmothers and their children were severed, and a long-standing family structure was destroyed. Indian men who were married to more than one wife were told to divest their extra relatives. **Vine Deloria, Jr.**, recalled the tearful response of the Kiowa chief Quanah Parker, who, when told that he must give up his extra wives, "told the [Indian] agent that, if he must give them up, he could not choose which one to surrender and that the agent must do it for him" (Deloria and Lytle 1983: 197).

The Allotment Act also authorized the secretary of the Interior Department to sell timber from allotted land and increased existing powers authorizing the government to lease land for the supposed "benefit" of the allottees. Income from such activities was deposited in a Bureau of Indian Affairs account, called **Individual Indian Monies** (IIM), to be paid to allottees only if the bureau deemed them "worthy." A scandal subsequently ensued in Oklahoma when full-blooded members of the Five Civilized Tribes in Oklahoma Territory died of starvation despite the fact that they had IIM accounts worth hundreds of thousands of dollars. The BIA had been diverting their income to pay for construction of schools and churches.

According to legal scholar Charles F. Wilkinson, "Allotment and the other assimilationist programs that complemented it devastated Indian land base, weakened Indian culture, sapped the vitality of tribal legislative and judicial processes, and opened most Indian reservations for settlement by non-Indians" (1987: 19).

U.S. political leaders understood this to be the upshot of allotment at the time. President Theodore Roosevelt, for example, said that "the General Allotment Act is a mighty pulverizing engine to break up the tribal mass. It acts directly upon the family and the individual" (Johansen 1997: 21). Over the generations, many individual allotments were subdivided into minuscule plots by inheritances, rendering many of them nearly useless for agriculture.

If the goal of allotment was to turn native people into yeoman farmers in the Jeffersonian image, the experiment was an unmitigated failure. Many peoples who had practiced agriculture themselves preferred their own farming methods, especially in the West, where lands that often were racked by drought were simply unsuited for agricultural methods developed in Europe and refined in humid eastern North America. In addition, farming the staples of life (especially corn) often was closely associated with religious practices; among the **Hopis** and **Pueblos**, for example, the breaking of the ground with a plow was considered a sacrilege comparable to slashing the breast of Mother Earth. For peoples who had never farmed, the situation was often worse. Conversion of Native American land into individual allotments did not lead to family self-sufficiency. For the Cheyennes and Arapahoes, only sixteen years passed between their confinement on reservations in 1875 and allotment of their lands in 1891. Except for the most assimilated mixed-bloods, they had not made the transition from independent nomadism to settled commercial farming, nor had many of the men come to accept agricultural labor as anything more than complete humiliation.

Some native peoples' unwillingness to accept allotment occasionally erupted into violence. At the turn of the century, Chitto Harjo, a full-blooded **Creek**, established the Snake Society as a native-controlled government. Harjo and his followers asserted that the United States could not annul legally signed treaties without the consent of native signers, despite the 1871 legislation by which Congress had unilaterally done just that. In 1901, the reorganized Creeks rejected allotment. Harjo's band assaulted some Creeks who had accepted individual parcels of land. The "Snake Uprising" was crushed quickly by federal troops as resistance to allotment began to spread to the **Cherokees** and **Choctaws**, who, like the Creeks, were descended from people who had been forced to march the **Trails of Tears** from the Southeast in the 1830s. For years after their turn-of-the-century uprising was crushed, many of the Snakes refused to live on their allotments. Instead, they camped on church, school, communal, or government property. Their example was followed by some other members of the Five Civilized Tribes, some of whom even refused to cash royalty checks for oil found under the lands that had been assigned individually.

The breakdown of Native American real estate, Native American governments, and family relations was the stated aim of allotment legislation. BIA publications acknowledge that the thrust of U.S. Indian policy in the 1870s and 1880s was to "further minimize the functions of tribal leaders and tribal institutions and to continually strengthen the position of the government representative and his subordinates, and to improve the effectiveness of their programs to break down traditional patterns within the Indian communities" (Johansen 1997: 21).

Some non-Indian people protested allotment and other forms of assimilation. Ethnologist Lewis Henry Morgan, known as the founder of American anthropology, predicted that a result of allotment for the Indian "would unquestionably be, that in a very short time he would divest himself of every foot of land and fall into poverty" (Johansen 1997: 21). Morgan was echoing the minority opinion of the Congressional Committee of Indian Affairs on the Allotment Act:

The real purpose of this bill is to get at the Indian lands and open them up to settlement. The provisions for the apparent benefit of the Indians are but the pretext to get his lands and occupy them. . . . If this were done in the name of greed, it would be bad enough; but to do it in the name of humanity, and under the cloak of an ardent desire to promote the Indian's welfare by making him like ourselves whether he will or not, is infinitely worse. (Johansen 1997: 21)

While allotment impoverished many Indians, as Morgan foresaw, the Bureau of Indian Affairs prospered. By 1934, with Indian real estate comprising less than half the area it had before allotment began, the BIA increased its staff (6,000 people) and its budget ($23 million a year) 400 percent.

FURTHER READING

Deloria, Vine, Jr., and Clifford Lytle. *American Indians, American Justice.* Austin: University of Texas Press, 1983.

Jackson, Helen Hunt. *A Century of Dishonor: A Sketch of the United States Government's Dealings with Some of the Indian Tribes.* New York: Harper and Brothers, 1881.

Johansen, Bruce E. "Taking Indians for a Ride: The BIA's Missing $204 Billion," *Native Americas* 14:1 (Spring 1997): 14–23.

McLaughlin, Michael R. "The Dawes Act, or Indian General Allotment Act of 1887: The Continuing Burden of Allotment." *American Indian Culture and Research Journal* 20:2 (1996): 59–105.

Nabokov, Peter, ed. *Native American Testimony.* New York: Viking, 1991.

National Resources Board, Land Planning Committee. *Indian Land Tenure, Economic Status, and Population Trends.* Washington, DC: U.S. Government Printing Office, 1935.

Tyler, S. Lyman. *A History of Indian Policy.* Washington, DC: Bureau of Indian Affairs, 1973.

Washburn, Wilcomb. *The Assault on Indian Tribalism: The General Allotment Law (Dawes Act) of 1887.* Philadelphia: J. B. Lippincott, 1975.

Wilkinson, Charles F. *American Indians, Time, and the Law: Native Societies in a Modern Constitutional Democracy.* New Haven, CT: Yale University Press, 1987.

AMERICAN INDIAN POLICY REVIEW COMMISSION

Beginning in the middle 1960s, confrontations over treaty rights and federal Indian policy became commonplace across the United States. In the Northwest, "fish-ins" provoked examination of century-old treaties. **Alcatraz** was occupied in 1969, the Bureau of Indian Affairs headquarters offices in 1972, and Wounded Knee a year later. The American Indian Policy Review Commission was convened by the federal government after that decade of unrest to examine the federal government's role in perpetuating poverty and injustice among Native Americans.

The commission, which was chaired by Senator James Abourezk, often worked with the U.S. Commission on Civil Rights. With task forces composed almost entirely of Native Americans, including some of the 1970s best-known activists, the AIPRC investigated social and economic conditions on reservations. In some respects, it found that little had changed since compilation of the federal government's **Meriam Report** in the 1920s. American Indians were still among the worst-paid and housed people in the United States on the average, especially if they lived in rural areas. Health care was still falling short of needs. A 1977 report of the AIPRC found that the 1974 Self-determination Act had failed to bring true self-government to Indian reservations. The AIPRC also looked at the growing use of Indian nations as "energy colonies" as coal and uranium mining increased following the oil shortages of the 1970s. **Vine Deloria, Jr.** and Clifford Lytle provided this evaluation of the AIPRC:

Unfortunately, the commission was mired in the infighting of national Indian politics from the very beginning and never recovered from these fatal wounds it received while yet in its conception. . . . The commission itself did not attend any field hearings . . . but instead delegated this responsibility to eleven "Task Forces." . . . The Task Forces staggered from one end of the country to the other in search of data and some of them compiled a considerable amount of material. . . . Staff work was haphazard and sporadic at best. . . . Almost all the recommendations made by Indians at the field hearings were ignored, and a very fragmentary and highly political agenda was substituted in their stead. (1983: 23)

FURTHER READING

American Indian Policy Review Commission. *Report on Federal, State, and Tribal Jurisdiction: Final Report: Task Force Four.* Washington, DC: U.S. Government Printing Office, 1976.
Deloria, Vine, Jr., and Clifford Lytle. *American Indians, American Justice.* Austin: University of Texas Press, 1983.

AMERICAN INDIAN RELIGIOUS FREEDOM ACT 42 U.S.C. § 1996 (1978). *See* **Religious Freedom**.

APACHE POLITICAL AND LEGAL TRADITIONS
Apache society was centered around groups of two to six matrilocal extended families, a unit sometimes called a *gota*. Members of the *gota*

lived together, and members of the different households cooperated in the pursuit of game and the raising of crops. A *gota* was usually led by a headman who assumed his status over several years by general **consensus** of the extended families in the *gota*. The headman in some cases inherited the title of "true chief." He would not retain the position, however, unless he displayed leadership. If no qualified headman was raised through inheritance, a consensus would form in favor of another leader who would be informally "elected" by members of the *gota*. Headmen were invariably male, but women exercised influence as political advisors, and it was their society and kinship lineages that maintained the Apaches' matrilineal society.

A headman could wield considerable influence, but only if the people in the extended families he led were willing to follow his advice, which could include detailed lectures on how to hunt, the techniques of agriculture, and who should work with whom. He also coordinated labor for hunting, foraging, and farming, advised parties engaged in disputes, and was sought out for advice regarding spousal choices. At times, the wife of a chief would become, in effect, a subchief. As a chief aged, he was not only charged with maintaining exemplary behavior, but with identifying young men who might become leaders in the future. He was expected to tutor younger men in the responsibilities of leadership. A chief was also charged with aiding the poor, oftentimes by coordinating distribution of donations from more affluent members of the *gota*. If two or more *gotas* engaged in conflict, their headmen were charged with resolving the dispute.

Each Apache was a member not only of a *gota*, but also of one of sixty-two matrilineal clans that overlapped the individual settlements. Members of one's clan (and, in some cases, others identified as being close to it) helped each other in survival tasks and usually did not intermarry. Such a system resembles that of many peoples in the eastern woodlands (**Cherokees**, **Wyandots**, and **Iroquois**, for example). Even the ways in which Apaches raised up chiefs generally recalls the system of the Iroquois, under which a person could "inherit" a title (from membership in a clan, not head to head); other Iroquois sachems were named to office by the Grand Council solely on the basis of their leadership qualities. Unlike the Iroquois and Wyandots, however, the Apaches did not maintain a formal political structure beyond the local level.

Among some Apaches, magic (or the fear of becoming the target of sorcery) was called into service as a social-control device, especially in the case of conflict between members of different kin groups. Social control was also maintained by positive means; a person who behaved according to socially cohesive norms was said to have access to one or more of several forms of "power," which insulated the person from misfortune and calamity. "Power" in several forms ("Wind Power," "Mountain Lion Power," and "Fire Power" are three examples) could be acquired by anyone who displayed the proper behavior, but such acquisition was expensive in terms of goods, time, and energy. A person who was acquiring a given power learned it from a shaman who already had it, a procedure requiring hundreds of hours of tutoring, for which the supplicant paid in horses, food, or other goods. Shamans usually were said to have acquired one or more forms of power through dreams or visions, followed by exhaustive attention to a corpus of chants and prayers. This was no small task. Acquisition of Black-tailed Deer Power required memorization of nearly sixty chants, each containing twenty or more half-hour verses. Less than letter-perfect performance was said to insult the power.

FURTHER READING

Baldwin, Gordon C. *The Warrior Apaches*. Tucson: University of Arizona Press, 1965.
Debo, Angie. *Geronimo: The Man, His Time, His Place*. Norman: University of Oklahoma Press, 1976.
Worcester, Donald A. *The Apaches: Eagles of the Southwest*. Norman: University of Oklahoma Press, 1979.

ARIZONA V. CALIFORNIA 373 U.S. 546 (1963)

Arizona v. California contained an elaboration of the Supreme Court's doctrine governing Indian water rights laid down in **Winters v. United States** (1908), in which residents of the Fort Belknap Reservation in Montana were held to be entitled to enough water to carry on their lives in a productive manner. As part of an overall plan adjudicating water rights in the lower Colorado River basin, the Supreme Court decided in *Arizona v. California* that Indian nations' water rights were reserved under the Winters Doctrine at the time reservations were created. *Arizona v. California* defined this standard as enough water to sustain all practicably irrigable acreage, the goal being to make reservation land habitable and productive.

Trends in Indian water-rights law since *Arizona v. California* indicate that water rights may be reserved for uses other than agriculture, such as fishing (*see **Pyramid Lake Paiute Tribe v. Morton***, 354 F. Supp. 252 [D.D.C. 1972]). Beginning in the 1970s, Native American goals of economic self-sufficiency have been an added factor in encouraging use of water under the Winters Doctrine and subsequent rulings. The court in *Arizona v. California* held that neither Congress nor the president would have meant to establish reservations without access to enough water to sustain the people living on them.

Winters Doctrine rights have been held to apply to underground water as well as surface supplies, as at Death Valley National Monument in *Cappaert v. United States*, 426 U.S. 128 (1976). Winters rights also are transferred if land is allotted. Winters rights also may be leased to non-Indians as part of a lease of Indian-owned land, as in *Skeem v. United States*, 273 F.2d 93 (9th Cir. 1921).

FURTHER READING

Burton, Lloyd. *American Indian Water Rights and the Limits of Law.* Lawrence KS: University Press of Kansas, 1991.

ARTICLES OF CONFEDERATION
Article IX of the Articles of Confederation vested the Continental Congress with "the sole and exclusive right and power of . . . regulating the trade and managing all affairs of Indians not members of any of the states; provided, that the legislative right of any state within its own limits not be infringed or violated." This was similar to the provision that **Benjamin Franklin** wrote into the **Albany Plan of Union** at the behest of the Iroquois and other Native Americans.

Many people contributed to the creation of the Articles of Confederation, but Benjamin Franklin was the predominant intellectual force behind the design for a loose confederation of states that resembled his Albany Plan of Union. It was a federal system that he had remarked "had subsisted ages" among the Iroquois. The system was not as durable for the new United States; it was replaced by the **Constitution** in 1789.

ASSIMILATION
Much of U.S. policy toward American Indians has been based on assumptions that the greater social good demanded that Indians become absorbed into "mainstream" society. A number of policies, from the establishment of schools and churches to the allotment of Indian land, have been implemented with the ulterior motive of assimilation.

During much of its first century under the Constitution, the United States dealt with Indian nations as semisovereign political entities by **treaty**. The legal interpretation of this relationship was set down by Chief Justice **John Marshall** in his **Marshall Trilogy**. In 1871, however, Congress stopped treaty making and embarked on a number of other measures aimed at assimilation of Indians into the "mainstream" culture. At the time, assimilation often was advanced by reformers as a desirable alternative to extinction.

Many Indians did not desire the future that was being constructed for them by powers beyond their control. Gen. Philip Sheridan, one of the principal U.S. Army commanders during the Indian wars of the western plains, remarked in 1878, as the wars were ending: "We took away their country and their means of support, broke up their mode of living, their habits of life, introduced disease and decay among them[,] and it was for this and against this that they made war. Could anyone expect less?" (Morris 1992: 376).

Nevertheless, as early as 1819, the U.S. Congress passed an act to establish a "civilization fund" for Indians, notably for the construction of schools by benevolent societies. The act urged that the schools be used to introduce among the Indians "habits and arts of civilization, including "agriculture . . . and . . . teaching their children in reading, writing, and arithmetic." The act asserted that its provisions would be "for the purpose of providing against the further decline and final extinction of the Indian tribes." Congress allotted $10,000 for the fund's first year.

Assimilation was the goal of a paternalistic educational system established for Indian young people late in the 1870s by Gen. Richard Henry Pratt, a reformer who coined the assimilationist slogan "Kill the Indian, save the man," which was used to convince Congress to appropriate money for Indian education that had spread to a nationwide complex of schools by 1900. Pratt's Indian schools were run on army-style boot-camp discipline, the idea being to make the Indian children anew in the image of churchgoing small farmers with the rudiments of an Anglo-American cultural heritage. Discipline was sometimes personal and petty. Albert White Hat, an instructor of Lakota at Sinte Gleska University on the Rosebud Reservation in South Dakota, recalled instances at St. Francis Indian School in which he and his classmates had their mouths washed out with soap for speaking their native language. In 1872, the commissioner of Indian affairs was quoted as saying that the reservation must become "a legalized reformatory," where Native Americans would adopt non-Indian ways "peaceably if they will, forcibly if they must."

Some supporters of assimilation put the case for it in more ethnocentric terms, such as the Office of the Commissioner of Indian Affairs in 1901:

Indian dances and so-called Indian feasts should be prohibited. In many cases these dances and feasts are simply subterfuges to cover degrading acts and disguise immoral purposes. You [Indian agents] are directed to use your best efforts in the suppression of these evils.

The rules for the court of Indian offenses on the Pine Ridge Reservation in 1908 included a ban on "the sun dance and all other similar dances and so-called religious ceremonies." An Indian convicted of dancing could, on the first offense, be deprived of rations for up to ten days. A second offense called for deprivation of rations for fifteen to thirty days, or for up to thirty days in the agency prison.

In 1875, Congress moved to make Indians on reservations subject to federally supervised policing. Family, religious, and economic affairs of Indians were strictly regulated by the Bureau of Indian Affairs in 1882, and Congress set up mechanisms to enforce an individualized property-holding ethic among Indians in the General **Allotment Act** of 1887.

From the points of view of many Native Americans, assimilation was the essence of political oppression on a very personal level. In the early 1940s, Winnebago Reuben Snake attended a mission school in Neillsville, Wisconsin, directed by Jacob Stucki, a medical doctor and minister in the United Church of Christ. Snake recalled that "the founder of the school had raised his children among the Winnebago so that they would all be fluent in the Winnebago language. But the rule enforced at the school was that we couldn't speak our own native language. We had to speak English. We couldn't practice any of our cultural activities, because they would be condemned as pagan. . . . That was my first experience with hypocrisy, of the whites, preaching one thing and doing another" (1996: 49).

As assimilation was being legislated, the Supreme Court denied citizenship to Indians who wished to take the policy to its logical conclusion. In 1884, in **Elk v. Wilkins**, Indians were denied the right to vote, despite the wording of the recently passed Fourteenth Amendment.

FURTHER READING

Barsh, Russel, and James Henderson. *The Road: Indian Tribes and Political Liberty*. Berkeley: University of California Press, 1980.

Morris, Roy, Jr. *Sheridan: The Life and Wars of General Phil Sheridan*. New York: Crown Publishers, 1992.

O'Brien, Sharon. *American Indian Tribal Governments*. Norman: University of Oklahoma Press, 1989.

Pommersheim, Frank. *Braid of Feathers: American Indian Law and Contemporary Tribal Life*. Berkeley: University of California Press, 1995.

Snake, Reuben. *Reuben Snake, Your Humble Serpent: Indian Visionary and Activist, as Told to Jay C. Fikes*. Santa Fe, NM: Clear Light, 1996.

ASSINIBOINE POLITICAL TRADITIONS

The basic political unit among the Assiniboine was the band, which might comprise two hundred to eight hundred people living in families averaging eight each. Bands were autonomous and sovereign, even when they met for ceremonies, including their annual sun dance. Unlike the **Cheyennes**, who also used the band as a basic political unit, the Assiniboines had no central council.

Membership of Assiniboine bands was fluid. At marriage, a couple could migrate with either the husband's or the wife's band. Assiniboine bands constantly gained or lost individual members based on personal preferences. If major differences arose between two factions of a single band, one would usually volunteer to leave and form a group of its own.

Within the band, a chief's authority was limited. When U.S. commissioners appointed the Assiniboine Crazy Bear as a representative at the **Treaty of Fort Laramie** in 1851, for example, they did not understand that he could speak only for himself and members of his band who agreed with him, not for all of the Assiniboine bands. Most major policy decisions within a given band were made by its council, a loose association of men in the band who had distinguished themselves in hunting and war.

The band chief, who was elected by acclamation, acted as a chief executive of the council and held responsibility for directing the band's military (or soldier) society to enforce the council's decisions. A chief was held to certain behavioral standards, those that Assiniboines believed constituted a "good man." Such a man put the welfare of the band above that of himself and his own family. He was kind, generous, and skilled at solving disputes by negotiation. If the chief was wealthy, he was expected to be generous with presents. He was also expected to be modest—and the higher his esteem, the more modest his behavior was expected to be. The chief determined the line of march on migrations, set the place and time to make camp, controlled the dispatch of war parties, and decided when to call the band council into session.

FURTHER READING

Rodnick, David. "Political Structure and Status among the Assiniboine Indians." *American Anthropologist* 39 (1937): 408–416.

AZTEC (MEXICA) POLITICAL TRADITIONS

In the Aztecs' complex society, located in the Valley of Mexico, each person was born into a social class. At the head of this sociological pyramid was the king (*tlatoani* or *tlacatecuhtli*), a descendant of the Toltec prince Acamapichtli, who, in turn, was said to have been descended from Quetzalcoatl, the principal god of the Toltecs. Aztec history described how the prince had come to Tenochtitlan to found the city's royal line from unions with twenty wives, probably one from each *calpulli* (clan).

The nobles (*pipiltin*) were distinguished by the legal permission afforded them to own land in their own names upon adulthood. They also were taught to use glyphs (a form of Aztec writing), along with cultural arts and religion. They held the highest judicial, military, civil, and religious posts, but membership in this class (all of whose members also were offspring of the Toltec prince who sired the king) did not guarantee a prestigious office. Office required leadership skills. Nobles who did not have such skills might end up being palace servants, or even being unemployed. Below the nobles stood a class of knights (*caballeros pardos*), who had been raised to their standing, usually from the lower classes, because of valor in warfare.

The commoners or working class (*macehualtin*) were educated to farm communal lands or to ply trades. They could not own land (farms were the property of the *calpulli*), but they could consume, sell, or exchange what they produced from it. A talented member of this class could rise to the high offices of his *calpulli* and thereby in practice outrank a noble with no official position. A separate class (sometimes called a propertyless proletariat) owned no land, but also had no masters. Typically, members of this class might work as craftspeople or day laborers.

Aztec serfs (*mayeques*) could sometimes work their way out of this status into the working class. Aside from the noble ranks, Aztec class structure was sometimes fluid: people could rise and fall on merit or luck. Serfs were assigned to certain plots of land and were paid with a portion of their produce from it. If land was sold, the serfs assigned to it were considered part of the transaction. Besides agricultural work, serfs were expected to render menial services to their masters. Men might haul water or build a house; women might prepare meals. A large number of Aztec serfs were commoners from conquered nations; some native Aztec commoners even tried to pass as serfs to avoid paying taxes.

Slaves could be assigned to any job by their masters, but the master owned only the labor of the slave, not his or her life. A slave could own a residence and could not be traded or sold to another master without consent. The status often was temporary; a slave could even own the services of another slave.

The Aztecs governed themselves according to a clan-based system that included aspects of **consensus** and hierarchy. This system did not fit any European category of government. The state was comprised of twenty clans, or *calpulli*, each of which elected officials similar to county clerks or aldermen. Each clan also elected a speaker (*tlatoani*), who sat on a supreme state council. From these leaders, four were appointed to executive posts. In Tenochtitlan, one of these four, called *tlacatecuhtli* (chief of men) or *hueytlatoani* (revered speaker) was chosen to be chief executive, a lifetime appointment.

Some Spanish accounts refer to the government as a "republic," while others designate leaders as "kings." Elected along kin lines, Aztec leaders enjoyed total authority once they were elevated to supreme office. Ownership of most land rested with the clans. This concept often confused the Spanish, who were accustomed to individual or royal ownership.

Another concept that sometimes confused the Spanish, who came from a male-dominated society, was the influence of Mexica women. The Mexica language referred to a woman as "the owner of a man." Some Spanish observers remarked on the role of Aztec women, who often held high positions in the Aztec religious order. Women and men treated each other as equals at social occasions and affairs of state; a woman who died in childbirth was spoken of with the same reverence as a soldier who had died in battle. Aztec women were masters of the home and the marketplace; they also worked as artists, artisans, seamstresses, and salespeople. An Aztec woman of the elite class could also own property in her own name.

FURTHER READING

Leon-Portilla, Miguel. *The Aztec Image of Self and Society: An Introduction to Nahua Culture.* Salt Lake City: University of Utah Press, 1992.
———. *Pre-Columbian Literature of Mexico.* Norman: University of Oklahoma Press, 1969.
Mochtezuma, Eduardo Matos. "Templo Mayor: History and Interpretation," in *The Great Temple of Tenochtitlan: Center and Periphery in the Aztec World*, ed. Johanna Broda, David Carrasco, and Mochtezuma. Berkeley: University of California Press, 1988.
Molina Montes, Augusto F. "The Building of Tenochtitlan." *National Geographic* (December 1980), 753–775.

B

BANISHMENT

Traditional Native American justice usually emphasized restitution rather than retribution. Retribution, sometimes in starkly personal terms, often did play a role in serious crimes, especially murder. An extremely antisocial person might be exiled from the community to a near-certain death, also a form of retribution. Banishment was often viewed as worse than execution, since a person without a community often ceased to exist as a human being. In most cases, members of the families involved sought to arrive at mutually agreeable compensation to restore the equilibrium of social relations within the group.

Among some native peoples, such as the **Cheyenne**, a banishment also was accompanied by a purification ceremony to remove the disruption in the harmony of the people. The Cheyenne purified themselves through a ritual that anthropologist E. Adamson Hoebel called Renewal of the Medicine Arrows. Everyone in a native group except the accused (usually a murderer) was required to be present. Military societies compelled attendance. Absolute silence was maintained at the gathering for several hours as the feathers of the Cheyennes' sacred medicine bundle (which were said to have been bloodied by the crime) were replaced.

A banished Cheyenne could request reinstatement from the nation's Council of Forty-four if he had been able to survive on his own or in the company of friendly Arapahoes or Sioux. The appeal had to be approved by the victim's family. Even after reinstatement of most civil rights, a murderer was reminded of his crime for his entire remaining lifetime, as other Cheyenne barred him from smoking a common pipe or eating from a common bowl.

Banishment was used as an experimental punishment at least once in the 1990s. In Everett, Washington, two Tlingit teenagers, Simon Roberts and Adrian Guthrie, were sentenced to eighteen months' banishment on an island off the southeast coast of Alaska by state judge James Allendoerfer after they were convicted of severely beating a pizza deliveryman. Before the sentence was completed, however, Judge Allendoerfer ordered the two boys to prison in the Shelton, Washington, state correctional center. Guthrie was sentenced to thirty-one months and Roberts to fifty-five months.

FURTHER READING

Hoebel, E. Adamson. *The Law of Primitive Man*. Cambridge, MA: Harvard University Press, 1954.

BILL OF RIGHTS, NATIVE AMERICAN PRECEDENTS

Thomas Jefferson, the primary author of the Bill of Rights, described American Indian societies in ways strikingly similar to his visions of the state he hoped to erect, modified to suit a people of Old World ancestry. Writing to James Madison on January 30, 1787, from Paris, Jefferson examined three forms of societies:

1. Without government, as among our Indians. 2. Under governments wherein the will of every one has a just influence, as is the case in England in a slight degree, and in our states in great one. 3. Under governments of force, as is the case in all other monarchies and in most of the other republics. (Boyd, 11: 92–93)

"It is a problem, not clear in my mind, that the 1st condition [the Indian way] is not the best," Jefferson wrote. "But I believe it to be inconsistent with any great degree of population." American Indians and their societies figured into conceptions of life, liberty, and happiness in the minds of Jefferson and **Benjamin Franklin**, who operated in many ways as Jefferson's revolutionary mentor. Both sought to create a society that operated as much as possible on **consensus** and public opinion, while citing the same mechanisms in native societies. Both described Indians' passion for liberty while making it a patriotic rallying cry; they admired Indians' notions of happiness while seeking a definition that would suit the new nation. Franklin wrote:

All the Indians of North America not under the dominion of the Spaniards are in that natural state, being restrained by no Laws, having no Courts, or Ministers of Justice, no Suits, no prisons, no governors vested with any Legal Authority. The persuasion of Men distinguished by Reputation of Wisdom is the only

Means by which others are govern'd, or rather led—and the State of the Indians was probably the first State of all Nations. (Lynd 1968: 85)

Jefferson said much the same in his *Notes on Virginia*. This wording was inserted into the 1787 edition, as the Constitutional Convention was meeting. Native Americans, wrote Jefferson, had never

submitted themselves to any laws, any coercive power and shadow of government. Their only controls are their manners, and the moral sense of right and wrong. . . . An offence against these is punished by contempt, by exclusion from society, or, where the cause is serious, as that of murder, by the individuals whom it concerns. Imperfect as this species of control may seem, crimes are very rare among them. (Jefferson [1784]: 93)

The lesson here seemed clear to Jefferson: "Insomuch that it were made a question, whether no law, as among the savage Americans, or too much law, as among the civilized Europeans, submits man to the greater evil, one who has seen both conditions of existence would pronounce it to be the last" (Ford, 395n.).

Jefferson discussed the political system of the **Iroquois Confederacy** in his *Notes on Virginia* and then diffused his observations and ideas to many influential people, including Marquis de Lafayette, James Madison, and Franklin. *Notes* ran through several editions, was quickly translated into French, and proved popular enough to be pirated. The book was current reading in the United States at the time of the Constitutional Convention, a period that Jefferson himself spent in France.

Writing to Edward Carrington in 1787, Jefferson linked freedom of expression with public opinion as well as happiness, citing American Indian societies as an example:

The basis of our government being the opinion of the people, our very first object should be to keep that right; and were it left to me to decide whether we should have a government without newspapers or newspapers without a government, I should not hesitate for a moment to prefer the latter. . . . I am convinced that those societies [like the Indians] which live without government enjoy in their general mass an infinitely greater degree of happiness than those who live under European governments. (Boyd, 11: 49)

"Without government" could not have meant without social order to Jefferson. He and Franklin knew native societies too well to argue that Native Americans functioned totally without social cohesion, in the classic Noble Savage image as autonomous wild men of the woods. Jefferson, Franklin, and Paine had experience with native leaders as treaty negotiators, a peer relationship from which each observed Native American political systems and other aspects of culture for several decades.

FURTHER READING

Boyd, Julian, ed. *The Papers of Thomas Jefferson*. Vol. 11. Princeton, NJ: Princeton University Press, 1950–1974.

Ford, Paul L., ed. *The Writings of Thomas Jefferson*. New York: J. P. Putnam's Sons, 1892–1800.

Grinde, Donald A., Jr., and Bruce E. Johansen. *Exemplar of Liberty: Native America and the Evolution of Democracy*. Los Angeles: UCLA American Indian Studies Center, 1991.

Jefferson, Thomas. *Notes on the State of Virginia* [1784]. Ed. William Peden. Chapel Hill: University of North Carolina Press, 1955.

Lynd, Staughton. *Intellectual Origins of American Radicalism*. New York: Random House, 1968.

BLACK HILLS, LEGAL STATUS

The Black Hills (or *paha sapa*, "hills that are black") have been deemed sacred land in the oral history of the **Sioux** since about 1800, after the Sioux migrated to the area to avoid Euro-American settlement in their former homeland north and west of the Great Lakes. The Sioux firmly controlled the Black Hills in 1874, when Anglo-American settlers, enticed by an expedition into the hills under command of George Armstrong Custer, found rich deposits of gold in the area.

The Black Hills were reserved for the Sioux in the **Fort Laramie Treaty** of 1868, which was signed after Red Cloud and other Sioux leaders mounted attacks against the U.S. Army serious enough to cause the United States to abandon its forts along the Bozeman Trail. The Treaty of Fort Laramie was a rare instance in which the United States negotiated a peace in which it gave the Indians everything they asked, and asked no quid pro quo in return.

Following Custer's intrusion into the Black Hills in 1874, reports of gold and other exploitable minerals drew large numbers of non-Indians. By 1875, the United States was attempting to acquire the land from the Sioux. The Fort Laramie Treaty of 1868 barred land cessions by the Sioux without the consent of three-quarters of the adult men covered by the treaty. Negotiators for the United States were unable to get more than 10 percent of Sioux men to approve of selling the Black Hills. In the context of these events, a Sioux-Cheyenne alliance defeated Custer's forces at the Battle of the Little Bighorn in 1876. Disregarding the treaty provision and exploiting a volatile political atmosphere following Custer's defeat, the U.S. Congress in 1877 ratified transfer of the land.

In 1946, with the creation of the **Indian Claims Commission**, the Sioux again pressed for annulment of the 1877 act of Congress taking the Black Hills. After two decades, the Indian Claims Commission validated the Sioux claim. This time, the U.S. Claims Commission also upheld the Sioux claim on the grounds that the original expropriation of the Black Hills was an illegal "taking" within the meaning of the **Fifth Amendment** to the U.S. Constitution.

In 1980, the U.S. Supreme Court affirmed the ruling in *United States v. Sioux Nation*. The Sioux were therefore owed $17.5 million for the land value at the time of the taking, plus interest at 5 percent a year. By the late 1990s, the total, with interest accrued, had risen to roughly $400 million as the Sioux debated whether to press for return of the land or accept the cash settlement.

FURTHER READING

Ball, Milnar. "Constitution, Court, Indian Tribes." *American Bar Foundation Research Journal*, no. 1 (Winter, 1987): 1–140.
Cadwallader, Sandra, and Vine Deloria, Jr., eds. *The Aggressions of Civilization: Federal Indian Policy since the 1880s*. Philadelphia: Temple University Press, 1984.
Johansen, Bruce E., and Roberto F. Maestas. *Wasi'chu: The Continuing Indian Wars*. New York: Monthly Review Press, 1979.
Lazarus, Edward. *Black Hills, White Justice: The Sioux Nation versus the United States, 1775 to the Present*. New York: HarperCollins, 1991.

BLOOD QUANTUM

Native American nations and bands within the United States set their own standards for membership, usually as a measure of "blood quantum," or percentage of a person's ancestry from that band or nation. Some accept a quantum as low as 1/32 (3 percent), but most set the standard at about one-quarter (25 percent). Some native groups also apply patriarchal or matriarchal rules of descent, which have been upheld by the U.S. Supreme Court, notably in *Santa Clara Pueblo v. Martinez*.

BOLDT, GEORGE (1903–1984)

On February 12, 1974, in *United States v. Washington*, U.S. District Court Judge George Boldt ruled that Indians were entitled to an opportunity to catch as many as half the fish returning to off-reservation sites that had been the "usual and accustomed places" when treaties were signed with Puget Sound Native Americans in the 1850s. The case became an object of major controversy between Indians and commercial and sports fishermen.

Boldt had put three years into the case; he used two hundred pages to interpret one sentence of the treaty in an opinion that some legal scholars say is the most carefully researched, thoroughly analyzed decision ever handed down in an Indian fishing-rights case. The nucleus of Boldt's decision had to do with nineteenth-century dictionaries' definitions of "in common with." Boldt said that the phrase meant "to be shared equally." During the next three years, the Ninth Circuit Court of

Appeals upheld Boldt's ruling, and the U.S. Supreme Court twice let it stand by refusing to hear an appeal.

Judge Boldt's ruling had a profound effect not only on who would be allowed to catch salmon in Puget Sound, but on racial relations generally. Bruce J. Miller characterized the situation in the *American Indian Culture and Research Journal*:

The relative powerlessness of the Indian communities left non-Indians unprepared for the sudden turn of events brought about by the Boldt decision, and the shocked white community reacted immediately. Non-Indians, who had long come to regard the salmon harvest as virtually their own, were suddenly faced with the possible prospect of being forced out of the fishing industry, or [of] facing large reductions in their catch. Hostility became so serious that Indians armed their fish camps after enduring attacks on themselves and their equipment. Many whites displayed their reaction to the decision with bumper stickers proclaiming "Can Judge Boldt" on their cars. A widely held view was that the Boldt decision had given an unfair advantage to Indians in the fisheries. (1993:77)

State officials and the fishermen whose interests they represented were furious at Boldt. Rumors circulated about Boldt's sanity. It was said that he had taken bribes of free fish and had an Indian mistress, neither of which was true. Judge Boldt was hung in effigy by angry non-Indian fishermen, who on other occasions formed "convoys" with their boats and rammed Coast Guard vessels that had been dispatched to enforce the court's orders. At least one coastguardsman was shot.

FURTHER READING

American Friends Service Committee. *Uncommon Controversy: Fishing Rights of the Muckleshoot, Puyallup, and Nisqually Indians.* Seattle: University of Washington Press, 1970.

Barsh, Russel L. *The Washington Fishing Rights Controversy: An Economic Critique.* Seattle: University of Washington School of Business Administration, 1977.

Brack, Fred. "Fishing Rights: Who Is Entitled to Northwest Salmon?" *Seattle Post-Intelligencer Northwest Magazine,* January 16, 1977.

Brown, Bruce. *Mountain in the Clouds.* New York: Simon & Schuster, 1982.

Miller, Bruce J. "The Press, the Boldt Decision, and Indian-White Relations." *American Indian Culture and Research Journal* 17:2 (1993): 75–98.

Roderick, Janna. "Indian-White Relations in the Washington Territory: The Question of Treaties and Indian Fishing Rights." *Journal of the West* 16:3 (July 1977): 23–34.

United States v. Washington, 384 F. Supp. 312 (1974).

BRYAN V. ITASCA COUNTY 426 U.S. 373 (1976)

Itasca County, Minnesota, sought to impose a personal property tax on reservation Indians, arguing that **Public Law 280** granted that right if a state had assumed civil jurisdiction. The U.S. Supreme Court disagreed, arguing that P.L. 280 conferred adjudicatory jurisdiction only. Taken to the extreme that Itasca County advocated, reservations would have become subject to all non-Indian law and would have lost their distinct historical characteristics.

This case arose because the language of P.L. 280 stipulates that civil jurisdiction in states that assume it under the law provides that the "civil laws of [the] State . . . shall have the same force and effect within Indian Country as they have elsewhere within the State." The personal property on which Itasca County sought to impose taxation was not being held in trust by the federal government, so it was argued that the tax was permissible under P.L. 280. The U.S. Supreme Court rejected this contention, holding that

nothing in its legislative history remotely suggests that Congress meant [that] the Act's extension of civil jurisdiction to the states should result in the undermining or destruction of such tribal governments as did exist and the conversion of the affected tribes into "little more than "private, voluntary organizations," . . . a possible result if tribal governments and reservation Indians were subordinated to the full panoply of civil regulatory powers, including taxation, of state and local governments.

BURKE ACT 34 Stat. 182 (1906)

The General **Allotment Act** (1887) prescribed that individual acreage granted to Indians was to be held in trust for twenty-five years, or until at least 1912 for the earliest allottees under the act. In 1906, however, Congress passed the Burke Act, which allowed transfer of land titles in fee simple to Indians judged "competent." If judged competent, the Native American landowner was then forced to pay taxes on the land or sell it.

BURSUM BILL (1922)

Senator Holm O. Bursum of New Mexico introduced the Bursum Bill in an attempt to quiet title to the lands of the New Mexico **Pueblos**. The bill would have required people living in the Pueblos to prove title to the land they occupied, something that was often nearly impossible because the Pueblos' residency predated the imposition of Spanish and U.S. legal systems. The bill was meant to give non-Indian immigrants an advantage over the Pueblos in competition for land. This bill passed the Senate on September 11, 1922, but popular outrage among the Pueblos kept it from being passed in the House of Representatives. The Bursum Bill has been characterized by Pueblo scholar Joe Sando as a blatant land grab by political interests. The controversy that followed debate over the Bursum Bill ultimately led to establishment of a special board to adjudicate disputes over land between Pueblos and non-Indians.

FURTHER READING

Sando, Joe. *Pueblo Nations: Eight Centuries of Pueblo Indian History.* Santa Fe, NM: Clear Light, 1992.

C

CALIFORNIA INDIANS, POLITICAL AND LEGAL TRADITIONS

At the time of the first sustained contact with the Spanish in the sixteenth century, Native American peoples living in present-day California numbered more than 400,000, in several hundred distinct cultures, many of which numbered only a few hundred people each. Political and legal organization was often very well developed at the village level, but only rarely exceeded the scale of small, loose confederacies. This lack of political organization made California Indians easy prey for virtual slavery on Spanish missions. Later, after the United States seized California from Mexico in 1848, the in-migration prompted by the gold rush obliterated most surviving Native Americans in California. By 1900, the Bureau of Indian Affairs found fewer than 17,000 native people surviving there. Most social, political, and legal organization was lost, but some of it can be gleaned from studies in anthropology.

The principles of Yurok law were described by anthropologist A. L. Kroeber in his classic *Handbook of the Indians of California* (1925). All rights and all conflicts were held to be personal; there was, in effect, a civil code, but not a criminal one. There also was no punishment among the Yurok, according to Kroeber, because they had no state to inflict or enforce it. Additionally, individual revenge was not sanctioned because the Yurok believed that revenge merely created another offense. All offenses were held to be valued in money (or goods representing money), and a payment was negotiated by the offending and offended parties. After the agreed payment had been made, the Yurok believed that the damage had been remedied. Even the harboring of bad feelings was considered improper in Yurok society.

Nearly all value could be measured in money by the Yuroks, and debt was the only way a person could fall into slavery. Land deemed valuable for hunting was privately owned among the Yurok, whose society was sharply class ranked, with little opportunity for social mobility. Material wealth was prized and avidly sought. The Yuroks shared these values with other northern California native bands, such as the Hupa. Kroeber described the headman of a Hupa village as usually the wealthiest, the holder of substantial property, including hunting and fishing rights to large areas. For their obedience, the headman owed the other villagers food in time of scarcity and arbitration (an arrangement of money payment) in times of trouble. Both property and political power were inherited in the male line. Hupa villages had no councils, although the headman sometimes would consult with the wiser men of the village before making important decisions. The headmen also played an important judicial function among the Shasta, in northern California. Their chiefs were responsible for setting the amount of payment due for injury. If an offender could not meet the price, the chief might loan or grant him the money, thereby enhancing his power over the offender.

In central California, a Yuki chief was also invariably described as a rich man who was a natural leader, hospitable, and generous with his assets in time of need, but not a fool with his fortune. A Yuki chief was selected by acclamation of his village and could be deposed when his popular support ebbed. While the chief would decide when the time for war had come, he would not go into battle himself. He also supervised ceremonial dances. In many cases, according to Kroeber, the chief demonstrated his readiness for leadership by organizing his kinfolk to erect a dance-house to which they could then assert ownership.

Among the Pomo, who lived along the northern California coast, two groups of chiefs were recognized. A "major chief" was elected by **consensus** to lead a group of villages that acted as a political unit. Each of the individual extended families within this loose confederation was led by a subchief (called a "surrounding chief"). The surrounding chiefs made up a council that consulted with the major chief. The major chief presided at ceremonial occasions and was charged with "lecturing to" his people, but he had no powers of direct control other than his powers of persuasion.

Yokut chiefs (in present-day southern California) were chosen by consensus for their ability to acquire wealth as well as their knowledge of spiritual matters. The Yokuts had a well-developed governmental organization, with several established political roles other than that of the chief. One role was that of the herald, who announced policy decisions and collected shell-money for ceremonies. Another position (which was held for life) was that of the clown, whose business it was to mock sacred ceremonies and act nonsensically.

FURTHER READING

Kroeber, A. L. *Handbook of the Indians of California.* Washington, DC: Interior Department, 1925.

CALIFORNIA V. CABAZON BAND OF MISSION INDIANS 480 U.S. 202 (1987)

The U.S. Supreme Court upheld reservation Indians' right to conduct gambling free of state control in *California v. Cabazon Band of Mission Indians*, despite the fact that California claims civil and criminal jurisdiction under **Public Law 280**. The situation regarding P.L. 280 is exceedingly complex. In California, according to a number of court rulings, state criminal jurisdiction is concurrent with that of Native American governments; regulatory issues have been held to be outside of state jurisdiction.

This case arose after California asserted a right to regulate gambling (including card games and bingo) on the reservations of the Cabazon and Morongo bands of Mission Indians. California asserted that the Indian gaming enterprises violated state law, which prohibited bingo except for charitable purposes. Riverside County also asserted that Indian gaming violated local ordinances that regulated bingo and prohibited games of chance played with cards.

A lawsuit was filed in federal court to turn aside the state's assertion of jurisdiction. The Supreme Court found that since California does not prohibit all gambling, its statute was regulatory (civil) rather than prohibitive (criminal) in nature. The state was therefore found to have no jurisdiction in the matter, because the Court held that "state regulation would impermissibly infringe on tribal government."

CANASSATEGO (Onondaga) (c. 1690–1750)

Canassatego was tadadaho (speaker) of the **Iroquois Confederacy** in the middle of the eighteenth century and a major figure in diplomacy with the French and English colonists. His advice that the colonies should form a union on the Iroquois model influenced the plans of **Benjamin Franklin** for colonial union as early as 1754. Later in the century, a fictional Canassatego became a figure in English social satire and other literature.

In 1744, Pennsylvania officials met with Iroquois sachems in council at Lancaster, Pennsylvania. This meeting was one of a number of significant diplomatic parlays between British colonists, the Iroquois, and their allies that preceded and helped shape the outcome of the French and Indian War. At the meeting, Canassatego and other Iroquois complained that the colonies, with no central authority, had been unable to restrain invasion of Native American lands by settlers. In that context, Canassatego advised the colonists to form a union emulating that of the Iroquois:

Our wise forefathers established Union and Amity between the Five Nations. This has made us formidable; this has given us great Weight and Authority with our neighboring Nations. We are a powerful Confederacy; *and by your observing the same methods our wise forefathers have taken*, you will acquire such Strength and power. Therefore whatever befalls you, never fall out with one another. (emphasis added) (Van Doren and Boyd 1938: 75)

Richard Peters, delegate from Pennsylvania, described Canassatego at Lancaster as "a tall, well-made man," with "a very full chest and brawny limbs, a manly countenance, with a good-natired [*sic*] smile. He was about 60 years of age, very active, strong, and had a surprising liveliness in his speech" (Boyd 1981: 244–245).

At the time of the Lancaster Treaty Council, Franklin, a Philadelphia printer, was publishing the transcripts of Indian treaty councils as small booklets that enjoyed a lively sale in the colonies and in England. The **Lancaster Treaty** was one of several dozen treaty accounts that he published between 1736 and 1762. Franklin read Canassatego's words when they issued from his press, and he became an advocate of colonial union by the early 1750s, when he began his diplomatic career as a Pennsylvania delegate to the Iroquois and their allies. Franklin urged the British colonies to unite in emulation of the Iroquois Confederacy in a letter to his printing partner James Parker in 1751, and when he drew up his **Albany Plan of Union** in 1754.

After he advised colonial leaders to form a federal union at the Lancaster Treaty Council of 1744, Canassatego also became a British literary figure, the hero of John Shebbeare's *Lydia, or, Filial Piety*, published in 1755. The real Canassatego had died in 1750. With the flowery eloquence prized by romantic novelists of his time, Shebbeare portrayed Canassatego as something more than human—something more, even, than the "Noble Savage" that was so popular in Enlightenment Europe. Having saved the life of a helpless English maiden from the designs of a predatory English ship captain en route, Canassatego, once in England, became judge and jury for all that was contradictory and corrupt in mid-eighteenth-century England.

Disembarking, Shebbeare's Canassatego meets with a rude sight: a ragged collection of dwellings "little better than the Huts of Indians," and men rising from the bowels of the earth, dirty, broken, and degraded. Asking his hosts for an explanation, Canassatego is told that the men have been digging coal. The Iroquois sachem inquires whether everyone in England digs coal for a living, and reflects that he is beginning to understand why so many English have fled to America.

By Shebbeare's fictional account, Canassatego came to England not only as a tourist, but also to present a petition of grievances on behalf of his people. Continually frustrated in his efforts to do so, he finds England's leaders to be persons of small measure. The prime minister, in particular, strikes Canassatego as "ungrateful, whiffling, inconsistent, [a man] whose words included nothing to be understood . . . the farce and mockery of national prudence." Exasperated, Canassatego asks, "Can it be . . . that this man can direct the business of a people?" (Shebbeare 1974: Act III, 264).

By and by, Canassatego meets Lady Susan Overstay, a woman of rank and breeding who is overly conscious of her lofty station in society. Faced with a windy exposition by Lady Overstay on the quality of her breeding, Canassatego replies that in his country no one is born any better than anyone else, and that wisdom, courage, and love of family and nation, as well as other virtues of the mind and body, are "the only qualities that give authority and esteem among the Indians" (Bissell 1925: 206).

The character of Canassatego that Shebbeare created says a lot about what addled Europe late in the age of monarchy. It says as much about what people yearned for: freedom from oppressive taxation and the falseness of social convention, from a caste system that enriched a few and impoverished many. It would be a mere century from the needling of a fictional Indian to the first publication of The Communist Manifesto.

Canassatego's words echoed to the eve of the American Revolution, amplified by Franklin's talents as author and publisher. In 1775, Canassatego's thirty-one-year-old advice was recalled at a treaty between colonial representatives and Iroquois leaders. The treaty commissioners told the sachems that they were heeding the advice Iroquois forefathers had given to the colonial Americans at Lancaster, Pennsylvania, in 1744. At this point, the commissioners quoted Canassatego's words:

Brethren, We the Six Nations heartily recommend Union and a good agreement between you our Brethren. Never disagree but preserve a strict Friendship for one another and thereby you as well as we will become stronger. Our Wise Forefathers established Union and Amity between the Five Nations. . . . We are a powerful Confederacy, and if you observe the same methods . . . you will acquire fresh strength and power. ("Proceedings . . ." 1775)

FURTHER READING

Bissell, Benjamin. The American Indian in English Literature of the Eighteenth Century. New Haven: Yale University Press, 1925.

Boyd, Julian. "Dr. Franklin, Friend of the Indian." In *Meet Dr. Franklin*, ed. Roy Lokken, Jr. Philadelphia: Franklin Institute, 1981.

Grinde, Donald A., Jr., and Bruce E. Johansen. *Exemplar of Liberty: Native America and the Evolution of Democracy*. Los Angeles: UCLA American Indian Studies Center, 1991.

"Proceedings of the Commissioners Appointed by the Continental Congress to Negotiate a Treaty with the Six Nations, 1775." Papers of the Continental Congress, 1774–89. National Archives (M247, Roll 144, Item No. 134). See Treaty Council at German Flats, New York, August 25, 1775.

Shebbeare, John. *Lydia, or Filial Piety*. [1755]. New York: Garland Publishing, 1974.

Van Doren, Carl, and Julian P. Boyd, eds. *Indian Treaties Printed by Benjamin Franklin, 1736–1762*. Philadelphia: Historical Society of Pennsylvania, 1938.

Wallace, Paul A. W. *Indians of Pennsylvania*. Harrisburg: Pennsylvania Historical and Museum Commission, 1961.

CHARRIER V. BELL 496 So. 2d 601 (1986) (*cert. denied*, Louisiana Supreme Court)

An amateur archaeologist dug up 150 Native American graves on private lands in Louisiana, then tried to sell two and one-half tons of burial goods to a museum. The museum expressed doubts that the archaeologist would be able to present clear title, so he filed suit in state court claiming ownership of the remains and burial objects.

Louisiana district and appellate courts denied the plaintiff's assertion that he owned the remains, despite his assertions that they were of unknown origin, more than two hundred years old, and from private lands. The court held that title for the burial goods rested with the descendants of the people buried there. This ruling applied common law concerning the disposition of the dead and burial goods and presaged the adoption of laws in the late 1980s and early 1990s to rebury Indian remains and funerary objects that had been held by museums and historical societies or displayed as tourist attractions (*see* **Repatriation**).

CHECKERBOARD PATTERN

"Checkerboarding" is a colloquial term used to describe a pattern of landownership that has become established on many Indian reservations where a large proportion of land has been sold in small parcels to non-Indians over time. Because of laws that treat Indians and non-Indians differently (*see*, for example, *Oliphant v. Suquamish* and *Montana v. United States*), such ownership patterns make Native American law enforcement and other assertions of **sovereignty** and territorial integrity very difficult.

The General **Allotment Act** (1887) has been a major source of checkerboarding, as Indians sold their allotted land to non-Indians in a piecemeal fashion. At Pine Ridge, for example, more than 50 percent of the land is used by non-Indian farmers and ranchers, while Indians use less than 1 percent of it. In 1968, $170 million was earned from agricultural activities on Indian trust land; Indians were paid less than a third of the total.

FURTHER READING

Schusky, Ernest L. *The Right to Be Indian*. San Francisco: American Indian Educational Publishers, 1970.

CHEROKEE NATION V. GEORGIA 30 U.S. (5 Pet.) 1 (1831)
Following the discovery of gold in 1829, Georgia attempted to assert authority over the Cherokee Nation, which comprised several economically self-sufficient towns with their own farms, mills, animal herds, government, and written language devised by Sequoyah. The assertion of authority by Georgia set the stage for a key test of federal-state relations in the decades before the Civil War, as the Cherokees resisted removal to **Indian Territory** in *Cherokee Nation v. Georgia* and **Worcester v. Georgia** (1832).

The Cherokees sued in federal court under a clause in the **Constitution** (Article III, section 2) that allows foreign citizens or states to seek legal redress against states in the Union. In this case, the Cherokees were suing as an independent nation seeking redress because the state of Georgia had extended its power over Cherokee territory, extinguished the authority of the Cherokee government, and executed one of its citizens. Chief Justice **John Marshall** skirted the issue by deciding that the Cherokee were not an independent country, but instead a "domestic dependent nation." Marshall thus threw the case out of court, deciding that the Cherokees had no grounds on which to sue under the Constitution.

Writing for the majority in *Cherokee Nation v. Georgia*, Marshall said that the Cherokees possessed a limited **sovereignty**: "They may, more correctly, perhaps be denominated domestic dependent nations. . . . Their relation to the United States resembles that of a ward to his guardian." These phrases, interpreted by the Bureau of Indian Affairs, became the legal justification for the colonial system that was being imposed on Indians as Anglo-American settlement exploded across North America in the nineteenth century.

In *Cherokee Nation v. Georgia*, the justices of the Supreme Court took a variety of positions on the issue of Native American sovereignty that mirrored societal attitudes toward that issue. While Justices Marshall and John McLean held that Indians lived in domestic dependent nations, Justices Smith Thompson and Joseph Story held that the Cherokees were a sovereign nation. Justice Henry Baldwin wrote that they had no sovereignty at all, and Justice William Johnson believed that the Cherokees had no sovereignty in his time, but that they possessed an inherent political power that could "mature" into more complete independence in the future.

CHEROKEE NATION V. HITCHCOCK 187 U.S. 294 (1902)

Over the opposition of the Cherokees, Ethan Hitchcock, the secretary of the interior, pressed to lease some of their lands for mining. The Cherokees challenged this action as a deprivation of property without due process of law. The U.S. Supreme Court denied the Cherokees' position, finding no question of taking (or, by implication, deprivation of due process of law).

The Court found that the statute in question, which had been passed by Congress in 1898 (30 Stat. 495), related "merely to the control or development of the tribal property." Control over administrative disposition of the land fell within the law, according to the Court's ruling, despite the fact that the Cherokees opposed it. The Court ruled that the action in question fell under an act of Congress and was therefore an exercise of the Congress's **plenary power** over Indian affairs, and thus a political question not open to judicial review. This case was often cited as a basis for both the plenary power and political-question doctrines in subsequent rulings.

CHEROKEE POLITICAL AND LEGAL TRADITIONS

The Cherokee, who called themselves Ani-Yunwiya ("the real people" or "the principal people"), were organized in settlements scattered in fertile bottomlands among the craggy peaks of the Great Smoky Mountains. In the early eighteenth century, the Cherokee Nation comprised sixty villages in five regions, with each village controlling its own affairs. The Cherokees took public opinion so seriously that they usually split their villages when they became too large to permit each adult a voice in council, so the number of villages varied over time.

Villages sent delegates to a national council only in times of national emergency. The **Choctaws**, like the Cherokees, elected leaders from each town or village and sent them to a central council, a system that has been characterized as "amazingly efficient," combining "elected officials, unlimited debate, civilian rule, and local self-government," according to scholars Jesse O. McKee and Jon A. Schlenker (1980: 17). Cherokee villages averaged 300 to 400 persons each; at about 500 people, a village usually split in two. It may have been this political organization that **Thomas Jefferson** had in mind when he penned the following comment regarding a proposal to make the states several times larger than the original colonies:

This is reversing the natural order of things. A tractable people may be governed in large bodies but, in proportion as they depart from this character, the extent of their government must be less. We see into what small divisions the Indians are obliged to reduce their societies. (Koch and Peden 1944: 408)

In Cherokee society, each adult was regarded as an equal in matters of politics. Leadership titles were few and informal, so when Europeans sought "kings" or "chiefs" with whom to negotiate treaties, they usually did not understand that a single person could not compel allegiance or obedience of others. The Cherokees made a conscious effort to keep government to a minimum, in the belief that personal freedom would be enhanced.

According to John Phillip Reid, "The closest approach to a permanent government body, at any level of their society [was] the town council. . . . It was a matter not of legislation; it was a matter of consensus." In the debates that led to **consensus**, according to Reid, "Women were equal to men in every respect. They could speak in the council house . . . and they enjoyed the same sexual license as their men" (1976: 4–5). Duane Champagne, director of UCLA's American Indian Studies Center, warned against overstating the role of women in Cherokee society. "Not any women could speak in council, but specifically designated ones. A women's council appointed according to clan could address the council on issues that concerned the women or other national issues of importance. . . . Men did most of the talking."

A Cherokee headman belonged to a specific clan; he was assisted by a second from the same clan. When a change of leadership was called for, clan elders agreed with the village community as a whole on a successor. Often, the second was groomed for the position. While some European commentators of the time held that the Cherokees and neighboring Native American nations were without government or law, Reid wrote that "the Cherokees did have a national law: a law derived from rules of conduct and attitudes of mind concerning their kinship system" (Reid 1976: 4–5).

As among the **Iroquois**, each Cherokee was a member of a matrilineal clan: Wolf, Deer, Bird, Blue, Red Paint, Wild Potato, or Twisters. The clans formed an intervillage kinship system that linked them in peaceful coexistence. As with many other **confederacies**, a clan system among the Cherokees bound the individual villages together. A man or woman outside his or her own village knew that members of the same clan would be awaiting him or her in other villages to provide hospitality and other support. The clan system cemented the confederacy, giving it a strength and enduring quality that prevented a high degree of local autonomy from degenerating into anarchy. In village councils, each clan caucused before decisions were reached by consensus in a general session.

As they had among the Iroquois before the organization of **Degana-widah**'s confederacy, the clans among the Cherokee had a judicial function. They avenged crimes against their members. If a member of one clan killed a member of another, a life was owed. The power of this sanction was so strong that when it was combined with many other aspects of Cherokee society that restrained violence, the resulting murder rate was insignificant. In Cherokee society, a decent person was one who sought consensus, agreed with the majority, and avoided physical conflict. People who were antisocial by these standards faced ridicule, gossip, and eventual ostracism from the community.

George Milliken Johnson, a surgeon who lived with the Cherokees during the middle of the eighteenth century, observed that "subjugation is what they are unacquainted with . . . there being no such thing as coercive Power among them" (Grinde and Johansen 1991: 34–35). Another observer of the Cherokees commented at about the same time: "It is by native politeness alone . . . that the chiefs bind the hearts of their subjects, and carry them wherever they will" (34–35).

Some similarities between the political systems of the Cherokees, Iroquois, and **Wyandots** (Hurons) probably were not accidental, since all three groups were linked by common ancestry. Floyd G. Loundsbury, a linguist, traced the Iroquois and Cherokee linguistic base to a shared language that split between 3,500 and 3,800 years ago. It is believed that the Cherokees migrated southeastward from the Ohio valley, where they had shared the basics of their language with both the Iroquois and the Wyandots, with some movement taking place as late as 1700. About that time, some of the Tuscaroras moved from an area near Cherokee country to become the sixth nation of the Iroquois.

Like the Iroquois, the Cherokees frowned on concentration of material wealth. Henry Timberlake speculated that the Cherokees buried valuables with the dead to prevent development of a class structure based on inherited wealth, to make "merit the sole means of acquiring power, honor and riches" (Grinde and Johansen 1991: 34–35). According to Timberlake's account, the Cherokees maintained a ceremony to provide for the poor. During a special war dance, each warrior was called on to recount the taking of his first scalp. During the ceremony, anyone with something to spare, "a string of wampum, piece of [silver] plate, wire, paint, lead," heaped the goods on a blanket or animal skin that had been placed on the ground. Afterwards, the collection was divided among the poor of the community, with a share reserved for the musicians who had provided entertainment during the ceremony.

When council meetings were held, a large proportion of the men, women, and children of a village (as many as four hundred people) would gather in the council house; each clan sat together, facing the "beloved old men." The council held no coercive power. Important matters were discussed in the council as a whole, after which the clans caucused individually so that everyone could speak and reach a consensus. Each clan reported its consensus to the village council as it was reached. The council as a whole could adopt a consensus from those of the various clans, or not. If not, there was no binding national consensus, and each clan or group of individuals acted on its own.

Cherokee council meetings could last for several days or even weeks. Debate was usually quiet, with participants trying to avoid direct conflict with other residents of the village. Speeches and debate continued until a consensus was reached. While most of the speechmaking was done by men, women often were active behind the scenes. In addition to the matrilineal nature of the clans, home life was matrilocal among the Cherokee of the Smoky Mountains.

Cherokee political and social ritual displayed a striking affection for the number seven. Not only were there seven clans and seven members on the inner council, but the council house had seven sides (one for each clan). The Great New Moon Feast (the Cherokee New Year, held in the autumn) was preceded by seven days of hunting, seven prominent men were selected to organize the feast, and seven honorable women were picked to prepare it. At dawn on the day of the feast, seven ears of corn (and bits of other crops) were offered to a perpetual fire in the council house. After a sacred dance by the women, the priest-chief led participants to a river that had been scattered with medicinal leaves, where people bathed seven times so that they would be purified and restored. In the evening, the people of the settlement shared a communal banquet.

The Great New Moon Feast opened the most important ritual occasion in Cherokee life, a rite of interpersonal healing. The dates of the ritual were set by the priest-chief and inner council of "beloved men." Seven days before the ritual began, seven men went out to hunt; as the men hunted, seven women selected by the priest-chief and his assistants danced in the village. Seven men were appointed to clean the council house while all village officials fasted. On the seventh day of this ritual, the men who had been cleaning the council house extinguished the central, ceremonial fire of the settlement, after which all families doused their own blazes. The women of each household then relit home fires from a rekindled central blaze. The people then followed the priest to the river and immersed themselves seven times, stripping away their old clothes, as the current swept them downstream. The expressed aim of the entire ritual was renewal of village unity and eradication of anger among villagers that might otherwise be directed at each other.

The fact that the most important peacemaking rituals of the year were held during the council's meeting was probably not accidental. The participation of the entire village in a mass exercise emphasizing unity and eradication of bad feelings allowed the people to get through an otherwise tense time without undue animosity. After the unity ritual ended, the hunters returned with fresh game, signaling the transition from a season of political debate and ritual to the part of the Cherokees' annual cycle where the emphasis was on provision of food and other essentials of daily life.

FURTHER READING

Corkran, David H. *The Cherokee Frontier: Conflict and Survival, 1740–62.* Norman: University of Oklahoma Press, 1962.

Gearing, Fred. *Priests and Warriors: Social Structures for Cherokee Politics in the Eighteenth Century.* Memoir 93, American Anthropological Association, Vol. 64, No. 5, Part 2, October 1962.

Grinde, Donald A., Jr, and Bruce E. Johansen. *Exemplar of Liberty: Native America and the Evolution of Democracy.* Los Angeles: UCLA American Indian Studies Center, 1991.

Koch, Adrienne, and William Peden, eds. *The Life and Selected Writings of Thomas Jefferson.* New York: Modern Library, 1944.

Kupferer, Harriet J. *Ancient Drums, Other Moccasins: Native North American Cultural Adaptation.* Englewood Cliffs, NJ: Prentice-Hall, 1988.

McKee, Jesse O., and Jon A. Schlenker. *The Choctaws: Cultural Evolution of a Native American Tribe.* Jackson: University Press of Mississippi, 1980.

Mooney, James. *Myths of the Cherokee.* In J. W. Powell, Nineteenth Annual Report, Bureau of American Ethnology. Washington, DC: Smithsonian Institution, 1897–1898, part 1.

Perdue, Theda. *Slavery and the Evolution of Cherokee Society.* Knoxville: University of Tennessee Press, 1979.

Reid, John Phillip. *A Better Kind of Hatchet: Law, Trade, and Diplomacy in the Cherokee Nation during the Early Years of European Contact.* University Park: Pennsylvania State University Press, 1976.

———. *A Law of the Blood: The Primitive Law of the Cherokee Nation.* New York: New York University Press, 1970.

CHEROKEE TOBACCO, THE 78 U.S. (11 Wall) 616 (1871)

In *The Cherokee Tobacco,* the Supreme Court held that subsequent congressional action controls a prior Indian treaty. In other words, an Indian treaty may be abrogated by subsequent unilateral congressional action.

In this case, the Court upheld a federal tax on tobacco sold on Cherokee territory despite a treaty providing an exemption. Cherokees Elias Boudinot and Stand Watie refused to pay taxes required by the Internal Revenue Act of 1868 on tobacco raised on the Cherokee Nation because they believed that the Cherokees were exempted from such taxation by the treaty, which had been signed in 1866. This case was an example of judicial deference to the legislative branch in cases affecting American Indians that evolved into the **plenary power** doctrine three decades later in *Cherokee Nation v. Hitchcock* (1902).

CHEYENNE POLITICAL AND LEGAL TRADITIONS

The Cheyennes maintained a powerful central government that united the various Cheyenne bands as well as family-based affinities. At the head of this organization was the Council of Forty-four, on which civil chiefs served ten-year terms. After serving a ten-year term, a Cheyenne chief appointed his own successor, usually from within his own band, but never his own son. The Cheyennes built this and other checks into their system to prevent the rise of a hereditary ruling class. A chief also could not appoint himself to a new term, although he could be "held in the lodge," or reappointed at a future date by another retiring chief. The Council of Forty-four was led by five priest-chiefs. The five "sacred chiefs" remained on the council, with the consent of the rest of its members, after they had completed their ordinary ten-year terms. The leader of the five, who was called Sweet Medicine Chief, acted as a religious intermediary between the Cheyenne and their Creator. He was said to represent Sweet Medicine, the Cheyenne culture hero, who filled a role something like that of **Deganawidah** among the **Iroquois**. The four sub-chiefs, whose names evoked ritual spiritual personages, acted as the head chief's assistants.

Cheyenne oral history holds that Sweet Medicine gave the people a sacred bundle of four arrows (probably about the year 1775), a symbol of a code of laws believed to have been handed down from the Creator or Supreme Being. The Cheyennes' acceptance of the sacred bundle formed a covenant—the Cheyennes believed that they would prosper if they adhered to the laws of the sacred bundle. Later, the prophet Erect Horns brought to the people the sacred buffalo hat and the sun dance. The buffalo hat (sometimes called the "holy hat") was said to ensure survival and well-being of the group, while the sun dance ensured world renewal.

Cheyenne military societies served as police, as well as organizers of war parties. The six societies were called Fox, Elk, Shield, Bowstring, Dog, and Northern Crazy Dogs. These societies maintained order during communal hunts and ceremonial rituals. Discipline meted out by the military societies was swift and unequivocal, especially when a transgression involved jumping the gun during buffalo hunts, when the coordinated action of everyone in the group was held to be sacrosanct. An elderly Cheyenne, Stump Horn, gave an account in 1935 in which Shield Soldiers found two young men who had started the buffalo hunt before the rest of the people, as described by anthropologist E. Adamson Hoebel:

A Shield Soldier chief gave the signal to his men. They paid no attention to the buffalo, but charged in a long line on the two violators of the rules. Little Old Man [a Shield Soldier] shouted out for everyone to whip them: "Those who fail or hesitate shall get a good beating themselves." The first men to reach the spot shot and killed the horses from under the hunters. As each soldier reached the miscreants, he slashed them with his riding whip. Then some seized the guns of the two and smashed them. (1954: 151)

The military societies of the Cheyennes were open to all men in the nation and were more egalitarian than the police societies of the Lakota. All of these societies grew out of the horse culture of the Plains. As a civil function, the military societies often carried out the council's orders. As the periods of peace dwindled with the onset of the Euro-American invasion, the police societies evolved into war societies that assumed much of the authority of the Council of Forty-four.

The number four occurs time and again in Cheyenne social relations, religion, and government, similar to the number seven among the **Cherokees**; the Council of Forty-four carried on this tradition. Anthropologists refer to the Cheyenne social system as "religiously integrated." Membership on the council was drawn from the ten traditional Cheyenne bands, but membership in a band was voluntary, not a factor of kinship ties, as among the Iroquois and **Wyandots**. While kinship ties did not define membership in a band or representation on the council, they still played an important role in day-to-day Cheyenne politics and economic activity. When a man addressed the council, the other members assumed that he was speaking on behalf of his extended family. The Council of Forty-four appointed one of the Cheyenne soldier societies to manage the annual buffalo hunt, the premiere economic activity. The ten traditional bands and affiliated kinship groups managed their own economic resources, including the redistribution of food to feed people, such as orphans, the elderly, and the poor, who could not provide for themselves.

Members of the Council of Forty-four were male. One description of a Cheyenne chief's demeanor sounds remarkably similar to the behavior that was expected of Iroquois sachems under their Great Law of Peace:

A chief must be brave in war, generous in disposition, liberal in temper, deliberate in making up his mind, and of good judgement. A good chief gives his whole heart and his whole mind to the work of helping his people, and strives for their welfare with an earnestness and a devotion rarely equalled by other rulers of men. Such thought for his fellows was not without its influence on the man himself. After a time, the spirit of goodwill which animated him became reflected in his countenance, so that, as he grew old, such a chief came to have a most benevolent and kindly expression. Yet, though simple, honest, generous, tender-hearted, and often merry and jolly, when occasion demanded, he could be stern, severe, and inflexible of purpose. Such men, once known, commanded general respect and admiration. (Hoebel 1954: 145)

Generosity was a key attribute of a Cheyenne leader, because he was charged with caring for widows and orphans. A chief also was called on to resolve disputes, so people who were good at mediation were usually chosen over those who were not. According to **Vine Deloria, Jr.**, and Clifford Lytle, "A chief would often suffer loss himself as a means of resolving a dispute so that it would not disrupt the camp. In the most serious of disputes, the entire council would act to mediate."

The Council of Forty-four engaged in lengthy debates whenever it needed to make major policy decisions or adjudicate a serious crime. By custom, each speaker was allowed to discourse until he finished, without interruption, followed by a period of silent reflection to consider his remarks before the next speaker began. Arguing or exchange of angry words was considered to be extremely bad form in council. After they reached a decision by **consensus**, the chiefs sent out riders mounted on horseback to announce it. Each chief then returned home to explain the council's actions, which sometimes were changed if large numbers of people disagreed.

While all the chiefs were men, women served in influential advisory roles. As in many other native nations, the general tenor of the society, including political decision making, was set by women. While men did most of the speaking in council, they could not act without the general consent of the women.

A Cheyenne who killed another Cheyenne was not killed, but was ostracized and considered impure. The murderer was banished, and for seven years no Cheyenne was allowed to give him aid or assistance. A murderer was usually left to fend for himself on the open plains. In some cases, the murderer was allowed to petition for readmittance to the community by bearing a sacred and symbolic gift to the family of the victim. The gift was a sign from the murderer that he would accept the rules of Cheyenne society. If the family and the Council of Forty-four accepted the gift, the murderer was allowed to return to Cheyenne society.

The Cheyennes also practiced a form of religious asylum. Anyone being pursued for a crime (even the most serious, such as horse theft or murder) could take shelter in the home of the priest-chief who held the Holy Hat. Once inside the Hat Keeper's lodge, the miscreant would be given free passage out of Cheyenne territory. When the Cheyennes were moving, without fixed lodgings, this power was exercised by the wife of the Hat Keeper, who could declare asylum by embracing a person who was being pursued on a criminal charge.

FURTHER READING

Champagne, Duane. *American Indian Societies: Strategies and Conditions of Political and Cultural Survival.* Cambridge, MA: Cultural Survival, 1989.

Grinnel, George Bird. *The Cheyenne Indians: Their History and Ways of Life.* 1923. New York: Cooper Square Publishers, 1962.

Hoebel, E. Adamson. *The Law of Primitive Man.* Cambridge, MA: Harvard University Press, 1954.

Llewellyn, Karl N., and E. A. Hoebel. *The Cheyenne Way: Conflict and Case Law in Primitive Jurisprudence.* Norman: University of Oklahoma Press, 1941.

McNickle, D'Arcy. *They Came Here First: The Epic of the American Indian.* New York: Harper & Row, 1975.

CHICKASAW POLITICAL AND LEGAL TRADITIONS

The first recordings of the Chickasaw people are from the expedition of Hernando de Soto dating from about 1539–1540. The Soto accounts say that the Chickasaw were a numerous people with large areas under cultivation, and their leader was carried about on the shoulders of men. Although there is little more information given by the Soto manuscripts, the Chickasaw principal chief appears to have been a "god-king" who was honored as a sacred person. Most likely the Chickasaw shared in the Mississippi Culture of A.D. 800 to A.D. 1600, which was characterized by increasing dependency on agriculture, religious centralization, powerful priesthoods, and towns centered around platform mounds. As in later years, the Chickasaw were most likely organized into two phratries consisting of numerous matrilocal and matrilineal clans. Most likely the Chickasaw population was larger before 1600 than when better records became available in the early 1700s. According to Mississippi Culture legends, the principal chief and in many cases his sister were given the right to rule after the Creator, having lived for a while upon the earth, returned to the heavens. The two phratries of clans were hierarchically arranged, with the Imosaktca moiety and the clan of the principal chief at the highest rank. The head warrior or Tishomingo, second warriors, leading second chiefs, and head priests and their assistants were selected from specific clans. The clans had hereditary rights to appoint certain priests, leaders, warriors, and assistants. The national council was composed of the leading chiefs, priests, warriors, and leaders of the clans. During the Mississippi Culture period, it is not clear how much political and religious authority the principal chief commanded. Certainly he held a position of respect, honor, and sacredness and played a major role in a cycle of religious festivals, most likely associated with the changing seasons, fertility of crops, and good luck in the hunt. Priests managed the ceremonial cycles, performed healing rituals, kept track of time through knowledge of the rotation of heavenly bodies, and prophesied future events. Although the Mississippi Culture tradition indicates that the principal chief had a sister or consort who coruled, there is no record outside of legend for such a person or role in Chickasaw political history. Women were influential in clan relations and had much to do with the organization of households and cultivating and harvesting the crops.

By the 1690s, when records of English traders become available, the Chickasaw were no longer living in the Mississippi Culture tradition. Between 1500 and 1600, the Mississippi Culture imploded, most likely because of the introduction of disease by colonists. The diseases spread inland decades before any European saw the region, and many of the Mississippi Culture towns were decimated, possibly suffering losses as high as 90 percent in many cases. The rapid population decline was associated with the rebellion of subordinate towns and chiefdoms, increased warfare, and spatial decentralizations where the people moved away from the religiously centralized towns of mounds to smaller and more scattered towns. Since so many people died, including many priests and elders, much knowledge of the Mississippi Culture period was lost and not passed on to the survivors. When, in the 1690s, English traders recorded their visits to the Chickasaw, there appears to have been little oral tradition of the Mississippi Culture period, and society was no longer arranged around sacred mounds. In the 1690s, the principal chief was no longer carried about by men, and he was no longer considered a sacred person. He was still regarded as the hereditary leader of the Chickasaw people, but he lacked coercive powers beyond those granted by **consensus** among the national leaders and clan leaders. The political, religious, and warrior leaders were selected from specific clans, and the national council was formed by the gathering of the national leaders and clans. Agreements were made by consensus; a disagreeing clan was not bound by the decision of the majority. Priests seemed to play a less prominent role than in the sacred hierarchy of the Mississippi Culture period, but holy men were still highly regarded as prophets, ritual specialists, and healers, as well as protectors of the ritual and moral purity of the community. Holy men among the Chickasaw remained influential well into the nineteenth century, if not longer.

Community norms and religious sanctions served to inhibit most ritual and moral infractions. In the Chickasaw worldview, the Creator, or Great Composite Being, was a benevolent gift giver and would not allow misfortune to be visited upon a moral and just people. Those people who broke sacred law, botched rituals, committed adultery, or engaged in other immoral acts endangered the entire community with the withdrawal of divine favor. Droughts, defeat in battle, early death, disease, accidents, floods, and other misfortunes were interpreted as the result of impure acts among the people of the community. When such collective misfortunes occurred, the people often accused the priests or holy men of improper ritual performance or immoral acts that desecrated the annual ceremonies of purification and caused harm to the community.

The Great Composite Being would not harm a moral people, so the fault was with the improper or sacrilegious acts of the people. Since a prophet or holy man could be killed by the community members if he was found guilty of impure actions, the priests often defended their actions and cast blame upon the moral and religious behavior of the people. Often clan matrons took up this theme, castigated the community for any wrongdoing, and implored it to do better in the future. Ceremonies of ritual purification and better moral conduct were then believed to be necessary to regain the favor, blessings, and protection of the Creator and his intermediary spirit manifestations. After the annual Green Corn Ceremony, all transgressions, except murder, were forgiven as the entire nation or town was purified by the ceremony.

Transgressions of property and personal injury were managed by clan elders. If the issue arose between kin, people of the same clan, the elders managed the issue internally. When an issue arose between members of two clans, clan leaders and elders discussed the issue, and the offending party made an agreed-upon restitution. In cases of murder, the offended clan had the right to take the life, or "spirit," of the murderer. If the murderer was considered a person of little consequence, then the offended clan had the right to take the spirit of a person of equal repute to the victim among the members of the offending clan. Revenge was considered necessary; otherwise, the spirit of the victim was believed to linger nearby and cause harm to the family for failure to seek revenge. The older brother of the victim performed the ritual of avenging his younger kin's death. In the Chickasaw kinship system, many people whom Americans consider cousins on their mother's side are considered brothers and sisters among the Chickasaw. The murderer, or his replacement, was required to attend a public ritual execution on an agreed-upon day. If the murderer or ritual victim ran away, then the clan was required to supply a substitute. Any person who did not meet his or her obligations to voluntarily surrender to the ritual execution was considered a coward, who jeopardized the lives of kin, and was ostracized. Failure among the murderer's kin to meet the obligations of revenge execution prevented them from passing onto the good hunting ground after death, so the fulfillment of the revenge execution obligation was spiritually motivated. Tradition has it that few people failed to meet their kin obligations in matters of revenge. After the revenge execution, peace was restored. Usually no more killings occurred, and social relations were prevented from breaking into a war of all against all.

The Chickasaw political and legal structure remained generally intact from the 1690s until the early 1840s. After signing a treaty to remove west of the Mississippi River in 1837, for want of land, the Chickasaw joined the **Choctaw** Nation in Indian Territory, present-day eastern

Oklahoma. According to their agreement with the Choctaw, the Chickasaw would join the Choctaw Nation and observe the Choctaw constitution and law. Many Chickasaw conservatives still preferred the kin-based political order and through the late 1840s and early 1850s sought separation from the Choctaw Nation, where they were outnumbered by three to one. In 1855, the Chickasaw made a treaty with the United States and Choctaw and formed an independent nation. The Chickasaw quickly formed a constitutional government with courts and abolished the kin-based political and legal order. Over the years, the Chickasaw wrote increasingly complicated legal codes, which in large part resembled those of the United States. The Chickasaw constitutional government remained in power until it was abolished by the U.S. government in 1907. During this period, the Chickasaw still observed many moral, religious, and social rules of Chickasaw culture. Chickasaw courts ruled on cases of murder, but a convicted murderer was not held in jail until his execution, but rather was given six months to put his affairs in order. On an appointed day, a convicted murderer was obligated to voluntarily surrender for execution at a public place. Most Chickasaw convicted murderers honored the traditional moral code to pay a spirit with a spirit.

FURTHER READING

Adair, J. *The History of the American Indians.* London: Edward and Charles Dilly, 1775.

Baird, W. David. *The Chickasaw People.* Phoenix, AZ: Indian Tribal Series, 1974.

Champagne, Duane. *Social Order and Political Change: Constitutional Governments among the Cherokee, Choctaw, Chickasaw, and Creek.* Stanford, CA: Stanford University Press, 1992.

Chickasaw Nation. *Constitution, Laws, and Treaties of the Chickasaws.* Wilmington, DE: Scholarly Resources, 1975.

Gibson, Arrell. *The Chickasaws.* Norman: University of Oklahoma Press, 1971.

Nairne, T. *Nairne's Muskhogean Journals: The 1708 Expedition to the Mississippi River.* Ed. A. Moore. Jackson: University Press of Mississippi, 1988.

DUANE CHAMPAGNE

CHOCTAW POLITICAL AND LEGAL TRADITIONS

The Choctaws, who originally occupied the central and southern portions of present-day Mississippi, maintained a decentralized government of towns and villages with four geographical groups, which evolved into three districts after prolonged contact with Europeans. French writers in the 1700s indicated that one head chief presided over the entire Choctaw nation, but his power was limited to his personal influence and persuasion. Most governmental business was accomplished at the district level, where a head chief was elevated by a system that was partially hereditary and partly based on his personal abilities. Each town also had a head chief who was loosely under the authority of the district leader. The town chief generally had several assistants, such as a speaker (who arranged ceremonies, feasts, and dances), a war chief, and two war captains, who mobilized the village in time of war.

A council of a Choctaw district, or the nation as a whole, was called by the responsible head chief. Runners carrying bundles of sticks describing the time of meeting summoned chiefs from the Choctaw villages, who gathered on an appointed day. Like the **Iroquois** and many other Native American peoples who relied on **consensus** in their councils, the Choctaws prized oratory. Many people often gathered to hear the chiefs debate the issues before the council and to take part in dancing and feasting that usually accompanied council meetings. The council dealt with policies that affected all the Choctaw villages, such as war and peace and other matters of foreign relations. The council also sometimes was called upon to exercise a judicial role in case of intervillage disputes. The role of the council was to ensure peace and harmony between the various villages.

Murder was considered the paramount crime among the Choctaw and was usually avenged by the family of the victim. The murderer usually considered surrender a duty of honor. In the rare instance that the murderer failed to surrender in the customary manner, another member of his family could serve as an acceptable substitute. "Murder" was defined broadly by Anglo-American standards, including accidental killing and, in some cases, deaths attributed to another's witchcraft.

Interpersonal animosity that could not be ameliorated any other way might be addressed by a duel designed so that both opponents would die. The two might shoot at each other, with the survivor being killed by the first victim's next of kin. At other times, the opponents stood facing each other as their seconds shot them. Pushmataha, a well-known district chief during the early nineteenth century, was said to have purchased a barrel of gunpowder after an Anglo-American man called him a coward. He then invited the white man to join him on top of the barrel as he prepared to light a fuse to it. In this case, the Anglo refused the dare, and Pushmataha did not light the fuse.

FURTHER READING

Debo, Angie. *The Rise and Fall of the Choctaw Republic*. Norman: University of Oklahoma Press, 1961.

COHEN, FELIX (1907–1953)

Felix Cohen was the author of the *Handbook of Federal Indian Law* (1942), a basic reference book of this field for decades. Cohen also served as associate solicitor of the Interior Department and chaired the department's Board of Appeals. He played an instrumental part in drafting the **Indian Reorganization Act** (1934) and the legal infrastructure for the **Indian Claims Commission**, founded in 1946. Cohen was especially active in securing for American Indians the right to vote and Social Security benefits.

Cohen also authored a number of books, including *Ethical Systems and Legal Ideals* (1933) and *Combating Totalitarian Propaganda: A Legal Appraisal* (1944). In his introduction to *The Legal Conscience*, a collection of Cohen's papers, Eugene V. Rostow wrote that "Felix Cohen died at forty-six. But he had already moved mountains as a public servant, as a practitioner, and as a law teacher and philosophical scholar of law" (Cohen 1960: xvi).

Cohen was a son of Morris Raphael Cohen, philosopher, writer, and professor at City College, New York City. In 1951, Cohen coauthored a book with his father, *Readings in Jurisprudence and Legal Philosophy*. The younger Cohen was born in New York City and earned an A.B. degree in 1926 (summa cum laude) from City College, where, as a student, he edited a student newspaper, *The Campus*. Cohen earned a Ph.D. from Harvard in 1929 and an LL.B. from Columbia Law School in 1931.

Cohen also was a student of Native American societies and a social critic. On one occasion, Cohen compared Native American influence on immigrants from Europe to the ways in which the Greeks shaped Roman culture:

When the Roman legions conquered Greece, Roman historians wrote with as little imagination as did the European historians who have written of the white man's conquest of America. What the Roman historians did not see was that captive Greece would take captive conquering Rome [with] Greek science [and] Greek philosophy. (1952: 180)

Cohen wrote that American historians had too often paid attention to military victories and changing land boundaries, while failing to see that "in agriculture, in government, in sport, in education, and in our views of nature and our fellow men, it is the first Americans who have taken captive their battlefield conquerors." American historians "have seen America only as an imitation of Europe," Cohen asserted. In his view, "The real epic of America is the yet unfinished story of the Americanization of the white man."

In 1952, Cohen argued that

it is out of a rich Indian democratic tradition that the distinctive political ideals of American life emerged. Universal suffrage for women as for men, the pattern of states that we call federalism, the habit of treating chiefs as servants of the people instead of their masters, the insistence that the community must respect the diversity of men and the diversity of their dreams—all these things were part of the American way of life before Columbus landed. (1952: 179–180)

Cohen resigned from government service in 1948 to practice American Indian law in the New York City–Washington, D.C., firm of Riegelman, Stasser, Schwartz, and Spiegelberg. He often represented the interests of the Montana Blackfeet, Oglala Sioux, All-Pueblo Council, and San Carlos Apache. Cohen also served as a visiting professor of law at Yale University and City College and taught at Rutgers Law School and the New School for Social Research.

Cohen died of cancer on October 19, 1953, at his home in New York City. No cause of death was listed in public reports of the time. At Cohen's funeral in Washington, D.C., pallbearers included Felix Frankfurter, an associate justice of the U.S. Supreme Court, Senator Hubert H. Humphrey, **John Collier**, former commissioner of Indian affairs, and Oliver LaFarge, author and president of the Association on American Indian Affairs. Three days after his death, the *New York Times* editorially eulogized Cohen, saying that his death "comes at a time when the American Indian can least afford to lose a stalwart friend." The editorial mentioned efforts to alienate Indian land through **termination** legislation and efforts to allow state control over Native American lands, later expressed in **Public Law 280**. Eugene Rostow evaluated Cohen's career:

Felix Cohen was a teacher of power and purpose. He talked with his students as equals. He left them with a renewed awareness of the issues in law that spell the difference between life and death. . . . [H]is writings have been a force in the world's literature of legal philosophy and jurisprudence. In my judgement, his has been, and will remain, one of the best-balanced and one of the most creative voices in the literature of what is loosely called American legal realism. (Cohen 1960: xvi)

FURTHER READING

Cohen, Felix. "Americanizing the White Man," *American Scholar* 21:2 (1952), 177–191.

———. *Ethical Systems and Legal Ideals.* 1933. Westport, CT: Greenwood Press, 1976.

———. *Handbook of Federal Indian Law.* Washington, DC: Interior Department, 1942.

———. *The Legal Conscience: Selected Papers of Felix S. Cohen.* Ed. Lucy Kramer Cohen. New Haven, CT: Yale University Press, 1960.

Cohen, Morris R., and Felix Cohen. *Readings in Jurisprudence and Legal Philosophy.* Boston: Little, Brown, 1951.

COLLIER, JOHN (1884–1968)

As commissioner of Indian Affairs for most of Franklin Delano Roosevelt's administration, John Collier is best known as the prime originator of the **Indian Reorganization Act** (IRA) (1934), which generally recognized native peoples' right to exist in distinct groups on their own land—under certain governmental controls.

Collier was born in Atlanta in 1884, the fourth of seven children. His father, John A. Collier, was a well-known banker and lawyer who served four years as Atlanta's mayor. In the late 1890s, however, the elder Collier became involved in a financial scandal that led to his suicide three years after John Collier's mother, Susie Rawson Collier, died in 1897 of addiction to laudanum, a drug then used as a relaxant. Collier was shocked by the sudden deaths of both his parents, but he finished high school in Atlanta. Using money from his father's estate, Collier registered at Columbia University as a student in 1902.

In 1907, Collier joined the People's Institute of New York City. The institute was an educational institution with a political agenda: to replace the Tammany Hall governance system in the city. It was reformist and mildly socialist, favoring popular election of senators, women's suffrage, and public ownership of municipal utilities. By 1903, six years after its founding, the People's Institute had held more than 120 public lectures in the Cooper Union to audiences totalling more than 120,000 people, many of them recent Irish and Jewish immigrants.

Mabel Dodge, a close friend of Collier's during these years, characterized him as "a small blond Southerner, intense, preoccupied, and always looking windblown on the quietest day. Because he could not seem to love his own kind of people, and as he was full of a reformer's enthusiasm for humanity, he turned to other races and worked for them" (Philp 1977: 16–17). After seven years of intense work at the People's Institute, Collier resigned and (as he did periodically during his adult life) sought solitude for months at a time camping in the wilderness.

Collier returned to work at the People's Institute, but later split with it and formed his own Training School for Community Workers. This school lost most of its funding and political support at the onset of U.S. involvement in World War I, when Tammany Hall resumed power in New York City. In 1919 the training school closed and Collier moved to Los Angeles to become director of the California adult-education program. A year later, his salary was removed from the state budget for political reasons, after which Collier once again sought solace in the wilderness, this time in Mexico and the U.S. Southwest.

During this trip he came to know the **Pueblos** of Taos and began a lifelong advocacy of American Indian policy reform. Collier was a prime mover in the **Committee of One Hundred** and a leading advocate of reform efforts throughout the 1920s that produced such documents as the **Meriam Report** (1928), which indicted government treatment of Indians during the early reservation era. During the early 1920s, Collier played a leading role in opposition to the **Bursum Bill** that would have deeded much of the Pueblos' land to non-Indian occupants. Later, he criticized the assimilationist **Indian Rights Association** and its leader, Herbert Welsh, for continuing to favor laws banning Pueblo dances.

Collier was appointed commissioner of Indian affairs shortly after Roosevelt's initial election in 1932. The IRA was passed in 1934, and the administrative mechanism established by the General **Allotment Act** (1887) was dismantled.

During the implementation of the "Indian New Deal," Native American opposition to John Collier's programs gave initial impetus to pan-Indian organizations such as the American Indian Federation (AIF). Many pan-Indian organizations attacked Collier's programs as "Communistic." Joseph Bruner (Creek), president of the AIF, believed that Collier "unfurled the red flag of race-prejudice" when he advocated the adoption of the IRA. Leaders of the AIF such as Bruner (who was active in the Society of Oklahoma Indians) and **Thomas L. Sloan** (Omaha and former president of the **Society of American Indians**) were active in earlier pan-Indian groups that had believed in a strong Indian voice in Bureau of Indian Affairs (BIA) activities but had become disillusioned. In fact, even former BIA employees like D'Arcy McNickle voiced disillusionment with the implementation of the IRA. While roughly half the Indian bands and nations recognized by the BIA voted to establish Indian Reorganization Act governments, the act was criticized by Rupert Costo, a leader among the Mission Indians of California, as nothing but a subtler form of government tyranny over Native Americans. Costo called the IRA "the Indian Raw Deal."

Collier retired from government service during World War II, but remained a constant critic of federal Indian policy for many years afterwards, especially as it swung from Roosevelt's liberalism to enactment of the Termination Act in 1953. Collier died at Taos Pueblo on May 8, 1968.

FURTHER READING

Collier, John. "The Indian in a Wartime Nation." *Annals of the American Academy of Political and Social Science* 223 (September 1942).

Kelly, Lawrence C. *The Assault on Assimilation: John Collier and the Origins of Indian Policy Reform.* Albuquerque: University of New Mexico Press, 1983.

Philp, Kenneth R. *John Collier's Crusade for Indian Reform, 1920–1954.* Tucson: University of Arizona Press, 1977.

Smith, Jane F., and Robert M. Kvasnicka, eds. *Indian-White Relations: A Persistent Paradox.* Washington, DC: Howard University Press, 1976.

COLVILLE CONFEDERATED TRIBES V. WALTON 647 F.2d 42 (9th Cir.), *cert. denied* 454 U.S. 1092 (1981)

Indian water rights apply for uses other than agriculture, the federal courts ruled in *Colville Confederated Tribes v. Walton*. The purpose for which the reservation was established, to provide a home for Indians, was liberally construed to benefit them. Under this ruling, the Colvilles were entitled to enough water to maintain a fishery as well as agriculture. The court ruled that Indians do not lose their water rights by changing the economic purposes for which they are used.

In this case, the courts also ruled that Winters Doctrine water rights can be transferred to non-Indians who purchase allotted land (*see Winters v. United States*). The case was brought after a non-Indian purchased three allotted tracts from an Indian who had irrigation established on it. The non-Indian's continued use of irrigation water was deemed justifiable.

COMANCHE POLITICAL AND LEGAL TRADITIONS

Individual freedom is held paramount above all else in Comanche society, where the lack of governmental control brings to mind Thomas Paine's slogan in *Common Sense* (1776) that that government is best that governs least. Comanche hunting bands were led by headmen who were elected informally, usually by acclamation. Anthropologist E. Adamson Hoebel commented that in Comanche society, "The headman was a magnet at the core of the band, but his influence was so subtle that it almost defied explicit description. He worked through precept, advice, and good humor, expressing his wisdom through well-chosen words and persuasive common sense" (1954: 132). The headman was charged with negotiating **consensus** in a society in which all men (but not women) had a say on important issues.

Comanche society (in which women were excluded from political decision making) had no public officials with an ability to promulgate or enforce a given body of law. Such law as the Comanches possessed was, according to Hoebel, "hammered out on the hard anvil of individual cases by claimant and defendant pressing the issue in terms of Comanche notions of individual rights and tribal standards of right conduct" (1954: 133).

Comanche political institutions were informal and fluid, but structure did exist. The political and social system was based on nuclear families and extended from them to extended families and bands (called "rancherías" in Spanish). The Comanches as a whole comprised roughly ten bands whose relations, according to Kavanagh, ranged "from mutual support and intermarriage to professed if not explicit antagonism" (55). Allied bands sometimes sent leaders to common councils.

Comanche headmen met in informal councils at the local and band levels to deal with internal and external problems. In some of the bands, there is evidence that men assumed specialized roles as war and peace chiefs. Archival records (especially those maintained by the Spanish) indicate that band members elected their chiefs, although how election was carried out is unknown. One observer, George W. Bonnell, in 1838 described the Comanches as "perhaps the most perfect democracy on the face of the earth; everything is managed by primary assemblies, and the people have a right to displace a chief and elect a successor at pleasure."

For more than a century, Anglo-American anthropologists have sketched the attributes that contributed to leadership in Comanche society. A man or a woman could attain honor and respect through *puha*, or acquiring medicine power; men also could attain leadership roles through valor in warfare. The most distinguished warriors were rewarded with the status of *tekwuniwapl*, meaning "warrior" or "hero." A political leader often carried the title of *paraibo*, meaning "chief" or "one with authority." Individual Comanches also acquired respect by becoming members of groups that anthropologists call *sodalities*, associations of people with a shared purpose. Most *paraibos* had councils of advisors, and medicine people with similar *puha* often functioned in groups. Soldier societies functioned in a similar manner. These groups often had names such as "Wolves," "Swift Fox," or "Little Ponies." Some of the sodalities also performed policing functions. As among many peoples on the Northern Plains, such policing was most necessary to maintain the discipline of communal buffalo hunts.

Although the Comanches had no formalized legal system, they had many opportunities to adjudicate disputes spurred by excessive practice of individuality, from taking another man's horses to stealing his wife. So many Comanche men pursued other Comanches' wives that some anthropologists speak of "wife absconding" (women were not taken from their husbands with their consent) nearly as ritual behavior among them. In extranational affairs, the Comanche also were noted for being quarrelsome. Their oral history accounts of past battles often began with the phrase "Once there was a bunch of Comanches out looking for trouble."

FURTHER READING

Hoebel, E. Adamson. *The Law of Primitive Man*. Cambridge, MA: Harvard University Press, 1954.
———. *The Political Organization and Law-ways of the Comanche Indians*. 1940. Memoirs of the American Anthropological Association, no. 54. Menasha, WI: AAA, 1976.
Kavanagh, Thomas W. *Comanche Political History: An Ethnohistorical Perspective, 1706–1875*. Lincoln: University of Nebraska Press, 1996.

COMMITTEE OF ONE HUNDRED

By 1923, an organized committee of influential Indians and non-Indians, which called itself the Committee of One Hundred, was lobbying for more respectful and humane treatment of surviving American Indians. **John Collier** was an early member, with William Jennings Bryan, Clark Wissler, General John J. Pershing, Bernard Baruch, William Allen White, and the **Iroquois** Arthur C. Parker. Parker was elected presiding officer at a convention in Washington, D.C., during December 1923. Under his aegis, in 1924, the group published its findings under the title *The Indian Problem*. This document formed the basis for the better-known **Meriam Report** four years later.

CONFEDERACY

All along the Atlantic seaboard, Indian nations had formed confederacies by the time they encountered European immigrants, from the Seminoles in what is now Florida (Crèvecoeur called them "a federated republic") and the **Cherokees** and **Choctaws** in the Carolinas to the **Iroquois** and their allies, the **Wyandots** (Hurons), in the Saint Lawrence Valley and the Penacook federation of New England, among many others. Anthony F. C. Wallace found that

ethnic confederacies were common among all the Indian tribes of the Northeast. . . . Village bands, and tribes speaking similar languages, holding similar customs, and sharing a tradition of similar origin usually combined into a loose union that at least minimized warfare among themselves. The Illinois Confederacy, the "Three Fires" of the Chippewa, Ottawa and Pottawatomi, the Wapenaki Confederacy, the Powhatan Confederacies, the tripartite Miami—all the neighbors of the Iroquois—were members of one confederation or another. (1970: 42)

Each of these native confederacies had its own variation on the common theme of counsellor democracy, but most were remarkably similar in broad outline. By the late eighteenth century, as resentment against England's taxation flared into open rebellion along the Atlantic seaboard, the colonists displayed widespread knowledge of native governmental systems. **Thomas Jefferson, Benjamin Franklin**, and others the length of the coast into the Saint Lawrence Valley all saw governmental systems that shared many similarities. For examples of confederacies, see entries under **Iroquois Confederacy, Wyandot,** Cherokee, **Sioux,** and **Cheyenne**.

FURTHER READING

Colden, Cadwallader. *History of the Five Indian Nations Depending on the Province of New-York in America.* 1727 and 1747. Ithaca, NY: Cornell University Press, 1968.

Crèvecoeur, St. Jean de. *Journey into Northern Pennsylvania and the State of New York.* 1801, in French. Trans. and ed. by Percy G. Adams. Ann Arbor: University of Michigan Press, 1964.

Grinde, Donald A., Jr., and Bruce E. Johansen. *Exemplar of Liberty: Native America and the Evolution of Democracy.* Los Angeles: UCLA American Indian Studies Center, 1991.

Richter, Daniel K., and James Merrell, eds. *Beyond the Covenant Chain.* Syracuse, NY: Syracuse University Press, 1987.

Wallace, Anthony F. C. *The Death and Rebirth of the Seneca.* New York: Vintage, 1970.

CONSENSUS, NATIVE AMERICAN MODELS

From the eastern seaboard to the Plains and the Southwest, the consensus model of government was used by many native bands and nations. With the exception of the indigenous nations of Mesoamerica, most of the Northwest Coast peoples, and a few others, most Native American nations ordered their political lives using systems best characterized as forms of counsellor democracy.

The complexity of the system varied according to the number of people using it. People who relied solely on hunting for their sustenance (and who usually lived in small, scattered settlements that moved with the seasons) tended to have the least elaborate, and most direct, forms of democracy. Those who combined hunting with agriculture, and who often lived in larger, more permanent settlements, utilized forms that were often more elaborate in custom and ritual, and that sometimes substituted forms of representation for direct participation. In all systems, however, public forums were held at least occasionally that enabled people who did not hold office to voice their views. In some systems, such as that of the Iroquois, public officials could be impeached for errant behavior.

Having generalized, we also must consider an important caveat regarding any generalization about native peoples in North America. The continent comprises some eight million square miles varying in nearly every conceivable manner of geography, topography, and climate. At least four hundred to five hundred distinct native peoples inhabited most parts of this land mass, speaking several hundred distinct languages. These numbers may even have been higher, because we can "count" only those cultures that have survived one hundred to five hundred years of colonization or that, not having survived, have left us a historical record of some detail.

Even among peoples who are often grouped into a single "Indian nation" by scholars (such as the **Pueblos** and the Mayas), individual villages, towns, and cities exercised considerable control over the ways in which they chose to make decisions and solve interpersonal problems. These systems sometimes evolved in ways distinct even from those in nearby settlements. The nature and variety of rituals was (and remains) richly complex. When studying any aspect of Native American history and prehistory, one must recognize that the "culture areas" defined by scholarship tend to simplify a vastly more complicated reality.

The nature of participatory government among Native Americans has been a subject of comment by nonnative scholars and explorers during much of the history of contact between New World and Old. The democratic nature of many of these cultures has often, in the past, been attributed to their small size. Calling it "primitive democracy" or "forest democracy" tends to attribute the nature of decision making to small numbers and simplicity of life. In reality, as we learn more about how native peoples in North America ordered their societies, that impression is being replaced by a knowledge of how elaborate many of these structures became, and how native peoples chose the system of decision making that best suited them. Because they could choose, the systems varied widely. Although the ritual context of governance varied widely among native nations in North America, public participation seems to have been a common denominator among those who used the consensus model.

The Northwest Coast peoples' rigid, class-conscious society was strikingly dissimilar to most native social organization across North America outside of Mexico and Central America. Nearly everywhere else, indigenous people regarded each other as equals (sometimes with a mild degree of status and inherited rights); they usually maintained societies in which consensus was used in decision making. Structures and customs used to achieve consensus varied widely. In some societies, such as the **Cree**, a decision-making apparatus existed only informally even at the local level.

In the highly developed confederacies along the eastern seaboard with which immigrants from England and France had early contact, an elaborate corpus of custom and law maintained political structures that bound together networks of villages and maintained peace between them. Such systems could be found not only in the east, but also among some Plains peoples, such as the **Cheyenne**, who maintained a vigorous central council that brought together leaders from several disparate settlements. In the case of the **Iroquois Confederacy**, historically the best-known system of this type, a body of myth and ritual supported a formal corpus of law and belief that united not only villages, but nations of native peoples in a federal structure.

CONSTITUTION, U.S., PRECEDENTS IN NATIVE AMERICAN LEGAL PRACTICES

In 1787, on the eve of the Constitutional Convention, John Adams published his *Defence of the Constitutions of the Governments of the United States of America*. Although Adams was selected as a Massachusetts delegate to the Constitutional Convention, he chose not to attend and published his lengthy essay instead. The *Defence* was much circulated in the convention and formed a basis for the definition of the new federal system. On June 6, 1787, James Madison, while reporting the opening of the Constitutional Convention to **Thomas Jefferson**, wrote that "Mr. Adams' Book . . . has excited a good deal of attention." Madison believed that Adams's *Defence* would be read and "praised, and become a powerful engine in forming the public opinion" (Boyd, 11: 401–402).

Adams's *Defence* was a critical survey of world governments. He included a description of the **Iroquois** and other Native American governments in his analysis. In his preface, Adams mentioned the Inca, the Manco Capac, and the political structure "of the Peruvians." He also noted that native groups in "North America have certain families from which their leaders are always chosen." Adams believed that American Indian governments collected their authority in one center (a simple or unicameral model), and he also observed that in American Indian governments "the people" believed that "all depended on them" (Adams 1851: 292). Later in the preface, Adams observed that **Benjamin Franklin**, the French *philosophes*, and other "great philosophers and politicians of the age were "attempting to . . . set up governments of . . . modern Indians" (296).

According to Adams, the French philosopher Turgot believed that the new American constitutions that Franklin showed him were "an unreasonable imitation of the usages of England." Turgot, like Franklin, objected to the perpetuation of bicameral legislatures by the American states and reserved praise only for the unicameral legislature found in the new Pennsylvania State Constitution of 1776. The Pennsylvania Constitution also contained a Council of Censors that functioned similarly to the Council of Elders of the Iroquois. The Council of Censors' duties included inquiring into whether the constitution was "preserved inviolate . . . and whether the legislative and executive branches have discharged their duty" as guardians of the people. Like the Iroquois League, the Pennsylvania Constitution provided that "the doors of the . . . general assembly, shall be and remain open for the admission of all persons who behave decently."

In his *Defence of the Constitutions of the Governments of the United States*, Adams implied that Turgot's preference for the Pennsylvania Constitution was probably the result of conversations with Franklin. Adams believed that "Americans are advised" by Turgot, Franklin, and others to go back to the political structures of ancient Germans and modern Indians. While he was critical of this suggestion, Adams argued that "the three powers [of government] are strong in every tribe." Adams also talked of the importance of certain families in American Indian governments. Adams was familiar with the opinions of Richard Price, the radical British thinker, who had received a letter from Turgot in

1778 on the nature of American constitutions. Price believed that Americans had established forms of "government more equitable and more liberal than any the world has yet known." He also believed that as a result of the American Revolution the "Britons themselves will be the greatest gainers" (Price 1784). It is very likely that Franklin favored unicameral legislatures because of his experience in Pennsylvania and his exposure to the ideas of the Iroquois. Certainly, this was what Adams tried to imply in his *Defence*. The Iroquois governmental system helped reinforce Franklin's belief (similar to that of Tom Paine and Thomas Jefferson) that the best government governed least—and with the simplest bureaucratic machinery.

Adams, an ardent believer in the fundamentals of the British Constitution, opposed Franklin's intimation that the new government should resemble the native **confederacies**, but he did believe that it would be productive to have "a more accurate investigation of the form of governments of the . . . Indians" (1851: 296). In addition, Adams argued that it would be "well worth the pains . . . to collect . . . the legislation of the Indians" (298) for study while creating a new constitution. Adams believed that in studying American Indian governments such as the League of the Iroquois, Americans could observe the best examples of governmental separation of powers. In fact, Adams stated that separation of powers in American Indian governments "is marked with a precision that excludes all controversy" (511).

Indeed, Adams pointed out that American Indian governments were so democratic that the "real sovereignty resided in the body of the people." Personal liberty was so important to American Indians, according to Adams, that Mohawks might be characterized as having "complete individual independence" (511).

While discussing the Mohawks, Adams referred to "fifty families governed by all authority in one centre" (511). This statement reflects the extent of Adams's knowledge of the structure of the Iroquois Confederacy. In fact, Adams noted rather casually the number of Iroquois sachemships that were delineated by Lewis Henry Morgan, pioneer ethnographer of the league, more than sixty years later. Adams's insight indicates that the founders knew a great deal more about the Iroquois governance system than has been previously acknowledged. The fact that Morgan arrived at similar conclusions without reference to Adams's and other founders' observations provides independent verification of such knowledge. However, the extent of Adams's understanding of the nature of Iroquois government is less important than the awareness that there were profound intellectual connections between Native Americans and the Founding Fathers. Essentially, Adams's insights about Indian governments were really personal and cultural manifestations of a lengthy and sustained dialogue between Euro-Americans and Native Americans.

Adams's knowledge of Iroquois and other American Indian confederacies can be seen in his reference to the sachemship system in American Indian governments, which also resembles Morgan's work. Adams wrote that a sachem was elected for life and lesser "sachems are his ordinary council." In this ordinary council, all "national affairs are deliberated and resolved" except declaring war, when the "sachems call a national assembly round a great council fire." At this council, the sachems "communicate to the people their resolution, and sacrifice an animal" (511, 566–567). The animal sacrifice is doubtless a reference to the "white dog ceremony" of the Iroquois, also described by Morgan more than six decades after Adams. Adams further described Iroquois custom when he stated that "the people who approve the war . . . throw the hatchet into a tree" and then "join in the subsequent war songs and dances." Adams also exhibited an understanding of the voluntary nature of Iroquois warfare when he asserted that those who disapproved of the decision to go to war "take no part in the sacrifice, but retire" (511, 566–567).

Adams was critical of such European thinkers as Turgot, John Locke, and David Hume. Adams felt that their theories of government were too abstract and that European thinkers did not know enough about Native American societies and republican governments. In an analysis of the Iroquois and other native governments, Adams saw American Indian governments as a window to the premonarchical past of Europeans. The founders looked to American Indian ideas about government because they believed that American Indian societies possessed a democratic heritage that European society had largely lost. Adams and other thinkers of the time were critical of all governments, but when they rejected the monarchy and the aristocratic House of Lords of the British Constitution, they often turned to American Indian governmental structures to seek alternatives. Firsthand knowledge of American Indian governments helped Americans like John Adams in political discussions of emerging republicanism during the eighteenth century. Examples from native America thus framed their debates.

Adams' *Defence* was no unabashed endorsement of native models for government. Instead, he refuted the arguments of Franklin and Turgot, who advocated a one-house legislature resembling the Iroquois Grand Council, a model that had been used in the **Albany Plan of Union** and the **Articles of Confederation**. Among Europeans, Adams did not trust the **consensus** model that seemed to work for the Iroquois. Adams believed that without the checks and balances built into two houses, the system would succumb to special interests and dissolve into anarchy or despotism. When Adams described the Mohawks' independence, he exercised criticism, while Franklin wrote about Indian governments in a much more benign way. Adams believed:

Is it not sublime wisdom, to rush headlong into all the distraction and divisions . . . which are the certain consequence of the want of order and balances, merely for the sake of the popular caprice of having fifty families governed by all authority in one centre? Even this would not satisfy; the fifty families would soon dissolve their union, and nothing would ever content them short of the complete individual independence of the Mohawks; for it may be depended on, that individual independence is what every unthinking human heart aims at, nearly or remotely. (511)

Adams sought to erect checks on the caprice of the unthinking heart and cited the Iroquois Grand Council (the fifty families) as a negative example, ignoring the fact, as Franklin wrote to James Parker in 1751, that it "has subsisted ages." Franklin was more of a utopian: he still sought a government based upon the best in human nature, calling its citizens to rise to it. He did not fear unrestrained freedom as did Adams. The United States, having tasted revolution and the better part of a decade under the Articles of Confederation, seemed ready in 1787 to agree with Adams, whose advocacy of two houses prevailed over Franklin's unicameral model. Still, the example of native liberty exerted a telling pull on the national soul, and conceptions of native America played an important role in these debates. The fact that Adams repeatedly called upon native imagery even in opposition to its use is proof of how widely these ideas were discussed. Furthermore, Adams specifically stated that many thinkers of the era liked the governmental structures of Native Americans. Since Adams's *Defence* was "much circulated in the [Constitutional] convention," it seems that his portrayal of the crosscurrents of ideas at the time is an accurate reflection of the thinking of the era.

Given the nature of Adams's *Defence*, there can be no doubt that Native American governmental structures and ideas were part of the process of constitution making. Even though John Adams and Thomas Jefferson disagreed fundamentally about the nature of government, both men used American Indian ideas and customs to support divergent points of view. This insight leads to the realization that both men were in agreement over the source of distinctly American ideas even though they interpreted that source very differently. In the end, it is significant that American Indian ideas and political structures, as perceived by Adams and Jefferson, were used to construct a uniquely American political system.

FURTHER READING

Adams, John. *The Works of John Adams*. Vol. 4. Boston: Little-Brown, 1851.
Boyd, Julian, ed. *The Papers of Thomas Jefferson*. Princeton: Princeton University Press, 1950.

Grinde, Donald A., Jr., and Bruce E. Johansen. *Exemplar of Liberty: Native America and the Evolution of Democracy.* Los Angeles: UCLA American Indian Studies Center, 1991.

Price, Richard. *Observations on the Importance of the American Revolution.* Boston: Powars & Willis, 1784.

CONSTITUTION, U.S., PROVISIONS RESPECTING NATIVE AMERICANS

Native Americans are mentioned twice in the U.S. Constitution, adopted in 1789. Article I, section 8, clause 3, authorizes Congress to regulate commerce with Indian nations. This is the "commerce clause," the legal taproot of the **plenary power** ascribed by U.S. federal courts to Congress since about 1900. Article II, section 2, clause 2, empowers the president to make treaties (with all other nations, including Indians) with the consent of the Senate. Treaties are held by the Constitution to be one of the components of the supreme law of the land.

The phrase "Indians not taxed" was used to differentiate Native American people living in areas effectively controlled by the United States from those living under their own governments at the time the Constitution was ratified. At that time, European-American settlement comprised a thin ribbon along the eastern seaboard. Most of the area designated as the "United States of America" in the Treaty of Paris (1783)—and nearly all of the area west of the Appalachians' spine—was still **Indian Country**, occupied by native peoples (some facing increasing pressure from illegal immigration from the east). Indians living under Native American land and jurisdiction also were not to be taxed by any state, except Indians came to be taxed by relinquishing their collective sovereignty or by individually emigrating to state lands.

The Constitution's language reserving to the federal government the power of negotiating treaties with Native American nations reflected **Benjamin Franklin**'s advice three decades earlier in the **Albany Plan of Union** (1754), when the **Iroquois** advised the English colonies to centralize their trade policy. This measure also corrected a vague passage in the **Articles of Confederation** in which the Congress was authorized to "manage the affairs" of the Indians. The Articles of Confederation did not forbid the states from making international treaties, so some states began to regard themselves as sovereign in relations with Indians. This conflict between state and federal power outlasted the Articles of Confederation and became manifest in the assertion of state power by Georgia over the **Cherokees** that led to the **Trails of Tears**, as well as the landmark cases *Cherokee Nation v. Georgia* (1831) and *Worcester v. Georgia* (1832).

FURTHER READING

Barsh, Russel, and James Henderson. *The Road: Indian Tribes and Political Liberty*. Berkeley: University of California Press, 1980.

COURTS OF INDIAN OFFENSES

Courts of Indian offenses as well as Indian police were established and supervised by the Bureau of Indian Affairs during the early decades of the Plains reservations, beginning in 1883. Traditional political and legal institutions had broken down or were outlawed by the government, and no other formal institutions of arbitration existed at the time. These informal courts usually began when Native American leaders who had disputes with each other appealed to the reservation agent for mediation. The Indian police were created in a similar manner, because the laws could be more easily enforced through them than at the hands of federal troops, the only other available option during the early years of the reservation system.

Courts of Indian offenses were sometimes called "CFR courts" because they operated according to regulations printed in the *Code of Federal Regulations*. Traditional Indians often looked at these courts as an imposition of the dominant society's laws because much of their business had to do with outlawing Native American rites, dances, and other customs. The courts of Indian offenses usually had Indian judges, but they were appointed by the reservation agent and served at his pleasure.

To enhance the credibility of these courts, Indian agents often appointed well-known Indian leaders, such as Quanah Parker, to serve on them. Parker served as a judge from 1886 to 1898. Wooden Leg, a Cheyenne veteran of the Battle of the Little Bighorn, served as a judge in the Cheyenne Court of Indian Offenses. As a judge, Wooden Leg was told at one point that the Bureau of Indian Affairs had issued an edict allowing Indian men only one wife each. This was part of a general governmental offensive against polygamy that also affected the Mormon settlers of Utah.

Wooden Leg was charged with enforcing the new rule. He sent a Cheyenne police officer to gather all men who had more than one wife, and gave them the news. Initially, most of them resisted, but they then came up with strategies for telling Indian agents that the extra wives were really in-laws. In some cases, a man would maintain two households under different names with one wife in each of them. Wooden Leg later related a story of how he pondered telling his two wives of the order. He was stricken with remorse as his younger wife, who had no children, was moved out of his house. "A few years later, I heard that she was married to a good husband. Oh, how glad it made my heart to hear that!" (Johansen and Grinde 1997: 428).

The **Indian Reorganization Act** (IRA) (1934) abolished courts of Indian offenses and laid the legal basis for the modern Native American court system. The IRA allowed a court system closer to traditional models, but by the time it was enacted, decades of assimilative policies had destroyed memory of many of the old systems. During the subsequent decades, a court system evolved that carried attributes of both the traditional, mediation-centered system and the adversarial Anglo-American justice system. Indian courts are usually informal. Judges often help both sides present their positions, and lawyers are sometimes not allowed to participate. Few of the courts keep written records, and written judgments are the exception rather than the rule.

FURTHER READING

Deloria, Vine, Jr., and Clifford Lytle. *American Indians, American Justice.* Austin: University of Texas Press, 1983.
Johansen, Bruce E., and Donald A. Grinde, Jr. *The Encyclopedia of Native American Biography.* New York: Henry Holt, 1997.
Nabokov, Peter, ed. *Native American Testimony.* New York: Viking, 1991.

COVENANT CHAIN
The covenant chain was a widely used metaphor for colonial alliance with neighboring Native American nations, particularly the **Iroquois**, before the American Revolution. The metaphor was sometimes extended to the idea of an alliance or confederation between the colonies. **Benjamin Franklin**, for example, used a covenant-chain image in designs for early U.S. coins. Colonial leaders had been using the covenant-chain image for decades, since letters convening the Albany Congress of 1754 (*see* **Albany Plan of Union**) from the various colonies spoke of "burying the hatchet"—a phrase that entered idiomatic English from the Iroquois Great Law—as well as "renewing the covenant chain."

Iroquois imagery was used by James Wilson to explain the process of territorial expansion and the establishment of new states. Wilson made it clear that the eastern states should not expand their western boundaries, and instead new semi-independent states ought to be created. Wilson believed that in order to have the respect of western settlers, new government officers should be

chosen by the people to fill the places of greatest trust and importance in the country; and by this means, *a chain of communication and confidence* will be formed between the United States and the new settlements.

To preserve and strengthen this chain it will, I apprehend, be expedient for Congress to appoint a minister for the new settlements and Indian Affairs. (Grinde and Johansen 1991: 296)

In using covenant-chain imagery, Wilson was echoing the rhetoric of Iroquois and American diplomacy. Since Wilson served on many Indian committees in the Continental Congress and had met with the Iroquois on several occasions, he seems to have been impressed by Iroquois ways concerning the rights of the people and territorial expansion. In December 1787, the *American Museum* published a poem that used chain imagery as a model to unite the vast United States. In part, the poem stated:

> In federal laws connect the wide domain,
> And bind the Union with a deathless chain.

FURTHER READING

Grinde, Donald A., and Bruce E. Johansen. *Exemplar of Liberty: Native America and the Evolution of Democracy.* Los Angeles: UCLA American Indian Studies Center, 1991.

CREE POLITICAL AND LEGAL TRADITIONS

Among the Crees, a sub-Arctic people who inhabited the southern reaches of Hudson Bay in present-day Ontario and Quebec, there was no central political organization, as among the **Iroquois** and **Wyandots** (Hurons) to the south. Even the individual bands or hunting parties had little or no organized political structure. Such a lack of structure is sometimes called "atomistic" by scholars; it is the closest that actual native governance comes to the stereotype of the "Noble Savage."

Instead of a formal council, Cree bands informally selected a wise elderly man, usually the head of a family, as a source of advice. He exercised informal, limited influence. As with the sachems of the more organized farming and hunting peoples to the south, these informal leaders usually did not relish the exercise of power, probably because most of the people who sought their advice resented any attempt to dictate. According to John J. Honigmann, who studied the Cree social structure, "Too great evidence of power is resented and feared by those whom it affects" (1957: 369).

Cree life was marked only rarely by multifamily celebrations or rituals. Social life and social control were usually a function of the extended family. Outside the family, a Cree might appear ambivalent or reticent, usually out of respect for others' autonomy. People who transgressed social norms of interpersonal behavior became targets of gossip or sorcery of a type that was used widely across the continent. Although their society was family based, the Crees recognized no clan or other kinship system between different bands. The society thus did not have the interconnections between settlements offered by the clans of the Iroquois, Wyandots (Hurons), and **Cherokees**.

FURTHER READING

Honigmann, John J. "Interpersonal Relations and Ideology in a Northern Canadian Community." *Social Forces* 35 (1957): 365–370.

CREEK (MUSCOGEE) POLITICAL AND LEGAL TRADITIONS

The Creek **confederacy**, a loose alliance of between fifty and eighty villages when Europeans first made contact with it, divided between "Red" towns and "White." Red towns declared wars on behalf of the confederacy and conducted foreign relations. White towns held civil councils, conducted adoption ceremonies, and enacted laws for the confederacy.

To prevent the two groups from splitting apart, competitive ball games were held between Red and White towns. These sporting matches were reputed to be quite fierce; **Vine Deloria, Jr.**, and Clifford Lytle commented in *American Indians, American Justice* (1983) that "to hear some tribal traditions about these ball games, one would wonder whether a formal war would not have been more humane since these games made the average professional football game appear mild indeed" (85).

Each Creek town was governed by a council of leaders (*miccos*), who chose one of their number as an executive or spokesman. A *micco*, usually a male elder who headed a family, served for life on condition of honorable behavior. When a *micco* became too old to take an active part in the affairs of the community, he became a member of a group of senior *miccos* who acted as advisors and presided at ceremonial occasions.

Immigrant European Americans were confused by the Creek system, as they insisted on speaking to one Creek "leader." Over time, the Creeks evolved a single national council of *miccos*, mainly to deal with the incursions of non-Indians.

As in many other Native American confederacies, the main mechanism of leadership in Creek society was the building of **consensus**. The Creeks' Grand Council brought together leaders from each town (or *talwa*) in the national confederation. The council usually met in the summer, on an occasion marked by social and religious, as well as political, significance. The members of the council debated measures of national importance, such as war and peace, the signing of treaties, and the admission of new villages into the confederation. The council left matters of local concern to the villages affected, establishing a federal system like that of the **Iroquois** and other Native American nations that exercised political decision making by consensus.

Each *talwa* had its own town council that debated local measures and also acted as a forum (or court) for adjudicating disputes between individuals that could not be solved by the clans. A *talwa* might be as small as a hundred people or as large as a thousand. Four of the *talwas* (Koweta, Tukabahchee, Knsita [also called Cussetah], and Abihka) were called "Mother talwas," comprising the primary centers for commerce and political affairs within the Creek Nation.

Creek clans resembled those of the Iroquois and many other eastern

North American confederacies. They were matrilineal (descent follows the female line) and exogamous (one may not marry within his or her clan). A large family would be related by marriage to a number of different clans, which tended to reinforce political ties within the confederacy. Most interpersonal conflict was handled by clan members; only in unusual circumstances was a dispute taken up by the *talwa* council.

Each *talwa* had two primary leaders advising the head *micco*, one a civil chief and the other a leader in war. According to Sharon O'Brien, "The civil chief, or *micco*, received ambassadors, negotiated treaties, dispensed food from the public granaries, and established feast days to celebrate successful hunts." War leaders, wrote O'Brien, "organized warriors for battle, maintained public order, and arranged the important stickball games between Red and White towns" (1989: 21–22). In White towns, according to O'Brien, the Red clan members chose the *micco* from among the White clans' membership. In Red towns, White clan members chose the *micco* from among the Red clans. Both civil and war chiefs were usually people who had earned their people's trust over many years of community service, and who could be relied upon to exercise good judgment in a crisis. *Miccos* led because their people supported them; if they lost that support, they were expected to leave the position.

The oldest man in each clan was regarded as a teacher and, when occasion required, as a judge. According to O'Brien, "It was his job to talk with clan members who behaved improperly and to determine punishments in the case of serious offense." Fines sometimes were imposed for minor offenses, such as shirking responsibility at work or failure to participate in ceremonies. Only if the clans failed to solve a dispute did the *talwa* council become involved as a court of appeal.

The Creek system also employed a spokesman for the *talwa* council (chiefly of the *miccos*) who was responsible for carrying the decisions of the leaders and council to the people of the *talwa*, filling the role of communication media in modern U.S. society. This person was expected to be well informed on all aspects of Creek law and custom.

In Creek society, punishment was based not only on the nature of the crime, but also on the community standing of the offender. In a case of theft, a repayment of double value was usually required. In addition, if the accused was of low esteem, he might be delivered by his clan for whipping by the offended parties. If he was of ill repute, a person accused of murder might be killed by members of the offended clan. A major object of punishment was to restore societal harmony. Once a sentence was finished, the person serving it was again presumed innocent.

If large groups of people within a village came to intractable disagreement with another faction, Creek law allowed a solution: one of the parties could leave and form its own village with its own governing council. Once this happened, the two factions were expected to restore harmony within the Creek Nation by again becoming friendly. To carry a grudge was deeply offensive to the Creek emphasis on honest dealing and social cohesion.

FURTHER READING

Deloria, Vine, Jr., and Clifford Lytle. *American Indians, American Justice.* Austin: University of Texas Press, 1983.

O'Brien, Sharon. *American Indian Tribal Governments.* Norman: University of Oklahoma Press, 1989.

Swanton, John R. *Early History of the Creek Indians and Their Neighbors.* Bulletin no. 73 of the Bureau of American Ethnology. Washington, DC: Bureau of American Ethnology, 1922.

Worcester, Donald E., ed. *Forked Tongues and Broken Treaties.* Caldwell, ID: Caxton, 1975.

CROW POLITICAL AND LEGAL TRADITIONS

Before sustained contact with European Americans, the Crows were unified more by a common language and shared culture than by any sense of political unity among dispersed bands of hunters. While the Crows were "a self-governing community," according to historian Frederick Hoxie, "and their numbers, wealth, and military power warranted a respectful label . . . the Crows of 1805 were not a modern nation [in the European sense]" (1995: 116).

The basic unit of Crow political society was the band, comprising, on average, one hundred individuals in several families. Groups of bands met occasionally, but unlike the **Sioux** and **Cheyenne**, they had no centralized council. The membership of the bands was fluid, as some families spent periods on their own, captives were adopted, and visitors (such as many early fur traders) arrived and became part of the various communities.

Indian agent A. R. Keller in 1879 wrote that he could find no overall political order within the Crows as a whole. He wrote that bands consisted of ten to thirty lodges. "Little authority is exercised or possessed by any chief over his followers," Keller continued (Hoxie 1995: 116). Leadership was informal and fluid and was generally bestowed for merit in the hunt or warfare. Such a diffusion of leadership often perplexed U.S. treaty commissioners, who found it difficult to pinpoint leaders with whom to negotiate treaties. The presence of settlers, armed forces, and negotiators from the United States prompted the emergence of a more identifiable leadership system by the mid-nineteenth century. The same circumstances also sparked rivalries between leaders who wished to cooperate with the invaders and those who did not.

Among the traditional Crow, a leader was called *batsé tse* ("a valiant man") once he had performed four feats at least once: leadership of a successful raid, removal of a horse from an enemy camp, being the first to touch ("count coup") an enemy, and snatching an enemy's bow or gun. The Crows' military aristocracy became members of an informal band council that selected one of its members as an executive. This headman led by consensus and had no power of fiat. He decided when and where to pitch camp and each spring appointed one of the band's military societies to act as police.

The police, which resembled the Cheyenne and Sioux practice, exercised authority at the time of the annual communal buffalo hunt. Anyone who engaged in hunting before the body of the band was severely beaten, his weapons were crushed, and his illegally gotten game was confiscated. Otherwise, the police of the band also negotiated interpersonal disputes and generally acted to maintain social order, especially during ceremonies.

The band headman also appointed a herald or "crier," who, Lowie wrote, "reported aloud any matters of public interest." At times, the crier announced that he was relaying the opinion of the chief; otherwise, he was a freelance broadcaster of news and other people's speculations.

FURTHER READING

Hoxie, Frederick. *Parading through History: The Making of the Crow Nation in America, 1805–1935*. New York: Cambridge University Press, 1995.
Lowie, Robert H. *The Crow Indians*. 1935. New York: Holt, Rinehart, and Winston, 1966.

CURTIS, CHARLES (Kansa [Kaw] and Osage) (1860–1936)

As a Republican politician, Charles Curtis served as a member of the U.S. House of Representatives, a U.S. senator, and vice president of the United States. Born on Indian land later incorporated into North Topeka, Kansas, Charles Curtis was the son of Oren A. Curtis (an abolitionist and Civil War Union cavalry officer) and Helen Pappan (Kaw/Osage). His mother died when he was three, and he was raised under the care of his maternal grandmother on the Kaw Reservation and in Topeka. Following an attack on Kaw Indians at Council Grove by **Cheyenne** militants, Curtis, who was one-eighth Indian, left the Indian mission school on the Kaw Reservation in 1868 and returned to Topeka, where he attended Topeka High School. For several years as a young man, he was a jockey and worked odd jobs until he met A. H. Case, a Topeka lawyer. Studying the law and working as a law clerk, Curtis was admitted to the Kansas bar in 1881.

Entering politics as a Republican, Curtis was elected county prosecuting attorney in 1884 and 1886. From 1893 to 1907, he served seven terms in the U.S. House of Representatives. He authored the **Curtis Act** of 1898 that dissolved Native American governments and permitted the institution of civil government within **Indian Territory**. The Curtis Act tried to force **assimilation** on American Indian peoples. It brought the allotment policy to the Five Civilized Tribes of Oklahoma, who had been exempt from the Dawes Severalty Act (**Allotment Act**) of 1887. That act empowered the Dawes Commission (former Senator **Henry L. Dawes** was chairman), created in 1893, to extinguish native title to lands in Indian Territory. Once Native American title had been eliminated, Dawes proceeded with allotment of reservation lands to individuals. Curtis's endeavors to foster detribalization, allotment, and assimilation were opposed by many of the leaders of Indian Territory. In essence, the Curtis Act paved the way for Oklahoma statehood in 1907 by destroying Native American land titles and governments.

Curtis served in the U.S. Senate from 1907 to 1913 (he was the first U.S. senator of American Indian ancestry) and from 1915 to 1929. During his tenure in the Senate, he was Republican party whip (1915–1924) and then majority leader (1924–1929). As chairman of the Senate Committee on Indian Affairs in 1924, Curtis sponsored the **Indian Citizenship Act**, which made American Indians U.S. citizens and yet still protected their property rights. After an unsuccessful campaign for the presidential nomination, he ran for Vice President with Herbert Hoover in 1928. He served as vice president from 1929 to 1933. He was a deft politician who used his Indian background for personal advantage, even though his political adversaries called him "the Injun." Although he was a fiscal conservative, he supported veterans' benefits, farm relief, women's suffrage, and national prohibition.

The Hoover-Curtis ticket's bid for a second term in 1932 was defeated by Franklin Delano Roosevelt. Upon his retirement in 1933, Curtis had served longer in the nation's capital than any other active politician at the time. After leaving public office, he headed the short-lived National Republican League and practiced law in Washington, D.C. He was also president of a gold-mining company in New Mexico. In 1936, Curtis died of heart disease.

FURTHER READING

Unraw, William E. *Mixed-Bloods and Tribal Dissolutions: Charles Curtis and the Quest for Indian Identity*. Lawrence: University of Kansas Press, 1989.

DONALD A. GRINDE, JR.

CURTIS ACT (1898) 30 Stat. 495

Following the passage of the General **Allotment Act** in 1887, Congress in 1898 passed the Curtis Act, which opened the Five Civilized Tribes' land in Oklahoma to allotment. The Curtis Act also terminated their governments, including a school system that at the time was producing more graduates who were prepared for higher education (by seminaries, in this case) than the neighboring state of Texas.

The Curtis Act established and regulated townsites, provided for leases of mineral rights, and provided for allotment of Indian land in the area that would soon become the state of Oklahoma. The act also abolished courts that native peoples in Indian Territory had maintained since they were forced from their homelands during the removal period.

D

DAWES, SENATOR HENRY (1816–1903)

U.S. Senator Henry Dawes of Massachusetts was the principal author of the General **Allotment Act**, which was designed to break down common landholdings among Indians and replace them with individual family farms. The idea, born of late-nineteenth-century non-Indian "reform" efforts, was designed to transform Indians into self-sufficient farmers.

FURTHER READING

Josephy, Alvin, Jr. *The Indian Heritage of America*. New York: Bantam, 1969.
Nabokov, Peter, ed. *Native American Testimony*. New York: Viking, 1991.

DECLARATION OF INDEPENDENCE, NATIVE AMERICAN INFLUENCES ON

American Indians and their societies figured into conceptions of life, liberty, and happiness in the mind of **Thomas Jefferson**, who authored the Declaration of Independence, and **Benjamin Franklin**, who operated in many ways as Jefferson's revolutionary mentor. A major debate at the time resulted in the phrase "happiness" being substituted for "property," in which the two founders' description of American Indian societies played a provocative role. Both sought to create a society that operated as much as possible on **consensus** and public opinion, while citing the same mechanisms in native societies. Both described Indians' passion for liberty while making it a patriotic rallying cry; they admired Indians' notions of happiness while seeking a definition that would suit the new nation. Franklin wrote:

All the Indians of North America not under the dominion of the Spaniards are in that natural state, being restrained by no Laws, having no Courts, or Ministers of Justice, no Suits, no prisons, no governors vested with any Legal Authority. The persuasion of Men distinguished by Reputation of Wisdom is the only Means by which others are govern'd, or rather led—and the State of the Indians was probably the first State of all Nations. (Ramsay 1968: 85)

Jefferson wrote much the same in his *Notes on Virginia*. This wording was inserted into the 1787 edition, as the Constitutional Convention was meeting. American Indians, wrote Jefferson, had never

submitted themselves to any laws, any coercive power and shadow of government. Their only controls are their manners, and the moral sense of right and wrong. . . . An offence against these is punished by contempt, by exclusion from society, or, where the cause is serious, as that of murder, by the individuals whom it concerns. Imperfect as this species of control may seem, crimes are very rare among them. (Jefferson [1784]: 93)

The lesson here seemed clear to Jefferson:

Insomuch that it were made a question, whether no law, as among the savage Americans, or too much law, as among the civilized Europeans, submits man to the greater evil, one who has seen both conditions of existence would pronounce it to be the last. (Ford 1892–99: 195n.)

As they decried contemporary Europe, architects of the new nation such as Franklin, Jefferson, and Thomas Paine described American Indian societies in ways strikingly similar to their visions of the state they hoped to erect, modified to suit a people of Old World ancestry. Jefferson wrote, "The only condition on earth to be compared with ours, in my opinion, is that of the Indian, where they have still less law than we" (Commager 1975: 119). When Paine wrote that "government, like dress is the badge of lost innocence" (1892: 1), and Jefferson said that the best government governs least, they were recapitulating their observations of Native American societies directly, or through the eyes of European philosophers such as Locke and Rousseau. Writing to Edward Carrington in 1787, Jefferson linked freedom of expression with public opinion as well as happiness, citing American Indian societies as an example:

The basis of our government being the opinion of the people, our very first object should be to keep that right; and were it left to me to decide whether we should have a government without newspapers or newspapers without a government, I should not hesitate for a moment to prefer the latter. . . . I am convinced that those societies [like the Indians] . . . enjoy in their general mass an infinitely

greater degree of happiness than those who live under European governments.
(49)

FURTHER READING

Commager, Henry Steele. *Jefferson, Nationalism, and the Enlightenment.* New
     York: George Braziller, 1975.
Ford, Paul L. *The Writings of Thomas Jefferson.* Vol. 3. New York: G. P. Put-
     nam's Sons, 1892–1899.
Jefferson, Thomas. *Notes on the State of Virginia.* 1784. Ed. William Peden.
     Chapel Hill: University of North Carolina Press, 1955.
Jefferson to Carrington, January 16, 1787. In *The Papers of Thomas Jefferson,*
     ed. Julian P. Boyd. Vol. 11. Princeton, NJ: Princeton University Press,
     1950–1974.
Paine, Thomas. "Common Sense." In *The Political Works of Thomas Paine.*
     New York: Peter Eckler, 1892.
Ramsay, Allan. "Thoughts on the Origin and Nature of Government." In *Intel-
     lectual Origins of American Radicalism,* ed. Staughton Lynd. New York:
     Random House, 1968.

DEGANAWIDAH (Wyandot [Huron]) (fl. 1100–1150)

The **Iroquois Confederacy** was founded by the Wyandot prophet Deganawidah, who is called "the Peacemaker" in oral discourse among
many Iroquois. Deganawidah enlisted the aid of a speaker, Aionwantha
(sometimes called Hiawatha), to spread his vision of a united Haudenosaunee confederacy.

Deganawidah needed a spokesman (Hiawatha) in the oral culture of
the Iroquois because he stuttered so badly he could hardly speak, a
manifestation that Iroquois oral history attributes to a double row of
teeth. The confederacy was founded before the first European contact
in the area, possibly as early as A.D. 900 or as late as A.D. 1500. Deganawidah sought to replace blood feuds that had devastated the Iroquois
with peaceful modes of decision making. The result was the Great Law
of Peace (sometimes called the Great Binding Law) of the Iroquois,
which endures to this day as one of the oldest forms of participatory
democracy on earth. The confederacy originally included the Mohawks,
Oneidas, Onondagas, Cayugas, and Senecas. The sixth nation, the Tuscaroras, migrated into Iroquois country in the early eighteenth century.

Together, Deganawidah and Hiawatha developed a powerful message
of peace. Deganawidah's vision gave Hiawatha's oratory substance.
Through Deganawidah's vision, the constitution of the Iroquois was formulated. In his vision, Deganawidah saw a giant white pine reaching
to the sky and gaining strength from three counterbalancing principles
of life. The first axiom was that a stable mind and healthy body should
be in balance so that peace between individuals and groups could occur.
Second, Deganawidah stated that humane conduct, thought, and speech

were a requirement for equity and justice among peoples. Finally, he foresaw a society in which physical strength and civil authority would reinforce the power of the clan system.

With such a powerful vision, Deganawidah and Hiawatha were able to subdue the evil Tadadaho and transform his mind. Deganawidah removed evil feelings and thoughts from the head of Tadadaho and said, "Thou shalt strive . . . to make reason and the peaceful mind prevail." The evil wizard became reborn into a humane person charged with implementing the message of Deganawidah. After Tadadaho had submitted to the redemption, Onondaga became the central fire of the Haudenosaunee, and the Onondagas became the "firekeepers" of the new confederacy. To this day, the Great Council Fire of the confederacy is kept in the land of the Onondagas.

FURTHER READING

Colden, Cadwallader. *The History of the Five Indian Nations Depending on the Province of New-York in America.* 1727. Ithaca, NY: Great Seal Books, 1958.

Dennis, Matthew. *Cultivating a Landscape of Peace.* Ithaca, NY: Cornell University Press, 1993.

Fenton, William N. *The Roll Call of the Iroquois Chiefs.* Washington, DC: Smithsonian Institution, 1950.

———. "Seth Newhouse's Traditional History and Constitution of the Iroquois Confederacy." *Proceedings of the American Philosophical Society* 93:2 (1949): 141–158.

The Great Law of Peace of the Longhouse People. Rooseveltown, NY: White Roots of Peace, 1971.

Hale, Horatio. *The Iroquois Book of Rites.* 1883. New York: AMS Press, 1969.

Hamilton, Charles. *Cry of the Thunderbird.* Norman: University of Oklahoma Press, 1972.

Henry, Thomas R. *Wilderness Messiah.* New York: Bonanza, 1955.

Hewitt, J. N. B. *A Constitutional League of Peace in the Stone Age of America.* Washington, DC: Smithsonian Institution, 1918.

———. *Iroquois Cosmology.* Washington, DC: Smithsonian Institution, 1903.

———. *Legend of the Founding of the Iroquois League.* Washington, DC: Smithsonian Institution, 1892.

Tehanetorens. *Wampum Belt.* Onchiota, NY: Six Nations Museum, n.d.

Wallace, Paul A. W. *The White Roots of Peace.* Santa Fe, NM: Clear Light, 1994.

Waters, Frank. *Brave Are My People.* Santa Fe, NM: Clear Light, 1993.

Wilson, Edmund. *Apologies to the Iroquois.* New York: Farrar, Straus, and Cudahy, 1960.

DELORIA, VINE, JR. (Yankton Sioux) (b. 1933)

Vine Deloria, Jr., rose to prominence with Native American **self-determination** movements during the 1960s and 1970s, becoming a widely respected professor and author as well as legal and social critic.

He is one of the founders of Native American studies as a field of scholarly inquiry in the late twentieth century.

Deloria was born in Martin, South Dakota; he served in the Marine Corps between 1954 and 1956 before he earned a B.S. degree at Iowa State University (granted in 1958) and a B.D. at the Lutheran School of Theology in 1963. After that, Deloria served as executive director of the **National Congress of American Indians**.

As early as the 1950s, Deloria was engaging in criticism of the **Indian Claims Commission**, arguing that it was a device by which to avoid treaty issues, not solve them. He pointed out that laws and regulations announced as "help" to Indians often perpetuated colonialism. Historically, Deloria argued, the rights of Native Americans have trailed those of other social groups in the United States. For example, slavery of Alaska natives was not outlawed until 1886, two decades after the Civil War.

Deloria's writings also compare the metaphysics of Native American and European points of view, especially in religious matters. In *God Is Red*, he contrasted Native American religion's melding of life with a concept of sacred place to the artifices of Christianity and other "Near Eastern" religions. Deloria compared the nature of sacredness in each perceptual realm. His discussion of sacredness led to ecological themes in Native American religions. Deloria also compared the ways in which each culture perceives reality—Europeans seeing time as lineal and history as a progressive sequence of events; most Native American cultures as neither of these. Christianity usually portrays God as a humanlike being, often meddlesome and vengeful, whereas many Native American religions place supreme authority in a great spirit or great mystery symbolizing the life forces of nature.

The great mystery became an ecological metaphor as Deloria explained ways in which Native American religions weave a concept of cycles into life, reinforcing reverence for the land and the remains of ancestors buried in it, contrasted to Europeans' ability to move from place to place without regard for location, until the reality of the American land and its often unwritten history begins to absorb them. What follows was described by Deloria as a "surplus of shamans," lost European souls trying to put down ideological roots in American soil.

In the late twentieth century, Deloria continued to write a number of books and articles in scholarly journals that often took issue with ethnocentric interpretations of reality. Many of them criticized U.S. Indian policy. His early books, such as *Custer Died for Your Sins* (1969), *We Talk, You Listen* (1970), and *Of Utmost Good Faith* (1971), continued to spread to new, younger audiences. On January 6, 1994, Deloria's home in Boulder, Colorado, was ravaged by a fire that destroyed his archives, including his personal library of more than one thousand books. Deloria's computer, containing five chapters of a work in progress, also was destroyed in the fire.

FURTHER READING

Deloria, Vine, Jr. *Behind the Trail of Broken Treaties*. New York: Delacorte, 1974.
———. *Custer Died for Your Sins: An Indian Manifesto*. Norman: University of Oklahoma Press, 1988.
———. *The Indian Affair*. New York: Friendship Press, 1974.
Deloria, Vine, Jr., ed. *American Indian Policy in the Twentieth Century*. Norman: University of Oklahoma Press, 1985.
Deloria, Vine, Jr., and Clifford Lytle. *American Indians, American Justice*. Austin: University of Texas Press, 1983.
———. *The Nations Within*. New York: Pantheon, 1984.

DESKAHEH (LEVI GENERAL) (1873–1925)

Deskaheh was speaker of the **Iroquois** Grand Council at Grand River, Ontario, in the early 1920s, when Canadian authorities closed the traditional Longhouse, which had been asserting independence from Canadian jurisdiction. The Canadian authorities proposed to set up a governmental structure that would answer to its Indian affairs bureaucracy. With Canadian police about to arrest him, Deskaheh escaped from Canada and traveled to the headquarters of the League of Nations in Geneva, Switzerland, with an appeal for support from the international community.

Several months of effort did not win Deskaheh a hearing before the international body, in large part because of diplomatic manipulation by Great Britain and Canada, governments that were being embarrassed by Deskaheh's mission. Lacking a forum at the League of Nations, Deskaheh and his supporters held a privately organized meeting in Switzerland that drew several thousand people who roared approval of Iroquois **sovereignty**.

In his last speech, March 10, 1925, Deskaheh had lost none of this distaste for forced acculturation:

Over in Ottawa, they call that policy "Indian Advancement." Over in Washington, they call it "Assimilation." We who would be the helpless victims say it is tyranny. . . . If this must go on to the bitter end, we would rather that you come with your guns and poison gas and get rid of us that way. Do it openly and above board. (Fadden n.d.: 14)

As he lay dying, relatives of Deskaheh who lived in the United States were refused entry into Canada to be at his bedside. Deskaheh died two and one-half months after his last defiant speech. His notions of sovereignty have been maintained by many Iroquois into contemporary times. The Iroquois Grand Council at Onondaga issues its own passports, which are recognized by Switzerland and several other countries, but not by the United States or Canada.

FURTHER READING

Fadden, Ray. *Deskaheh: Iroquois Statesman and Patriot.* Rooseveltown, NY: Akwesasne Notes, n.d.
Deskaheh (Levi General) and Six Nations Council. *The Redman's Appeal for Justice.* Brantford, Ontario: Wilson Moore, 1924.
Rostkowski, Joelle. "The Redman's Appeal for Justice: Deskaheh and the League of Nations." In *Indians and Europe*, ed. Christian F. Feest. Aachen, Germany: Edition Herodot, 1987.

DINEBEIIN A NAHIILNA DE AGADITAHE

Translated as "Attorneys Who Contribute to the Economic Revitalization of the People," Dinebeiin a Nahiilna de Agaditahe (DNA) is the name of the Navajo Nation's Indian Legal Services program, which was started in 1967. The program is noted for adapting traditional Navajo (Dine) legal practices to modern conditions. The program's head office is in Window Rock, Arizona, but it has offices widely dispersed across the Navajo Nation. The attorneys and legal advocates of DNA have been generally known for their harmonious relationships with Native American courts, but in one instance Theodore Mitchell, director of DNA, was ordered off the reservation after a disagreement with the Navajo council. Mitchell took the case to court; a district court in *Dodge v. Nakai*, 298 F. Supp. 26 (D. Ariz. 1969), found the expulsion to be illegal.

DOCTRINE OF DISCOVERY

A year after Christopher Columbus's first voyage to the New World, in 1493, Pope Alexander IV issued two opinions that shaped European nations' perceptions of their "rights," under church law, to discover and occupy lands in the New World. In the Papal Bull *Inter Caetera*, Spain was granted all lands not governed by a "Christian prince" as of Christmas Day, 1492. This bull was modified in *Inter Caetera II*, which allocated to Spain all such lands west of a north-south line running one hundred leagues west of the Azores and Cape Verde Islands. Lands east of that line were reserved for Portugal.

The Spanish Crown was very legalistic and very concerned that its Indian policy pass muster with the church's moral dictates. A debate raged beginning about the year 1500 over whether the native peoples of the New World possessed souls and could be regarded as "human" by European standards. The church, after lengthy debate, found that the natives did indeed possess souls, and that these souls were fit for conversion to Christianity.

Once that question had been settled, European kings, popes, and savants wrestled with the question of how their nations could "discover" and then "own" lands that were obviously already occupied by the native peoples of the Americas. Around 1550, the Spanish king Charles V initiated a debate over these questions in which the priest Bartolomé de Las Casas argued for Indian rights and another theologian, Sepulveda, argued against. The Spanish theologian **Francisco de Vitoria** wrote that "in the absence of a just war . . . only the voluntary consent of the aborigines could justify the taking of American land" (Deloria and Lytle 1983: 3).

The same basic debate took place a century later as the English colonized the area they came to call "New England." **Roger Williams**, also a theologian, was asked by Puritan authorities to write an opinion regarding who owned the land on which the new colonies had begun. When he came to the conclusion that the native inhabitants owned the land, the authorities prepared to exile Williams to England. Hearing of these plans, he escaped and founded the colony of Providence Plantations with Indian aid. This colony later became known as Rhode Island.

The Doctrine of Discovery held that the native peoples of the New World were childish beings in need of the "benefits" of European civilization, a point of view that also informed English colonial policy in North America. Native American peoples whose land was at issue under the Doctrine of Discovery were not consulted in the formulation of it. Instead, the doctrine was formulated to describe Native American ownership (usually defined as "aboriginal title") within the framework of European and European-American legal systems. The doctrine had nothing to do with ways in which Native Americans perceived land use.

The Doctrine of Discovery has been used to justify the taking of land from Native Americans by degrading their rights of ownership to "aboriginal title," which may be rescinded in a "just" war, that is, one that the aggressor did not provoke. This interpretation of the Doctrine of Discovery became a major basis of Spanish and English and then of U.S. Indian policy. Under this policy, the Bureau of Indian Affairs was said to hold the Indians' land in "**trust**," with the Indians as "wards," a legal rationale used to foster policies meant to change the Indians' social lives, legal systems, and economic practices to conform to mainstream American standards through such policies as allotment (*see* **Allotment Act**), as well as the maintenance of boarding schools and other institutions meant, as some "reformers" phrased it late in the century, to "Kill the Indian and save the man."

When U.S. Supreme Court Chief Justice **John Marshall** ruled in the three cases comprising the **Marshall Trilogy** that Indian title predated that of the United States, and that the Indians were "domestic dependent nations" under the "guardianship" of the United States, he was wrestling with the same legalities that had informed the debates of Vitoria, Las Casas, and Williams. Legal scholar **Felix Cohen** summarized issues related to the Doctrine of Discovery:

Since the Indians were true owners, Vitoria held discovery can be justified only where property is ownerless. Nor could Spanish title to Indian lands be validly based upon the divine rights of the Emperor or the Pope, or upon the unbelief or sinfulness of the aborigines. Thus, Vitoria concluded, even the Pope has no right to partition the property of the Indians, and in the absence of a just war, only the voluntary consent of the aborigines could justify the annexation of their territory. (Deloria 1974: 89–90)

FURTHER READING

Cohen, Felix. *Handbook of Federal Indian Law*. Washington, DC: Interior Department, 1942.
Deloria, Vine, Jr. *Behind the Trail of Broken Treaties: An Indian Declaration of Independence*. New York: Delacourte, 1974. Austin: University of Texas Press, 1985.
Deloria, Vine, Jr., and Clifford Lytle. *American Indians, American Justice*. Austin: University of Texas Press, 1983.

DOOLITTLE COMMITTEE (1865–1867)

In 1865, Sen. James Doolittle of Wisconsin was appointed to head a joint special committee of Congress investigating the demise of Native Americans. The committee, which issued its report in 1867, investigated reasons why Indian populations were declining rapidly in the face of rapid westward expansion by European Americans. Among its findings were that

the Indians everywhere, with the exception of tribes within the Indian territory, are rapidly decreasing in numbers from various causes, by disease; by intemperance; by wars among themselves and with the whites; by the steady and relentless emigration of white men into the territories of the west, which, confining the Indians to still narrower limits, destroys that game which, in their normal state, constitutes their principal means of subsistence. (Prucha 1975: 102–105)

The tone of the report was accommodating toward Indians, but was also overtly racist, as it associated the Indians' demise with the "irrepressible conflict between a superior and an inferior race." Nevertheless, the report found that "in a large majority of cases Indian wars are to be traced to the aggressions of lawless white men" (102–105). The report traced the rapid decline in populations of large animals, especially the buffalo, to the rapid spread of settlement, including the construction of a transcontinental railroad. It provided detailed descriptions of corruption within the Indian Bureau and suggested more intense oversight by Congress.

FURTHER READING

Prucha, Francis Paul, ed. *Documents of United States Indian Policy*. Lincoln: University of Nebraska Press, 1975.

DRAPER V. UNITED STATES 164 U.S. 240 (1896)

Fourteen years after *United States v. McBratney* (1882) legitimized the use of state criminal jurisdiction on one reservation, the Supreme Court, in *Draper v. United States*, extended state power to prosecute crimes anywhere in **Indian Country**. The Court, likely swayed by assumptions that the General **Allotment Act** would disassemble the Native American estate anyway, upheld state power despite the fact that Montana had been admitted to the United States with Indian lands remaining "under the absolute jurisdiction and control of the Congress of the United States."

DUNDY, ELMER S. (1830–1896)

Elmer S. Dundy was a federal judge in Omaha who ruled during 1879, in the case of the Ponca **Standing Bear**, that Indians must be treated as human beings under U.S. law. The ruling implicitly denied the U.S. Army's presumed right to relocate individual Native Americans against their will.

Hearing of the travail of Standing Bear and his people as they camped near Omaha, local citizens obtained a writ of habeas corpus and brought the army into the federal court of Judge Dundy, who ruled: "An Indian is a person within the meaning of the law, and there is no law giving the Army authority to forcibly remove Indians from their lands" (Massey 1979: 6). Ironically, the case was prepared with the help of the old Indian fighter George Crook, who was swayed by the manifest injustice of the case. The harsh treatment of the Ponca also received publicity in Omaha newspapers that was wired to larger newspapers on the East Coast, causing a storm of protest letters to Congress.

Shortly after the ruling, Standing Bear's brother Big Snake tested it by moving roughly one hundred miles within **Indian Territory**, from the Poncas' assigned reservation to one occupied by **Cheyennes**. He was arrested by troops. On October 31, 1879, Ponca Indian Agent William H. Whiteman called Big Snake a troublemaker and ordered a detail to imprison him. When Big Snake refused to surrender, contending that he had committed no crime, he was shot to death. Big Snake did not realize that Dundy's ruling had been written to apply only to his brother's band. If Dundy had written his ruling to apply to all Indians, the army's policies might have been crippled. Later, the U.S. Senate called for an investigation of the shooting and other aspects of the Poncas' tragedy.

FURTHER READING

Massey, Rosemary. *Footprints in Blood: Standing Bear's Struggle for Freedom and Human Dignity*. Omaha, Nebraska: American Indian Center of Omaha, 1979.

DURO V. REINA 495 U.S. 676 (1990)

In *Duro v. Reina*, the Supreme Court held that a Native American court lacked jurisdiction over an Indian from another native nation who was charged with murder. A fourteen-year-old boy had been shot to death on the Salt River (Pima/Maricopa) Reservation. Both parties in this case were nonmembers of the jurisdiction. This case shares some similarities with **Oliphant v. Suquamish** (1978).

E

ECHO HAWK, JOHN (Pawnee) (b. 1945)

As an attorney, and as executive director of the **Native American Rights Fund** (NARF) since the middle 1970s, John Echo Hawk has made the organization a national force in Native American legal affairs. From land rights and water rights to the reburial of Native American bones and burial artifacts, the Native American Rights Fund has helped shape law and public opinion in late-twentieth-century America.

Echo Hawk was born in Albuquerque, New Mexico, and earned a bachelor's degree from the University of New Mexico in 1967. He earned a law degree from the same university in 1970, the same year he began his career at the Native American Rights Fund as a staff attorney.

John Echo Hawk worked closely with **Walter Echo Hawk** as NARF played a major legal role in negotiations with the Smithsonian Institution in 1989 for the return of Native American artifacts and human remains to native nations and peoples. Both were national leaders in efforts to pass federal laws protecting Native American graves.

ECHO HAWK, LARRY (Pawnee) (b. 1948)

After serving as attorney general of Idaho, Larry Echo Hawk in 1994 ran for governor of Idaho as a Democrat. He lost to Republican Phil Batt in a nationwide Republican landslide, scuttling Echo Hawk's hopes to become the first Native American state governor in the United States. Echo Hawk advocated environmental issues, consumer protection, and crime victims' rights.

Echo Hawk was born at Cody, Wyoming, and grew up in Farmington, New Mexico, one of six children of a full-blooded **Pawnee** father and a German mother. Echo Hawk's father was a land surveyor and worked in the oil-supply business. The father was a severe alcoholic until he was converted to Mormonism. Larry is a brother of **John Echo Hawk** and a cousin of **Walter Echo Hawk**.

Larry Echo Hawk won a football scholarship to Brigham Young University, where he played quarterback and earned an undergraduate degree in 1970. He also earned a juris doctor degree in 1973 at the University of Utah. Echo Hawk's legal career began with California Indian Legal Services. After that, Echo Hawk practiced law privately in Salt Lake City.

Echo Hawk served as general counsel for the Shoshoni-Bannock at Fort Hall for nine years before he served a term as Bannock County prosecutor. He also served in the Idaho House of Representatives after election in 1982 and reelection in 1984. In the Idaho House, a body with eighty-four members, he was one of seventeen Democrats. In 1991, Echo Hawk became the first Native American in the United States to be elected to a state attorney general's position. Echo Hawk spoke at the 1992 Democratic National Convention and was the first Native American to head a state delegation to that convention.

Echo Hawk is a holder of the George Washington University Martin Luther King Award for contributions to human rights and is fond of quoting King in his speeches, in which he often speaks of the motivating power of dreams. "It was beyond my wildest dreams [as a child] that I would someday be a lawyer, and a state attorney general," Echo Hawk said. He credits his father for the strength of his values and dreams. Larry Echo Hawk's great-grandfather, a well-known warrior among the Pawnees in Nebraska, was the first to carry the name "Echo Hawk." It was said that the hawk was the symbol of a renowned warrior, so he was first given that name. Hawk did not talk much about his exploits, but others among the Pawnees spread the word, which was said to "Echo." Thus he became known as "Echo Hawk." Larry Echo Hawk, who took a post as professor of law at Brigham Young University after his defeat in the race for Idaho's governorship, says, "There is no higher calling than using one's life to help others in need."

FURTHER READING

Echo Hawk, Larry. Speech. Omaha, Nebraska, May 2, 1996.

ECHO HAWK, WALTER (Pawnee) (b. 1948)

As senior staff attorney with the **Native American Rights Fund** for many years, Walter Echo Hawk earned a reputation as one of the best-known attorneys in the United States in cases involving the disposition of human remains and burial artifacts. He was one of the leading people behind a major effort to return such remains and artifacts from museums and historical societies to Native American people. Echo Hawk, who has served on the **Pawnee** Supreme Court, also has litigated cases concerned with religious freedom, water rights, prisoners' rights, and **treaty** rights.

Echo Hawk was born on the Pawnee reservation near Pawnee, Oklahoma. He earned an undergraduate degree in political science at Oklahoma State University in 1970 and a law degree from the University of New Mexico in 1973. Shortly thereafter, Walter Echo Hawk joined **John Echo Hawk** at the Native American Rights Fund. His work sometimes involved the Pawnee, as when he negotiated the closure of Pawnee burial pits that had been opened to public viewing in Kansas. Echo Hawk also played a key role in the passage in 1989 by the Nebraska state legislature of a law requiring the return of human remains and burial objects held by the Nebraska State Historical Society. Many of these remains were Pawnee in origin. This state law was a model used by the Smithsonian Institution and other museums in negotiating the return of Indian remains and artifacts nationwide beginning about 1990.

FURTHER READING

Echo Hawk, Walter. "Loopholes in Religious Liberty." *Cultural Survival Quarterly* 17:4 (1994): 62–65.

———. "Native American Religious Liberty: Five Hundred Years after Columbus." *American Indian Culture and Research Journal* 17:3 (1993): 33–52.

———. "Who Owns the Past? How Native American Indian Lawyers Fight for Their Ancestors' Remains and Memories." *Human Rights* 16:3 (1989): 24–29, 53–55.

———, guest editor. "Repatriation of Native American Remains" (special issue). *American Indian Culture and Research Journal* 16:2 (1992).

Echo Hawk, Walter, and C. Echo Hawk. *Battlefields and Burial Grounds: The Indian Struggle to Protect Ancestral Graves in the United States*. Minneapolis: Lerner Publications, 1994.

Echo Hawk, Walter, and Jack F. Trope. "The Native American Graves Protection and Repatriation Act: Background and Legislative History." *Arizona State Law Journal* 24: 1 (Spring 1992): 35–77.

ELK V. WILKINS 112 U.S. 94 (1884)

The U.S. Supreme Court held in *Elk v. Wilkins* that an Indian is not made a citizen by the Fourteenth Amendment to the U.S. **Constitution**. This position held even if the Indian was living apart from his nation or band. The Court also ruled that acts of Congress do not generally apply to Indians unless they are specifically mentioned.

At issue was the constitutional status of American Indians for purposes of citizenship and voting. The Fourteenth Amendment granted citizenship to "all persons born or naturalized in the United States, and subject to the jurisdiction thereof." Did American Indians fall under this definition? A federal district court ruled that it did not apply to Indians who had not been "born subject to its jurisdiction—that is, in its power and obedience" (*McKay v. Campbell*, 16 Fed. Cas. 161 [1871] [No. 8840]).

John Elk had been born outside of U.S. jurisdiction, but moved to Omaha as an adult and lived what the court described as a "civilized" life. He sought to become a citizen and exercise the right to vote in Omaha elections during 1880. The Supreme Court ruled that the Fifteenth Amendment (which grants the right to vote to all citizens regardless of race) did not apply in Elk's case, because he was not born in an area under U.S. jurisdiction. Therefore, Elk was not a citizen within the meaning of the Fourteenth Amendment. The fact that Elk had abandoned his Indian relatives and lifeways did not matter to the Court. Elk's citizenship and voting rights were denied because the Court held that an affirmative act was required of the United States before an Indian could become a citizen. The Supreme Court's opinion cited a dozen treaties, four court rulings, four laws, and eight opinions of the U.S. attorney general requiring "proof of fitness for civilization" as a precondition of granting Indians citizenship and voting rights.

Elk v. Wilkins posed an intriguing irony in late-eighteenth-century America, when the ideological landscape even of "friends of the Indian" promoted assimilation as an alternative to extermination. At a time when assimilation was at high tide, an individual Indian who wanted voting rights was being told that he was, in essence, a foreigner.

Six years after John Elk's desire for citizenship was denied, Congress passed the Indian Territory Naturalization Act (26 Stat. 81, 99–100), which allowed any Indian living in **Indian Territory** to apply for citizenship through the federal courts. The aim of this act was to break down communal loyalties among Native Americans in Indian Territory as it moved toward statehood as Oklahoma.

FURTHER READING

Deloria, Vine, Jr. *Behind the Trail of Broken Treaties: An Indian Declaration of Independence*. 1974. Austin: University of Texas Press, 1985.

EX PARTE CROW DOG 109 U.S. 556 (1883)

In *Ex Parte Crow Dog*, the U.S. Supreme Court denied federal jurisdiction over the murder of an Indian by another Indian on Indian land, citing treaties. The Supreme Court found that U.S. courts tried Indians "not by their peers, nor by the customs of their people, nor the law of their land, but by superiors of a different race, according to the law of a social state of which they have an imperfect conception, and which is opposed to the traditions of their history."

Congress reacted to this ruling by passing the **Major Crimes Act of 1885** (23 Stat. 385, U.S.C. § 1153), which subjected reservation Indians to federal prosecution for murder and other crimes. *Ex Parte Crow Dog* may be compared to *United States v. McBratney*, in which the Supreme Court two years earlier had found that Native American courts lacked jurisdiction in cases involving non-Indians accused of crimes against other non-Indians on Indian land.

Crow Dog was born at Horse Stealing Creek, Montana Territory, into a family of esteemed warriors. Before submitting to reservation life, he made his reputation in battle. When the Sioux were confined on reservations following the Custer battle, dissension rose between some of their leaders. On one occasion, Spotted Tail was accused by Red Cloud of pocketing the proceeds from a sale of native land. Crow Dog heard rumors that Spotted Tail was selling Lakota land to the railroads and building himself an enormous mansion with the proceeds. Such displays of favoritism toward Spotted Tail by the United States deeply angered and offended many of the traditional leaders. In addition, rumors abounded that Spotted Tail had slept with Crow Dog's wife.

In mid-July 1880, Spotted Tail was called before the general council by Crow Dog's White Horse Group, where he denied the charges. The council voted to retain Spotted Tail as head chief, but Crow Dog continued to assert the chief's complicity in various crimes against the people. Crow Dog carried out his own death sentence on Spotted Tail on August 5, 1881. At the time, Crow Dog was chief of the Rosebud Reservation's Indian police.

Blood money was paid, a Brule tradition, for the crime. Crow Dog was later arrested and convicted of murder in the federal territorial court at Deadwood, Dakota Territory. He was sentenced to hang. A marshal allowed Crow Dog to return home to finalize his private affairs before reporting to the gallows. During a snowstorm the day he was supposed to report back to the marshal, local settlers were wagering long odds that Crow Dog would not appear. Instead, Crow Dog appeared as agreed and created a sensation among the Anglos, who now looked at him as a paragon of honesty, a hero, rather than as the murderer of Spotted Tail, who had been very popular among the immigrants. Attorneys volunteered to submit a writ of habeas corpus on Crow Dog's behalf to the U.S. Supreme Court, which ruled that the territorial government had no jurisdiction over the crime. The writ of habeas corpus was issued and Crow Dog was set free.

Later, Crow Dog was one of the leaders in diffusing the Ghost Dance among the Lakota. Crow Dog adopted the religion from Short Bull. Crow Dog vociferously opposed army occupation of South Dakota Indian reservations and was one of the last holdouts after the massacre at Wounded Knee during December 1890. Crow Dog spent the last years of his life in relative peace on the Rosebud Sioux Reservation, South Dakota.

FURTHER READING

Harring, Sidney L. *Crow Dog's Case: American Indian Sovereignty, Tribal Law, and United States Law in the Nineteenth Century*. New York: Cambridge University Press, 1994.

F

FEDERAL ACKNOWLEDGMENT PROGRAM (1978)

The Federal Acknowledgment Program, administered by the Bureau of Indian Affairs, established procedures whereby a Native American band or nation can become a legal entity in the eyes of the U.S. government. The program was begun in 1978 to recognize Native American groups not acknowledged by prior treaties or other agreements. When the program was begun, about two hundred Indian groups existed within the borders of the United States without federal recognition, while about five hundred were recognized. Almost a hundred groups began the long process of certification; by the middle 1990s, several dozen had completed it. To be recognized, a Native American organization must submit a petition that documents its existence and operation as a governmental authority from historical times to the present.

One example of a recently recognized Native American group is the Ponca of Nebraska, who in the 1990s were establishing a reservation on the Niobrara River in northern Nebraska. These are descendants of the **Poncas** who were forced from their homeland by the U.S. Army in the 1870s, and whose situation became a part of American Indian law in the case of *United States ex rel. Standing Bear v. Crook* (1879).

FURTHER READING

O'Brien, Sharon. "Federal Indian Policy and Human Rights." In *American Indian Policy in the Twentieth Century*, ed. Vine Deloria, Jr. Norman: University of Oklahoma Press, 1985.

FEDERAL ENCLAVES ACT (1817) 18 U.S.C. 1152

Passed as the General Crimes Act, the Federal Enclaves Act was the first law providing federal jurisdiction over crimes committed by Indians in **Indian Country**. This law pertained to crimes by Indians against non-Indians and vice versa, but did not apply to Indians who were accused of crimes against other Indians. Indians already punished under Native American law also were excluded, as were offenses over which jurisdiction was reserved under specific treaties. This act, an extension of federal jurisdiction in Indian Country, has held sway as valid legal doctrine, with minor modification, since the early nineteenth century. In its contemporary form, this law holds as follows:

Except as otherwise expressly provided by law, the general laws of the United States as to the punishment of offenses committed in any place within the sole and exclusive jurisdiction of the United States, except the District of Columbia, shall extend to Indian Country. . . . This section [18 U.S.C. § 1152] shall not extend to offenses committed by one Indian against the person or property of another Indian, or to any Indian committing any offense in the Indian Country who has been punished by the local law of the tribe, or to any case where, by treaty stipulations, the exclusive jurisdiction over such offenses is or may be secured to the Indian tribes respectively.

FEDERAL PREEMPTION DOCTRINE

Growing out of Justice **John Marshall**'s opinion in *Worcester v. Georgia* (1832), the Federal Preemption Doctrine holds that the U.S. **Constitution** delegates regulation of Indian affairs to the federal government rather than to the individual states. This doctrine may be traced legally to some examples even before the founding of the United States, such as the **Albany Plan of Union** (1754), in which **Benjamin Franklin** described unitary control over Indian affairs so that Indians would not be forced to deal with the governments of several different British colonies.

The doctrine underlies nearly two centuries of law and confines state intervention into Indian civil or criminal jurisdiction to areas expressly allowed by federal legislation, such as **Public Law 280**, which allowed some states to assume jurisdiction over Indian reservations within their borders. State power over Indian lands and resources has been asserted several times, often illegally, according to federal courts. Many of these challenges have involved states trying to open new sources of tax revenue. Courts often use an "infringement" test to determine whether a specific assertion of a state's rights will diminish a Native American group's ability to govern itself.

FIFTH AMENDMENT (U.S. Constitution, Bill of Rights)

The Fifth Amendment has been used in Indian law to argue that compensation is due for illegal usurpation of lands and resources. In some cases (such as ones involving the **Trade and Intercourse Acts**, first passed in 1790), the doctrine of illegal taking has been used to regain for Native Americans lands alienated as many as two hundred years earlier. See especially ***United States v. Creek Nation*** (1935).

FLETCHER V. PECK 10 U.S. (6 Cranch) 87 (1810)

Fletcher v. Peck was the first case directly related to American Indian law to be adjudicated by the U.S. Supreme Court, and the first to strike down a state action. The Court held that the state held Indian lands in fee simple subject to Indian rights of occupancy, and, according to Holt and Forrester (in *Digest of American Indian Law*, 1990), "Thus, the State could grant the land subject to Indian title" (3).

FURTHER READING

Holt, H. Barry, and Gary Forrester. *Digest of American Indian Law: Cases and Chronology*. Littleton, CO: Fred B. Rothman, 1990.

FOUR MOTHERS, THE

The Four Mothers, a reference to the sacred, cardinal directions, was the name of the post-Tecumseh Native American resistance movement among woodland peoples. The Four Mothers was most active during the harshest century of invasion, from just prior to removal until just before the **John Collier** era. The Four Mothers consistently opposed U.S. policies of land seizure and forced assimilation. Growing out of the remnants of the earlier Black Drink resistance (which Gregory Dowd has recently documented in *A Spirited Resistance*), the Four Mothers movement found itself dealing with the policies of Manifest Destiny. The name of the movement transmuted from Black Drink to Four Mothers sometime during and after removal.

By the late 1820s in the Old Northwest, the movement concentrated on thwarting missionary attempts at conversion and enumeration of the captive populations, especially on church-run reservations in western Pennsylvania and Ohio. Although frustrated missionaries typically accused Four Mothers leaders of attempting to drive out Christians in order to enrich themselves by selling liquor, in fact, followers of the Four Mothers were old-time traditionals who eschewed the European vision medium of alcohol, along with European religion. Between 1824 and the removal era, De-Un-Kot, a Wyandot shaman of the **Iroquois** League remnants in Ohio, used Four Mothers resistance tactics to keep people from allowing themselves to be enrolled (that is, to become "dead bugs on bark") on reservation lists and to persuade them to resist conversion to Christianity. He did this by scheduling competing, runner-announced, traditional ceremonies to coincide with Christian services, forcing a public choice of loyalties. At one point, De-Un-Kot and his lieutenants came into Methodist Sunday services in full regalia. He disrupted Christian teachings by calmly reciting, in Wyandot, oral traditions that the people seemed in danger of forgetting. Refusing census, enrollment, and conversion by holding onto tradition was to become a basic tenet of the Four Mothers in **Indian Territory** after removal.

Between 1800 and removal in the South, Kee-Too-Wah band **Cherokees** and, especially, the **Creeks** and Seminoles continued the old Black Drink resistance under inspired leaders such as Osceola, whose name means "Black Drink Singer." During removal, the Four Mothers secretly helped people avoid transport west of the Mississippi. About one-fourth of the Cherokee, **Chickasaw, Choctaw**, and Creek fled to the safety of the mountains and the swamps, while the Seminole remained in the Florida Everglades. In the North, meantime, approximately one-quarter to one-third of the so-called Wyandot (actually Haudenosaunee League remnants in Ohio) escaped removal, many by hiding in and near the Great Black Swamp in northwest Ohio, where soldiers could not follow with horses and heavy, wheeled wagons.

After removal, the main leadership of the Four Mothers passed into Oklahoma, along with the Creek "Harjo" ("Recklessly Brave Ones") and Cherokee Kee-Too-Wah and Nighthawks. The transported "Wyandot"— Seneca and Wyandot remnants of the league—had their hands full in Kansas, where the U.S. government was attempting to declare them "non-Indians," reusing the strategy by which it had recently defined the Florida Seminole out of existence. Simply surviving both the new environment and the Civil War took up most of the elders' attention. A brief respite from Eurocultural pressures ensued.

The infamous Dawes era (1887–1934), a forced-assimilation scheme of the U.S. government that upped the ante to complete cultural destruction by way of allotment, brought the Four Mothers back into high relief. To the old tenets of refusing census, enrollment, and conversion was added a fourth, the refusal to accept the Dawes Land Allotment. With the aid of the Four Mothers, Native Americans evaded federal "Indian agents" and the census takers, clung to their traditional names, thwarted Dawes enrollment, and prevented delivery of allotment deeds for eleven years. As during removal, the Four Mothers kept people in hiding, if need be. So successful was the Four Mothers in preventing implementation of the **Allotment Act** (Dawes Act) that in 1898, Congress was forced to pass the **Curtis Act**, mandating allotment, whether or not the allottee agreed to it.

During the mayhem, murder, and land fraud facilitated by the Dawes Act, the Four Mothers finally registered as a blip on the federal consciousness, leading historian Angie Debo to assert, inaccurately, that the group was first formed in 1895. In fact, the Four Mothers had been active for most of the nineteenth century. In 1895, the Four Mothers incorporated as a dues-paying organization to raise the funds necessary for relief of the desperate poverty caused by the Dawes Act and to underwrite its most audacious effort yet: the attempt to create a pan–Native American state called **Sequoyah** out of the Oklahoma Territory. This effort resurrected a hope once cherished by the "Moravian Delaware" (actually, Western Door members of the Haudenosaunee League) based on a 1778 promise from the revolutionary government. As recorded by John Heckewelder, the government pledged to reward the "Christian" Delaware with actual statehood in return for their neutrality during the Revolution. (Instead, they and other Western Door members were rewarded with confinement on an Ohio reservation in 1797.)

Now vigorously headed up by the Creeks, the Four Mothers pulled together the Choctaw, Chickasaw, Cherokee, Seminole, and other fragments of transported nations in an "Indian Territory" statehood drive. Without any "guidance" from the various "Friends of the Indian" groups in the East—indeed, without their knowledge—the Four Mothers researched the legal requirements of federal statehood and then crafted and implemented a statehood petition that met all tests of eligibility under U.S. law. In 1905, the "Last Council of the Creek Nation" (before it was "legally" dissolved by the U.S. government) voted to put the Four Mothers petition on the Oklahoma territorial ballot, one year before Eurosettlers could put forward their own statehood initiative. The Sequoyah State Constitution Issue appeared on the territorial ballot for the election of November 7, 1905. It "passed" with the combined vote of Euro- and Native American citizens of the territory. The Four Mothers then presented its ratified Sequoyah State Constitution to the U.S. Congress, as provided in the U.S. **Constitution**. Federal legislators did not even consider the petition. Despite the fact that there had been no errors in the Four Mothers' process, Congress illegally set the Sequoyah statehood petition aside. In 1906, it accepted, instead, the Euro-drafted Oklahoma statehood petition, even though a fully legal, prior petition was still before it.

The Four Mothers officially surfaced again in 1906 before the Senate Select Committee taking public testimony in preparation for recognizing "white" Oklahoma statehood. These hearings provided the first inkling that the federal government had of the existence of the Four Mothers resistance movement, despite the fact that 24,000 impoverished Native Americans were paying dues to the Four Mothers by 1906. Native speakers, some of them (like Chitto Harjo) actually wanted "renegades" at the time, testified at these hearings regarding the history of the Four Mothers movement. Eufaula Harjo explained the rationale behind refusing enrollment and allotment. Chitto Harjo began his testimony, "I am telling you now about what was done since 1492," but the chairman unceremoniously stopped him, claiming that he was pushing the issue too far into the past. Undaunted, Chitto Harjo insisted, "I am going to make a foundation for what I have to say," and started anew with the broken Removal Treaty of 1832.

The Four Mothers began receding into the background after Oklahoma was granted statehood in 1907. In 1908, it rallied to oppose the imposition of U.S. citizenship on Oklahoma Native peoples, a position it continued to press through 1910. Although the Four Mothers never yielded on any of its positions, and there are records of dues payments continuing at least through 1915, the group gradually went into abeyance with the loss of Sequoyah statehood in 1906 and the death of Chitto Harjo in 1911. By 1934, when the Dawes era was officially terminated (after almost all allotted land had passed fraudulently into Euro-American hands), the Four Mothers was no longer spoken of.

FURTHER READING

Debo, Angie. *And Still the Waters Run*. Princeton: Princeton University Press, 1940.

Dowd, Gregory Evans. *A Spirited Resistance: The North American Indian Struggle for Unity, 1745–1815*. Baltimore: Johns Hopkins University Press, 1992.

Garland, Hamlin. "The Final Council of the Creek Nation." In *Hamlin Garland's Observations on the American Indian, 1895–1905*. Ed. Lonnie E. Underhill and Daniel F. Littlefield, Jr., 184–192. Tucson: University of Arizona Press, 1976.

Heckewelder, John. *Thirty Thousand Miles with John Heckewelder*. Ed. Paul A. W. Wallace. Pittsburgh: University of Pittsburgh Press, 1958.

Marsh, Thelma R. *Moccasin Trails to the Cross: A History of a Mission to the Wyandott [sic] Indians on the Sandusky Plains*. Upper Sandusky, OH: United Methodist Historical Society of Ohio, 1974.

U.S. Congress. Senate. *Report of the Select Committee to Investigate Matters Connected with Affairs in the Indian Territory with Hearings, November 11, 1906–January 9, 1907*. 59th Cong., 2nd sess. S. Rep. 5013, pts. 1 and 2. 2 vol. Washington, DC: U.S. Government Printing Office, 1907.

BARBARA A. MANN

FRANKLIN, BENJAMIN (1706–1790)

Benjamin Franklin's life was frequently intertwined with the lives, societies, and affairs of Native Americans. As a printer, he published accounts of Indian treaties for more than two decades. Franklin began his diplomatic career by representing the colony of Pennsylvania at councils with the Iroquois and their allies. His designs for the **Albany Plan of Union** and later the **Articles of Confederation** contain elements of the Native American systems of confederation that he had come to know as a diplomat. Franklin also speculated liberally in Native American land as he helped to frame the documents that form the basic law of the United States.

Born in Boston, Franklin worked with his brother James as a printer until the age of seventeen. In 1723, he left Massachusetts for Philadelphia, where he became a successful printer and made his mark on history as an inventor, statesman, and philosopher.

Franklin's earliest contacts with Indians occurred in Philadelphia, where his printing company published the Indian treaties entered into by the colonial Pennsylvania Assembly. He was later a delegate to the 1753 treaty with the Ohio Indians at Carlisle, Pennsylvania. In 1744, at the **Lancaster Treaty** Council, **Canassatego**, an Onondaga sachem, urged the colonies to unite in a manner similar to that of the **Iroquois Confederacy**. Franklin learned of Canassatego's words when he published the treaty proceedings. Franklin's press issued Indian treaties in small booklets that enjoyed a lively sale throughout the colonies. Beginning in 1736, Franklin published Indian treaty accounts on a regular basis until the early 1760s, when his defense of Indians under assault by frontier settlers at Lancaster cost him his seat in the Pennsylvania Assembly. In "Narrative of the Late Massacres in Lancaster County" (1763), Franklin condemned the massacre of Christianized Conestoga Indians by a mob from Paxton, Pennsylvania. He called these vigilantes "Christian white savages." He also argued that liquor and disease, brought on by increasing contact with non-Indians, would cause the Indians' decline in North America. When the Paxton Boys marched on Philadelphia to exterminate the city's Indians in February 1764, Franklin led a delegation to the Indian camp and counselled peace.

In 1776, Franklin ardently supported the idea of American independence, and his revised Albany Plan of Union became the basis for the new American nation's first instrument of government, the Articles of Confederation. It is known that he based some of his political concepts about governmental unity on the Iroquois League of Six Nations.

In Europe, Franklin was a wry advocate of America and its peoples, European derived and native. While serving as ambassador to France, **Thomas Jefferson** was fond of relating the story of a dinner attended by Franklin, a few other Americans, and French degeneracy-theory advocates while Franklin was representing the new nation in France. Franklin listened to Abbé Raynal, a well-known proponent of American degeneracy, describe how Europeans would be stunted by exposure to the New World. Franklin listened quietly, then simply asked the French to test their theory "by the fact before us. Let both parties rise," Franklin challenged, "and we shall see on which side nature has degenerated." The table became a metaphorical Atlantic Ocean. The Americans, on their feet, towered over the French. "[The] Abbé, himself particularly, was a mere shrimp," Jefferson smirked.

Franklin used his image of Indians and their societies as a critique of Europe's social and legal systems:

The Care and Labour of providing for Artificial and fashionable Wants, the sight of so many Rich wallowing in superfluous plenty, while so many are kept poor and distress'd for want; the Insolence of Office . . . [and] restraints of Custom, all contrive to disgust them [Indians] with what we call civil Society. (Laberee 1950–: 381)

Franklin described Indians' passion for liberty while making it a patriotic rallying cry; he admired Indians' notions of happiness while seeking a definition that would suit the new nation. Franklin wrote of Native American legal behavior:

All the Indians of North America not under the dominion of the Spaniards are in that natural state, being restrained by no Laws, having no Courts, or Ministers of Justice, no Suits, no prisons, no governors vested with any Legal Authority. The persuasion of Men distinguished by Reputation of Wisdom is the only Means by which others are govern'd, or rather led—and the State of the Indians was probably the first State of all Nations. (Ramsay 1968: 85)

As U.S. ambassador to France, Franklin often wrote about Indians. Indeed, among the French *philosophes*, he was known as the "Philosopher as Savage." In his tract "Remarks Concerning the Savages of North America" (1784), Franklin asserted cultural relativity regarding Indians vis-à-vis Europeans. Although sometimes paradoxical in his outlook, Franklin often compared the virtues and shortcomings of both Indian and non-Indian cultures, asserting that Indian ideas and customs had great wisdom and value. Franklin died in 1790, shortly after he helped fashion the U.S. **Constitution**, which he had helped shape with his ideas of an amalgam between Native American and European cultures.

FURTHER READING

Aldridge, Alfred O. *Benjamin Franklin: Philosopher and Man*. Philadelphia: J. B. Lippincott, 1965.

———. "Franklin's Deistical Indians." *Proceedings of the American Philosophical Society* 94 (August 1950): 398–410.

Franklin, Benjamin. *The Autobiography of Benjamin Franklin*. Ed. John Bigelow. Philadelphia: J. B. Lippincott, 1868.

Grinde, Donald A., Jr., and Bruce E. Johansen. *Exemplar of Liberty: Native America and the Evolution of Democracy*. Los Angeles: UCLA American Indian Studies Center, 1991.

Labaree, Leonard, and William B. Willcox (Whitfield J. Bell after 1962), eds. *The Papers of Benjamin Franklin*. Vol. 17. New Haven, CT: Yale University Press, 1950– .

Ramsay, Allan. "Thoughts on the Origin and Nature of Government. In *Intel-*

lectual Origin and Nature of Government, ed. Staughton Lynd. New York: Random House, 1968.

Van Doren, Carl, and Julian P. Boyd, eds. *Indian Treaties Printed by Benjamin Franklin, 1736–1762*. Philadelphia: Historical Society of Pennsylvania, 1938.

G

GAGE, MATILDA JOSLYN (1826–1898)

Matilda Joslyn Gage compared the status of women in **Iroquois** society with that of other women in nineteenth-century America in her most important book in what Sally R. Wagner called "the first wave of feminism," *Woman, Church, and State* (1893). In that book, Gage acknowledged, according to Wagner's research, that "the modern world [is] indebted to the Iroquois for its first conception of inherent rights, natural equality of condition, and the establishment of a civilized government upon this basis" (Grinde and Johansen 1991: 226–227).

Gage was probably one of the three most influential feminist architects of the nineteenth-century women's movement, with **Elizabeth Cady Stanton** and Susan B. Anthony, according to Wagner, whose research was among the first to provide a scholarly basis for a resurgent feminist movement in the late twentieth century. Gage was later "read out" of the movement and its history because of her radical views, especially regarding oppression of women by organized religion.

Knowledge of the Iroquois' matrilineal system of society and government was widespread among early feminists, many of whom lived in upstate New York. The early feminists learned of the Iroquois not only through reading the works of Lewis Henry Morgan, Henry Schoolcraft, and others, but also through direct personal experience. With Stanton and Anthony, Gage coauthored the landmark *History of Woman Suffrage*. In her last book, *Women, Church, and State*, Gage opened with a chapter on "the matriarchate," a form of society she believed existed in a number of early societies, specifically the Iroquois. Gage discussed several Iroquois traditions that tended to create checks and balances between the genders, including descent through the female line, the ability of women to nominate male leaders, the fact that women had a veto power over decisions to go to war, and the woman's supreme authority in the household. Gage also noted that Iroquois women had rights to their property and children after divorce.

Gage herself was admitted to the Iroquois Council of Matrons and was adopted into the Wolf Clan with the name Karonienhawi, "she who holds the sky." Wagner asserted that "Nineteenth century radical feminist theoreticians, such as Elizabeth Cady Stanton and Matilda Joslyn Gage, looked to the Iroquois for their vision of a transformed world" (Grinde and Johansen 226–227).

As contemporaries of Morgan, Friedrich Engels, and Karl Marx, Gage and the other founding mothers of modern feminism in the United States shared a chord of enthusiasm at finding functioning societies that incorporated notions of gender equality. All seemed to agree that the native model held promise for the future. Gage and Stanton looked to the native model for a design of a "regenerated world." "Never was justice more perfect, never civilization higher than under the Matriarchate," Gage wrote. "Under [Iroquois] women the science of government reached the highest form known to the world" (Gage 1980: 9–10). Writing in the *New York Evening Post*, Gage contended that "division of power between the sexes in this Indian republic was nearly equal."

FURTHER READING

Allen, Paula Gunn. *The Sacred Hoop: Recovering the Feminine in American Indian Traditions.* Boston: Beacon Press, 1986.

Brown, Judith K. "Economic Organization and the Position of Women among the Iroquois." *Ethnohistory* 17: 3–4 (Summer–Fall 1970): 151–167.

Carr, Lucien. *The Social and Political Position of Women among the Huron-Iroquois Tribes.* Salem, MA: Salem Press, 1884.

Gage, Matilda Joslyn. *Woman, Church, and State.* 1893. Watertown, MA: Persephone Press, 1980.

Grinde, Donald A., and Bruce E. Johansen. *Exemplar of Liberty: Native America and the Evolution of Democracy.* Los Angeles: UCLA American Indian Studies Center, 1991.

Landsman, Gail. "Portrayals of the Iroquois in the Woman Suffrage Movement." Paper presented at the Annual Conference on Iroquois Research, Rensselaerville, NY, October 8, 1988.

Stanton, Elizabeth Cady, Susan B. Anthony, and Matilda Joslyn Gage. *History of Woman Suffrage.* Salem, NH: Ayer Co., 1985.

Wagner, Sally Roesch. "The Iroquois Confederacy: A Native American Model for Non-sexist Men." *Changing Men*, Spring–Summer 1988, 32–33.

————. *The Untold Story of the Iroquois Influence on Early Feminists*. Aberdeen, SD: Sky Carrier Press, 1996.

GENOCIDE

"Genocide" has been defined by the United Nations as "a denial of the right of existence of entire groups of human beings, as homicide is the denial of the right to live of individual human beings." Although the word is practically never used in American Indian law, legal activists sometimes contend that the sum total of U.S. Indian policy during the last two centuries has been genocidal. The United Nations has endorsed the position that genocide is harmful to human society as a whole, and that it is an international crime.

The United Nations Convention on Genocide was passed by that body in 1948, but was not considered seriously by the U.S. Senate until 1970, after seventy-four other nations had signed it. Opponents of the genocide convention were able to prevent its ratification from 1949, when President Harry S. Truman submitted it, until 1986, when despite Senator Jesse Helms's opposition the measure was finally ratified by the Senate. At that time, ninety-seven other nations had signed the genocide convention, despite the fact that every sitting president had supported it.

H

HANDBOOK OF FEDERAL INDIAN LAW (FELIX COHEN)

The *Handbook of Federal Indian Law*, first published in 1942 by the U.S. Department of the Interior, is the most complete compilation of U.S. law pertaining to Native Americans to that time. The *Handbook* was republished (and, in some cases, revised) several times after **Felix Cohen**'s death in 1953, as it was widely used by judges and attorneys at bar in all of the U.S. federal courts. Between 1958 and 1985, according to legal scholar Charles F. Wilkinson, Cohen's handbook was cited in more than one hundred opinions issued by federal and state courts (1987: 174). "Handbook" is something of a misnomer in this case, since the book comprises roughly 660 encyclopedia-sized pages of very dense type.

FURTHER READING

Wilkinson, Charles F. *American Indians, Time, and the Law: Native Societies in a Modern Constitutional Democracy.* New Haven: Yale University Press, 1987.

HANDSOME LAKE (GANEODIYO) (Seneca) (c. 1733–1815)

"Handsome Lake" is a reference to Lake Ontario. The name acts as a position title, one of fifty, in the Grand Council of the Haudenosaunee (**Iroquois**) League. The individual commonly known to American history as Handsome Lake bore the personal name of Ganeodiyo. He was elected to the seat of Handsome Lake through his maternal lineage.

There had been dozens of Handsome Lakes before him, the first being a supporter of the Great Peacemaker, but the title was retired at the death of Ganeodiyo, an honor earlier bestowed only on the Peacemaker. Ganeodiyo was the great-great-grandson of Elizabeth, a Wolf Clan keeper of women's traditions, a brother (or half-brother, as Europeans count it) of the Seneca sachem Cornplanter, an uncle of Red Jacket, and an ancestor of the ethnohistorian Arthur C. Parker.

Handsome Lake was born at Conawagus, a Seneca village near contemporary Avon, New York, on the Genesee River. He and many other Senecas sided with the British in the French and Indian War and the American Revolution. After that war, many Iroquois and other Native Americans who had supported the British were forced into Canada or onto small, impoverished reservations in the United States. Handsome Lake's revival occurred in an atmosphere of dissension within a fractured Iroquois League.

Handsome Lake's early life reflected the disintegration of his people. His birthplace was taken by whites, and Handsome Lake was forced to move to the Allegheny Seneca reservation. The Seneca ethnologist Arthur C. Parker characterized Handsome Lake as "a middle-sized man, slim and unhealthy looking . . . [who became] a dissolute person and a miserable victim of the drink" (Johansen and Grinde 1997: 160).

After four years on his back in a small cabin, Handsome Lake began having a series of visions with which he later rallied the Iroquois at a time when some of them were selling their entire winter harvest of furs for hard liquor, turning traditional ceremonies into drunken brawls, and, in winter, often dying of exposure in drunken stupors. The Iroquois population in upstate New York had declined to roughly four thousand people by this time. By the spring of 1799, Handsome Lake experienced considerable remorse over his alcoholism, but did not stop drinking until he was nearly dead, "yellow skin and dried bones."

A nationalistic figure in a religious context, the prophet Handsome Lake finally stopped his own heavy drinking and later committed to writing the Code of Handsome Lake (*see* **Handsome Lake, Code of**). He persuaded many other Iroquois to do the same. Handsome Lake achieved some political influence among the Senecas, but his popularity slid because of his ideological rigidity. In 1801 and 1802, Handsome Lake traveled to Washington, D.C., with a delegation of Senecas to meet with President **Thomas Jefferson** and to resist the reduction of their people's landholdings.

FURTHER READING

Johansen, Bruce E., and Donald A. Grinde, Jr. *The Encyclopedia of Native American Biography*. New York: Henry Holt, 1997.

HANDSOME LAKE, CODE OF

The religion of Handsome Lake, which began as a series of visions in 1799, combined Quaker forms of Christianity with Native American traditions. Its influence is still strongly felt among the traditional Iroquois, who often call the Code of Handsome Lake "The Longhouse Religion."

The Code of Handsome Lake, developed by the Seneca **Handsome Lake** (c. 1733–1815), combines European religious influences (especially those practiced by the Quakers) with a traditional Iroquois emphasis on family, community, and the centrality of the land to the maintenance of culture. It is a legal as well as a religious code in that its main emphasis is on correct interpersonal behavior.

The largest following for Handsome Lake occurred after his death. Many Iroquois accepted rejection of alcohol, and his concepts of social relationships, as well as concepts of good and evil that closely resemble Quakerism, which Handsome Lake had studied. Handsome Lake also borrowed heavily from the Iroquois Great Law of Peace, emphasizing its values of reciprocity and mutuality. Handsome Lake also popularized concepts such as looking into the future for seven generations and regard for the earth as mother. These ideas have since become part of pan-Indian thought across North America and, from there, were incorporated into late-twentieth-century popular environmental symbolism.

The Code of Handsome Lake is still widely followed (as the Longhouse Religion) in Iroquois country. By the late twentieth century, roughly a third of the 30,000 Iroquois in New York State attended Longhouse rites.

FURTHER READING

Deardorff, Merle H. *The Religion of Handsome Lake: Its Origin and Development.* Bureau of American Ethnology Bulletin no. 149. Washington, DC: Bureau of American Ethnology, 1951.

Parker, Arthur. *The Code of Handsome Lake, the Seneca Prophet.* New York State Museum Bulletin No. 163. Albany: New York State Museum, 1913.

———. *Parker on the Iroquois.* Ed. William Fenton. Syracuse, NY: Syracuse University Press, 1968.

Wallace, Anthony F. C. *The Death and Rebirth of the Seneca.* New York: Knopf, 1970.

HARJO V. KLEPPE 420 F. Supp. 110 (D.D.C. 1976)

A federal district court in Washington, D.C., ruled in 1976 that the Bureau of Indian Affairs had ignored the government of the **Creek** Nation for sixty years, thereby abusing its **trust** responsibility. In the opinion of the court, the BIA's refusal to deal with a government legally constituted under treaty was "bureaucratic imperialism," in which "the

influence and control of the [BIA] over . . . the Creek national government between 1920 and 1970 was exercised wholly without the benefit
of any specific congressional mandate." William Bryant, the district
court judge who handed down the ruling in *Harjo v. Kleppe*, maintained
that the Bureau of Indian Affairs had turned the office of head chief of
the Creek Nation into its own private fiefdom, appointing leaders with
such disregard of public opinion that the BIA had violated the Five
Tribes Act, which permitted the Creeks to retain their government.

HARMONY ETHIC, CHEROKEE

The **Cherokee** occasionally went to war with other native nations, but
within their settlements, the highest value was placed on what was
sometimes called a "Harmony Ethic." This code of behavior placed a
great deal of emphasis on eliminating interpersonal conflict, especially
face-to-face anger; it may be compared in some ways to the Iroquois
code of behavior developed in the Great Law of Peace and the Code of
Handsome Lake (see **Handsome Lake, Code of**). The Harmony Ethic
governed the way in which Cherokees treated each other, and how they
defined their relationship with nature.

In Cherokee society, a person was conditioned by social norms to
avoid giving offense to others. A good person was supposed to avoid
expressing anger or causing others to become angry; a leader earned
respect by listening carefully and not expressing his views until he had
heard all sides in a conflict. A third person often was brought in to
resolve conflicts between two individuals in this manner. If a conflict
was not reconciled, the two parties often went about their business,
studiously avoiding each other.

In the face of conflict, the Harmony Ethic directed both parties to
withdraw. If a conflict could be resolved through generosity, a good
Cherokee was expected to give of himself and his belongings to retain
a semblance of social well-being. This value was especially evident with
respect to sharing of food; the Cherokee language contains a special
word that indicates stinginess with food, as compared to stinginess with
other possessions.

A person who engaged in behavior contrary to the Harmony Ethic
would at first become the target of gossip and ostracism. If verbal methods of social control failed, and if a pattern of antisocial behavior became entrenched, the people who were offended by it might hire a
conjurer, whose rituals were said to prepare the way for the offending
person to become seriously ill, with death the eventual result in the
most extreme cases. Even when preparing to kill such a person, however, a third party was always engaged. Face-to-face conflict was
avoided at all costs.

HAUDENOSAUNEE (IROQUOIS) WOMEN, LEGAL AND POLITICAL STATUS

October 12, 1492, is not the first day of Native American history. Indeed, mounting evidence (some of it from a Pennsylvania habitation site) shows Native America to be at least 50,000 years old and, based on the Hueyatlaco site at Valsequillo, Mexico, perhaps as much as 250,000 years old. Thus Europeans have been in contact with woodlanders for less, and perhaps far less, than 1 percent of their existence. Even were European accounts of Native America culturally neutral, which they are not, so slight an acquaintance could not provide conceptual depth. Therefore, our discussion of Haudenosaunee women starts with the people's own stories.

The legal status of women in Haudenosaunee culture was originally encoded in two forms: oral traditions and **wampum**. Native oral traditions are ancient learning stories, articulating cultural principles and sociopolitical relationships. Wampum writing is a more recent development, having begun around a thousand years ago. Iridescent purple and white wampum beads, either stringed or knotted into belts, were a precontact form of emblematic writing based on color coding of complex cultural metaphors. The wampum belts of the Great Law encoded the laws of women's powers. We turn first to the Keepings (oral traditions) of the Haudenosaunee Epochs, or Cycles of Time.

The Cycles of Time: Learning Tools

In the First Cycle of Time, inexpressibly long ago, the earth was a water globe. Sky People possessed of extensive *orenda* (psychic spiritual access) lived in Sky World, their moving home among the stars. Due to the dishonest machinations of Sky Woman's husband and his circle of advisors, all jealous of her strong dream *orenda*, Sky Woman was either tricked into falling or was pushed from Sky World down to the Earth below. Birds alerted the other earth animals that she was falling, and they all held a council to see what should be done. In compassion for her plight, the birds held her aloft on their interlocking wings while the water animals created dry land for her on the back of the great Turtle who still swims endlessly, holding North America—Turtle Island—above sea level.

Sky Woman carried the seeds of agriculture along with her from Sky World to earth; in particular, in her right hand, she clasped the Three Sisters: the Younger Sisters, Beans and Squash, and the Elder Sister, Corn; and in her left, Sacred Tobacco. Pregnant before she left Sky World, she gave birth on Turtle Island to her beloved daughter, the Lynx. Together, Sky Woman and the little Fat-Faced Lynx explored the length and breadth of Turtle Island, planting their seeds and naming all the creatures. The Lynx eventually married a shape-shifting earthling and died before her time in childbirth, to the indescribable grief of her mother. Buried in the earth, the Lynx became associated with "Mother Earth." The Haudenosaunee thus trace their descent through the womb of the Lynx to the womb of Sky Woman and, with her, back to the stars.

Now called "Grandmother," Sky Woman reared the Lynx's twin boys, the sibling rivals, Sapling and Flint. At puberty, although still listening to Grandmother, these youths went off on their own, the younger seeking out his father. Eventually, the brothers came to blows with one another. In the end, Sapling threw a mountain down on Flint, imprisoning him inside. Flint became associated with the West, and Sapling with the East. Just before her death, Grandmother scattered the stars of the Milky Way so that people could see the path home. After her death, Sapling lifted Grandmother up as the Moon, where she now smiles down on her descendants as "Grandmother Moon."

In the Second Cycle of Time, a thousand years ago, the people were in great tribulation. War ravaged the clans, under the strongman leadership of the madman-cannibal Atotarho (Flint in new flesh). The Lynx returned for the sake of the community, to help see the people through the founding of the League. Now called the "Jigonsaseh," or the "New Face," she collaborated with her elder son Sapling, returned as the Peacemaker, and his speaker-friend Hiawatha to establish the Great Law of Peace, or the Constitution of the Five Nations, the Elder Brothers, Mohawk, Onondaga, and Seneca, and the Younger Brothers, Oneida and Cayuga. The Tuscarora joined the Younger Brothers between 1711 and 1735, becoming the Sixth Nation of the Haudenosaunee.

Before proceeding on his mission, the Peacemaker consulted Jigonsaseh. Jigonsaseh negotiated the women's sections, called "Clans and Consanguinity" by Seth Newhouse, into the Peacemaker's proposed law. One important step Jigonsaseh took was to refuse food to war parties, thus impeding the war effort. It was also she who suggested the final peace proposal, acceptable to all—including Atotarho, also her cosmic son. Upon her death, "Jigonsaseh" became the position title bestowed on the powerful Head Clan Mothers of the League.

We are now in the Third Cycle of Time, the era of "contact" generally connected with the appearance of **Handsome Lake** (c. 1733–1815), the "Seneca Prophet." With the Revolution and formation of the United States, the Ohio-Pennsylvania Haudenosaunee were cut off from their eastern counterparts in New York and Canada. Handsome Lake rallied the defeated and demoralized New York and Canadian Haudenosaunee, with mixed results, by promulgating the *Gaiwiio*, or "Good Message." His "Longhouse Religion" has been both praised for preserving elements of tradition and rebuked for cooperating with the U.S. government and "Christianizing" his culture.

The Fourth Cycle of Time is yet to come. The prophecies state that the Haudenosaunee will resume their former cultural prominence. Morally and physically sickened by their own culture and guided by the smoke rising from the Fire at Onondaga, Europeans will trace the Shining Roots of Peace back to spirituality in the Great Law of Peace. This will occur amidst considerable environmental havoc: Turtle Island will be partially submerged in a cataclysm marking the beginning of the Fourth Epoch.

All Native American stories are learning stories, articulating cultural principles. The women's powers established in these epochal stories cover matrilineage; reciprocity and gendered roles; faith keeping; sexual relations and childrearing; ownership of agriculture and annual ceremonies; peace keeping; name keeping, an extensive area itself, including adoptions; funerals; nomination of candidates, advisors, and speakers; and impeachment of wrong-headed public officials.

Matrilineage: The Mother-Daughter Relationship

The deathless bond between Sky Woman and the Lynx, in life and in their later relationship as Mother Earth and Grandmother Moon, emphasized the primacy of the mother-daughter relationship in Haudenosaunee society. This story articulated the concept of descent and inheritance through the female line in kinship groups, or clans, headed by women called "Clan Mothers." Sky Woman's delight at the birth of her infant daughter further articulated the principle of matrilineage.

In practice, this meant that matrilineal clans formed the backbone of society, with inheritance passing through matrilineal grandmothers to mothers to daughters. Traditionally, rejoicings at the birth of a girl exceeded those at the birth of a boy. While boys were valued, the most crucial community link remained that of a girl through her mother, or alternately, through the siblings of her mother. Boys identified with and inherited through their mothers. Extended families traditionally lived together by matrilineage in "longhouses," structures made of sapling poles shingled over with bark. Women owned the longhouses and their contents, except for any hunting or war implements that might belong to specific men. Each longhouse was managed by its Clan Mother, who rose to the position as the eldest, most self-disciplined, and wisest woman of the house's primary lineage. Clan Mother management of the longhouse was one of the points the Haudenosaunee had in mind in calling themselves the "People of the Longhouse."

At the founding of the League, there were fifteen original, matrilineal clans, whose names were carefully preserved by Seth Newhouse. By the time Lewis Henry Morgan studied the League in 1851, however, clan ranks had been thinned by three centuries of European disease, warfare, and **genocide**. Morgan heard of only eight clans. Although many scholars today depict these "eight clans" as static and inviolable, clans are actually fluid and quite flexible. As Annemarie Shimony showed, there is considerable historical change as new clans such as the Hawk start up, old clans like the Cayuga Eels go into abeyance, and still other clans recombine for ceremonial convenience. Members are frequently adopted or "borrowed" back and forth to preserve certain lineages. Some Western scholars now claim that matrilineage was never complete, and that patrilineage had always been practiced as well. The data they rely upon derive from the contact era, notably *after* foreign agents of cultural change had done everything in their power to disrupt Haudenosaunee culture. In particular, matrilineage, with inheritance through the daughter, was legally replaced by patrilineage, with inheritance through the son. Given missionary and later federal interference, lasting nearly four hundred years, it would be surprising had patrilineal descent not crept in here and there, but to assert that this is evidence of precontact patrilineage is insupportable.

Today, after two centuries of U.S. and Canadian meddling and muddling, many—though not all—have forgotten their lineages and clans. Vestiges of social organization by clan have been preserved through the clan groupings fundamental to Handsome Lake's "Longhouse Religion." In addition, Haudenosaunee descendants outside of the Longhouse are now retracing and reclaiming their matrilineal identities.

Reciprocity and Gendered Roles

The First Family story sets forth the crucial Haudenosaunee principle of reciprocity, as shown in the eternal balance of the Twins. Although missionaries tinkered with the Twins, dichotomizing them into a Manichean opposition of Good (Sapling) versus Evil (Flint), the authentic story presented the Twins as *complementary halves of one constantly self-replicating whole*, with each Twin balancing the other. Theirs is not a divisive duality, but a cooperative mutuality. Accordingly, each clan is "half" of a whole composed of itself and the complementary clan on "the other side." Inside the longhouse, mutuality is pragmatized by household fires running down the center aisle, shared by families who face each other "across the fire," just as collected clan halves face each other during seasonal ceremonies.

Reciprocity went hand in hand with the equitable distribution of goods, the responsibility of Clan Mothers. In 1580, Montaigne recorded that "visiting" Haudenosaunee were appalled to find that "one half" of the French lived in great affluence, content to allow its "other half" to live in profound poverty. Gratified, Montaigne explained, "In their language, they have a way of calling men the half of one another [*ils ont une façon de leur langage telle, qu'ils nomment les hommes moitié les uns des autres*]" ([1580]: 244). European disparities were unknown in Iroquoia where, under the expert administration of the civic-minded Clan Mothers, clan halves shared and shared alike, notably through the custom of "gifting," or ritualized gift giving, regular festivals at which each clan was obliged to give its best goods away to its other half, receiving the other's best in return. In practical terms, gifting ensured that wealth circulated evenly.

Also modeled on the Twins' principle of two-as-one, the sexes observed separation in all activities. Women sought out the company of women, men of men. This held true for political, economic, and social activities, with work strictly segregated by gender: men owned the hunt and women owned the farm; men tended the forest and women tended the fields. Gendered role separation should not be construed as a sign of women's oppression or social inferiority to men. The male-female line does not divide Haudenosaunee culture into competing sexes, nor does the presence of two necessarily mean that one must subjugate the other, as it does for Westerners. Haudenosaunee gendering is reciprocal: the *two halves* are necessary to the *one balanced whole* of community. Gendered role separation is simply another expression of the mutuality principle.

Faith Keeping

Spiritual matters are not separate from civic (including legal) matters in Haudenosaunee culture; indeed, spirituality is seen as the animating principle of the Great Law, or Constitution of the Five (Six) Nations. Nor is there any mind-body split. Spirit and matter interact easily and naturally. Traditionally, women prominently guided spirituality. In addition to selecting every religious leader, or "Keeper of the Faith," they regularly acted as those leaders themselves. At least half of all Keepers of the Faith are female, and before contact, the percentage was probably much higher.

This role reflects the traditions of Sky Woman and the Lynx, who were both skilled medicine women. While still in Sky World, Sky Woman excelled at dream work. In the mornings, she would "comb out the hair" of various relatives. "To comb out the hair" means to straighten out impressions, usually through analogy, and to follow out the associational links among ideas. When applied to dreams, "combing" means to walk through the "Open Doors" of *orenda*, that is, to interact with the spiritual knowledge present in them. For her part, the Lynx was able to commune with Earth Spirits, a shamanic role connected to visions and floral medicine. Dreams were, and remain, major venues of spiritual knowledge. Ever since Jean de Brebeuf wrote his garbled version of dream combing as satanic soul communion in 1669, European observers have been attempting to interpret this practice in Western terms. Three hundred years later, Anthony Wallace erroneously cross-identified Native American dream work with psychoanalysis, but there is no common ground between the two practices beyond the fact that both start—or in the case of psychoanalysis, *may* start—with a remembered dream (59–75).

It is an error to portray dream telling as a child's game of twenty questions, as many scholars do. It is, in fact, an exercise in divination, done by someone other than the dreamer, using what Westerners would probably regard as ESP. In dreams, a nonhuman, self-aware, independent, and, most important, *real* entity is in contact with the dreamer. The dream is wholly true, not imaginary. It may contain instructions, prescriptions, predictions, or sacred sanctions. Even a dream that appears to zero in on the life of one dreamer contains implications for the whole community, and the whole community must be involved in acknowledging, reenacting, or—in some instances—subverting its content. The purpose of dream telling is connected to **consensus**; the perfect community has One Mind, in the recurrent phrase of the traditional Thanksgiving Address.

Because dream combing was frowned upon by missionaries as intercourse with the devil, and because it showcased the abilities of women, the Longhouse Religion downplayed it. Although the Longhouse Religion did continue the practice of selecting Faith Keepers, it rearranged the meaning of the post to that of "deaconship," while allowing men as well as women to appoint "deacons." Dream combers were split from "deacons" and rather slightingly dubbed "fortune tellers," while the practice of dream combing was relegated to a minor function during the Midwinter Ceremony. In Ohio and Pennsylvania, non-Longhouse traditionals continued the earlier, more frequent, and respected dream work.

Medicine women dealt, and still deal, in the powerful properties of plants, the traditional purview of women. Floral remedies dip straight into *orenda*, for, like the Lynx before them, medicine women commune with the Spirit of the plant. Their "old Indian medicine" has some claim to being considered medicine in the modern sense. For instance, it cured Cartier's crew of "*la grande vérole*" (literally, "the big pox," probably scurvy) in 1535 (Cartier xxxvi, 79–80). Montaigne, quoting his Haudenosaunee "houseguest," spoke of women preparing a root drink for regularity, a laxative to strangers, but comfortable for those accustomed to it. In addition to curing, medicine power could be turned against enemies physically. Although bodily damage might be done, the individual's spirit was never in jeopardy.

Before contact, medicine women were taken for granted. Some might be feared and/or depicted figuratively as cannibals in certain traditions, but socially, medicine women were accepted and, depending on their use of power, honored. After contact, given the primitive condition of European medicine, all plant work was dubbed "witchcraft" by superstitious colonists. Medicine women were liable to be denounced as "witches," especially if they were extending a strong challenge to the missionaries. Over time, the European concept of "witchcraft" crept into Haudenosaunee consciousness. As part of his collaboration with the Europeans, Handsome Lake would accuse dissenting women of "witchcraft," although he would later rebuke his followers for taking it upon themselves to whip "witches." It was not only assimilationists who borrowed the notion of "witchcraft," however; non-Longhouse traditionalists also used it. The "Shawnee Prophet" Tenskwatawa, a contemporary of Handsome Lake, also held "witch hunts"—only in this instance, a traditionalist was rooting out assimilationists.

Sexual Relations

Like Sky Woman and the Lynx, Haudenosaunee mothers and daughters remained together for life. Matrilineage meant that marriage was a minor event in a woman's life. She neither left home nor lost identity. Instead, the husband was taken into the longhouse of his mother-in-law. Nevertheless, he too retained his identity through his own mother. Neither mother of the bride nor mother of the groom lost "dibs" on her child because neither child was "given in marriage." Marie Laure Pilette was quite right to reject the Levi-Straussian marriage formula as a process of male giving and taking, for, as she so aptly put it, in Haudenosaunee marriage "there was neither male giver nor male taker" of women; "there were only female lenders [*il n'y a ni preneur, ni donneur, mais des prêteuses*]" of offspring (Pilette 52).

There was also a caution in the Lynx's marital story: it ended in the tragedy of her premature death, not because she engaged in premarital sex, but because she failed to receive her mother's subsequent permission to marry the earthling. Premarital sex was accepted. Sometimes, girls did not marry until they were pregnant. Once a marriageable girl had let her preference be known, her Mothers (her biological mother, maternal aunts, and grandmother and/or Clan Mothers) approached the Clan Mothers of the boy in question, bearing gifts. If the boy's Mothers, or the boy himself, objected, his Mothers rejected the suit, releasing the girl's Mothers to seek out a new match.

Before European interference in such "filthy Indian practices," it was common for a new young couple to undertake a trial marriage, living together experimentally to see whether they suited one another. If not, they split. On the other hand, if the arrangement proved agreeable to all parties, the youngsters were formally viewed as married. They lived with the maternal family of the girl. Children of the marriage belonged to the wife's lineage through her mother and matrilineal grandmothers. While fathers were not personally slighted, the most important adult male role model in the lives of children was their maternal uncle. A biological father fulfilled the role of social father for his own sisters' children.

Divorce, remarriage, extramarital sex, and polyandry were also traditional. Before a couple had children, divorce was a simple matter of one partner rejecting the other, a not-infrequent event, with the wife (or her mother) usually the instigating party. After children were born, however, both clans would try to maintain the relationship if it looked at all salvageable, although no partner was ever forced to remain in an untenable marriage, no matter how much the other partner might wish to continue the relationship. The former husband returned to his matrilineage, while children of the relationship stayed with their mother's family. Rejected men displaying jealousy were deeply scorned and prevented from acting possessively. John Heckewelder recorded this custom with bewilderment, and Mary Jemison (c. 1742–1833), a Scots-Irish Seneca adoptee, with approval. She related that her second husband, Hiokatoo, was so outraged by a jealous (European) neighbor beating his "unfaithful" wife that he took it upon himself—and his tomahawk—to restrain the man (Seaver 65).

Extramarital or, more accurately, serial-and multimarital sex was practiced both by men and women. Men away on long hunts might take a hunting bride, a relationship often arranged by his wife's Clan Mothers. Hunting marriages ended with the hunt. Especially among the Seneca, women might have more than one husband, for any duration of time at their pleasure, to the scandal of the missionaries. Haudenosaunee men never engaged in rape.

Childrearing

Children abound in First Cycle stories: the Lynx is a child until she becomes a child-bride; her twin sons are infants who grow into curious, quarrelsome boys. These children were allowed to explore at will, make mistakes, and take the consequences, under the unobtrusive eye of an undemonstrative Grandmother. At puberty, the boys went off on their own, with one going to his father for advice.

As modeled in this portion of tradition, women kept and raised the children, both male and female, until puberty. At that point, the girls stayed with their mothers learning women's roles, just as the Lynx had stayed with Sky Woman. Boys, on the other hand, left the custody of women, reverting to all-male company and learning men's roles, as did the Twins. Like Grandmother, Haudenosaunee parents were tender and "permissive" with children, seeking to instill values of self-control, foresight, and independent judgment through unimpeded exploration, rather than blind, fearful obedience enforced through corporal punishment. Hence adults supervised children constantly, but from a discreet distance, never intervening in their activities unless a child was about to injure herself or himself or others—including animals and plants. Desirable (communally beneficial) behaviors were verbally encouraged through public praise; conversely, undesirable behaviors were discouraged through verbal shaming.

Physical punishment was rare, consisting of cold water tossed on a child, or perhaps feet dipped in water. A child might be threatened with a complete dunking in the local stream, but this threat was seldom realized, and never in cold weather. Early Europeans, whose methods of childrearing were exceptionally brutal, controlling, and punitive, were disgusted by Haudenosaunee "leniency." Missionary and later federal "Indian schools" set out to "correct" this "deficiency" by beating children cruelly for the slightest infraction. By the nineteenth century, European abusiveness had worked its way into some Haudenosaunee families, and new stories were invented to justify mild beatings; however, the old ways were and still are preferred. Bearing twins—two children at once—had killed the Lynx. The lesson was that having too many children, especially too close together, was bad for a woman. Traditionally, Haudenosaunee women spaced their children out at intervals of three to five years, with some women choosing to stop at one child, after the example of Sky Woman. Women's control of their own bodies is, therefore, an ancient Haudenosaunee principle, and numerous traditional medicines were (and are) available as contraceptives and abortifacients. Handsome Lake, exhibiting Christian influence, inveighed against "cutting the child off in the womb," but women largely ignored his injunctions. A favorite method of birth control was late weaning. Women would keep a child at the breast as long as five years, a practice that continued into the first half of the twentieth century, until bottle feeding was promoted by health officials. Many women are now returning to breast feeding.

Ownership of Agriculture

Earth animals created Turtle Island specifically for Sky Woman. The Three Sisters—corn, beans, and squash—were the sacred sustenance of the fields that, along with tobacco, were brought by Sky Woman from Sky World. Farming was, therefore, always in the purview of women. So fundamental was this rule that it was firmly reiterated in the provisions of the Great Law that recognize women's ownership of the land and agriculture. Women's mound farming was not "horticulture" or "gardening," as many scholars insist on calling it, but agriculture on a massive scale. Yield rates were extraordinary, far in excess of contemporary European yield rates. Denys Delage cited the average good yield rate in Europe as 6:1, with the best yield on record (Holland's) as 15:1. "In America, the average yield rate of corn easily reached, at least on the best lands, 200:1, that is, twenty-seven bushels to the acre [*En Amé-*

rique, le taux de rendement du blé d'Inde atteint facilement, en moy-enne, sur les meilleures terres 200 pour 1, soit 27 boisseaux à l'acre]" (Jensen 53). Joan Jensen documented the high levels of food reserves that women warehoused. On the orders of General George Washington in 1779, the Revolutionary Army destroyed some Seneca granaries. By the army's own count, they contained 60,000 bushels of corn, 2,000–3,000 bushels of beans, uncounted melons, and 1,500 orchard trees. This was the surplus of one part of one nation; there were five other nations in the League at this time. At contact, two-thirds of the Haudenosaunee food supply came from farming. Based on such statistics as these, there can be no further argument: Haudenosaunee women were engaged in *agriculture.*

Women performed all farm labor from planting, hoeing, and weeding to harvesting and storing. (Men originally cleared trees from the land, as the forest was their purview.) In addition to the Three Sisters and tobacco, women cultivated melons and sunflowers. Female work crews, under the team leadership of an elected manager, worked communal fields, although, in what was probably a postcontact behavior, families might work individual plots and keep the produce for themselves. Surplus harvest was carefully stored in underground pits, lined with bark, the dried crops layered inside and then covered over with earth to prevent detection by animal or human foragers.

Mary Jemison is often quoted to show that farm work performed by women was actually light. This is in reply to the commonplace charge that Haudenosaunee men were lazy brutes who treated their wives like "beasts of burden," an allegation still recklessly repeated today as proof that women were inferior to men in Haudenosaunee culture. This is a complete error, based on an ethnocentric misperception. In Europe, farming was dirty work done only by men at the bottom of the social ladder, while hunting was an entertainment reserved to the leisure classes. Hence, when Europeans saw women farming and men hunting, they leapt to the invidious conclusion that leisured Haudenosaunee men lived off the hard labor of "their degraded wives." Not so: Farming was a privileged relationship among Mother Earth, the Three Sisters, and Haudenosaunee women.

Women managed the harvests and surpluses and oversaw the distribution of all food supplies, including game garnered in the hunt. (Upon returning from a hunt, the men would turn over their game to the Clan Mothers.) Because it dealt with food, Clan Mothers were in charge of the famous Haudenosaunee "hospitality" that freely fed and accommodated visitors. By logical extension of food-distribution rights, passing war parties depended upon resident Clan Mothers to feed them. Reciprocally, the warriors could not harm the village of a Clan Mother who fed them, even if the village belonged to the enemy. Control of the

food supply also gave women a tacit veto over warfare: Should the
women refuse warriors food, after the example of the Second Epoch
Jigonsaseh, the war could not continue.

Handsome Lake, at the instigation of Quaker missionaries, attempted
to make men, not women, the farmers. The Clan Mothers strenuously
resisted. His vision of the Corn Maiden, Spirit of the Elder Sister Corn,
must be understood in this light. The Corn Spirit lingered about the
planting mounds, cementing the spiritual relationship among women,
Mother Earth, and the crops. On summer nights, female Keepers of the
Faith would walk among the budding mounds, dragging their cloaks
and sprinkling tobacco to complement and compliment the spirits of
the Sisters. Not even Handsome Lake dared to accost Sister Corn at
night, but he did walk boldly into women's fields in the daytime, where,
he said, he was encouraged by the whispering spirit of Sister Corn and
caressed by her leaves. By claiming the approval of Sister Corn, he was
claiming the highest possible sanction for abrogating women's ownership of agriculture. The Clan Mothers did not accept his story.

Annual Ceremonies

Because of their ownership of agriculture, any ceremony including
food preparation and distribution was under the regulation of Clan
Mothers, whose responsibility it was to set the time and place of the
event and to arrange for runners to "go around" announcing it. Predom-
inantly male rituals, such as False Face and Thunderer ceremonies,
were under male control, except for food distribution.

The traditional round of the agricultural season was Maple Gathering
(March–April); Strawberry Festival (June); Raspberries Are Ripe (July);
Green Bean Ceremony (August); and the Green Corn Ceremony, the
most important agricultural festival of the year, which happened in two
stages, first the Little Green Corn, or Green Corn Testing, followed
quickly by the main Green Corn Ceremony (all falling late August
through early September). Ceremonial observances also existed for various growing stages: Planting, Sprouting, First and Second Hoeings, and
so on. The food of a plant is served at its ritual feast, with the Spirit of
that food thanked and encouraged. For instance, Green Beans are
served, and the Spirit of Sister Bean acknowledged, at the Green Bean
Ceremony. The Harvest Ceremony (October/November) is not technically an agricultural ceremony, but a general Thanksgiving that marks
the end of the agricultural year. The Midwinter Ceremony, the most
important festival of the year, was once aimed at quickening agricultural
spirits, but is now tipped toward concepts of the Longhouse Religion.
For a good rundown of annual ceremonials as preserved by the Longhouse Religion, see Annemarie Shimony's *Conservatism among the Iroquois at the Six Nations Reserve.*

Political Powers

The Great Law confers an extensive array of governmental powers upon women. The familiar precept of halved-whole reciprocity extends into politics, particularly in gendering. The women's right of naming is also fundamental. Sky Woman and the Lynx originally named the creatures of the earth. Their female descendants continued the practice, most famously in adoption, but also in naming: children born into lineages, Clan Mothers, sachems (male civil councilmen), councilwomen, speakers, and advisors. Moreover, based on the tradition of Jigonsaseh as a peace mediator, women also named, and were named, Keepers of the Peace, or judges.

Name Keepers

Names and titles of office (ceremonial names) are on loan to an individual only during his or her lifetime. All names are "owned" by female Name Keepers, who bestow them according to the matrilineage of the recipient. At death, the personal name and any titles of the deceased recycle back into the Name Keepers' pool of family names and/or national titles for redistribution. The fifty titular sachemships are well recalled and still used. A similar, but today largely lost, set of matrons' titles also existed. One of the few women's titles still recalled is "the Jigonsaseh," or Head Clan Mother of the League. Open titles of office are conferred on new sachems in the Requickening Address, which completes the funeral rite for a deceased male official. The women's parallel retitling ritual has apparently been lost. Family names are reconferred on infants or children during either the Green Corn or the Midwinter festivals.

Theoretically, only one person at a time may use a name, and this rule was observed in traditional times. However, in the modern era, federally imposed amnesia has wiped out the memory of family names and women's titles, with the result that remembered names are overused. In addition, the confusion caused by the presence of the Haudenosaunee in both Canada and the United States has allowed two traditional six-nation councils to exist, the "fifty" hereditary sachemships being replicated on both sides of the border.

Adoption

As a family "naming" function, adoption belonged exclusively to women. The original purpose of adoption was to enhance the ranks of a clan or village by replacing lost members with newly life-quickened recruits. Contrary to vulgar stereotype, this was not necessarily accomplished through captives obtained in war. Adoptions have always been performed in times of peace, and "borrowing" individuals back and forth from one clan to shore up another is a traditional practice, still continued today. In colonial times, non-Haudenosaunees—Native American, African, or European—were freely adopted during times of peace.

The "captivity" mystique arose in response to "mourning wars." Just as women could veto war, they could also call for a "mourning war"—a misleading term. These were not "wars" in the European sense of large, standing armies visiting mass destruction to grab territory and loot. Clan Mothers wishing to increase the community's census "mourned" for the dead and called for replacements. A raiding party formed in response to collect a pool of eligible adoptees. The objective of mourning wars was to procure *live* prospective adoptees, not to "massacre" settlers. Once a good supply was gathered, the "war party" went home. The incidence of mourning wars surged after European disease and invasion ravaged the Haudenosaunee population.

Captives were presented to the Clan Mothers, who decided which ones were to be adopted into the Clan and whom they were to replace. Rejects were put to ritual death. Children and female captives were simply and gently inducted by the women. Adult male captives, on the other hand, had first to display their courage and stamina by running a gauntlet. Men could and sometimes did die from wounds sustained in the gauntlet, but most lived. Adoptees were taken into specific clans, not nations—that is, they became Turtles or Wolves, not Senecas or Mohawks—and literally took the place of some recently deceased kin.

Youthful captives were favored, as they were quickly and easily acculturated. Adult adoptees especially were placed on temporary probation before being fully trusted; however, upon adoption, every person was immediately accorded the utmost kindness and consideration. The European concept of "race" did not exist among the traditional Haudenosaunee. All adoptees, regardless of "race," were regarded as full members of the clan and expected to act as reciprocal kinsfolk. Nor was favoritism shown to born over adopted members. To the chagrin of Christian colonials, most adoptees, if given the choice, preferred to remain with the Haudenosaunee. Arthur C. Parker recorded a conversation Chateaubriand had in the 1790s with a French captive who assured him that he had been "happy only since I became a savage" (Parker [1926]: 150). Mary Jemison, adopted in at twelve, went into desperate hiding rather than be taken back to "civilization" (Seaver 26–27, 43–46).

In the mid-nineteenth century, federal intervention in clanship began to alter adoption. The Western concept of infant adoption into nuclear, patrilineal families was legally imposed, relegating traditional adoption to the sidelines. Under this pressure, adoption split into two basic modes: true, traditional adoption, which continued to carry the full, reciprocal expectations of yore; and goodwill adoptions, typically of Euro-American officials, anthropologists, and the like, which did not entail kinship reciprocity, but were merely for show. Today, traditional adoptions are on the upswing.

Funerals

Funerals are often erroneously grouped with "ceremonies," but they are actually extensions of naming. Women therefore traditionally managed (and still manage) funeral and mourning rites. Heckewelder devoted a chapter to the 1762 funerary rites for a Clan Mother (whose status he obdurately attributed to her husband, even as he noted that she held a "high" position). Interestingly, *female* runners announced her death. Clan Mothers, women, sachems, and warriors all joined in the funeral, conducted exclusively by the women. The burial occurred after 12:00 noon, with women forcibly interposing themselves between male undertakers and the corpse, imploring her spirit not to leave the people. Women then allowed men to place the body in the earth, but only women filled in her grave with their farming hoes. A large group of female mourners, of all ages, lamented her loss at the gravesite. After the funeral, a major wake feast and a gifting ritual were held. Women continued to hold formal mourning sessions for three weeks. Intriguingly, during this particular funeral, a tornado came up just as the grave cover had been secured with bark and leaves. Traditionally, tornados are powerful statements by the Thunderers, commonly of displeasure—in this instance, incurred perhaps by the presence of unadopted Europeans at the funeral. Heckewelder did not record the requickening ceremony, rebestowing her title, which probably occurred several months to one year later.

Nomination to Office

Clan Mothers alone nominated individuals to office by conferring matrilineal names-as-titles, on females at the local level and on males at the federal level. However, it is wrong to conclude from this, as some writers do, that the Haudenosaunee government was an "oligarchy." Titular positions may have been hereditary, but the pool of matrilineal candidates for these titles was very large, including every kinsperson from among the five (later six) nations, not to mention individuals from all of the affiliated nations—Lenne Lenape, Tutelo, Wyandot, and others. Furthermore, titles did not descend directly to a preordained heir. Indeed, it was (and is) *illegal* for a Clan Mother to nominate her own son or matrilineal nephew to office. She had to select a candidate from outside her own personal family. While the rules for nomination to Women's Councils have yet to be unearthed, it is likely that they followed the same regulations, with the nomination ban being on daughters and nieces. Hence clan nominations were comparable to modern party-endorsed candidates running for political office. Today, men can veto candidates and return the matter to the women for further deliberation, but in traditional times, women alone held the final say on nominations.

There were numerous Councils, which interfaced in stipulated ways. Because the Peacemaker first consulted Jigonsaseh, Women's Councils were the first to consider public matters on the local level of government, pulling grass-roots issues into public discourse. Once consensus was forged at the local level, women forwarded issues to their counterparts, the Council of Sachems at the federal level. Sachems could only consider matters put forward by Clan Mothers. Thus popular sovereignty was a guiding principle of the Six Nations. It is not entirely known how the Clan Mothers' Council functioned, but the Sachems' Council operated according to complex rules. Halved brotherhoods, working in subcommittees, forged compromises first among themselves, then "across the fire." The Brotherhoods' compromise decisions were submitted to the executive branch (Fire Keepers) for approval, veto, or tabling. It is likely that the Clan Mothers' Council was set up in a parallel fashion.

There were also feeder Councils of Warriors (men) and Farmers (women) who brought matters to the attention of their respective male or female halves. Some older sources record independent Councils of Elders, male and female, but it is likely that they meant the Sachems' and Clan Mothers' Councils. Generally, Councilwomen spoke the concerns of women, children, and plants, while Councilmen spoke the concerns of the men, including pubescent boys, the forest, and the animals.

Advisors and Speakers

Both Clan Mothers' and Sachems' Councils were attended by advisors, tapped to voice popular concerns, normally to specific Councilpersons. These advisors, male and female, were chosen on merit by the Clan Mothers. In addition to advisors, there were specially chosen Speakers who communicated with other Councils, non-Haudenosaunee nations, and, after contact, European powers. Europeans often mistook Speakers for "chiefs," not understanding that they were actually messengers whose task it was to repeat, perfectly, positions decided upon earlier in the appropriate male or female Council. As a result, Speakers such as Red Jacket are still miscalled "chiefs" by many scholars. Most known Speakers were men, like Red Jacket, who spoke for the Clan Mothers. This gave rise to another mistake in the literature, to wit, that women were "not allowed" to speak in men's Councils. In fact, the Clan Mothers spoke regularly, loudly, and clearly in Men's Councils through their Speakers—just as Men made presentations to Women's Councils through their Speakers (who may well have been female).

To understand the dynamics of Speakerhood, the principle of the One Mind must be grasped. The Thanksgiving Address, typically repeated before major events, is a gathering of spirits, a cosmic consensus intended to inspire cooperation among the beings of creation before any other business is attempted. Each invocation of the Address wraps up with the phrase "Now our minds are one." Speakers operated within this One-Minded space. The connection between Clan Mothers and their Speaker was, therefore, a sacred bond made of *orenda*. The degree to which the Speaker was faithful to the message was a measure of the Clan Mothers' ability to induce One-Mindedness. On the practical level, to have a Speaker was to have, and display, social status. On the spiritual level, to have a Speaker who was so reliable that it was not necessary to dog his steps was to display *orenda*. Thus that Clan Mothers depended entirely upon their Speakers to present their messages is not evidence of a social disability, but rather of their social importance and skill at Faith Keeping.

Impeachment

Clan mothers also could (and still can) dename people, either personally or on the civic level. As provided in the Great Law, Clan Mothers had the power to impeach any male officeholder run amok. Traditionally, offenders were rebuked thrice before impeachment proceeded. Treason, incompetence, or bad faith were grounds for impeachment. After contact, conversion to Christianity was considered treasonable, and Clan Mothers impeached even high officials for it. For instance, in the mid-nineteenth century, the matrilineal Onondaga Sachem Albert Cusick—often misidentified as "Tuscarora" through his patrilineage—was deposed from his hereditary title for converting to Christianity. In a minuscule number of cases, Clan Mothers were also deposed. In 1671, a Mohawk Clan Mother was impeached for converting. On a personal level, the Great Law provided for Clan Mothers to banish from the clans any treasonous adoptees, that is, any who repatriated, or any who showed themselves to be unworthy, that is, unwilling to assimilate.

Keepers of the Peace

Finally, women named, and were, Keepers of the Peace. The principle of female dispute mediation is patterned on the example of the Second Epoch Jigonsaseh, who mediated for the people. Women ran the judiciary based on analogies drawn from hair combing and corn pounding. On the spiritual level, being hair combers made women Keepers of the Faith, but on the civic level, it made them Keepers of the Peace, mediators who could straighten out entanglements. At the same time, women's talking through problems was comparable to "corn pounding," the process by which corn kernels were pounded smooth by macelike drop-pounders. By analogy, disputes were conceived of as rough corn kernels that could be pounded smooth enough to pass through the body of the people without giving them intestinal gripes. Through the naming principle, women held the right to appoint the judges who would pound disputes smooth, that is, intervene in and settle any internal dispute. Because it was Hiawatha ("He Who Combs") who untangled Atotarho's hair/thoughts, judges could be male as well as female.

Their actual sex notwithstanding, all judges were ceremonially referred to as "Women." Upon being named a Woman, the incumbent was handed a skirt and a cornpounder as emblems of office, causing another fractured—and this time hilarious—misinterpretation by Europeans, who typically choked upon seeing men proudly wearing their skirts of office. In 1724, Joseph Lafitau struggled to explain the "Men Dressed as Women" in a section tentatively translated as "Transvestites" by William Fenton two and one-half centuries later. For his part, John Heckewelder always regarded the practice of "making women" (appointing judges) as the final word in "Iroquois treachery." He was deeply disturbed that the whole Lenni Lenape (Delaware) Nation had been adopted into the league as "Women" and spent a great deal of ink denouncing this supposed neutering of Lenni Lenape men. (It apparently never occurred to him that half of the Lenni Lenape were always women.) In the era of forced **assimilation**, the practice of "making women" was suppressed by missionaries and federal agents, but women unobtrusively continued this and many other traditional practices.

Contact and Cultural Loss

From first contact until well into the twentieth century, Christian Europeans were intent upon re-forming the Haudenosaunee in the Western image. High on the cultural hit list was the economic, political, and social power of Haudenosaunee women. Missionaries worked to suppress "demonic" learning stories featuring women as progenitors, while reconfiguring ("Christianizing") others to serve evangelical agendas. At the same time, Europeans reinterpreted wampum as money. Lineage wampum and belts of the Great Law were deliberately scattered, stolen, destroyed, or "collected."

Between missionaries, settlers, traders, and the military, traditional Haudenosaunee culture had already been seriously disrupted by the time of the Revolutionary War. With the founding of the United States, the New York Haudenosaunee were cut off from the Pennsylvania-Ohio

Haudenosaunee, who were then treated as a separate entity by the United States, just as Canada treated the Ontario Haudenosaunee as separate. The federal "Indian" reservation system was born alongside the U.S. government. In 1789, Congress created the New York Haudenosaunee reservations and ceded control of them to Quaker missionaries. In 1797, it created a reservation along the Muskingum River for the Pennsylvania-Ohio Haudenosaunee, controlled by the Moravian missionaries. Bureaucrats lumped the Ohio-Pennsylvania Haudenosaunee together with non-Haudenosaunee peoples, styling them all "Wyandot." They were "removed" during 1843–1845.

Federal policy was to "civilize and Christianize the Indians" by granting sweeping coercive powers to missionaries and bureaucrats. Women were deprived of their young children, who were kidnapped and confined in faraway "boarding schools" until the age of eighteen, where they were beaten and forbidden to speak home tongues or tell old stories. Women were prohibited from Keeping the Faith and forced instead to attend male-run Christian rites. Kinship was federally reorganized along patrilineal lines, with clan longhouses replaced by nuclear-family dwellings. Only Christian marriages were recognized. Missionaries attempted to overturn women's hoe farming and replace it with European male plow farming. Gifting rituals were also outlawed, with the stated end of destroying communalism in favor of "rugged" individualism. For the Haudenosaunee, "civilizing and Christianizing" continued, in various phases and disguises, from 1789 until the 1970s.

It was under this dire threat of cultural annihilation that Handsome Lake stepped forward to promote the *Gaiwiio*. To do so, he bowed to numerous Christianizing pressures concerning women's status. For instance, the first matrilineage—Sky Woman, the Lynx, and her Twins—was stripped down. Sapling, the Elder Twin, alone was kept, then represented in Christianized form as a supreme and lonely God. The Thanksgiving Address was reworked to acclaim this newly solitary "Creator," to the exclusion of other spirits. Creation was presented as a hierarchy, instead of a cooperative whole. Clan Mothers were frequently denounced as "witches." Handsome Lake cooperated with the Quakers to take hoes out of women's hands and place plows in men's. Appointments that had been the territory of Clan Mothers were now made jointly with, or even solely by, men. On the other hand, Handsome Lake must be credited with saving much of the memory of traditional culture, from the annual round of celebrations to a version of clan kinship, the Sachems' Council, older marriage rites, respect for nature, and, most important, the concept of reciprocity. Largely because of Handsome Lake, traditional practices were remembered and passed along in New York and Canada.

In Pennsylvania and Ohio, the parallel "civilizing and Christianizing" effort lacked a Haudenosaunee collaborator. Instead, some very uncooperative prophets, such as Wangomend, Coocooche, and Undekot, resisted federal efforts. Since Christianity was less successfully imposed in Pennsylvania and Ohio, the Longhouse Religion did not take much root there. The older stories were better remembered, and, as much as possible under occupation, Clan Mothers continued to wield their traditional powers. With removal, stories went west to Kansas and Oklahoma or else deep underground with removal resisters who defied the federal order by hiding out in their Ohio-Pennsylvania homeland. Today, the Longhouse Religion is primarily influential on the reservations of New York and Ontario, Canada. It has little influence in Ohio and Pennsylvania.

In his farewell address, the Peacemaker predicted the Third Cycle of Time and its agonies. He foresaw that a "White Panther" would emerge from the eastern sea to fall upon the people. This "Dragon of Discord" would disrupt traditional culture by instigating infighting among leaders. "Then heads will roll," he said, scattering the people west. Yet by remaining true to the precepts of the Great Law, the Haudenosaunee would rise again in the Fourth Cycle of Time. Heckewelder, quoting an unnamed Keeper, recorded the prophecy thus: "The great tortoise which bears this island upon his back, shall dive down into the deep," drowning all the Europeans, and "the Indians shall once more be put in possession of the whole country" (Heckewelder 345). Today, as the Third Cycle of Time draws to a close, the Grandmothers are speaking again in preparation for the resurgence of the people.

FURTHER READING

Anderson, Karen. *Chain Her by One Foot: The Subjugation of Women in Seventeenth-Century New France.* London and New York: Routledge, 1991.

Bonvillain, Nancy. "Iroquoian Women." In *Studies on Iroquoian Culture*, ed. Nancy Bonvillain, 47–58. Occasional Publications in Northeastern Anthropology, no. 6. Rindge, NH: Franklin Pierce College, Department of Anthropology, 1980.

Brown, Judith K. "Economic Organization and the Position of Women among the Iroquois." *Ethnohistory* 17 (1970): 151–167.

Charlevoix, Pierre de. *Journal of a Voyage to North-America.* 1761. Ann Arbor: University Microfilms, 1966.

Delage, Denys. "L'Amérique du Nord avant l'implantation européenne." In *Le pays renversé: Amérindiens et Européens en Amérique du Nord-Est, 1600–1664*, 47–88. Montreal: Boréal Express, 1985.

Foster, Martha Harroun. "Lost Women of the Matriarchy: Iroquois Women in the Historical Literature." *American Indian Culture and Research Journal* 19:3 (1995): 121–140.

The Great Peace Project. Six Nations. Internet, interactive website, http://www.WorkingWorld.ca/greatpeace.

Heckewelder, John. *An Account of the History, Manners, and Customs of the Indian Nations, Who Once Inhabited Pennsylvania and the Neighboring States.* 1819. New York: Arno Press, 1971.

Jensen, Joan M. "Native American Women and Agriculture: A Seneca Case Study." In *Unequal Sisters: A Multicultural Reader in U.S. Women's History*, ed. Ellen Carol DuBois and Vicki L. Ruiz, 51–65. New York and London: Routledge, 1990.

Lafitau, Joseph François. *Customs of the American Indians Compared with the Customs of Primitive Times.* 1724. Ed. and Trans. William N. Fenton and Elizabeth L. Moore. 2 vols. Toronto: Champlain Society, 1974.

Mann, Barbara A. "The Lynx in Time: Haudenosaunee Women's Traditions and History." *American Indian Quarterly*, in press.

"The Mohawk Creation Story." *Akwesasne Notes* 21:5 (Spring 1989): 32–39.

Montaigne, Michel Eyquem de. "Des cannibales." *Essais*. 1580. Vol. 1, 230–245. Paris: Éditions Garnier Frères, 1962.

Morgan, Lewis Henry. *League of the Iroquois.* 1851. Secaucus, NJ: Citadel Press, 1962.

Parker, Arthur C. *The Constitution of the Five Nations, or, The Iroquois Book of the Great Law.* New York State Museum Bulletin no. 184. Albany: University of the State of New York, 1916.

———. *The History of the Seneca Indians.* 1926. Port Washington, Long Island, NY: Ira J. Friedman, 1967.

Pilette, Marie Laure. "Oeuvre de chair: La petite histoire du pic mangeur d'hommes." *Anthropologica* 35:1 (1993): 39–57.

Seaver, James. *A Narrative of the Life of Mrs. Mary Jemison* [1823]. Syracuse, NY: Syracuse University Press, 1990.

Shimony, Annemarie. *Conservatism among the Iroquois at the Six Nations Reserve.* 2nd ed. Syracuse, NY: Syracuse University Press, 1994.

Wallace, Anthony F. C. *The Death and Rebirth of the Seneca.* New York: Knopf, 1970.

BARBARA A. MANN

HAWAII, LEGAL STATUS OF NATIVE CLAIMS

The 1893 overthrow of the Hawaiian monarchy by the United States was invalid under international law. Native Hawaiians have secured an apology from the U.S. House of Representatives for the overthrow and are pressing a land claim that would return 1.8 million acres (of Hawaii's 4.2-million-acre land area) to the jurisdiction of a government to be elected at a Native Hawaiian constitutional convention. During the late summer of 1996, about 30,000 Native Hawaiians voted by a margin of three to one to establish such a government. Roughly 40 percent of Native Hawaiians who were eligible to vote took part.

The land claim includes all state and federal lands on the islands, but leaves private owners untouched. The 200,000 acres presently occupied by U.S. military bases would be leased to the Department of Defense at market value for a fixed period of time.

This **sovereignty** movement had permeated the 200,000 members of Native Hawaiian society to a surprising extent by the 1990s, a hundred years after the United States colonized the islands. During 1995 and 1996, Native Hawaiians registered to vote in a referendum that will decide whether to initiate a native legislature to press the land claim and other issues. On September 9, 1996, an overwhelming majority of Native Hawaiians voted to elect delegates to a constitutional convention. This effort was being headed by the state government's Office of Hawaiian Affairs. In the 1990s, for the first time since 1893, the chief executive of Hawaii was an ethnic Hawaiian.

A modern "Hawaiian renaissance" began in the 1970s. The native language, which had nearly died, began to flourish again; Hawaiians, who had once thought themselves homeless in their own land, began to recapture their heritage. Teams of seafarers built canoes capable of traveling to Tahiti to renew ties with indigenous people there. They sailed practicing ancient navigational skills that tied together the people of widely dispersed islands centuries ago.

FURTHER READING

Weinberg, Bill. "Land and Sovereignty in Hawai'i: A Native Nation Re-emerges." *Native Americas* 13:2 (Summer 1996): 30–41.

HENDRICK (TIYANOGA) (Mohawk) (c. 1680–1755)

Tiyanoga, called Hendrick by the English, was a major figure in colonial affairs between 1710, when he was one of four Mohawks invited to England by Queen Anne, and 1755, when he died in battle with the French as an ally of the British. In 1754, Hendrick advised **Benjamin Franklin** and other colonial representatives on the principles of **Iroquois** government at the Albany Congress. Hendrick was a member of the Wolf Clan.

Hendrick knew both Iroquois and English cultures well. He converted to Christianity and became a Mohawk preacher sometime after 1700. In England, he was painted by John Verelst and called the "Emperor of the Five Nations." Hendrick was perhaps the most important individual link in a chain of alliance that saved the New York frontier and probably New England from the French in the initial stages of the Seven Years' War, which was called the French and Indian War (1754–63) in North America.

Well known as a man of distinction in his manners and dress, Hendrick visited England again in 1740. At that time, King George II presented him with an ornate green coat of satin, fringed in gold, which Hendrick was fond of wearing in combination with his traditional Mohawk ceremonial clothing.

A lifelong friend of Sir William Johnson, Hendrick appeared often at

Johnson Hall, near Albany, and had copious opportunities to rub elbows with visiting English nobles, sometimes as he arrived in war paint, fresh from battle. Thomas Pownall, a shrewd observer of colonial Indian affairs, described Hendrick as "a bold artful, intriguing Fellow" who "has learnt no small share of European Politics, [who] obstructs and opposes all [business] where he has not been talked to first" (Johansen and Grinde 1997: 165). Hector Saint Jean de Crèvecoeur, himself an adopted Iroquois who had sat in on sessions of the Grand Council at Onondaga, described Hendrick in late middle age, preparing for dinner at the Johnson estate, within a few years of the Albany Congress:

[He] wished to appear at his very best. . . . His head was shaved, with the exception of a little tuft of hair in the back, to which he attached a piece of silver. To the cartilage of his ears . . . he attached a little brass wire twisted into very tight spirals.

A girondole was hung from his nose. Wearing a wide silver neckpiece, a crimson vest and a blue cloak adorned with sparkling gold, Hendrick, as was his custom, shunned European breeches for a loincloth fringed with glass beads. On his feet, Hendrick wore moccasins of tanned elk, embroidered with porcupine quills, fringed with tiny silver bells. (Crèvecoeur 1926: 170)

In 1754, Hendrick attended the conference at Albany that framed a colonial plan of union (*See* **Albany Plan of Union**). By the time Hendrick was invited to address colonial delegates at the Albany Congress, he was well known on both sides of the Atlantic, among Iroquois and Europeans alike. Hendrick played a major role in convening the Albany Congress in large part because he wished to see his friend Johnson reinstated as the English superintendent of affairs with the Six Nations. Without him, Hendrick maintained that the **covenant chain** would rust. It was Johnson himself who conducted most of the day-to-day business with the Indians at Albany.

At the Albany Congress, Hendrick repeated the advice that **Canassatego** had given colonial delegates at Lancaster a decade earlier, this time at a conference devoted not only to diplomacy, but also to drawing up a plan for the type of colonial union the Iroquois had been requesting. The same day, at the courthouse, the colonial delegates were in the early stages of debate over the plan of union.

Hendrick was openly critical of the British at the Albany Congress and hinted that the Iroquois would not ally with the English colonies unless a suitable form of unity was established among them. Describing the proposed union of the colonies and the Six Nations on July 9, 1754, Hendrick stated, "We wish this Tree of Friendship may grow up to a great height and then we shall be a powerful people." Hendrick followed that admonition with an analysis of Iroquois and colonial unity and said, "We the United Nations shall rejoice of our strength . . . and

. . . we have now made so strong a Confederacy" (*Colonial Records of Pennsylvania* 98). In reply to Hendrick's speech on Native American and colonial unity, James DeLancey, acting governor of New York, said, "I hope that by this present Union, we shall grow up to a great height and be as powerful and famous as you were of old" (*Colonial Records* 98). Benjamin Franklin was commissioned to compose the final draft of the Albany Plan of Union the same day.

Hendrick died at the Battle of Lake George in the late summer of 1755, when Sir William Johnson defeated Baron Dieskau. The elderly Mohawk was shot from his horse and bayoneted to death while on a scouting party September 8.

FURTHER READING

Colonial Records of Pennsylvania. Vol. 6. Harrisburg, PA: Theo. Fenn & Co., 1851.
Crèvecoeur, St. Jean de. *Letters from an American Farmer.* New York: E. P. Dutton, 1926.
Jacobs, Wilbur R. *Wilderness Politics and Indian Gifts.* Lincoln: University of Nebraska Press, 1966.
Johansen, Bruce E., and Donald A. Grinde, Jr. *The Encyclopedia of Native American Biography.* New York: Henry Holt, 1997.
Wallace, Paul A. W. *The White Roots of Peace.* Philadelphia: University of Pennsylvania Press, 1946.

HENRY, PATRICK (1736–1799)

Patrick Henry advocated state subsidies for Indian-white marriages. In the fall of 1784, he introduced such a measure into the Virginia House of Delegates. The bill directed the state to pay an unspecified sum for the marriage and an additional sum on the birth of each child. In addition, Henry proposed that Indian-white couples live tax-free. Henry pushed the bill with his usual enthusiasm and oratorical flourish as it survived two readings. By the time it reached the third reading, Henry had been elected governor of Virginia. Without his support in the House of Delegates, the intermarriage bill died.

HOOVER COMMISSION (1949)

Presaging **termination** efforts of the 1950s, the Hoover Commission in 1949 issued a report calling for the full **assimilation** of Indians into the general population "as full, tax-paying citizens." As part of the commission's general effort to recommend reductions in the federal budget, its final report suggested that some Indian programs be transferred to state governments. The recommendations were not implemented, but with Republicans controlling Congress for the first time since the 1920s, the Hoover Commission's recommendations related to American Indians were made largely superfluous by passage of House Concurrent Resolution 83-108, the Termination Act.

HOPI POLITICAL AND LEGAL TRADITIONS

While some anthropologists have described Hopi society as apolitical, with social cohesion supplied by ties of its social structure at the village level, Peter M. Whiteley finds evidence of class division and administrative structures in Hopi villages. He argues that a class of "ruling people" made up of members of secret societies held title to ceremonies and clan secrets which "ordinary people" did not possess. "People with the authority of chiefs" often held titles related to the ceremonial system, including the power to determine when certain ceremonies would be performed.

Hopi villages recognized chiefs, but did not invest them with coercive power. The village chief was looked upon as more of a guide and advisor than an executive—and as an interpreter of tradition rather than as a maker of law. The chief employed administrative assistants, including a crier, who formally announced ceremonial occasions. A war chief also acted as village police captain when a need arose. Many Hopis are said to have avoided holding political office because the commitment was believed to be too great. Such office carried no special privileges, only added responsibilities. Otherwise, a leader was expected to cope with the demands of everyday life like ordinary Hopis.

Early Spanish observers remarked on the lack of political coordination between Hopi (sometimes called "Western Pueblo") villages. Councils of elders whose authority was generally rooted in religion led the individual villages. Even these early reports indicated that Hopi political life was based in spirituality, and that the underground kivas (which the Spanish called *estufas*) were centers of social and political, as well as religious, life. Spanish descriptions tend to ignore what observers could not easily see, such as diplomatic contacts between villages that paralleled extensive trade routes.

FURTHER READING

Rushforth, Scott, and Steadman Upham. *A Hopi Social History*. Austin: University of Texas Press, 1992.

Titiev, Mischa. *The Hopi: Indians of Old Oraibi: Change and Continuity*. Ann Arbor: University of Michigan Press, 1972.

Whiteley, Peter M. *Deliberate Acts: Changing Hopi Culture through the Oraibi Split*. Tucson: University of Arizona Press, 1988.

HURON CONFEDERACY, POLITICAL AND LEGAL TRADITIONS.
See **Wyandot Confederacy**.

I

IMPLIED CONSENT

In an attempt to address congressional acts and court decisions that limit Indian courts' jurisdiction over crimes committed by non-Indians in **Indian Country**, some tribes have enacted "implied consent" ordinances stating that any person who enters a reservation consents implicitly to the authority of Native American police and judicial institutions. The passage of such laws is related to the denial of Suquamish jurisdiction in *Oliphant v. Suquamish* (1978). A majority of states have passed similar laws related to the use of motor vehicles, but the Interior Department has stated that the Indian attempts to impose implied consent are legally invalid. The Suquamish reservation had such a law when Oliphant was charged, but the Supreme Court refused to uphold it.

INDIAN CHILD WELFARE ACT (1978) P.L. 95-608; 92 Stat. 3069; 25 U.S.C.A. §§ 1901–1963

The Indian Child Welfare Act restricted non-Indian social-service agencies' ability to place Indian children in non-Indian homes without the consent of their parents and their nations. The act also established jurisdiction with Native American courts for child custody. Under this act, state courts have no jurisdiction over adoption or custody of Indian children living on the reservation of their tribe unless a federal law (such as **Public Law 280**) states otherwise. The states also have no jurisdiction over children who are wards of tribal courts.

The Indian Child Welfare Act was enacted after many years of appeals to Congress from Indian parents and their tribes. By the late 1970s, 25 to 35 percent of Indian children were being removed from their homes, according to a report by the Association of Indian Affairs. In South Dakota, Indian children were placed in foster homes at a per capita rate twenty-two times that of other state residents. In California, Indian children were being placed in non-Indian homes 93 percent of the time.

The act implemented a policy earlier established judicially in *Fisher v. District Court*, 424 U.S. 381 (1976). The court stated: "The exclusive jurisdiction of the Tribal Court does not derive from the race of the plaintiff but rather from the quasi-sovereign status of the Northern Cheyenne Tribe under federal law."

The Indian Child Welfare Act gives tribes authority over all child-custody proceedings unless parents request state jurisdiction. The act includes foster-care placement, termination of parental rights, and adoptive placement. The act does not cover child-custody procedures attendant to divorce. It also allocated money for tribal family-service programs. In the 1980s and 1990s, several tribes established juvenile courts, group homes, foster homes, and adoption mechanisms.

FURTHER READING

O'Brien, Sharon. "Federal Indian Policy and Human Rights." In *American Indian Policy in the Twentieth Century*, ed. Vine Deloria, Jr. Norman: University of Oklahoma Press, 1985.

INDIAN CITIZENSHIP ACT (1924) 43 Stat. 253; 8 U.S.C. § 14d; 8 U.S.C.A. § 1401(a)(2)

Citizenship in the United States was extended to all Native Americans in the Citizenship Act of 1924, only four decades after the Supreme Court, in **Elk v. Wilkins** (1884), denied the petition of an individual Indian for the same rights. Ironically, citizenship had been offered to some tribes as early as 1850, sometimes on condition that their lands be allotted to private ownership. Three years after *Elk v. Wilkins*, in 1887, the General **Allotment Act** extended citizenship to Indians whose land would be divided and privatized. Many Native American people refused citizenship (or did their best to avoid it), especially after it was tied to the loss of communal land through allotment. Citizenship was to begin after the allotted land had been held in trust for twenty-five years. In 1890, as Oklahoma moved toward statehood, reservation residents in **Indian Territory** were offered citizenship if they applied to federal courts. In 1919, an act of Congress extended citizenship to Native American veterans of World War I.

The granting of U.S. citizenship dovetailed with the abolition of Native American national autonomy. Although citizenship for all Native Americans was not legislated until 1924, many native people had been made citizens (often without their consent) decades earlier. By 1924, two-thirds of American Indians had been extended citizenship piecemeal. Citizenship was extended to individual native people at the time that their land was allotted. In 1888, a year after passing the Allotment Act, Congress made native people who married U.S. citizens eligible for citizenship.

In 1901, Congress "awarded" citizenship to all native people living in what was then called Indian Territory, now Oklahoma. By 1907, when Oklahoma became a state, 1.3 million non-Indians lived there, many of whom had been drawn by the discovery of oil. Of at least 19.5 million acres of "Indian Territory" land under tribal title in 1898, almost 16 million acres had been allotted to individuals by 1907. After that, much of the newly allotted land inevitably made its way into non-Indian hands as oil-exploration leases, railroad rights of way, and cattlemen's pastures.

Some native peoples have rejected citizenship, notably members of the **Iroquois Confederacy** and other native people in New York State. During World War II, the Iroquois made a point of their sovereignty by declaring war on the Axis powers independently of the United States. Many Iroquois abstain from voting in state and national elections, and a number have refused to pay income taxes. Some of the Iroquois nations (Mohawk, Oneida, Onondaga, Tuscarora, Cayuga, and Seneca) issue their own vehicle license plates; the Iroquois Confederacy at Onondaga sends diplomats to other countries with their own passports.

INDIAN CIVIL RIGHTS ACT (1968) 25 U.S.C. § 1301

The Indian Civil Rights Act required that Indian nations and bands be bound generally by the **Bill of Rights**. It also provided for retrocession of **Public Law 280**, which had allowed several states to assume criminal and civil jurisdiction on Indian reservations. The act allowed retrocession of P.L. 280 only at the initiation of the states that had asserted jurisdiction. Like many laws passed by Congress regarding Indians, this one was a double-edged sword. While it extended the protections of the Bill of Rights to **Indian Country**, the Indian Civil Rights Act also imposed U.S. legal standards, even, in some cases, when they conflicted with native traditions.

The language of the Indian Civil Rights Act has been limited severely by subsequent court decisions, the most important of which is *Santa Clara Pueblo v. Martinez* (1978), which held that the equal-protection clause does not apply in Indian Country. The practical effect of this and other rulings has been to make the application of the law subject, in many cases, to traditional Native American cultural and political practices. In **Native American Church v. Navajo Tribal Council**, the guarantees of the First Amendment were found not to apply on Indian reservations. Commented legal scholar William C. Canby, Jr., "The effect of this ruling [Santa Clara] . . . is to eliminate the jurisdictional base upon which most decisional law under the Indian Civil Rights Act has rested" (Canby 1981: 217).

Although the Indian Civil Rights Act closely resembles the U.S. **Constitution**'s Bill of Rights, it does not replicate it. For example, the act protects the free exercise of religion, but does not prohibit the establishment of a religion by a tribe. The reasoning here is that in many Indian cultures political activity cannot be easily divorced from religious practice, so a rigid state-church division in this area would fundamentally alter the entire structure and practice of government in many Native American communities. The Indian Civil Rights Act also guarantees counsel to the accused, but "at his own expense." Under U.S. law, a person accused of a crime that may result in imprisonment is required to be furnished with legal counsel, with the court footing the bill if the accused is not able. Congress did not include this clause in the Indian Civil Rights Act because many tribal courts could not afford it, and because not enough lawyers practice in Indian Country to make such a practice workable.

The Indian Civil Rights Act repeats the language of the Constitution, with some notable exceptions meant to preserve the tribes' cultural integrity. Even with these modifications, the Indian Civil Rights Act posed some ticklish issues of tribal sovereignty. See, for example, **Santa Clara Pueblo v. Martinez**.

No matter how standards are applied, many Native Americans point out that the Bill of Rights was extended to tribes without the type of consent that was required of the states in the process of original adoption.

Although it was motivated by an effort to extend the legal guarantees of citizenship to Indians, the Indian Civil Rights Act posed problems. For example, it mandated that informal, traditional means of resolving disputes be forsaken in favor of tribal courts modeled more closely on Anglo-American standards. "The cultural impact is even more significant," wrote **Vine Deloria, Jr**. He continued:

The intrinsic individualism of the Bill of Rights could endanger the remaining aspects of selfhood as conceived by specific Indian tribes. This is precisely the issue in the Santa Clara case where tracing membership patrilineally was regarded initially as being sexist in character. (1985: 30)

FURTHER READING

Ball, Milnar. "Constitution, Court, Indian Tribes." *American Bar Foundation Research Journal*, no. 1 (Winter 1987): 1–140.

Canby, William C., Jr. *American Indian Law in a Nutshell*. St. Paul, MN: West Publishing, 1981.
Deloria, Vine, Jr., ed. *American Indian Policy in the Twentieth Century*. Norman: University of Oklahoma Press, 1985.
Deloria, Vine, Jr., and C. Lytle. *The Nations Within*. New York: Pantheon, 1984.
Kickingbird, Kirke, Alexander Tallchief Skibine, and Lynn Kickingbird. *Indian Sovereignty*. Washington, DC: Institute for the Development of Indian Law, 1983.

INDIAN CLAIMS COMMISSION 60 Stat. 1049; 25 U.S.C. §§ 70–70
    The **Meriam Report** (1928) emphasized that no long-term solution of the "Indian problem" could occur without establishment of a commission to adjudicate outstanding claims. Several legislative attempts were made without success during the late 1920s and 1930s to create such a body. After World War II, however, the United States was facing pressure regarding treatment of minorities at home after having criticized the human-rights records of the Axis powers during the war. As a result, the Indian Claims Commission (ICC) was established by Congress in 1946.
    By 1946, much of the impetus of the Indian New Deal had ended, but the creation of the ICC in that year represented the final reform measure of the era. Before the enactment of the ICC, American Indian nations had to get the consent of Congress through special legislation in order to sue the federal government for violations of **treaties** and agreements. The Indian Claims Commission Act created a three-person commission to hear and determine claims existing prior to the bill's passage. The Congress felt that the ICC was to be part of a process that would enable Native American groups to become autonomous.
    A special tribunal was required to settle Indian claims because claims based on violation of Indian treaties had been barred from the jurisdiction of the general U.S. Court of Claims in 1863. Absent special congressional action, Indians in effect had no forum under U.S. law in which to present their claims until the Indian Claims Commission Act was passed in 1946. Under the act, suits were allowed by tribes, bands, or other "identifiable" groups of Indians. Appeals were permitted to the general Court of Claims and, by certiorari, to the U.S. Supreme Court. The Indian Claims Commission Act consolidated federal legal actions related to Indian claims for illegal taking of land, which heretofore had been dealt with through 142 different statutes. Congress created the ICC in an effort to extinguish all outstanding claims.
    The ICC expired in 1978, at which time the 102 cases remaining on its docket were transferred to the U.S. Court of Claims. Between 1946 and 1975, the commission awarded $534 million to Indian claimants, $53 million of which was paid in attorney's fees. In all, the commission

docketed 605 individual claims cases, nearly half of which resulted in monetary awards. The commission had originally been created for five years, but the volume of cases and the complexity of the commission's proceedings caused its bureaucratic life to be extended four times. Even so, when jurisdiction was transferred by Congress to the general Court of Claims, only 40 percent of the petitions filed had been adjudicated. The claims that were settled were paid conservatively, with land usually being valued at its cost when it was taken, usually in the late nineteenth century, without the benefit of several decades of increasing prices and land values. Many of the settlements came to less than $1 per acre.

Many non-Indian people in the late 1940s and 1950s believed that the Indian Claims Commission led to the termination of federal supervision over American Indian tribes. U.S. Senator Arthur V. Watkins, Republican of Utah, believed that Indian claims were the basis for federal "decontrol" (a term Watkins used). The Seneca activist Alice Lee Jemison prophesied the impact of termination legislation when she declared that the

present proposals will accomplish only one thing with any certainty—the termination of Federal expenditures for the benefit of the Indians, and will leave the Indians suspended in a twilight zone of political nonentity, partly tribal, partly state. . . . [T]wenty years from now, another Congress will be considering measures to correct the mistakes of this experiment.

FURTHER READING

Barsh, Russel, and James Henderson. *The Road: Indian Tribes and Political Liberty*. Berkeley: University of California Press, 1980.

Cohen, Felix S. "Indian Claims." *American Indian* 2:3 (Spring 1945), 10.

Deloria, Vine, Jr. *Behind the Trail of Broken Treaties*. Austin: University of Texas Press, 1985.

Holt, H. Barry, and Gary Forrester. *Digest of American Indian Law*. Littleton, CO: Fred B. Rothman & Co., 1990.

Indian Claims Commission. *Annual Report*. Washington, DC: Indian Claims Commission, 1975.

O'Brien, Sharon. "Federal Indian Policy and Human Rights." In *American Indian Policy in the Twentieth Century*, ed. Vine Deloria, Jr. Norman: University of Oklahoma Press, 1985.

Watkins, Arthur C. "Termination of Federal Supervision: The Removal of Restrictions over Indian Property and Person." In *The Rape of Indian Lands*, ed. Paul W. Gates. New York: Arno Press, 1979.

INDIAN COUNTRY

Following the arrival of Europeans and their descendants along the eastern seaboard of North America and the Saint Lawrence River Valley in the seventeenth century, "Indian Country" has been a term employed in legal discourse to define territory for the purported exclusive use and benefit of Native Americans. In contemporary legal usage (as in 18 U.S.C. § 1151), "Indian Country" is defined as all land within federally recognized Indian reservations, all "dependent Indian communities," and all allotted land held in **trust** by the United States. Under this definition, land owned by non-Indians may be defined as being Indian Country if it lies within the boundaries of reservation lands. Rights of way running through Indian lands also are included.

One of the earliest usages of the term "Indian Country" to embrace a large area was the British Royal **Proclamation of 1763**, which sought to contain Euro-American settlement east of the crest of the Appalachian Mountains. The Proclamation of 1763 and later demarcations of Indian Country usually were issued by European sovereigns (or the United States) in an attempt, usually futile, to contain the illegal rush of their own populations into areas not yet ceded by Indians through treaties or warfare. The **Trade and Intercourse Acts**, passed by the U.S. Congress as early as 1790, attempted to make illegal the pell-mell transfer of Indian land to European-American settlers without federal approval. Such acts usually were honored most often in the breach, a major reason that Indian nations have recovered land under these laws even two centuries after their enactment. The Trade and Intercourse Acts attempted, usually in legally imprecise language, to set limits on non-Indian settlement by demarcating areas said to be Indian Country. The term was used to describe land owned and occupied by Indians, regardless of its position vis-à-vis an absolute boundary.

By the early nineteenth century, Indian Country was being defined by U.S. legal authorities as land west of the Mississippi River (later, the Missouri). The Five Civilized Tribes and other Indian tribes who gave up their homelands after having been promised land in **Indian Territory** signed treaties stating that their land would not be annexed by the states. Within half a century, the government's definition of Indian Country changed again as settlement surged westward across the continent. From the late nineteenth through the mid-twentieth centuries, various measures were taken to divide and diminish Indian Country, through allotment (*see* **Allotment Act**), **termination**, and other congressional acts). In 1948, the U.S. government established yet another definition of Indian Country (18 U.S.C. § 1151), providing that all lands, however owned, within the exterior boundaries of all federal Indian reservations, however created, comprised Indian Country under criminal law. The statute was extended to civil jurisdiction by the U.S. Supreme Court in *DeCoteau v. District County Court*, 420 U.S. 425, 427 n. 2 (1975).

"In 1882," commented Fred Ragsdale, professor of law at the University of New Mexico, "the Supreme Court decided *United States v.*

McBratney, a case that changed [the definition of] Indian Country from a geographical concept to something else—exactly what else is a difficult question." Ragsdale continued:

Today, except when used for questions of federal criminal jurisdiction, "Indian Country" is about as provisional as "Marlboro Country," that is, it is an image, or a state of mind, or a sociological phenomenon to many. Indian Country is an incredibly complex jurisdictional issue disguised in a colorful phrase. (Deloria 1985: 69)

FURTHER READING

Deloria, Vine, Jr., ed. *American Indian Policy in the Twentieth Century.* Norman: University of Oklahoma Press, 1985.
Wilkinson, Charles F. *American Indians, Time, and the Law: Native Societies in a Modern Constitutional Democracy.* New Haven, CT: Yale University Press, 1987.

INDIAN DEFENSE LEAGUE OF AMERICA

Shortly after 1920, a wave of sympathy emerged in response to the cruelties imposed on native people during the reservation era. This manifestation of political opinion produced the **Meriam Report** (1928), as well as the **Indian Reorganization Act** (1934). The Indian Defense League of America was a key catalyst in reform efforts during these years.

During the 1920s, the Indian Defense League began to protest the violation of **treaty** rights, particularly with reference to eastern tribes. The Indian Defense League was organized by Clinton Rickard, a Tuscarora chief, and David Hill, a Mohawk from the Six Nations Reserve at Brantford, Ontario. The league was begun as an agency to provide legal representation for Indian people who were too poor to afford it.

The actions of Indians in the Indian Defense League beginning in the 1920s were complemented by those of non-Indians. By 1923, an organized committee of influential Indians and non-Indians, the **Committee of One Hundred**, was lobbying for more respectful and humane treatment of American Indians. **John Collier** was an early member, with William Jennings Bryan, Clark Wissler, General John J. Pershing, Bernard Baruch, William Allen White, and the Seneca Arthur C. Parker. Parker was elected presiding officer at a convention in Washington, D.C., during December 1923. Under his aegis, in 1924, the group published its findings under the title *The Indian Problem.* This document formed the basis for the better-known Meriam Report four years later.

The Indian Defense League also organized protests. Native people, many of them **Iroquois**, refused to pay customs duties or to surrender passports at the U.S.-Canadian border, because they believed both actions to be violations of the **Jay Treaty** (in the United States) and the

Treaty of Ghent (in Canada). The activist tactics of the league continued through the 1950s, when the group was called the League of North American Indians.

In 1957, the Indian Defense League helped to energize traditionalist resistance; the League of North American Indians, another group, also became active. Tuscarora Wallace "Mad Bear" Anderson (born 1927) was one of the most noted Native American rights activists in the 1950s, before a general upsurge in native **self-determination** efforts in the 1960s. Anderson later evolved into a noted spokesman for native **sovereignty** in international forums. Anderson was born in Buffalo, New York, and raised on the Tuscarora reservation near Niagara Falls. He served in the U.S. Navy during World War II at Okinawa. He later also served in Korea. Anderson became an activist after his request for a GI Bill loan to build a house on the Tuscarora reservation was rejected.

Mad Bear led protests against Iroquois payment of New York State income taxes in 1957. At the height of the protest, several hundred Akwesasne (St. Regis) Mohawks marched to the Massena, New York, state courthouse, where they burned summonses issued for unpaid taxes. In 1958, Anderson played a leading role in protests of a 1,383-acre seizure of Tuscarora land by the New York Power Authority for construction of a dam and reservoir. Anderson and other Iroquois deflated workers' tires and blocked surveyors' transits. When the Tuscaroras refused to sell the land, a force of about 100 state troopers and police invaded their reservation. Anderson met the troopers and police with 150 nonviolent demonstrators who blocked their trucks by lying in the road.

During March 1959, Anderson was involved in a declaration of sovereignty at the Iroquois Six Nations Reserve in Brantford, Ontario, the settlement established by Joseph Brant and his followers after the American Revolution. The declaration prompted an occupation of the reserve's Council House by Royal Canadian Mounted Police.

During 1967, Anderson formed the North American Indian Unity Caravan, which traveled the United States for six years as the types of activism that he had pioneered spread nationwide; Anderson also gathered opposition to **termination** legislation and carried it to Washington, D.C., from 133 Native American nations and bands, effectively killing the last attempt to buy out reservations in the United States. In 1969, he helped initiate the takeover of **Alcatraz Island**. During the 1970s and 1980s, Anderson spent much of his time as a merchant seaman, visiting most major ports in North and South America and making contacts among indigenous peoples of the hemisphere.

INDIAN DEPREDATION ACT 26 Stat. 851–854 (1891)

Passed by Congress under pressure by non-Indian settlers the year after the massacre at Wounded Knee, the Indian Depredation Act authorized non-Indians to sue Indians for damages alleged to have occurred during the Indian wars. Any Indian tribe that signed agreements with the United States and asserted friendship with its government was made liable under this act for almost unlimited damages. All claims for losses after July 1, 1865, were authorized in the Court of Claims. The Indian Depredation Act gave rise to many lawsuits of dubious legality, including many claims against the Sioux for losses due Euro-Americans prospecting in the **Black Hills**, which were (and remain) under Sioux ownership. Most of the claims were filed between 1891 and 1919.

FURTHER READING

Skogen, Larry C. *Indian Depredation Claims, 1796–1920.* Norman: University of Oklahoma Press, 1996.

INDIAN GAMING REGULATORY ACT (1988) 25 U.S.C. 2701–2721

The Indian Gaming Regulatory Act set forth regulations for operation of gambling in Indian Country, including the necessity of compacts with the governments of states in which gambling was to occur. The act said that Native American groups could begin regulated gaming subject to negotiation of compacts with states that surrounded their reservations. Gambling also was becoming an issue on native reservations throughout the United States at this time. On some reservations, the introduction of commercial gaming was a great boon. In others, it sparked community conflict.

Commercialized gambling is not a part of most Native American traditions, although many have traditions that include games of chance, often in connection with sacred ceremonies. Such gaming does not carry the connotations of sinfulness that are attached to commercialized gaming by many Euro-Americans.

The recent history of reservation gambling began in 1979, when the Seminoles became the first Indian tribe to enter the bingo industry. The state of Florida challenged the legality of the games, only to have the Fifth Circuit Court of Appeals rule that Seminole bingo could continue because the federal government had never transferred to Florida jurisdiction that would have allowed the state to enforce its civil laws on Indian lands. To show how complicated Indian law can get, the Seminole decision hinged on a finding of the court that Indian bingo in Florida fell under civil jurisdiction, not criminal law. If the Fifth Circuit had ruled that the bingo games fell under criminal law, the state's jurisdiction would have applied because Florida is a **Public Law 280** state. Federal P.L. 280 allowed states to extend criminal jurisdiction over Indian reservations. In 1968, the law was amended to require a native nation's consent before the state could assume jurisdiction. After 1968, the assumption of tribal criminal jurisdiction by states effectively stopped. The states that had taken jurisdiction before 1968 were allowed to keep it, however.

By early 1985, 75 to 80 of the 500 recognized Indian tribes in the United States were conducting some sort of game of chance. The proliferation of gambling on native reservations came at a time when gambling was expanding from a few enclaves, such as Reno and Las Vegas, Nevada, to become a more broadly accepted feature on the social landscape across the United States. Reservations, many of them within an hour's drive of major metropolitan areas, became small islands where many state prohibitions on gambling did not apply. In the mid-1990s, 90 of 557 recognized Indian groups were hosting games of chance, according to the National Indian Gaming Association. These operations comprised 200 sites in 19 states, with revenue of roughly $2.6 billion a year, according to *Gaming and Wagering Business* magazine.

By the fall of 1988, the Congressional Research Service estimated that more than 100 Indian nations and bands participated in some form of gambling, which grossed as much as $255 million a year. The CRS report said:

Indians tend to see gambling as a source of revenue consistent with the private enterprise motif emphasized by the administration, but states object that such activities involve non-Indian customers, are inconsistent with state regulations, and present a variety of law-enforcement problems as a result. . . . concern has been expressed by some, including the Department of Justice, that such Indian gambling may invite the infiltration of organized crime. (Walke 1988: 3)

Individual prizes in some reservation bingo games were reported to be as high as $100,000, while bingo stakes in surrounding areas under state jurisdiction were sometimes limited to $100. Marion Blank Horn, principal deputy solicitor of the Interior Department, described the fertile ground gambling enterprises had found in Indian country:

The reasons for growth in gambling on Indian land are readily apparent. The Indian tribal governments see an opportunity for income that can make a substantial improvement in the tribe's [economic] conditions. The lack of any state or Federal regulation results in a competitive advantage over gambling regulated by the states. These advantages include no state-imposed limits on the size of pots or prizes, no restrictions by the states on days or hours of operations, no costs for licenses or compliance with state requirements, and no state taxes on gambling operations. (Walke 3)

FURTHER READING

Dahl, Dick. "Law Practice: The Casino Boom Is Forging New Relationships between American Indians and the Law." *American Bar Association Journal*, May 1995, 86.

Murphy, M. Maureen. "Gambling on Indian Reservations." Congressional Research Service, Library of Congress, April 26, 1985.

Seminole Tribe of Florida v. Butterworth, 658 F.2d 310 (5th Cir. 1981).

Walke, Roger. "Gambling on Indian Reservations: Updated October 17, 1988." Congressional Research Service, Library of Congress.

INDIAN LAW RESOURCE CENTER

In the late 1970s, the Indian Law Resource Center became one of the most prominent voices (with the **International Indian Treaty Council**) that used international forums, particularly within the United Nations, to raise issues related to Native American **treaty** rights. The Indian Law Resource Center played a key role in lobbying the United Nations to begin its Working Group on Indigenous Populations.

The Indian Law Resource Center also aided in preparing American Indians' cases for the Fourth **Russell Tribunal**. Because of its participation in controversial issues, the Indian Law Resource Center has probably received more attacks from conservatives than any other Indian law advocacy group.

INDIAN REORGANIZATION ACT (1934) 25 U.S.C. § 7

The Indian Reorganization Act (IRA), passed during Franklin Delano Roosevelt's presidency, eliminated the allotment system and established Native American governments for some reservations under systems that were partially self-governing. The IRA also sought to protect (and in some cases enlarge) Native American land bases that had been eroded by allotment and other measures; it also established hiring preferences for Native Americans within the Bureau of Indian Affairs. **Vine Deloria, Jr.**, has called the IRA "perhaps the most fundamental and far-reaching piece of legislation passed by Congress in this century." Although it was criticized by some Native American groups, some of the IRA's changes were widely acclaimed. For example, native peoples were allowed by this act to resume their ceremonies openly.

Before passage of the IRA, Indian nations had been operated more or less as colonial enclaves by the United States. They were legally held to be subject to Congress and the president, delegated through the Bureau of Indian Affairs. According to legal scholars Russel Barsh and James Henderson, "No local laws or assemblies were recognized, and a special police force was established to maintain federal supremacy. Traditional leadership was deposed, prosecuted, and sometimes killed when in conflict with federal Indian policy" (1980: 209). Under the IRA, colonialism was relaxed somewhat. Leaders were no longer appointed, but were elected under constitutions that themselves were subject to U.S. government veto. In many cases, even individual ordinances passed by councils were subject to Interior Department review.

Franklin Delano Roosevelt brought **John Collier** into his administration to construct the "Indian New Deal" during the 1930s. Collier had been involved in efforts to liberalize Indian policy since the 1920s.

The IRA was introduced by Representative Edgar Howard of Nebraska and Senator Burton K. Wheeler of Montana and became known popularly as the "Wheeler-Howard Act." The initial drafts of the fifty-page bill were the work mainly of John Collier, whom Roosevelt had appointed commissioner of Indian affairs. Before its provisions were modified during debates in the House and Senate, the IRA declared a federal policy that American Indians be encouraged to establish and control their own governments. Another part of Collier's draft mandated that Indian schools develop materials relevant to Native American histories and cultures. The third title of the original bill stopped allotment of Indian land and restored title to "surplus" lands still held by the government, as well as creating reservations for Indian groups left without land by the usurpations of the previous century. Collier's bill also called for a court of Indian affairs. After compromise in the legislative process, many of Collier's ideas were discarded. Even so, the IRA established a new framework for Indian affairs, a hybrid of Collier's ideas and the older paternalistic system, limited self-government within a prescribed structure subject to the approval of the Interior Department. Allotment was stopped, and some small steps were taken to augment Native American landholdings.

Indian nations and bands were given two years after the passage of the IRA to accept or reject its provisions. Some of those that rejected the IRA pointed out that the requirement that the federal government approve a native group's policies on land use, selection of legal counsel, and other matters (including their constitutions) was heavy-handed. While the act rhetorically upheld native **self-determination**, it imposed a federal veto power over most major (and many minor) decisions that each native government had proposed.

Frank Fools Crow, a Sioux, described the effects of the Indian New Deal in this way: "Being beaten in war was bad enough. Yet being defeated and placed in bondage by programs we could not understand . . . is worse, especially when it is done to one of the most powerful, independent, and proudest of the Indian nations of North America" (Mails 1990: 146–147). Fools Crow believed that for the **Sioux** people, the "years from 1930–1940 rank as the worst ten years I know of." Fools Crow stated that the traditional family structure was crumbling because

individual independence and . . . irresponsibility was being encouraged among the young people. Bootleggers were after the Indian's money, and were hauling cheap wine and whiskey onto the reservation by the truckload. . . . Even the young women were drinking now, and this assured a future tragedy of the worst possible proportions. (Mails 146–147)

California was a center of opposition to John Collier's "Indian New Deal." One of the principal leaders of this opposition was Rupert Costo, a young Cahuilla who had attended college and had the respect of his people. Costo believed that the Indian New Deal was a "great drive to assimilate the American Indian." Costo felt that the IRA was a program to colonize Indians because "genocide, treaty-making and treaty-breaking, substandard education, disruption of Indian culture and religion, and the . . . Dawes Allotment Act" had failed. Costo knew that partial **assimilation** had already taken place in Indian societies through the use of "certain technologies and techniques," but he knew that total assimilation that meant "fading into the general society with a complete loss of" culture and identity was another thing altogether. Costo called the IRA "the Indian Raw Deal" (Mails 148).

By 1940, the IRA had come under enough criticism to prompt congressional hearings on its repeal. Alice Lee Jemison, a Seneca, told the committee that "there is no self-government in the act; all final power and authority remains in the Secretary of the Interior, which is exactly where it has always rested heretofore" (Jemison 1954: 3). As of that date, according to Indian law scholar Lawrence C. Kelly, 252 Indian nations and bands had voted on the IRA as required by the act, including 99 small bands in California with a total population of less than 25,000. Seventy-eight groups had rejected it. Nationwide, 38,000 Indians voted in favor of IRA governments, while 24,000 voted against. Another 35,000 eligible voters did not take part, most as a silent protest against the IRA.

FURTHER READING

Deloria, Vine, Jr. *Behind the Trail of Broken Treaties.* New York: Delacorte, 1974.

Hauptman, Laurence M. "Big Deal?" *Journal of Ethnic Studies* 9 (Summer 1981): 119–124.

———. *The Iroquois and the New Deal.* Syracuse, NY: Syracuse University Press, 1981.

Jemison, Alice Lee. Statement in "The First American." Washington, D.C., February 3, 1954.

Kelly, Lawrence C. "The Indian Reorganization Act: The Dream and the Reality." *Pacific Historical Review* 44 (August 1975): 291–312.

Kickingbird, Kirke, Alexander Tallchief Skibine, and Lynn Kickingbird. *Indian Sovereignty.* Washington, DC: Institute for the Development of Indian Law, 1983.

Mails, Thomas E. *Fools Crow.* Lincoln: University of Nebraska Press, 1990.

Parman, Donald L. *The Navajos and the New Deal.* New Haven, CT: Yale University Press, 1976.

Philp, Kenneth R. *John Collier's Crusade for Indian Reform, 1920–1954.* Tucson: University of Arizona Press, 1977.

Taylor, Graham D. *The New Deal and American Indian Tribalism: The Administration of the Indian Reorganization Act, 1934–45.* Lincoln: University of Nebraska Press, 1980.

DONALD A. GRINDE, JR., and BRUCE E. JOHANSEN

INDIAN RIGHTS ASSOCIATION

The Indian Rights Association was founded in Philadelphia, with substantial Quaker support, in 1882. During the ensuing years, the non-Indian organization became one of the most prominent advocates, with other "friends of the Indian," in support of allotment legislation, passed in 1887 (*see* **Allotment Act**), which mandated that communal native lands be broken up into individual tracts, with the balance of the land (often up to 90 percent of any given reservation) opened to non-Indian ownership. As provisions of allotment caused severe depletion of Indian landholdings and immeasurable poverty and suffering during the next half-century, the Indian Rights Association also evolved until, by the 1930s, it supported a limited form of tribal **self-determination** embodied in the **Indian Reorganization Act** (1934).

In the 1880s, however, the Indian Rights Association fully supported allotment as a means of "civilizing" American Indians by European-American social, legal, and political norms. The organization issued statements asserting that "the Indian as a savage member of a tribal organization cannot survive, ought not to survive, the aggressions of civilization." Herbert Welsh, founder of the Indian Rights Organization, was a fervent believer in the superiority of Western European over Native American cultures. His founding manifesto for the Indian Rights Association, *Four Weeks among Some of the Sioux . . .* (1882), extolled the potential of religious schools for "civilizing" the Plains Indians. Welsh's vision of the Indian future included complete **assimilation** into Anglo-American society.

In the 1920s, Welsh and others in the group's aging leadership confronted a new generation of Indian-rights advocates led by **John Collier** over the group's opposition to a number of **Pueblo** dances, which Welsh believed to be barbaric. Collier deeply admired native cultures and favored relaxation of bans on dancing and other ceremonies.

Internal policy squabbles notwithstanding, members of the Indian Rights Association mustered considerable non-Indian attention to reservation problems in the 1920s. By 1926, the Institute for Government Research (part of the Brookings Institution) undertook several studies of Indian policy that were consolidated in the **Meriam Report** (1928), a classic study that described in minute detail the condition of Indian life during the worst times of the reservation era. The Meriam Report helped create the popular consensus behind passage of the Indian Reorganization Act of 1934.

FURTHER READING

Cadwallader, Sandra L., and Vine Deloria, Jr., eds. *The Aggressions of Civilization: Federal Indian Policy since the 1880s.* Philadelphia: Temple University Press, 1984.
Welsh, Herbert. *Four Weeks among Some of the Sioux Tribes of Dakota and Nebraska, Together with a Brief Consideration of the Indian Problem.* Philadelphia: Indian Rights Association, 1882.

INDIAN TERRITORY (OKLAHOMA)

In 1830, the federal government passed general removal legislation aimed at annexation of land belonging to the "Five Civilized Tribes"— the **Cherokee, Choctaw, Chickasaw, Creek**, and Seminole—who were relocated in Indian Territory, later the state of Oklahoma. Many other native nations (such as the Osage, **Cheyenne**, and **Ponca**) also were removed to Indian Territory later in the nineteenth century as part of a federal policy aimed at concentrating all Native American populations in one geographical area. By 1883, twenty-five Indian reservations occupied by a total of thirty-seven native nations had been established in Indian Territory.

In most of the removal treaties, the government assured the Indians that they would have wide-ranging control over territory and resources in their new homes. For example, the **Treaty with the Choctaws** (September 27, 1830, 7 Stat. 333–342) pledged

jurisdiction and government of all persons and property that may be within their limits west, so that no Territory or State shall ever have the right to pass laws for the government of the Choctaw nation . . . and that no part of the land granted to them shall ever be embraced in any Territory or State.

Similarly, the **Treaty with the Creeks and Seminoles** (1856, 11 Stat. 699–707, Article IX) pledged "secure and unrestricted self-government and full jurisdiction over persons and property, within their respective limits."

Until late in the nineteenth century, the native nations in Indian Territory were self-governing in most major respects. The native nations in the area had set up formal governmental structures and judicial offices to settle disputes. During the middle of the nineteenth century, representatives from several native nations in Indian Territory had met and advanced the idea of an Indian state.

The removal treaties also pledged solemnly that the native nations in their new homes would never be enclosed in the borders of any state, the problem that had led to their eviction from their homelands in the Southeast. By 1890, however, this process was already beginning anew as large numbers of non-Indians moved into the area. The Organic Act of 1890 divided Oklahoma into a mainly non-Indian settler state and lands still reserved for Indians.

By late in the century, however, the discovery of oil and a lack of open land elsewhere in the United States gave rise to additional non-Indian in-migration that led to Oklahoma's admission to the United States as a traditional state in 1907. The introduction of railroads and other large non-Indian business enterprises in the area continued this trend. By 1889, more than 170,000 non-Indians had moved to Indian Territory, three times the Native American population at that time.

FURTHER READING

Burton, Jeffrey. *Indian Territory and the United States, 1866–1906.* Norman: University of Oklahoma Press, 1995.

Debo, Angie. *And Still the Waters Run.* Princeton: Princeton University Press, 1940.

Doran, Michael F. "Population Statistics of Nineteenth Century Indian Territory." *Chronicles of Oklahoma* 53: 4 (Winter 1975–1976).

Foreman, Grant. *A History of Oklahoma.* Norman: University of Oklahoma Press, 1942.

INDIAN TRIBAL GOVERNMENT TAX STATUS ACT (1983) 26 U.S.C. § 7871

In accordance with other measures passed after 1970, Congress attempted to enhance Native American **self-determination** with passage of the Indian Tribal Government Tax Status Act. The act allows deduction of taxes paid to tribal governments from federal income taxes, bringing treatment of these taxes into line with that of state and local government taxes. The act also allows deduction of charitable contributions to tribal governments and allows these governments to issue certain classes of tax-exempt debt obligations.

While the courts have refined Indians' tax-paying status, a number of Native Americans have refused to pay federal, state, or local taxes at all, citing tribal sovereignty or the clause in the **Constitution** that excludes "Indians not taxed." This practice is especially widespread among members of the **Iroquois Confederacy**. Several Iroquois have risked prison terms rather than pay taxes to the United States and its subordinate governments.

INDIANIZING

The American Indian was so tightly intertwined with images of liberty in the colonists' minds that both the Puritan and Jamestown colonists passed statutes against "Indianizing." "Such is the influence of this Wildernes[s] on inhabitants who were born here that it inclines them to an Indian way of life," Daniel Leeds wrote in his *Almanack for 1700*

(1980: 90). In 1642, the Connecticut General Court set a penalty of three years in the workhouse for any colonist caught "forsaking godly society." The rationale for the law was that "divers[e] persons depart from amongst us, and take up their abode with the Indians in a profane course of life." As early as 1612, the Jamestown colony prescribed the death penalty for "any man or woman [who] shall runne away from the Colonie, to Powhatan, or any Weroance else whatsoever."

FURTHER READING

"For the Colony of Virginia Britannia, Laws Divine, Lorall, & Martiall &c., Paragraph 29." Cited in *Tracts and Other Papers relating . . . to the origin . . . of the colonies in North America*, ed. Peter Force, vol. 3, n.p. New York: Peter Force, 1836–1846.

Leeds, Daniel. *An Almanack for . . . 1700*. New York, 1700, in *Proceedings of the American Antiquarian Society* 90: (April 1980): 90.

Trumbell, J. Hammon. *The Public Records of the Colony of Connecticut*. Hartford: Brown & Parsons, 1850–90. 1:78.

INDIVIDUAL INDIAN MONIES

Beginning in the term of **Andrew Jackson** and refined in the General **Allotment Act** (1887), accounts were created in the names of individual Native Americans into which the Interior Department deposited monies due them from use of land in the Indians' names. These deposits could be made for such things as the sale of timber, exploitation of mineral rights, or lease of the land for grazing, farming, or other uses. The Bureau of Indian Affairs maintained supervision of these Individual Indian Monies (IIM) accounts, from which Indians were allowed to draw only if the BIA deemed them "competent."

Mismanagement of the IIM accounts began early in the twentieth century when several full-blooded members of the Five Civilized Tribes in Oklahoma Territory were found dead of starvation despite the fact that they had IIM accounts worth hundreds of thousands of dollars. The BIA had been diverting their income to pay for construction of schools and churches.

Late in the twentieth century, the controversy over BIA handling of individual Indians' accounts arose again. With 300,000 individual account holders, the amount on deposit with the BIA has risen to about $450 million; tribal accounts held by the Interior Department total $2.3 billion. The BIA in 1994 investigated its own mismanagement, including investment of some Indian monies in failed savings and loans, and pledged reform. Astonished at the scope of the problem and the slow pace of change, the **Native American Rights Fund** in 1996 filed a class-action suit. Attorneys pointed to people such as Bernice Skunk Cap, an elderly Blackfoot, who lost her cabin to fire in 1994. Planning to build a new home, Skunk Cap applied to the BIA for $2,400 in her IIM account, but was told that she could have only $1,000 of it. She was forced to move into a nursing home.

"We have no idea how many thousands of Native Americans have been deprived of revenues that belong to them," said Sen. John McCain, Republican of Arizona, chairman of the Senate Indian Affairs Committee. "We should be ashamed of a system that is a living example of our nation's inattention to its trust obligations to Native Americans" (Johansen 1997: 19). A General Accounting Office (GAO) report said that resolving problems with the IIM and other trust funds "is a challenge of tremendous magnitude," in large part because record keeping has never met the minimal standards of the banking industry.

FURTHER READING

Johansen, Bruce E. "Taking Indians for a Ride: The BIA's Missing $2.4 Billion." *Native Americas* 14: 1 (Spring 1997): 19.

INSTITUTE FOR THE DEVELOPMENT OF INDIAN LAW
The Institute for the Development of Indian Law since its founding in 1971 has been a major advocate for tribal points of view in the courts of the United States. The institute researches legal cases, trains attorneys, and publishes in the field of American Indian law from its headquarters in Washington, D.C.

INTERNATIONAL INDIAN TREATY COUNCIL
As an advocacy group to bring questions of American Indian **sovereignty** and rights before international forums, the International Indian Treaty Council was first convened at a meeting of leaders from several tribes on the Standing Rock Sioux Reservation in 1974. During June of that year, four thousand Native Americans from ninety-seven tribes met at Standing Rock and issued "The Declaration of Continuing Independence." The declaration read, in part:

We reject all executive orders, legislative acts, and judicial decisions related to Native Americans since 1871, when the United States unilaterally suspended treaty-making relations with Native Nations. This includes, but is not limited to, the Major Crimes Act, the General Allotment Act, the Citizenship Act of 1924, the Indian Reorganization Act of 1934, [the] Indian Claims Commission Act, Public Law 280, and the Termination Act. All treaties between Native Nations and the United States shall be recognized without further need of interpretation. (Wing 1977: 3)

Later in the year, an International Indian Treaty Council office opened in New York City near the United Nations. The group, led by Cherokee Jimmie Durham, obtained nongovernmental organization observer status at the United Nations. By 1977, the IITC was prominent in testimony at United Nations hearings on the status of national minorities in Geneva, Switzerland, the same city in which **Deskaheh** had tried to present American Indian grievances to the League of Nations a half-century earlier.

FURTHER READING

International Indian Treaty Council. *The Third International Indian Treaty Conference, Standing Rock Sioux Reservation, Wakpala, S. D., June 15–19, 1977*. New York: IITC, 1977.

Wing, Marian, ed. *The Third International Indian Treaty Conference*. San Francisco: American Indian Treaty Council, 1977.

IOWA MUTUAL INSURANCE CO. V. LAPLANTE 480 U.S. 9 (1987)

Iowa Mutual denied insurance coverage to LaPlante, a Blackfoot who was injured while driving a cattle truck on the reservation. LaPlante filed suit in Blackfeet Tribal Court alleging bad faith on the part of Iowa Mutual. The insurance company's attorneys moved to dismiss LaPlante's suit for lack of jurisdiction, but the Blackfeet court continued to assert "subject matter" jurisdiction. The insurance company then filed suit in federal district court, which dismissed the suit for lack of jurisdiction.

The U.S. Supreme Court ruled in this case in conformity with *National Farmers Union Insurance Co. v. Crow Tribe* (1985) that remedies must be exhausted in a Native American court before a case may be appealed to the federal level. The Court held that there was no "indication that Congress intended . . . to limit the jurisdiction of tribal courts [and] . . . we decline to hold that tribal sovereignty can be impaired" as Iowa Mutual had sought. The insurance company was ordered to pay LaPlante's injury claim.

IRON CROW V. OGLALA SIOUX TRIBE 231 F.2d 89 (8th Cir. 1956)

In *Iron Crow v. Oglala Sioux*, the Eighth Circuit Court of Appeals upheld Native American governments' right to make and enforce their own laws. The court held that the U.S. **Constitution** recognized native nations as sovereign governments with "all the inherent rights of sovereignty," except when restricted by act of Congress (*see* **Plenary Power**). Basic among these powers are those of criminal jurisdiction (except as limited by **Public Law 280**) and taxation.

In this case, members of the Oglala Sioux went to court to enjoin the tribal council from enforcing its laws against adultery, as well as a tax placed on persons who leased Indian lands for grazing. While the court upheld the Oglala Sioux Tribe's authority to make and enforce its own laws, it also held that Indian governments possessed **sovereignty** restricted by the exercise of U.S. legislative and judicial power. What sovereignty an Indian government possessed was said to stem from its recognition by the United States. "This sovereignty," the court wrote, "is absolute excepting only as to such rights as are taken away by the paramount government, the United States." This sovereignty was said by the Eighth Circuit Court to be a matter of "inherent jurisdiction over all matters not taken over by the federal government." The court held:

From time immemorial, the members of the Oglala Sioux Tribe have exercised powers of local self-government, regulating domestic problems, and conducting foreign affairs, including, in later years, the negotiation of treaties and agreements with the United States. . . . We hold that Indian tribes, such as the defendant Oglala Sioux Tribe of the Pine Ridge Reservation, South Dakota, still possess their inherent sovereignty excepting only when it has been specifically taken from them, either by treaty or by Congressional act.

FURTHER READING

Barsh, Russel, and James Henderson. *The Road: Indian Tribes and Political Liberty*. Berkeley: University of California Press, 1980.

IROQUOIS (HAUDENOSAUNEE) CONFEDERACY

This entry concentrates on the traditional, male-oriented version of the Haudenosaunee (Iroquois) Confederacy's founding and operation. For the female version of these events, see the entry **Haudenosaunee (Iroquois) Women: Legal and Political Status** *by Barbara Mann.*

The Iroquois Confederacy was the best known to the European colonists of several Native American confederacies in large part because of the Haudenosaunees' pivotal position in diplomacy not only between the English and French, but also among other native nations. Called the Iroquois by the French and the Five (later Six) Nations by the English, the people who called themselves Haudenosaunee ("People of the Longhouse") controlled the only relatively level land pass between the English colonies on the eastern seaboard and the French settlements in the Saint Lawrence River Valley, the later route of the Erie Canal. The Iroquois' diplomatic influence permeated the entire eastern half of North America. Cadwallader Colden, who, in the words of Robert Waite, was regarded as "the best-informed man in the New World on the affairs of the British-American colonies" (Colden [1765]: v), provided the first systematic study of the Six Nations in 1727 and augmented it in 1747. In his *History of the Five Indian Nations Depending on the Province of New-York in America*, Colden, an adopted Mohawk, compared the Iroquois to the Romans because of their skills at oratory, warfare, and diplomacy, as well as the republican nature of their government. "When Life and Liberty came in competition, indeed, I think our Indians have outdone the Romans in this particular. . . . The Five Nations consisted of men whose courage could not be shaken" (Colden vi).

Describing the Iroquois' form of government extensively, Colden wrote that it "has continued so long that the Christians know nothing of the original of it. . . . Each Nation is an Absolute Republick by its self, governed in all Publick affairs of War and Peace by the Sachems of Old Men, whose Authority and Power is gained by and consists wholly in the opinions of the rest of the Nation in their Wisdom and Integrity." He continued, "They never execute their Resolutions by Compulsion or Force Upon any of their People" (xx). According to Colden, "The Five Nations have such absolute Notions of Liberty that they allow no Kind of Superiority of one over another, and banish all Servitude from their Territories" (xvii–xix).

Although some twentieth-century anthropologists maintain that the Iroquois League was not fully formed until Europeans made landfall in North America, the historical records these Europeans created contain no hint that the confederacy was in formation at that time. The consensus of writers who saw the confederacy in its full flower in the seventeenth and eighteenth centuries agreed that it formed before colonization. The oral history of the Iroquois indicates a founding date between A.D. 1000 and 1450. Lewis Henry Morgan and Horatio E. Hale estimated the founding date toward the end of that spectrum. William N. Fenton made his estimate of the founding of the Iroquois League even later. All of these estimates are educated guesses. In 1996, native oral tradition was combined with academic solar eclipse and archaeological data by Barbara Mann and Jerry Fields of the University of Toledo to make a case that the Great Law of Peace was ratified by the Iroquois in 1142 of the common era. The traditional use of the "black sun" (solar eclipse) that occurred during the Senecas' debate over ratification of the Great Law serves as a basis of this case.

The confederacy was formed by the Huron prophet **Deganawidah** (called "the Peacemaker" in oral discourse). Deganawidah enlisted the aid of a speaker, Aiowantha (sometimes called Hiawatha), to spread his vision of a united Haudenosaunee confederacy because Deganawidah stuttered so badly he could hardly speak. The confederacy originally included the Mohawks, Oneidas, Onondagas, Cayugas, and Senecas. The sixth nation, the Tuscaroras, migrated into Iroquois country in the early eighteenth century.

The Great Law of Peace outlined ways in which tribal councils would function within the Iroquois nations in a conscious effort to reduce conflict between the united nations of the confederacy. Social and political customs that grew out of this body of laws also reduced conflict between individuals and members of the various clans.

In his vision, Deganawidah saw a giant white pine reaching to the sky and gaining strength from three counterbalancing principles of life. The first axiom was that a stable mind and healthy body should be in balance so that peace between individuals and groups could occur. Second, Deganawidah stated that humane conduct, thought, and speech were a requirement for equity and justice among peoples. Finally, he foresaw a society in which physical strength and civil authority would reinforce the power of the clan system.

Deganawidah's tree had four white roots that stretched to the four directions of the earth. From the base of the tree, a snow-white carpet of thistledown covered the surrounding countryside. On top of the giant pine, an eagle perched. Deganawidah explained that the tree symbolized humanity, living within the principles governing relations among human beings. The eagle was humanity's lookout against enemies who would disturb the peace. Deganawidah postulated that the white carpet could be spread to the four corners of the earth to provide a shelter of peace and brotherhood for all humankind. Deganawidah's vision was a message from the Creator to bring harmony into human existence and unite all peoples into a single family guided by his three dual principles.

After Tadadaho accepted the will of the community, the clan leaders of the Five Nations (Mohawk, Oneida, Onondaga, Cayuga, and Seneca) were gathered around the council fire at Onondaga to hear the laws and government of the confederacy. The fundamental laws of the Iroquois Confederacy espoused peace and community, unity, balance of power, and natural rights of all people, as well as sharing of resources. Moreover, individual acts of violence were outlawed. Under the new law, when a person killed someone, the grieving family could forgo the option of exacting clan revenge (the taking of the life of the murderer or a member of the murderer's clan). Instead, the bereaved family could accept twenty strings of **wampum** (freshwater shells strung together) from the slayer's family (ten for the dead person and ten for the life of the murderer himself). If a woman was killed, the price was thirty wampum strings. Through this ceremony, the monopoly on legally sanctioned violence was enlarged from the clan to the league.

Peace among the formerly antagonistic nations was procured and maintained through the Haudenosaunee's Great Law of Peace (*Kaianerekowa*), which was passed from generation to generation by use of wampum, a form of written communication that outlined a complex system of checks and balances between clans and sexes. A complete oral recitation of the Great Law can take several days. Abbreviated versions of it have been translated into English for many years, but not until 1992 was a complete version published in English and Onondaga (see Woodbury). The fact that the Great Law is available in published form provides one reason why the Iroquois are cited so often today in debates regarding the origins of U.S. fundamental law. While many other native confederacies existed along the borders of the British colonies, many of the specific provisions of their governments have been lost.

To understand the provisions of the Great Law, one must understand the symbols it uses to represent the confederacy. One was the traditional longhouse. The confederacy itself was likened to a longhouse, with the Mohawks guarding the "eastern door," the Senecas at the "western door," and the Onondagas tending the ceremonial council fire in the middle. The primary national symbol of the Haudenosaunee was the Great White Pine, which serves throughout the Great Law as a metaphor for the confederacy. Its branches shelter the people of the nations, and its roots spread to the four directions, inviting other peoples, irregardless of race or nationality, to take shelter under the tree. The Haudenosaunee recognized no bars to dual citizenship; in fact, many influential figures in the English colonies and early United States, such as Colden, were adopted into Iroquois nations.

Each of the five nations maintained its own council, whose sachems were nominated by the clan mothers of families holding hereditary rights to office titles. The Grand Council at Onondaga was drawn from the individual national councils. The Grand Council also could nominate sachems outside the hereditary structure, based on merit alone. These sachems, called "pine tree chiefs," were said to have sprung from the body of the people as the symbolic Great White Pine springs from the earth.

Rights, duties, and qualifications of sachems were explicitly outlined, and the women could remove (or impeach) a sachem who was found guilty of any of a number of abuses of office, from missing meetings to murder. An erring chief was summoned to face charges by the war chiefs, who acted in peacetime as the people's eyes and ears in the council, somewhat as the role of the press was envisaged by **Thomas Jefferson** and other founders of the United States. A sachem was given three warnings and was then removed from the council if he did not mend his ways. A sachem guilty of murder not only lost his title, but also deprived his entire family of its right to representation. The women relatives holding the rights to the office were "buried," and the title was transferred to a sister family.

The Great Law stipulated that sachems' skins must be seven spans thick to withstand the criticism of their constituents. The law pointed out that sachems should take pains not to become angry when people scrutinized their conduct in governmental affairs. Such a point of view pervades the writings of Jefferson and **Benjamin Franklin**, although it was not fully codified into U.S. law until the Supreme Court decision in *New York Times v. Sullivan* (1964) made it virtually impossible for public officials to sue successfully for libel. Sachems were not allowed to name their own successors, nor could they carry their titles to the grave. The Great Law provided a ceremony to remove the "antlers" of authority from a dying chief. The Great Law also provided for the removal from office of sachems who could no longer adequately function in office, a measure remarkably similar to a constitutional amendment adopted in the United States during the late twentieth century providing for the removal of an incapacitated president.

The Great Law also included provisions guaranteeing freedom of religion and the right of redress before the Grand Council. It also forbade unauthorized entry of homes. All these measures sound familiar to U.S. citizens through the **Bill of Rights**.

The Iroquois Confederacy is fundamentally a kinship state. The Iroquois are bound together by a clan and chieftain system that is buttressed by a similar linguistic base. However, the League of the Iroquois is much more than just a kinship state. Through the "hearth" that consisted of a mother and her children, women played a profound role in Iroquois political life. Each "hearth" was part of a wider group called an *otiianer*, and two or more *otiianers* constituted a clan. The word *otiianer* refers to the female heirs to the chieftainship titles of the league, the fifty authorized names for the chiefs of the Iroquois, passed through the female side of the *otiianer*. The *otiianer* women selected one of the males within their group to fill a vacated seat in the league.

Such a matrilineal system was headed by a "clan mother." All the sons and daughters of a particular clan were related through uterine families that lived far apart. In this system, a husband went to live with his wife's family, and their children became members of the mother's clan by right of birth. Through matrilineal descent, the Iroquois formed cohesive political groups that had little to do with where people lived or from what village the hearths originated.

The oldest daughter of the head of a clan sometimes succeeded her mother at her death upon the judgment of the clan. All authority sprang from the people of the various clans that made up a nation. The women who headed these clans appointed the male delegates and deputies who spoke for the clans at tribal meetings. After consultation within the clan, issues and questions were formulated and subsequently debated in council.

Deganawidah provided strict instructions governing the conduct of the league and its deliberations. Tadadaho was to maintain the fire and call the Onondaga chiefs together to determine whether an issue was pressing enough to call to the attention of the council of the confederacy. If the proposed issue merited such consideration, the council would assemble and Tadadaho would kindle a fire and announce the purpose of the meeting. The rising smoke penetrating the sky is a signal to the Iroquois allies that the council is in session. The Onondaga chiefs and Tadadaho are charged with keeping the council area free from distractions.

The procedure for debating policies of the confederacy begins with the Mohawks and Senecas (the Mohawks, Senecas, and Onondagas are called the elder brothers). After being debated by the Keepers of the Eastern Door (Mohawks) and the Keepers of the Western Door (Senecas), the question is then thrown across the fire to the Oneida and Cayuga statesmen (the younger brothers) for discussion in much the same manner. Once consensus is achieved among the Oneidas and the Cayugas, the discussion is then given back to the Senecas and Mohawks for confirmation. Next, the question is laid before the Onondagas for their decision.

At this stage, the Onondagas have a power similar to judicial review: they can raise objections to the proposed measure if it is believed inconsistent with the Great Law. Essentially, the legislature can rewrite the proposed law on the spot so that it can be in accord with the constitution of the Iroquois. When the Onondagas reach consensus, Tadadaho gives the decision to Honowireton (an Onondaga chief who presides over debates between the delegations) to confirm the decision if it is unanimously agreed upon by all of the Onondaga sachems. Finally, Honowireton or Tadadaho gives the decision of the Onondagas to the Mohawks and the Senecas so that the policy may be announced to the Grand Council as its will. This process reflects the emphasis of the league on checks and balances, public debate, and consensus. The overall intent of such a parliamentary procedure is to encourage unity at each step. The rights of the Iroquois citizenry are protected by portions of the Great Law, which states, "Whenever an especially important matter . . . is presented before the League Council . . . threatening their utter ruin, then the chiefs of the League must submit the matter to the decision of their people" (Sec. 93).

Upon the death or removal of a confederacy chief, the title of the chief reverts to the women in his clan. The women protect this title and determine who will assume the position of chief. As in the power of removal, the women have the first priority in the installation of a new chief. The esteemed women of a clan gather when a title is vacant and nominate a male member to be chief. Next, the men of the clan give their approval. After this process, the nomination is then forwarded to the council of the league, where the new chief is installed.

Public opinion is of great importance within the League of the Iroquois. Iroquois people can have a direct say in the formulation of government policy even if the sachems choose to ignore the will of the people. The Great Law of Peace provides that the people can propose their own laws even when leaders fail to do so: "If the conditions . . . arise . . . to . . . change . . . this law, the case shall be . . . considered and if the new beam seems . . . beneficial, the . . . change . . . if adopted, shall be called, 'Added to the Rafters' " (Sec. 16). This provision resembles provisions for popular initiative in several states of the United States, as well as the mechanism by which the federal and many state constitutions may be amended.

If the council would not act on the will of the people, sachems faced removal under other provisions. Through public opinion and debate, the Great Law gave the Iroquois people basic rights within a distinctive and representative governmental framework. The Great Law solved disputes by giving all parties an equal hearing. Above all, thinking was the activity that went on underneath the Great Tree. For the Iroquois, the more thinkers who were beneath the tree, the better.

FURTHER READING

Colden, Cadwallader. *The History of the Five Indian Nations Depending on the Province of New-York in America.* 1727 and 1747. Ithaca: Cornell University Press, 1968.

————. *The History of the Five Indian Nations of Canada which Are Dependent on the Province of New York in America.* 1765. Vol. 2. New York: New Amsterdam Books, 1902.

Crèvecoeur, St. Jean de. *Journey into Northern Pennsylvania and the State of New York.* 1801, in French. Trans. and ed. by Percy G. Adams. Ann Arbor: University of Michigan Press, 1964.

Fenton, William N. "Seth Newhouse's Traditional History and Constitution of the Iroquois Confederacy." *Proceedings of the American Philosophical Society* 93:2 (1949): 141–158.

Great Law of Peace of the Longhouse People. Rooseveltown, NY: White Roots of Peace, 1971.

Grinde, Donald A., Jr. *The Iroquois and the Founding of the American Nation.* San Francisco: Indian Historian Press, 1977.

Grinde, Donald A., Jr., and Bruce E. Johansen. *Exemplar of Liberty: Native America and the Evolution of Democracy.* Los Angeles: UCLA American Indian Studies Center, 1991.

Hale, Horatio. *The Iroquois Book of Rites.* 1881. Toronto: University of Toronto Press, 1963.

Hertzberg, Hazel W. *The Great Tree and the Longhouse: The Culture of the Iroquois.* New York: Macmillan, 1966.

Howard, Helen A. "Hiawatha: Cofounder of an Indian United Nations." *Journal of the West* 10:3 (1971).

Jacobs, Wilbur R. "Wampum: The Protocol of Indian Diplomacy." *William and Mary Quarterly*, 3rd ser. 4:3 (October 1949): 596–604.

Johansen, Bruce E. *Forgotten Founders: Benjamin Franklin, the Iroquois, and the Rationale for the American Revolution.* Ipswich, MA: Gambit, 1982.

Lafitau, Rev. Joseph F. *Moeurs des sauvages amériquains, comparées aux moeurs première temps.* Vol. 1. Paris: Saugrain l'aîné, 1724.

Mann, Barbara, and Jerry Fields. "Sign in the Sky: Dating the League of Haudenosaunee." *American Indian Culture and Research Journal* 21:2
(1997): 105–163.

Morgan, Lewis Henry. *Houses and House-Life of the American Aborigines.* Chicago: University of Chicago Press, 1965.

Parker, Arthur C. *The Constitution of the Five Nations, or, The Iroquois Book
of the Great Law.* New York State Museum Bulletin no. 184. Albany:
University of the State of New York, 1916.

———. *Parker on the Iroquois.* Ed. William N. Fenton. Syracuse: NY: Syracuse
University Press, 1968.

Richter, Daniel K., and James Merrell, eds. *Beyond the Covenant Chain.* Syracuse, NY: Syracuse University Press, 1987.

Seaver, James. *A Narrative of the Life of Mrs. Mary Jemison* [1823]. Syracuse,
NY: Syracuse University Press, 1990.

Wallace, Anthony F. C. *The Death and Rebirth of the Seneca.* New York: Vintage, 1972.

Wallace, Paul A. W. *The White Roots of Peace.* Philadelphia: University of
Pennsylvania Press, 1946.

Woodbury, Hanni, ed. and trans. *Concerning the League: The Iroquois League
Tradition as Dictated in Onondaga by John Arthur Gibson.* Syracuse, NY:
Syracuse University Press, 1992.

J

JACKSON, ANDREW (1767–1845)

Andrew Jackson's name scorched the memories of Native American peoples for decades, first as an Indian fighter, then as president and advocate of removal, the policy that led to the many **Trails of Tears** in the 1830s. It was in the context of Jackson's policies that U.S. Supreme Court Chief Justice **John Marshall** honed the decisions that became, in many respects, the cornerstones of modern American Indian law (*see* **Marshall Trilogy**).

As a general in the U.S. Army, Jackson blazed a trail of fire throughout the South, refusing to retreat when his superiors ordered him to relent. In a battlefield confrontation with William Weatherford's **Creeks**, Jackson imprisoned assistants who advised retreat. In December 1813, Weatherford narrowly escaped capture. On March 27, 1814, Jackson, with 2,000 men, attacked Weatherford's force of 900, which was holed up in a stronghold at Horseshoe Bend in an area secured by river on three sides and a high log rampart on the fourth. Jackson sent men to seize a fleet of canoes that Weatherford had been keeping for escape, and then he set his men on the Creek encampment by announcing that "any officer or soldier who flies before the enemy without being compelled to do so by superior force . . . shall suffer death."

During July 1814, General Jackson returned to Horseshoe Bend for what was officially called a treaty conference with the defeated Creeks. The location was symbolic; Jackson relished rubbing in defeat on his enemies. The general, who never made a point of studying the cultures

of the Indians he subjugated, probably did not know that he was com-
pounding the Creeks' humiliation by holding the "treaty" on ground
they regarded as sacred. This meeting was not a treaty. It contained none
of the diplomatic equity that characterized eighteenth-century frontier
diplomacy. The Creeks were summoned to this parley on pain of death
by Jackson, who demanded twenty-three million acres—60 percent of
the area that would later become Alabama, as well as nearly a quarter
of Georgia. This was half the land under Creek control. When the Creek
chiefs asked for time to seek concessions and to think the matter over,
Jackson demanded an answer and hinted strongly that a negative reaction would be construed as a hostile act against the U.S. Army. As he
refused all concessions, Jackson wrote to his wife describing the destitution of the Creeks: "Could you only see the misery and the wretch-
edness of those creatures, perishing from want of food and picking up
the grains of corn scattered from the mouths of horses" (Tebbel and
Jennison 1960: 181).

Having subdued the Creeks, General Jackson next received orders to
quell what the War Department politely called "troubles" in Georgia,
principally among the Seminoles. By 1818, Jackson's troops were chas-
ing them into Florida, which was still under Spanish jurisdiction (the
area would be ceded to the United States in 1821). Having seized several
Spanish forts along the way, Jackson then withdrew and endured a debate over his extranational expedition in Congress. Jackson also reaped
popular acclaim from expansion-minded Americans and built his am-
bitions for the presidency.

The Seminoles, many of whom were descended from Creeks, had
elected to ally themselves with the Spanish rather than the United
States, an act of virtual treason to General Jackson. In addition, the Seminoles were giving shelter to runaway slaves. An active revolt was beginning to form among slaves themselves, one in which the Creeks
became actively involved, much to the chagrin of slave owners. The
pretext of Jackson's raid was recovery of "stolen property." After Florida was purchased from Spain by the United States, slave-hunting vigilantes invaded the area en masse, killing Seminoles as well as blacks.
Moving deep into the swamps of southern Florida (an area that, ironically, was being used as a removal destination for other groups of Native
Americans), the Seminoles fought 1,500 U.S. Army troops to a bloody
stalemate during seven years of warfare. They were never defeated and
never moved from their new homeland.

With nearly a million U.S. citizens in the Mississippi Valley by 1830,
the area was acquiring political leverage, which expressed itself with
the election of Andrew Jackson to the presidency. Eli Whitney's invention of the cotton gin in 1793 had opened the technological door to a
whole new age of agriculture on lands occupied by the Five Civilized

Tribes and other native peoples. President Jackson derived much of his political popularity from a wave of economic development across the South built on the economy of slavery, which demanded removal of the native peoples. Removal also was undertaken in part to sever a growing alliance between blacks and Indians that some whites feared might threaten them. Rather than the cotton belt, the alliance played out in the Everglades to which Jackson had chased the Seminoles when he was in the U.S. Army. Osceola, the famous Seminole leader, was of mixed African and Native American blood.

Before 1800, Euro-American settlement in the South had been limited mainly to the pine barrens of coastal Georgia, on land that was practically useless for farming before the advent of modern commercial fertilizers. The white settlers, seeing the value of the developing cotton culture, cast a covetous eye on the fertile inland valleys that were occupied by the Five Civilized Tribes, who had farmed them for hundreds of years. As the wave of land speculators and settlers moved in to evict them, the Creeks, **Cherokees, Choctaws, Chickasaws**, and others were building farms and towns in the European manner. The "civilized tribes" were well on their way to becoming some of the most prosperous farmers in the South.

Before their removal by force from their homelands, the Cherokees developed prosperous villages, a system of government modeled on that of the United States, a written language, and a newspaper. Sequoyah, who invented the Cherokee syllabary in 1821 after twelve years of work, was a warrior who had been crippled in a hunting accident.

After Spain ceded Florida to the United States, however, frontier general Andrew Jackson and other U.S. officials lost any remaining motive for treating the Indians as allies. From then on, they were defined as subjects, to be moved out as settlers rushed into the Southeast. Jackson's policy—"move the Indians out"—became the national standard after his election as president in 1828. Alabama had already been created in 1819 from Creek and Cherokee territory; Mississippi was created in 1817 from Choctaw and Chickasaw country. These two states, along with Georgia, passed laws outlawing Native American governments and making Indians subject to state jurisdiction, after which open season was declared on remaining native lands and estates. All these actions were in violation of treaties earlier negotiated with the federal government. President Jackson told the Indians that he was unable to stand by the treaties, very likely due to the pressures of states' rights, an emerging issue in the decades before the Civil War. Instead, Jackson proposed that the Indians be moved westward. At first, the moving of whole tribes was proposed as a voluntary act. In the meantime, land speculators and squatters closed a deadly vise on lands that had been home to the newly "civilized" tribes for thousands of years.

Whether in purposeful contravention of the treaties, or because he thought he had the right to personally annul them, Jackson within a decade cooperated with the land-industry business to move tens of thousands of native people from their homelands. Jackson, who as a general told his troops to root out Indians from their "dens" and kill Indian women and their "whelps," struck a slightly more erudite tone as president in his second annual message to Congress. He reflected on the fact that some white Americans were growing "melancholy" over the Indians being driven to their "tomb." These critics must understand, Jackson said, that "true philanthropy reconciles the mind to these vicissitudes as it does to the extinction of one generation to make way for another" (Stannard 1992: 240).

Jackson thought that Indian treaties were anachronisms. "An absurdity," he called them, "not to be reconciled with the principles of our government." He elaborated, before his election to the presidency, in a letter to President James Monroe (another advocate of Indian removal) in 1817:

The Indians are the subjects of the United States, inhabiting its territory and acknowledging its sovereignty. Then is it not absurd for the sovereign to negotiate by treaty with the subject? I have always thought, that Congress had as much right to regulate by acts of legislation, all Indian concerns as they had of territories, [and] are citizens of the United States and entitled to all the rights thereof, the Indians are subjects and entitled to their protection and fostering care. (McNickle 1975: 193)

The confusions of convoluted grammar aside, it is not easy to decipher what General Jackson was saying. Was he declaring the Indians to be citizens? Legally, that was not the case until a century later. Was he personally cancelling the treaties, which were signed by parties who had regarded the other as diplomatic peers barely two generations earlier? Whatever the nature of his rhetoric, the ensuing decades made clear, especially for the native peoples of the South, just what Jackson meant by "protection and fostering care."

FURTHER READING

McNickle, D'Arcy. *They Came Here First: The Epic of the American Indian*. New York: Harper & Row Perennial Library, 1975.

Stannard, David. *American Holocaust: Columbus and the Conquest of the New World*. New York: Oxford University Press, 1992.

Tebbel, John, and Keith Jennison.*The American Indian Wars*. New York: Bonanza Books, 1960.

Weeks, Philip. *Farewell, My Nation: The American Indian and the United States, 1820–1890*. Arlington Heights, IL: Harlan Davidson, 1990.

Wright, J. Leitch. *The Only Land They Knew: The Tragic Story of the American Indians in the Old South*. New York: Free Press, 1981.

Wright, Ronald. *Stolen Continents: The Americas through Indian Eyes Since 1492*. Boston: Houghton Mifflin, 1992.

JEFFERSON, THOMAS (1743–1826)

As the primary author of the **Declaration of Independence** and **Bill of Rights**, Thomas Jefferson often wove his perceptions of Native American polities into his conceptions of life, liberty, and happiness. Conversely, Jefferson described the class structure of Europe as "hammer and anvil," horses and riders, and "wolves over sheep." As a student of government, Jefferson found little ground less fertile than the Europe of his day. The political landscape of England was, to Jefferson, full of things to change, not emulate. Writing to John Adams, Jefferson said that force or corruption had been "the principle of every modern government, unless the Dutch perhaps be excepted." He continued:

I am sure you join me in the detestation of the corruption of the English government that no man on earth is more incapable than yourself of seeing that copied among us, willingly. I have been among those who have feared the design to introduce it here, and that has been a strong reason with me for wishing there was an ocean of fire between that island and us. (Malone 1962: 265–266)

Jefferson repeated the same sentiment to the Earl of Buchan: "Bless the almighty being who, in gathering together the waters of the heavens, divided the dry land of your hemisphere from the dry land of ours" (Commager 1975: 119). Americans had not only encountered a new vision of society in their experience with American Indians, but they also developed new concepts about landownership that were quite different from those of their European ancestors.

As they decried contemporary Europe, architects of the new nation such as **Benjamin Franklin**, Jefferson, and Thomas Paine described American Indian societies in ways strikingly similar to their visions of the state they hoped to erect, modified to suit a people of Old World ancestry. In many ways, these revolutionary Americans were taking up the argument of American freedom where **Roger Williams** left off. All were pragmatic enough to understand that a utopian vision of a society based on natural rights could not be instantly grafted onto thirteen recent British colonies. Writing to James Madison on January 30, 1787, from Paris, Jefferson examined three forms of societies:

1. Without government, as among our Indians. 2. Under governments wherein the will of every one has a just influence, as is the case in England in a slight degree, and in our states in great one. 3. Under governments of force, as is the case in all other monarchies and in most of the other republics. (Boyd 1950–1974: 92–93)

"It is a problem, not clear in my mind, that the 1st condition [the Indian way] is not the best," Jefferson wrote. "But I believe it to be inconsistent with any great degree of population" (Boyd 92–93). At the same time, most "Americans" (the word still sounded a little odd applied to people with European ancestors, rather than Indians) avidly sought relief not only from a raft of British taxes, but also from the entire European way of ordering society and government. This was to be Jefferson's "new chapter" in the history of humankind.

All during his life, Jefferson's political activities often delayed, but never defused, his interest in native societies. Entering Monticello, visitors in Jefferson's time were greeted in the Great Hall (or entryway) by walls laden with Native American artifacts. Jefferson was especially interested in native languages. For more than twenty years after he first discussed Indians' languages in *Notes on the State of Virginia* (1782), Jefferson collected Indian vocabularies, doing work similar to that of Roger Williams.

By 1800, Jefferson was preparing to publish what would have been the most extensive vocabulary of Indian languages in his time. It also was the year Jefferson was elected president, so his work was delayed until he left office in 1809. Jefferson packed his research papers at the presidential residence and ordered them sent to Monticello. Contained in the cargo were Jefferson's own fifty vocabularies, as well as several compiled by Lewis and Clark. Boatmen piloting Jefferson's belongings across the Potomac River ripped them open and, disappointed that they could find nothing salable, dumped the priceless papers into the river.

Jefferson's Declaration of Independence placed its case not before the Christian God, but before "Nature's God" and "the Supreme Judge of the World." Like others of the revolutionary generation, Jefferson usually called the deity just about anything except "God," including "the Great Spirit" and even "the Great Legislator." Jefferson's naturalistic conception of the deity provided him with a sense of universal morality very much like that of Roger Williams. Indeed, it took a sense of universal morality to believe that "all men are created equal." In theory, at least, this belief cut across racial and sexual lines, and no doubt Jefferson would have approved of efforts in centuries after his to address the practical contradictions such theory presented in his own time. Jefferson himself owned slaves. In Jefferson's time, only the most radical of visionaries (Paine among them) advocated emancipation of women.

Jefferson wrote *Notes on the State of Virginia* in part to refute the assertions of France's Comte de Buffon and others that the very soil, water, and air of the New World caused plants and animals (including human beings) to grow less rapidly and enjoy less sexual ardor than their Old World counterparts. The ongoing debate over the innate intelligence of American Indians also was factored into this debate, with Buffon and others asserting inferiority. Jefferson took the lead in countering the degeneracy theorists, maintaining that native peoples of

America enjoyed mental abilities equal to Europeans. In *Notes on Virginia*, Jefferson used the eloquent speech of Logan (delivered after whites had massacred his family) as evidence that American Indians were not short on intelligence and compassion. Portions of this speech were introduced to millions of elementary-school pupils during the nineteenth century in *McGuffey's Readers*.

America's revolutionaries never missed a shot at turning such theories on their heads. While serving as ambassador to France, Jefferson was fond of relating the story of a dinner attended by Franklin, a few other Americans, and French degeneracy-theory advocates while Franklin was representing the new nation in France. Franklin listened to Abbé Raynal, a well-known proponent of American degeneracy, describe how even Europeans would be stunted by exposure to the New World. Franklin listened quietly, then simply asked the French to test their theory "by the fact before us. Let both parties rise," Franklin challenged, "and we shall see on which side nature has degenerated." The table became a metaphorical Atlantic Ocean. The Americans, on their feet, towered over the French. "[The] Abbé, himself particularly, was a mere shrimp," Jefferson smirked.

Writing to Edward Carrington in 1787, Jefferson linked freedom of expression with public opinion as well as happiness, citing American Indian societies as an example:

The basis of our government being the opinion of the people, our very first object should be to keep that right; and were it left to me to decide whether we should have a government without newspapers or newspapers without a government, I should not hesitate for a moment to prefer the latter. . . . I am convinced that those societies [as the Indians] which live without government enjoy in their general mass an infinitely greater degree of happiness than those who live under European governments. (Boyd 49)

"Without government" could not have meant without social order to Jefferson. He, Franklin, and Paine all knew native societies too well to argue that native Americans functioned totally without social cohesion, in the classic Noble Savage image as autonomous wild men of the woods. All three had experience with native leaders as treaty negotiators, a peer relationship. Throughout the American Revolution, and into the early years of the United States, major native nations that bordered the colonies (later the United States) were a major focus of the nation's statecraft. It was clear that the **Iroquois**, for example, did not organize a **confederacy** with alliances spreading over much of eastern North America "without government." They did it, however, with a non-European conception of government, one of which Jefferson, Paine, and Franklin were appreciative students who sought to factor **natural law** into their designs for the United States during the revolutionary era.

Jefferson provided this description of Indian governance, which in some respects resembled the one the United States was erecting in his time, the pattern of states within a state that the founders called federalism:

The matters which merely regard a town or family are settled by the chief and principal men of the town; those which regard a tribe . . . are regulated at a meeting or a council of the chiefs from several towns; and those which regard the whole nation . . . are deliberated on and determined at a national council. (Ford 1892–99: 198–199n.)

By using "men," Jefferson glossed over the fact that women also played an important role in many of the Indian nations that bordered the new nation. In analyzing the nature of Native American polities, Jefferson rather accurately described the deliberations of native national councils that could have been drawn from many of the New England tribes, the Iroquois, Hurons, **Cherokees**, or **Choctaws**. He probably was making a generalized statement about most of the Indian nations he knew. Each Indian nation had its meetinghouse for government business, where

[in] council, it is common for the chiefs of the several tribes to consult thereupon with their counsellors, and when they have agreed, to deliver the opinion of the tribe at the national council; and, as their government seems to rest wholly on persuasion, they endeavor, by mutual concessions, to obtain unanimity. (Ford 198–199n.)

Jefferson denied reports that Indian sachemships were inherited, like European royal titles: "The sachem or chief of the tribe seems to be by election." Jefferson tended to ignore subtleties that distinguished the passage of power in native societies by popular election and inheritance. The Iroquois, for example, elected sachems from within bounds of families as defined by traditional titles that were inherited by the clan or extended family, not the individual.

FURTHER READING

Boyd, Julian P. *The Papers of Thomas Jefferson.* Vol. 11. Princeton, NJ: Princeton University Press, 1950–1974.

Commager, Henry Steele. *Jefferson, Nationalism, and the Enlightenment.* New York: George Braziller, 1975.

Ford, Paul L. *The Writings of Thomas Jefferson.* Vol. 3. New York: G. P. Putnam's Sons, 1892–1899.

Grinde, Donald A., Jr., and Bruce E. Johansen. *Exemplar of Liberty: Native America and the Evolution of Democracy.* Los Angeles: UCLA American Indian Studies Center, 1991.

Malone, Dumas. *Jefferson and His Time.* Boston: Little, Brown and Co., 1962.

JOHNSON AND GRAHAM'S LESSEE V. MCINTOSH 21 U.S. (8 Wheat.) 543 (1823)

The U.S. Supreme Court decision in *Johnson and Graham's Lessee v. McIntosh* for the first time formulated a national judicial viewpoint regarding Native Americans' legal relationship to the federal government. In this case, the Supreme Court ruled that Native Americans continued to possess a right of occupancy (sometimes called Indian title, aboriginal title, or original title) after contact with Europeans.

This case defined Indian title within the legal rubric of the **Doctrine of Discovery**, holding that a European discoverer might extinguish Indian title by purchase or conquest, and that once title had been gained, it was good against the claims of all other European nations, subject to Indian right of occupancy. At the same time, the Supreme Court held that this property right was well short of fee-simple ownership. The United States, for example, might extinguish this right without the just compensation mandated in the **Constitution** for the seizure of other lands.

Johnson v. McIntosh involved non-Indian plaintiffs who had derived the title of their land from direct grants from Native Americans obtained without the consent of the United States. The grants were made in 1773 and 1775, before the first **Trade and Intercourse Act** (1790) would have made them illegal. A competing land grant had been made to the defendant, McIntosh, by the United States. In *Johnson v. McIntosh*, Chief Justice **John Marshall** ruled as follows:

The person who purchases lands from the Indians, within their territory, incorporates himself with them, so far as respects the property purchased; holds their title under their protection, and subject to their laws. If they annul the grant, we know of no tribunal [in the United States] which can revise or set aside the proceeding.

The United States was held in this case to have no jurisdiction over Indian land simply because one of its citizens had an interest in it. This concept is basic to European concepts of international law. The United States, for example, does not acquire an interest in land that one of its citizens buys in Mexico.

Such a theory suited the legalities of the situation, but Marshall was still faced with the duality of "discovery" and conquest. According to Russel Barsh and James Henderson, "He fictionalized discovery into conquest. This, he freely confessed, [was] an unjust but expedient solution" (1980: 48). Marshall wrote:

However extravagant the pretensions of converting the discovery of an inhabited country into conquest may appear; if the principle has been asserted in the first instance, and afterwards sustained; if a country has been acquired and held under it; if the property of the great mass of the community originates in it, it becomes the law of the land, and cannot be questioned. . . . However this restriction may be opposed to natural right, and to the usages of civilized nations, yet, if it be indispensable to that system under which the country has been settled, and be adapted to the actual condition of the two people, it may, perhaps, be supported by reason, and certainly cannot be rejected by courts of justice.

Marshall held, in part, that

the rights of the original inhabitants were, in no instance, entirely disregarded; but were necessarily, to a considerable extent, impaired. They were admitted to be the rightful occupants of the soil, with legal, as well as just claim to retain possession of it and to use it according to their discretion; but their rights to complete sovereignty, as independent nations, were necessarily diminished, and their power to dispose of the soil at their own will to whomsoever they pleased was denied by the original fundamental principle, that discovery gave exclusive title to those who made it.

The Supreme Court's ruling in *Johnson v. McIntosh* shared some similarities with the Spanish doctrine enunciated in 1532 by **Francisco de Vitoria**, amended by Justice John Marshall in the first of three rulings (along with *Worcester v. Georgia* and *Cherokee Nation v. Georgia*) that would later be called the **Marshall Trilogy** because they shaped subsequent legal developments related to American Indians and their lands in the United States. In all three decisions, Marshall wrestled with the contradiction of one nation, the United States, usurping title of land long occupied by Indian nations. According to Marshall, Indian title was "impaired" (not extinguished) by European nations' assertions of discovery in America. According to **Vine Deloria, Jr.**, and Clifford Lytle, "While paying lip service to the European notion of discovery and continued Indian autonomy, Marshall reasoned that conquest gave the white settlers ownership and title to Indian lands." They continued:

Johnson v. McIntosh created a landlord-tenant relationship between the government and the Indian tribes. The federal government, as the ultimate landlord, not only possessed the power to terminate the "tenancy" of its Indian occupants but also could materially affect the lives of Indians through its control and regulation of land use. . . . This notion . . . constituted the basis on which the court in the Cherokee Nation cases developed its theory of guardianship over Indian affairs. (1983: 26–27)

FURTHER READING

Barsh, Russel Lawrence, and James Youngblood Henderson. *The Road: Indian Tribes and Political Liberty.* Berkeley: University of California Press, 1980.
Deloria, Vine, Jr., and Clifford Lytle. *American Indians, American Justice.* Austin: University of Texas Press, 1983.

JOHNSON-O'MALLEY ACT (1934) 25 U.S.C. §§ 452–457

The Johnson-O'Malley Act, as implementation legislation for the **Indian Reorganization Act**, encouraged Indian enrollment in state-controlled public schools by providing reimbursements for children residing on Indian lands that were exempt from state taxation. The act aided school districts whose tax bases were being eroded by the lack of ability to tax Indians.

JURISDICTION

Jurisdiction is the authority and ability of a governing body to promulgate and enforce measures with legal effect within a given territory. Questions of American Indian jurisdiction have been complicated by the fact that the federal, state, and Native American governments have been legally charged with different (and sometimes overlapping) responsibilities. The complexity of the law and the competitive nature of such disputes have made jurisdiction one of the most frequent causes for litigation in American Indian law.

Indian jurisdiction also is complicated by the fact that **Indian Country** is governed by more than one sovereign. While Native American governments possess attributes of **sovereignty** bestowing jurisdictional authority, the U.S. Congress, through its **plenary power**, reserves the right to change the division of jurisdiction in Indian Country between federal, Native American, and state governments.

Although Chief Justice **John Marshall** in *Worcester v. Georgia* (1832) wrote that state law has no power within Indian Country, Congress has attempted from time to time to restrict Native American governmental authority. Since the early years of the twentieth century, the U.S. Supreme Court has vested Congress with plenary power to determine Indian policy. Additionally, **Public Law 280**, for example, allowed the extension of state jurisdiction into large areas of Native American civil and criminal law, creating a jurisdictional maze in which the federal government was charged with prosecuting some crimes, while the state or Native American government prosecuted others. Legal treatment varies significantly based on whether a person is Indian or non-Indian and, in some cases, whether the person is a member of a particular Native American group.

In some cases, boundaries of non-Indian states and nations have been drawn without regard for the boundaries of Indian governments, creating monumental jurisdictional problems. One such example is the St. Regis (Akwesasne) Mohawk Reservation in upstate New York and Canada. Roughly half of this community of about 8,500 people lies in Canada, and half in the United States. The Canadian side's police force cannot reach portions of the territory it patrols without passing over the border. In addition, the Canadian side of Akwesasne is split between English-speaking Ontario and French-speaking Quebec.

FURTHER READING

Canby, William C., Jr. *American Indian Law in a Nutshell*. St. Paul, MN: West Publishing, 1981.
Johansen, Bruce E. *Life and Death in Mohawk Country*. Golden, CO: North American Press/Fulcrum, 1993.

K

KERR-MCGEE CORP. V. NAVAJO TRIBE OF INDIANS 471 U.S. 195 (1985)

The U.S. Supreme Court found in *Kerr-McGee Corp. v. Navajo Tribe of Indians* that the Navajo Nation had an inherent sovereign power to tax Indians and non-Indians doing business there. This case was notable because the Navajos have no **Indian Reorganization Act** government; an earlier ruling had held that the rights of Native American governments to levy taxes on severance of minerals applied only to those with governments formed under the Indian Reorganization Act.

L

LAND TENURE, NATIVE AMERICAN CONCEPTIONS OF

As European-American societies replaced those of Native Americans across North America, one conception of land tenure was replaced by another. The Sioux author Luther Standing Bear watched the last years of settlement on the Plains as he contrasted the Euro-American and Native American conceptions of the natural world of North America:

We did not think of the great open plains, the beautiful rolling hills, and winding streams with tangled brush, as "wild." Only to the white man was nature "a wilderness" and only to him was the land "infested" with "wild" animals and "savage" people. To us it was tame. Earth was bountiful, and we are surrounded with the blessings of the Great Mystery. (1978: 98)

This ethos was replaced by an attitude characterized by western historian Frederick Jackson Turner late in the nineteenth century as a commitment

to take possession without being possessed; to take secure hold on the lands beyond, and yet hold them at a rigidly maintained spiritual distance. It was never to merge, to mingle, to marry. To do so was to become an apostate from Christian history and to be kept in an eternal wilderness.

Tracing the roots of differences in Native American and European worldviews through American history does not take us far enough back in time, however. The real roots of this difference go back to the Bible, with its command to "subdue" the earth, and into the very bases of perception utilized by Native American and European cultures. Just as a command to subdue the earth implies separation between humankind and nature, straight-line thinking implies the "progress" and "development" necessary to the earth's subjugation. This is a foreign concept to the cyclical reality of many Native American cultures. The Mayan calendar provides an instructive example of this difference. While Mayan astronomers calculated a calendar that is slightly more precise than the one inherited from the Romans, we do not use it today because it was based on measuring time as a factor of two intersecting cycles, not as a straight-line passage from the immeasurable past into the indefinite future.

The landscape of the mind affects the use of land. The changes in the American landscape were described by the noted western historian Frank Waters, whose fourscore and ten years allowed him to witness many of the changes in the western United States:

That is exactly what the white conquerors did as they proceeded westward. They levelled whole forests under the axe, plowed under the grassland, dammed and drained the rivers, gutted the mountains for gold and silver, and divided and sold the land itself. Accompanying all this destruction was the extermination of birds and beasts, not alone for profit or sport, but to indulge . . . a wanton lust for killing. (1993:3)

The European immigrants' attitudes toward the American land and its peoples often contained a duality of love and hate, of a desire to preserve and to destroy. Hernán Cortés rhapsodized about the grandeur of Tenochtitlan before his soldiers sacked it in gold hunger. This ideological duality began, on the Atlantic coast, with the Puritans. To some of the immigrants, this was "New England," to be subjugated to the yoke of Christianity; to others, it was New Canaan, an escape into the wilderness from English orthodoxy.

In 1629, John Winthrop applied to America the biblical injunction to "multiply and subdue the earth" (Merchant 1993: 71–72). When Winthrop invoked the biblical injunction to subdue the earth, he wrote that the Bible commanded occupancy of a continent that had lain "empty and unimproved" (Merchant 71–72). The selectivity of Winthrop's perceptions is astounding, since he must have known that his colony had survived in large part because Squanto and other Native American peoples had taught the immigrants how to cultivate the environment by planting corn and other crops indigenous to America. Yet the rationale for conquest often argued that the immigrants were taking over land that had not been used—land that, by European standards, had lain uncultivated, unmined, unexploited, "undeveloped."

Other Europeans becoming Americans in "New England" sought to accommodate, to adapt, and to appreciate the land in terms expressed by its native inhabitants. **Roger Williams**'s Providence Plantations (later the state of Rhode Island) was founded with active Native American aid, as Williams conceived of political liberty in Native American terms. This duality in the American mind can sometimes be found in one person. In the eighteenth century, **Benjamin Franklin** evoked native examples of governance as he, along with many of his prominent fellows, speculated in native land.

The impulse to "develop" the "wilderness" propels "civilization," accompanied by the extraction of resources, which creates wealth in a market economy in which everything is defined as a commodity, and every commodity has a price. The beaver survived in large numbers in eastern North America until they were defined as a commodity by both Euro-American merchants and Native American hunters. The beaver was one example of a natural resource that became a commodity, one aspect of many that laid the financial basis for an explosion of colonization westward, over the Appalachians, after 1800. Alfred Crosby wrote in *The Columbian Exchange* (1972) that European-American expansion was much more than the movement of people; it also was the movement of domesticated animals, imported plants (including weeds), and diseases.

FURTHER READING

Cronon, William. *Changes in the Land: Indians, Colonists, and the Ecology of New England*. New York: Hill & Wang, 1983.
Merchant, Carolyn, ed. *Major Problems in American Environmental History*. Lexington, MA: D.C. Heath, 1993.
Standing Bear, Luther. *Land of the Spotted Eagle*. Lincoln: University of Nebraska Press, 1978.
Waters, Frank. *Brave Are My People: Indian Heroes Not Forgotten*. Santa Fe, NM: Clear Light, 1993.

LAWYER (HALLALHOTSOOT) (Nez Perce/Flathead) (c. 1795–1876)

The Nez Perce whom settlers called Lawyer negotiated treaties in the name of the Nez Perce that were repudiated by Chief Joseph before his Long March in 1877. Chief Joseph gave Lawyer that name because (as Joseph noted in a speech to Congress in 1879) "he talked too much" and gave away land that did not belong to him.

Lawyer was a son of Twisted Hair, a Nez Perce chief who had greeted Lewis and Clark, and his Flathead wife. Lawyer often worked as a guide and interpreter for missionaries and traders and became well known for his oratorical skill in both the English and Nez Perce languages.

Lawyer was designated as a representative of all the Nez Perce by Washington territorial governor **Isaac Stevens** at a treaty council in 1855. The outcome of that council was bitterly protested by Old Joseph,

his son Chief Joseph, and other nontreaty Nez Perces. During the ensuing Yakima War of 1855–1856, Lawyer's band protected Stevens from
attack by warriors seeking revenge for the death of Peopeomoxmox. In
1863, Lawyer signed another treaty and ceded even more land that Old
Joseph insisted was not his to give. By 1868, Lawyer himself was upset
at the number of treaties that had been broken, and he traveled to Washington, D.C., to protest. He died in 1876, one year before the Long March
of the nontreaty Nez Perces under Chief Joseph, Younger.

LONE WOLF V. HITCHCOCK 187 U.S. 553 (1903)

In *Lone Wolf v. Hitchcock*, the U.S. Supreme Court first enunciated a
federal **trust** responsibility for Indian affairs. This case is the source of
assertions that Congress enjoys a **plenary power** over Indian legislation.
In this opinion, the Supreme Court also asserted that Congress could
unilaterally abrogate treaties with subsequent legislation. The Court
held that Congress has "paramount power over the property of the Indians by reason of its exercise of guardianship over their interests, and
that such authority might be implied, even though opposed to the strict
letter of a treaty with the Indians."

According to **Vine Deloria, Jr.**, and Clifford Lytle in *American Indians, American Justice* (1983), *Lone Wolf v. Hitchcock* "remains the classic judicial statement articulating the doctrine of the plenary powers of
Congress over Indian affairs" (43). The Court held as follows:

The power exists to abrogate the provisions of an Indian treaty, though
presumably such power will be exercised only when circumstances arise that
would not only justify the government in disregarding the stipulations of the
treaty, but may demand, in the interest of the country and the Indians
themselves, that it should do so. When, therefore, treaties are entered into
between the United States and a tribe of Indians, it was never doubted that the
power to abrogate existed in Congress, and that in a contingency such power
might be availed of from such considerations of governmental policy,
particularly if consistent with perfect, good faith towards the Indians.

Lone Wolf v. Hitchcock arose after the federal government in 1892
attempted to allot 2.5 million acres of land belonging to the Kiowa,
Comanche, and other native nations, but was unable to obtain the consent of three-quarters of the adult males as required in the **Treaty of
Medicine Lodge** signed in 1867. Disregarding this, the Senate passed an
act that assumed the native nations' consent.

The struggle of native nations in the southern plains to maintain their
land base continued into the 1880s, when Lone Wolf and other leaders
bitterly fought allotment of their lands. Lone Wolf, a Kiowa chief, traveled to Washington, D.C., to lobby against allotment, but he arrived only
days after Congress had passed the General **Allotment Act** (1887). After

that, Lone Wolf sued the secretary of the interior, Ethan A. Hitchcock, to prevent implementation of allotment. Lone Wolf argued that the congressional act had violated both the Medicine Lodge Treaty and the **Fifth Amendment** to the U.S. **Constitution**, which guarantees due process of law, including compensation, when land is taken by the government.

The Supreme Court denied Lone Wolf's petition. Speaking for the Court, Justice Edward D. White ruled that in a pressing national emergency (as defined by Congress, not the Indians), the national legislature could confiscate Indian lands unilaterally. White seemed to indicate that the forced sale of the land was merely a change in form of Native American investment, not a violation of the treaty. The Court held the power of Congress over Indian affairs to be absolute, even to the point of abrogating treaties unilaterally, a practice that could be taken as breach of contract (and sometimes even as an act of war) in international law. In the Court's opinion, the breach was justified because of the Indians' status as "wards" of the federal government. Such governmental authority was said by the Court to be limited only by "considerations of justice as would control a Christian people in their treatment of an ignorant and dependent race." Legal scholar Ann Laquer Estin commented that the effect of *Lone Wolf. v. Hitchcock* and related decisions

was to reinterpret tribal property rights and political authority as a commodity granted the tribes by the federal government. This interpretation was a complete shift from the early decisions of the Supreme Court under John Marshall, which recognized inherent sovereignty in the Indian tribes and viewed treaties as narrow delegations from the tribe to the United States of specific and limited powers. (1984:237)

FURTHER READING

Barsh, Russel, and James Henderson. *The Road: Indian Tribes and Political Liberty.* Berkeley: University of California Press, 1980.

Canby, William C., Jr. *American Indian Law in a Nutshell.* St. Paul, MN: West Publishing, 1981.

Clark, Blue. *Lone Wolf v. Hitchcock: Treaty Rights and Indian Law at the End of the Nineteenth Century.* Lincoln: University of Nebraska Press, 1994.

Deloria, Vine, Jr., and Clifford M. Lytle. *American Indians, American Justice.* Austin: University of Texas Press, 1983.

Estin, Ann Laquer. *"Lone Wolf v. Hitchcock:* The Long Shadow." in *The Aggressions of Civilization: Federal Indian Policy since the 1880s,* ed. Sandra L. Cadwallader and Vine Deloria, Jr. Philadelphia: Temple University Press, 1984.

M

MAINE INDIAN CLAIMS SETTLEMENT ACT (1980) P.L. 96-420; 25 U.S.C. § 1721; 94 Stat. 1785

In an action taken under the federal **Trade and Intercourse Acts**, Maine Indians were provided with funds to purchase lands as their aboriginal title to roughly 60 percent of Maine was extinguished. The Maine case was one of several in which Native American nations sought and often received compensation in the late twentieth century based on sale of lands to states or individuals without the federal approval required by the Trade and Intercourse Acts, first passed in 1790, to keep state and private interests from disassembling Native American communal lands on a piecemeal basis.

The First Circuit Court of Appeals held in favor of Native American nations in Maine during 1975, setting in motion a negotiated settlement. Under the Maine Indian Claims Settlement Act, passed by Congress five years later, the Passamaquoddy and Penobscot, who had a claim to 12 million acres, much of Maine, under the 1790 Trade and Intercourse Act, received 300,000 acres (worth about $54 million at the time), as well as a $27-million trust fund to be used for economic development. This settlement was reached despite the fact that the two native nations had never been federally recognized.

FURTHER READING

Brodeur, Paul. "Annals of Law: Restitution." *New Yorker*, October 17, 1982, 76–155.

McLaughlin, Robert. "Giving It All Back to the Indians." *Atlantic Monthly* 239 (February 1977): 70–85.
"Symposium on Indian Law: The Eastern Land Claims." *Maine Law Review* 31: 1 (November 1979).

MAJOR CRIMES ACT (1885) 23 Stat. 362–385; 18 U.S.C. § 1153

After the U.S. Supreme Court in *Ex Parte Crow Dog* held that a Native American nation (in this case, the Sioux) retained jurisdiction over an Indian (Crow Dog) who was accused of killing another Indian (Spotted Tail), the U.S. Congress passed the Major Crimes Act of 1885, the first major federal law by which the federal government asserted jurisdiction over major crimes in **Indian Country**.

The Major Crimes Act, as later amended, gave the federal government jurisdiction over fourteen serious crimes, including murder, manslaughter, rape, incest, assault with intent to kill, arson, burglary, robbery, and kidnapping. The Supreme Court has generally held that while Native American governments may exercise limited jurisdiction over Indians accused of crimes against other Indians, they have almost no jurisdiction over non-Indians accused of the same crimes. See *Oliphant v. Suquamish* (1978).

The legislation that became known as the Major Crimes Act was actually attached as a rider to an appropriations bill with no hearings or other expression of opinion by the Indians who were affected. The number of crimes covered was later increased by Congress to fourteen, including carnal knowledge of "any female, not his wife, who has not attained the age of sixteen years," assault with intent to commit rape, assault with a dangerous weapon, assault resulting in serious bodily injury, and larceny.

The constitutionality of the Major Crimes Act was challenged in **United States v. Kagama** (1886), in which one Indian was accused of killing another on California's Hoopa Valley Reservation. The U.S. Supreme Court found that Congress had authority to pass the Major Crimes Act under the authority of earlier opinions by Justice **John Marshall** that held Indians to be wards under the guardianship of the United States. Late in the twentieth century, Native American courts were generally limited to trying cases with penalties of up to a $500 fine and/or six months in jail.

MANDAN POLITICAL AND LEGAL SYSTEMS

Political organization among the Mandans (who occupied present-day North and South Dakota) was restricted to the village level, with no central governance. The Mandans' village governance system included elements of representative democracy, but also recognized some degree of rank and economic status, which was often determined by a family's ownership of sacred medicine bundles that were vital to many Native American rituals. The owners of such bundles often built their lodges closest to the ceremonial center of a given village. Most Mandan villages resembled each other closely, with tightly packed family lodges clustered around the central plaza, which was usually at least one hundred feet across. Men selected from lodges that held sacred bundles comprised a council. These men selected from their number two men, one of whom displayed special talents at organizing war parties. The other leading chief's talent lay in his peaceful disposition and his ability to broker disputes, dispense wisdom, stage feasts and rituals, and greet diplomatic envoys from other places.

The two leading village chiefs wore elaborate costumes (including headdresses of buffalo horns) at official occasions, but their power was limited. A war chief who did not enjoy trust in the village might simply be deposed and replaced by another man who did. The mark of a successful peace chief was his ability to factor all points of view into consensus that would at least moderately satisfy everyone. Accumulation of power was frowned on in Mandan society, as in many others where a **consensus** model was used to govern.

Although Mandans recognized rank and status in their village lives, a person of either sex could be a leader in one of several secular societies that attended various facets of village life. In practice, leadership also was dispersed by the existence of thirteen matrilineal clans that overlapped village boundaries. Each clan selected its leaders (whose role, like that of the village chiefs, was mainly advisory). Clans regulated marriages and owned farming lands, ritual bundles, and family lodgings. The clans maintained a social-service system that cared for the poor and elderly, as well as orphaned children. In addition to reconciling wealth with need, clans also avenged wrongful deaths. As among many other native peoples across the continent, Mandan clans cut across village boundaries and provided social cohesion between villages, even though the Mandans had no central council of the type utilized by the **Iroquois** and **Wyandots** (Hurons), among others.

FURTHER READING

Bowers, Alfred W. *Mandan Social and Ceremonial Organization.* Chicago: University of Chicago Press, 1950.

MARSHALL, JOHN (1755–1835)

John Marshall, as chief justice of the U.S. Supreme Court, was the author of several decisions that still define Native American rights in the United States, most notably ***Worcester v. Georgia***, which upheld limited sovereignty for the **Cherokee** Nation in 1832. President **Andrew Jackson**, surrendering to states' rights interests in the South, ignored the decision and proceeded with plans to remove the **Cherokees** to **Indian Territory** (later Oklahoma). Jackson's actions later resulted in the Cherokees' **Trail of Tears**, as well as many other forced relocations of Indians.

Marshall's opinions outlining Native Americans' status in the U.S. legal system occurred as he defined the Supreme Court's place within U.S. political society. When Marshall became chief justice during 1801, the Supreme Court was little more than a clause in the **Constitution**. For nearly thirty-five years as chief justice, Marshall played a major role in defining the Court as an institution.

While Marshall's opinions were ignored by President Jackson, they shaped the relationship of the United States to Native American nations within its borders to the end of the twentieth century. The 1934 **Indian Reorganization Act** and legislative efforts promoting **self-determination** after the 1960s were based in part on Marshall's opinion that the rights of "discovery" did not extinguish the original inhabitants' "legal as well as . . . just claim to retain possession [of their land] and to use it according to their own jurisdiction." Marshall defined Indian nations not as totally sovereign, nor as colonies, but as "domestic dependent nations."

Marshall had long-running political differences with President Jackson, and he agonized over the conflicts between states' rights and Native American sovereignty. In 1831, in *Cherokee Nation v. Georgia*, Marshall held that the Cherokees had no standing at court to appeal the state of Georgia's seizure of their lands. This situation troubled Marshall so deeply that he said at one point that he thought of resigning from the Supreme Court over it. A year later, in *Worcester v. Georgia*, Marshall held unconstitutional the imprisonment by Georgia of a missionary (Worcester) who had tried to advise the Cherokees on their rights. Historians disagree over whether President Jackson actually said, "John Marshall has made his decision, now let him enforce it." Whether Jackson expressed himself in these words may be a moot point; his implementation of removal flew in the face of the law as interpreted by Marshall in *Worcester v. Georgia*. Marshall wrote, in part:

The Constitution, by declaring treaties already made, as well as those to be made, to be the supreme law of the land, has adopted and sanctified the previous treaties with the Indian nations. . . . The words "treaty" and "nation" are words of our own language, selected in our diplomatic and legislative proceedings, by ourselves, having each a definite and well-understood meaning. We have applied them to Indians, as we have applied them to the other nations of the earth; they are applied to all in the same sense.

Chief Justice John Marshall's rulings occupy a special place in the development of legal rationales for the system of law that developed as

American Indians were being relieved of their lands and independent lifeways. His opinion that Indian nations comprised "domestic dependent nations" laid the foundations of **trust** responsibility and the **wardship** system, although these legal doctrines were not fully developed until well into the twentieth century. Justice Marshall may have intended neither "wardship" nor "trust" as legal doctrines. He was trying to salvage a degree of sovereignty for the Cherokees and other peoples who were about to be "removed" to Indian Territory (later Oklahoma) by President (and former Indian fighter) Andrew Jackson. Jackson's conception of law had much more to do with power relationships than with a sense of justice. When Jackson ignored Marshall's ruling, the chief justice was greatly aggrieved and thought of resigning from the Supreme Court. Jackson's repudiation of the Court was clearly an impeachable offense under the Constitution, but the issue at hand (states' rights, asserted over the Cherokees by Georgia) was too incendiary in the pre–Civil War South to permit a serious debate on the issue.

FURTHER READING

Cherokee Nation v. Georgia, 30 U.S. (5 Pet.) 1 (1831).
Johnson and Graham's Lessee v. McIntosh, 21 U.S. (8 Wheat.) 543 (1823).
McNickle, D'Arcy. *Native American Tribalism*. New York: Oxford University Press, 1973.
Smith, Jean Edward. *John Marshall: Definer of a Nation*. New York: Henry Holt, 1996.
Worcester v. Georgia, 31 U.S. (6 Pet.) 515, 560 (1832).

MARSHALL TRILOGY
In legal analysis, "Marshall Trilogy" is used to describe as a group Chief Justice **John Marshall**'s rulings between 1823 and 1832 in *Johnson v. McIntosh, Cherokee Nation v. Georgia*, and *Worcester v. Georgia*. In these three cases, Marshall developed a legal doctrine that defined the relationship of the United States, the individual states, and Indian bands and nations. In these opinions, according to legal scholar Charles F. Wilkinson, "Marshall conceived a model that can be described broadly as calling for largely autonomous tribal governments subject to an overriding federal authority but essentially free of state control" (1987: 24).

The Marshall Trilogy is so important in American Indian law that the key precepts of its three opinions have been interpreted by lawyers, judges, legal scholars, and government officials in many different ways. The Bureau of Indian Affairs, for example, used the phrases "dependent," "pupilage," and "ward" to construct a cradle-to-grave social- and political-control system in which Indians have been regarded legally as incompetents or children would be in other social and legal contexts.

Many of Marshall's actual definitions of these key words may have been lost in interpretation during subsequent decades. The concept of "dependency," for example, was explained by Henry Wheaton, a friend of Marshall and a long-time reporter of the Supreme Court, as relating to international law. According to Wheaton, Marshall did not imply Indian inferiority (or a need for social and political control) in his use of the phrase "domestic dependent nations." Instead, he meant to stress the semisovereign nature of Native American nations and the need to gain consent of both parties before fundamentally changing a treaty relationship.

FURTHER READING

Wheaton, Henry. *Elements of International Law.* 1st ed. Boston: Dana, 1866.
Wilkinson, Charles F. *American Indians, Time, and the Law: Native Societies in a Modern Constitutional Democracy.* New Haven, CT: Yale University Press, 1987.

MCCARRAN WATER RIGHTS SUIT ACT (1952) 43 U.S.C. § 666

Also known as the McCarran Amendment, the McCarran Water Rights Suit Act sought to curtail the Indian water rights adjudicated in the Winters Doctrine (*see Winters v. United States*). This law waived U.S. sovereign immunity in cases involving water rights and provided that all water users would be bound by state-court decisions. The tone of this legislation was in line with House Concurrent Resolution 108 on **termination**, passed a year later, which encouraged the dismantling of Indians' remaining lands in the United States.

MCCLANAHAN V. ARIZONA TAX COMMISSION 411 U.S. 164 (1973)

McClanahan, an Indian who performed personal services on the Navajo reservation, filed suit after Arizona tried to collect state income tax from his pay. The state argued that the tax did not interfere with the operation of Native American governments according to precedent set by the Supreme Court in *Williams v. Lee* (1959). The Supreme Court rejected Arizona's argument and its premise. The Court held that the test did not apply to assertion of state jurisdiction over Indians. A balance of state and Native American interests was only appropriate when non-Indians were involved, the court ruled. Extant federal law as well as the history of Indian **sovereignty** indicated to the Supreme Court that Arizona had no power to impose its tax on an individual Indian's income earned for work performed in the Navajo Nation.

MEECH LAKE ACCORD (CANADA)

Canadian natives threw a political monkey wrench into the workings of the Meech Lake Accord during 1990. The accord was meant to satisfy

Quebec's demands for autonomy within the Canadian federation. Konrad Sioui, head chief of the Assembly of First Nations, indicated that the 1990 Quebec police raid at Oka had been in direct retaliation for the fact that Elijah Harper, the only native member of Manitoba's legislature, had led an effort against ratification of the Meech Lake Accord by its deadline of June 23. Harper's vote started a chain of procedural circumstances that kept the accord from going into effect. Native Americans in Canada have long been at odds with Quebec's demands for sovereignty, claiming that Quebec denies Native American sovereignty like the rest of Canada treats Quebec.

If it had been ratified, the accord would have given Quebec a "special status" designation in the Canadian confederation, while, at the same time, refusing to acknowledge native peoples' original occupancy of Quebec and the rest of Canada. Harper, who was first elected to Manitoba's legislature in 1981 from the northern riding (district) of Rupertsland (which includes his home of Red Sucker Lake), obstructed the accord precisely because Canadian natives were angered by their omission in it. Sioui also said that the entire Canadian governmental system for negotiating land claims ought to be revamped.

The rising tide of Native American anger across Canada was evidence of a belief that Quebec should not become a nation until it recognizes that it is built on land stolen from the first nations and that its economy is based on resources also taken from the native people. Native Canadians also were demanding that Quebec, and other provinces, be prepared to rectify past injustices.

Eighty-five percent of Quebec never has been ceded by treaty. While leaders of the Quebec independence movement had at least paid lip service to the idea that any constitution for an independent Quebec should respect native land claims as an issue of minority-group justice, probably very few French Canadians were prepared to meet the natives' assertion that their claim to the province did not extend much beyond the Montreal and Quebec City urban areas.

FURTHER READING

Johansen, Bruce E. *Life and Death in Mohawk Country*. Golden, CO: North American Press/Fulcrum, 1993.

MENOMINEE POLITICAL AND LEGAL TRADITIONS

With a sense of improvisation that might stymie anyone intent on defining regularity in political science, a Menominee chief was succeeded by his son—unless another person could muster enough popular support to wrest the title from him. Sometimes, the succession was in the female line instead. The Menominees seemed to bend their system to provide the leadership that they wanted at any given time. If a kinsman of the deceased chief claimed the title by heredity and many people thought him unfit, they would choose their own chief by their own methods.

Once selected, the chief led by persuasion. This held for the grand chief (the leader of the central Menominee council) as well as for sub-chiefs who led various bands within the nation. In the late nineteenth century, there were eleven bands of Menominee, each carrying the name of its chief (Oshkosh was an example). The head chief also employed a person known for his powers as an orator to act as a spokesman or official herald. When the Menominees needed a diplomat, this person often was called on to represent them with other nations. The orator was not usually eligible for the office of head chief or war chief, the other leading political office among the Menominee. As with many Menominee political customs, this one was flexible. If a majority of the people wanted the orator to succeed the head chief or war chief, the apparently "illegal" transfer of power could occur.

FURTHER READING

Hoffman, Walter James. *The Menomini Indians*. 1896. New York: Johnson Reprint Corp., 1970.

MENOMINEE TRIBE V. UNITED STATES 391 U.S. 404 (1968)

In *Menominee v. United States*, the Supreme Court held that Menominee hunting and fishing rights survived the **termination** of the Menominees by Congress. The Court said that Congress had made no such statement in the Menominee Termination Act. Thus Wisconsin was not allowed to enforce its fishing and game laws on individual Menominees. In *Menominee*, the Court declined "to construe the Termination Act as a backhanded way of abrogating the hunting and fishing rights of these Indians. . . . We find it difficult to believe that Congress, without explicit statement, would subject the United States to a claim for compensation by destroying property rights conferred by treaty."

The Termination Act had sought to keep such a thing from happening with a clause holding that after a native government had been terminated, "The laws of the several States shall apply to the tribe and its members in the same manner as they apply to other citizens and persons within their jurisdiction." The Court, however, held that hunting and fishing rights were included in original treaties; "the intention to abrogate or modify a treaty is not to be lightly imputed to Congress." In other cases, the Court has held that Congress may abrogate Indian treaties unilaterally; this point is an area of major debate among scholars of American Indian law. One may compare this ruling, for example, to **Montana v. United States**, adjudicated by the U.S. Supreme Court in

1981, in which aboriginal Crow land was awarded to Montana without compensation. The Court held that the bed of the Bighorn River was owned by the state despite a treaty signed in 1868 that reserved the land for the Crows.

In 1973, Congress passed legislation restoring a federal relationship with the Menominees, making them the first Native American nation to be restored after termination. Reservation status was restored on the Menominees' 233,900-acre land base in northern Wisconsin about forty miles west of Green Bay. By the late 1980s, the Menominees had established extensive gaming operations that funded new health and welfare measures and drew many people back to the reservation. By 1992, 7,100 people were enrolled as Menominees, twice the number before termination. About half lived on the reservation.

MERIAM REPORT (1928)

Shortly after 1920, a wave of sympathy emerged in response to the cruelties imposed on Native Americans during the nadir of the reservation era. This wave of political opinion produced the Meriam Report (1928), which documented the horrid condition of human health and welfare under the Bureau of Indian Affairs' **wardship**.

The Meriam Report also brought the argument on allotment full circle: from alleged harbinger of a new American Indian future to the dismal, culturally destructive real-estate agency it had become. The report laid the intellectual and political basis for the revolution that **John Collier** wrought in Indian affairs during the early 1930s. Collier himself called the Meriam Report "the most important indictment of the Bureau [of Indian Affairs] since Helen Hunt Jackson's *A Century of Dishonor* [1881]." Ironically, that book had been used in its time to advance the cause of allotment that was so soundly repudiated by the Meriam Report.

By 1923, an organized committee of influential Indians and non-Indians, the **Committee of One Hundred**, was lobbying for more respectful and humane treatment of surviving American Indians. Collier was an early member, with William Jennings Bryan, Clark Wissler, General John J. Pershing, Bernard Baruch, William Allen White, and the Iroquois Arthur C. Parker. Parker was elected presiding officer at a convention in Washington, D.C., during December 1923. Under his aegis, in 1924, the group published its findings under the title *The Indian Problem*. This document formed the basis for the better-known Meriam Report four years later. The report was an exhaustive, 870-page narrative and statistical portrait of American Indian life at the time sometimes called "the era of the vanishing race." It covered health, education, economic conditions, legal aspects, and missionary activities, among other matters. The Meriam Report found generally that the government was failing miserably at its professed goal of "protecting" Indians, their land, and resources. Of the **Allotment Act** (1887), the report said:

When the government adopted the policy of individual ownership of the land on the reservations, the expectation was that the Indians would become farmers. . . . It almost seems as if the government assumed that some magic in individual ownership of property would in itself prove an educational civilizing factor, but unfortunately this policy has for the most part operated in the opposite direction. (Meriam 1928: 7)

The Meriam Report provided graphic evidence of just how badly the federal government's Indian "wards" were being treated. Infant mortality on Indian reservations, for example, was found to be nearly three times that of European-descended Americans generally. Large numbers of Indians were dying from tuberculosis, trachoma, measles, and other diseases that had been largely eradicated in mainstream society. In this sea of disease, health services on reservations were ill equipped and lacked sufficient trained staff. Diets heavy on cheap-commodity carbohydrates were producing malnutrition in people who often were otherwise overweight. The government provided eleven cents a day to feed students at its boarding schools and skimped on equipment and salaries for teachers. Schools were often unsanitary. Per capita income for native reservation residents was less than $200 a year, at a time when national average earnings were $1,350. All of this resulted in an average life span among Indians of forty-four years.

According to the Meriam Report, the essential "Indian problem" was poverty caused by the fact that the U.S. government had done little to replace traditional native economies with self-sustaining structures that could provide Indians a livelihood. The report found that forced assimilation did little to improve Indians' economic conditions; many of its recommendations, such as an end to allotment, were essentially rearguard actions meant to ameliorate problems caused by forced **assimilation** during the previous century.

Belief that government should address its mistakes with regard to Indian affairs became a popular political theme after the release of the Meriam Report. Even before Collier (who had been accused of "Communist" tendencies during the "red scare" of the early 1920s) became commissioner of Indian affairs, a liberal tendency was evident under the otherwise conservative presidency of Herbert Hoover. Hoover drew Ray Lyman Wilbur from the presidency of Stanford University to become his secretary of the interior. Hoover also chose Charles J. Rhoades, a devout Quaker, as commissioner of Indian affairs. Rhoades enjoyed little success in his efforts to reform the federal bureaucracy to implement the Meriam Report. More fundamental reforms would have to wait until the presidency of Franklin D. Roosevelt, who would appoint John Collier as commissioner of Indian affairs.

FURTHER READING

Meriam, Lewis. *The Problem of Indian Administration.* Baltimore: Johns Hopkins Press, 1928.

MERRION V. JICARILLA APACHE TRIBE 455 U.S. 130 (1982)

Indian governments possess an inherent right to impose severance taxes on mineral development if they are organized under the **Indian Reorganization Act**, according to the Supreme Court ruling in *Merrion v. Jicarilla Apache Tribe.* The tax may be collected even if original lease agreements did not contain it. According to this ruling, a mineral tax is "an essential attribute of Indian **sovereignty**." The Court held that "the power to tax is an essential attribute of Indian sovereignty because it is a necessary instrument of self-government and territorial management."

MI'KMAW (MICMAQ) CONSTITUTIONAL LAW

A very ancient petroglyph in Nova Scotia depicts Mi'kma'ki, the Mi'kmaw world, as a series of concentric circles with the sun (*Naku'set*) and the moon (*Tepkunuset*) at its center (Figure 1). It is a model of the organization of the nation, read from the outside toward the middle.

The outermost ring is made up of small triangles, which represent the *wikuom*[1] or conical bark-lodges of individual Mi'kmaq families. All are connected, just as all Mi'kmaq families are connected by blood and marriage in a great circle of kinship.

The next ring consists of seven rounded hills and seven crosses. The hills represent the seven original *saqmawuti'l* or districts of the nation (Figure 2),[2] and the crosses are the seven *saqmaq*[3] or district chiefs. Long before it took on Christian associations, the equal-sided Mi'kmaw cross was a symbol of the four directions and gave its people wisdom, the strength to survive, and safety on their long voyages.

Within (or, more properly, above) the ring of seven districts and their chiefs is the sun, which represented the male creative power and the living force that connects all humans, animals and plants. Within the circle of the sun, the moon is the grandmother of all things, most sacred and powerful.

Spirit

Niskam,[4] the maker of the universe, is not a personality or thing but pure spirit. This pure spirit manifests in everything, including all of the seen and unseen forces that shape the world as we know it. The sun and the moon are male and female manifestations of *Niskam,* and the

Figure 1. The original seal of the Mi'kmaw Grand Council,
after a petroglyph at Kejimikujik National Park in Nova Scotia.

members of the Christian Holy Family are also manifestations of this
ever-present power as well.

The Mi'kmaw belief in spirits is quite strong even today, as can be
seen in the continued use of the old names for seasons of the year. Each
season within the annual cycle is named after the spirit of that season:
for example, *penatimuikus*, "the spirit of birthing," the time when new
life springs forth.

In the naming of things, a fundamental distinction is always made as
to animacy. An example would be a tree. While living and growing, it
is identified by its species name and the suffix *epit* ("is there"). Once it
has been cut down, it is described as *kmu'j* ("wood"), with the suffix
etek ("is there"). The terms *epit* and *etek* denote the animate (*epit*) or
inanimate (*etek*) nature of our surroundings.

Mi'kmaw believe that the spirit passes from this world to another at
the moment of death. The spirit will hesitate, however, as long as it is
concerned about the feelings of those whom it leaves behind. An elder
is therefore designated to assist the spirit's passage into the next world.
The elder will see to it that everyone at the bedside has accepted the

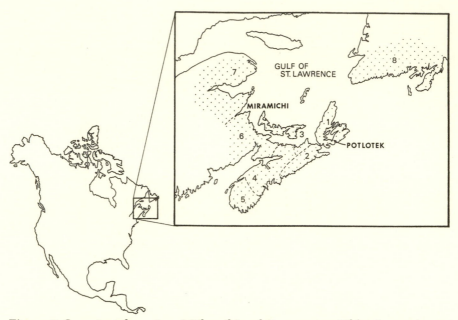

Figure 2. Seventeenth-century Mi'kma'ki and its *saqmawuti'l* (main provinces or districts). *Saqmawuti'l* referred to in the text are *Unama'ki* (1), *Epikoitik aq Piktuk* (3), *Kespe'k* (7), and *Ktaqamkuk* (8), which was originally attached to *Epikoitik aq Piktuk*.

passage. Anyone who is expressing his or her grief and can be heard by the dying person is asked to leave the room. He or she can return once he or she regains his or her composure and accepts what is about to happen. When the time comes, the elder begins to recite prayers in Mi'kmaq to encourage the dying person to "cross over" (*asoqama'si*).

Other members of the community also assist in the dying person's transition. It is believed that anyone who leaves the living world (*usitqamu*) with unpaid debts will have a troubled stay in the spirit world (*ski te'kmujewa'ki*). The entire community therefore makes sure that there are no unpaid debts in the deceased's name.

Justice

Everything, then, is connected. Whatever happens to one rock or tree or human being eventually affects everything else. This belief is central to Mi'kmaq conceptions of human responsibility and justice. Every action has far-reaching consequences, which must be weighed very carefully. At the same time, every human, like everything else in our world, is a mixture of both good and bad forces (*mntuewe'l*). No one is entirely bad, but each brings some unique good into the world as well. Justice depends on a willingness to accept humans as they were created and to discover the good in each of them.

This conception of justice is reflected in the autonomy generally afforded to children, who must be allowed to express their uniqueness, while learning to be self-confident and think independently (Battiste 1977). Children are warned of danger, but are rarely actually restrained. They are advised about good behavior and teased when they act poorly, but punishing them is viewed very unfavorably. Indeed, a child who is punished harshly is justified in moving to another household and will be protected by elders of the extended family.

At the same time, children are expected to learn two lessons, taught through words and example. One lesson is responsibility for the well-being of others. From the time they begin to walk, children are asked to help feed babies, elderly kin, and visitors. The other basic lesson is the insignificance of possessions. Children are encouraged to give away or share their food, clothes, and playthings. Selfishness is the object of general teasing and gossip. The freedom and lessons of childhood strengthen awareness of the interrelationship of all life, the reciprocal responsibilities of all creatures, and, above all, that to be human is to enjoy the freedom to act upon one's own conscience.

Today, and probably as long as the people have existed, gossip is the most widespread and most effective way of reinforcing the personal self-discipline expected of all adults. The principal institution of "social control" is discussion: in days past around a campfire, today at the dinner table or over tea in the course of the numerous social calls that Mi'kmaq enjoy each day. "It is an empirically based study of human behavior in an ecological flux, extremely intimate, critical, and moral" (Marshall 1996:24).

In these discussions, families will gain honor, respect, prestige, or disgrace and shame through the actions of their family. Hence it is necessary to keep one's own in line. Scolding and reproach by the heads of families is the key to social control, and in more drastic conditions a person may be asked to leave the household and not return. (Battiste 1977: 10)

In a society of pervasive emotional and economic interdependence, the most painful fate imaginable is a loss of respect and support from neighbors and kin.

Bernie Francis, a respected Mi'kmaw linguist, was recently asked by the Union of Nova Scotia Indians to explore the concepts of justice embedded in the language. He identified four key concepts: *ilsutekek, wi'kupaltimk, nijketekek*, and *apiksiktuek. Ilsutekek* can be translated "to make right" or "to judge correctly," according to the nature of a misdeed or injury. *Wi'kupaltimk*[5] has been translated as "a feast," but refers more specifically to a ceremony of reconciliation. *Apiksiktuek* ("that which forgives") and *nijketekek* ("that which heals") describe a paradigm of reconciliation and justice. Healing flows naturally from forgiveness; forgiveness is preferable to confrontation.

Until very recently, *wi'kupaltimk* was routinely practiced in many Mi'kmaq communities.[6] Bernie Francis recalled:

This feast happened on New Year's Day when members of our communities would meet at a designated place such as a church or a school. Women would bring cooked food and baked goods while tea was brewed on the spot. After eating, prayers would be offered by the entire group. It was immediately after this point that the "apiksiktatultimk" (the forgiveness part of the ceremony) would begin. While everyone stood in a circle the chief would be first to walk around to each and every person, shake his/her hand, sometimes embrace, and ask for forgiveness for past wrongs, for both intentional and for inadvertent ones. (This is one instance whereby a chief shows his/her humility by being off the pedestal.) The chief would be followed by the councillors who in turn would be followed by the remaining community members.

No one was accused or forced to lose face. Anyone who refused to show forgiveness, however, attracted attention and could expect to be "ostracised in a most inimitable way that only our people can do," as Francis observed.

Family and Territory

The family has always been the fundamental unit of Mi'kmaq social and economic organization, and each family was historically associated with a specific territory or harvesting area (*umitki*).[7] The humans and animals within a territory are kinfolk,[8] and this is why they have rights and responsibilities to one another, including the right to eat and be eaten. Each nation of the animals has its own chiefs and must be shown proper respect.

An early visitor was impressed by the fact that "they killed the animals only in proportion as they had need of them" (Denys 1672: 426). Wasting meat would result in animals hiding themselves and refusing to be taken. Responsible use of the living world (*netuklimkewe'l*)[9] meant harvesting and sharing the harvest for the common welfare of the whole family and community people. Harvesting seasons depended on the life cycles of each species. Fur animals were considered harvestable after weaning their young, when their pelts were in prime condition, usually in the season of *wikewikus* ("animal fattening season").[10] Consistent with *netuklimkewe'l*, families were often reassigned harvesting areas as their needs changed. Some areas were also understood to be open to all—for example, where there was an abundance of a particular kind of wood, or where certain berries or herbs grew in abundance.

Figure 3. The Mi'kmaw *umitki* (family hunting territories) in Nova Scotia which were still in use a century ago, as recorded by the Canadian anthropologist Frank Speck.

Birchbark maps were in common use for navigation and documenting harvesting rights long before the first Europeans arrived in Mi'kma'ki (LeClercq 1691: 153). Unlike Europeans, who think in terms of boundary lines that often disregard natural features of the landscape, Mi'kmaq think of a family territory as a network of connected bodies of water, with place names that precisely describe physical landmarks. Once you understand the meanings of Mi'kmaw place names, you will know that you have arrived at your chosen destination the moment you set eyes on it. Although the original distribution of Mi'kmaq family territories is no longer fully known, Figure 3 shows some of those that were still used a century ago (from Speck 1922).

Related families always lived in neighboring villages (*utanl*) and territories and shared an association with particular animals, plants, and spirits. For example, *muin* (bear) was the name of the clan of the late Kjisaqmaw Gabriel Sylliboy. Mi'kmaw who lived in the vicinity of Restigouche (*Listukuj*) used the salmon as a symbol on their canoes and in petroglyphs used to mark their territorial rights, while sturgeon, beaver, and deer were used elsewhere.

Crosses were also customarily used to mark claims. This is quite ironic, because it was also the custom of European kings. When Jacques Cartier erected a wooden cross at Miramichi on his 1534 voyage, he was confronted by a *saqmaw* who made a cross with his fingers and waved his hand along the shore, explaining that his own claim was better (Biggar 1924: 64–66).

Despite the close ties of every Mi'kmaq with a particular family and a specific territory, there was a complementary value of unstinting hospitality to travelers. This can still be seen today. A visitor will be offered food upon arrival, its nature and amount depending on the distance he or she has covered: the longer people have traveled, the hungrier they are presumed to be. Everyone is offered tea. To refuse these offers is a grave insult to the host and attracts criticism for being haughty and conceited, while visitors who accept these gifts are treated with warmth and kindness. Even if they have come on sensitive or controversial business, visitors are treated civilly over a cup of tea. As hunters, fishers, and traders (and, since the late nineteenth century, migrant farmworkers), Mi'kmaw people are always in motion and therefore rely continually on the hospitality of others, however distantly they may be related (Battiste 1977: 6).

Liability for wrongs was always shared within the extended family rather than being borne by the individual alone. In this way, everyone was equally responsible for encouraging proper behavior. Similarly, a wrong was best remedied by demonstrating repentance collectively: the offender's family offered presents to the family of the victim to make peace with them and avoid any possibility of revenge. Today, Mi'kmaw people are still likely to take the initiative on behalf of kinfolk to seek forgiveness or make some kind of restitution to avert grievances.

People with Big Hearts

The greatest compliment bestowed upon a Mi'kmaw man or woman has always been that he or she has a "big heart" (*meski'k ukamlamun*), meaning a spirit of generosity and compassion.

Those people who possessed the Big Hearts and followed the correct path were given the ability to communicate with the shadow soul of the forest and the streams. They provided for the others by hunting and fishing or by teaching others some of their gifts. They became the leaders of the families and clans, and later of the Council and nation. (Battiste 1984)

Leadership is more or less formal. Every family has its own good people ("uncles"), who are approached for advice. Respected, generous men were the recognized leaders (*sa'ya*) of families in the past. Then there were the *saqmaw* (the root of this word implies "elder"), or more formal leaders of individual villages or entire districts. A *saqmaw* had many important functions, such as organizing long-distance hunting and fishing enterprises and trade, redistributing harvesting areas within the community, ensuring respect for the creatures of the land and sea, mediating local quarrels, and speaking for his people in dealings with other parts of the nation.

Saqmaw had no coercive powers and could only propose and advise. A French explorer had this to say about a very influential *saqmaw* whom he had met:

This man made a point of honour to be always the worst dressed of his people, and to take care that they were all better clothed than he. He held it as a maxim, as he told me one day, that a ruler, and a great heart like his, ought to take more care for others than for himself, because, good hunter as he was, he always obtained easily everything which he needed for his own use, and that as for the rest, if he did not himself live well, he should find his desire in the affection and the hearts of his subjects. It was as if he wished to say that his treasures and riches were in the hearts and the affection of his people. (Le Clercq 1691: 235)

As Dorey explained, the *saqmaw* had no more wealth than ordinary Mi'kmaw, and no source of power or authority other than the quality of their ideas.

They had to display exemplary leadership qualities of honesty, wisdom and courage, otherwise their advice would not be heeded. There were no law enforcement or military structures or other authorities to enforce their decisions. Public opinion and acceptance of their leadership tempered any tendency to despotism. They extracted no payment or taxes to pay for their services although they could receive gifts and like all others, had to hunt and fish for their livelihood. (1994: 8–9)

The skills required to be a successful leader were learned from a very early age, as soon as a child showed a talent for this role. The leader might look first among his own children, but more often adopted a nephew or an orphan from another lineage. Succession to leadership therefore tended to pass from elder to younger within a household, but the apprentice was frequently not a lineal descendant and often not a blood relative at all.

Leaders also recruited young followers by serving as teachers and organizers and built up a large following over the years. Indeed, as Father Biard recognized (Biard 1616: 101), the wealth of a *saqmaw* was in the number of children he could raise.

Although there are fewer *saqmaw* today, and most local matters are administered by elected councils on the various Indian reserves where Mi'kmaw people live, the most influential people are still those known for their Big Heart, regardless of whether they have a formal title or public office. Contemporary *saqmaw* or *keptin*[11] likewise still play an important educational role with youth, derive their authority from the breadth of their generosity, and exercise leadership through listening and persuasion.

Grandmothers

Long ago the transformer *Kluskap* reshaped the land and rivers.[12] Although he had great power, he was always accompanied by Old Woman or Grandmother. Many stories refer to *Kukmijinu* or "Grandmother of All," and the sacred place associated with *Kluskap* on Cape Breton Island is known as *Kukmijinu kmtn* or "Grandmother Mountain." The spirits of the forest (*mi'kmuesu*), which often took pity on orphans or young men and lent them special powers, typically assumed a female form. Ceremonies traditionally required the consent and cooperation of women to prepare food and perform some of the dances (Lescarbot 1606: 236). Women still performed a ceremonial dance after the election of new *keptin* earlier this century (Parsons 1926). LeClercq (1691: 101–110) referred to "head women" who organized women's activities.

In everyday life, too, women have always functioned as the basic source of spiritual power and stability in the household and community (Battiste 1977: 12). The customary organization of Mi'kmaq society has been neither male-dominated nor female-dominated, but "complementary" (Barsh 1994). Mi'kmaw men and women have long been dependent on each other for the skills and labor required for success in the aboriginal subsistence cycle (Marshall 1996: 52). Women control major procreative resources such as human fertility and herbal medicine, and men control aggressive and destructive forces such as hunting, spirit powers, and war. Men may become *saqmaw*, but women, on the whole, have always been better organized. The basic cooperative unit in a traditional village or a contemporary Indian reserve is a group of related women who share their resources and responsibilities, including childrearing. Men are powerless to interfere.

According to at least one early observer, permission to marry was usually sought and received from the girl's mother, and the boy would hunt for his bride's family for some time as compensation (Diereville 1710: 137).[13] Elder women were also responsible for keeping records of clan structures and determining whether the young couple should marry and have children. In practical terms, they monitored the gene pool. The practice of working for the bride's family as compensation for the loss of her services is some indication of the esteem in which Mi'kmaq women were held by their families. Women were likewise always free to leave an unsatisfactory marriage (Lescarbot 1606: 236).[14]

The role of women has changed since Mi'kmaq embraced Catholicism in the seventeenth century. Close association between the Grand Council and the church increased the visibility and influence of men as leaders of Mi'kmaw communities. Since the British expulsion of French Catholics from Mi'kma'ki in the 1760s, the men who sit in Grand Council have also served when required as priests. The traditional complementary nature of Mi'kmaw society nonetheless survives in the form of elder women who serve as "prayer leaders," with broad customary authority to criticize the Grand Council and Catholic clergy. In Mi'kmaw doctrine, moreover, the focus of spiritual attention is the grandmother, St. Anne, who is the patron saint of the nation.

The People and the Nation

It is possible to speak of "the people" (*Inu*), or of the Mi'kmaq, a term implying friends or allies, a single historical nation. At one time, the ancestors of the people lived simply as neighbors who shared a similar language and way of life and were connected by trade. They united more than seven centuries ago during a time of bloody invasions by the *Kwetej* (Mohawks) and severe famine. The unifying force was a vision at Piktuk (modern-day Pictou Harbour, Nova Scotia).

In the depths of the people's bitter misfortune, *Naku'set*'s spirit visited an old man in his sleep. As the old man traveled through the dreamworld, he was approached by a youth bearing three small crosses. The youth explained that each cross had a purpose, and together they would help the people survive and prosper if used in accordance with *Naku'set*'s instructions (Battiste 1984). One cross would help the people prevail in times of war and conflict. The second would carry them safely across the ocean and the mountains on their long voyages. The third would lend wisdom to their councils.

When the old man awoke from this vision, he drew what he had seen on birchbark and journeyed from village to village, sharing *Naku'set*'s message. The people were galvanized and united under the sign of the three crosses to liberate themselves from the invaders. With wooden crosses guarding their villages, crosses tattooed on the chests of the warriors, and crosses painted on the bows of their sailing canoes, the allied people regained control of the territory of their ancestors and forged one nation.

The grandsons of the old prophet continued to enlarge the nation, establishing new alliances and settlements to the north (Newfoundland) and the west (Quebec). The crossing to Newfoundland was sixty-five miles, two days' voyage by sailing canoe, and the Mi'kmaq outpost there was still attached administratively to the *Epekoitik aq Piktuk* (Prince Edward Island and Pictou) district or *saqmawuti* when French explorers arrived in the sixteenth century. It later became a distinct *saqmawuti, Ktaqamkuk*, after Mi'kmaw settlement was facilitated by the acquisition of larger, heavier French sloops in the seventeenth century. The western settlements in Quebec were known as *Kespe'k* (or *Kespe'kewaki*), "the last land," which the French transcribed as Gaspe.

It was at Miramichi Bay, in *Kespe'k*, that the Mi'kmaw had their first encounter with Jacques Cartier in 1534. However, Mi'kmaw canoes had reportedly sacked and burned Basque and Portuguese fishing vessels on the Grand Banks at least a generation earlier (Martijn 1986). Thus the Mi'kmaw Nation had consolidated its vast Atlantic territory barely in time for Europeans' arrival.

The Grand Council

Like all wars, the war of liberation from the *Kwetej* scarred the spirits of the people. It unleashed a momentum of violence that soon threatened to plunge the nation itself into civil war. To invoke the power of the Third Cross and restore harmony, the *saqmaq* met secretly at Miramichi and formed a single Grand Council (*mawio'mi*) with the aim of securing the rights and lands of every family and district, keeping peace among the people, and defending the nation by building alliances with other nations (Battiste 1984).

As we will see, the council's name has been *Sante' Mawio'mi* (Holy Gathering) since the seventeenth century and the adoption of Catholicism as the state religion. The original name may very well have been *Sankew Mawio'mi*, which connotes a "Peaceful Gathering" or a "Peace Council." This reflects the way the Grand Council functions, building **consensus** and facilitating collective decision making. It is neither legislative nor adjudicative. Maintaining harmony among families is its goal.

The Grand Council began to meet annually at midsummer, gathering the people together to renew the kinship among clans and districts, to recount the ancient chronicles (*a'tukaqn*) of the nation, to settle disputes, and to review alliances or covenants that had been made with neighboring peoples (*l'napskuk*). The Grand Council also assumed the role of defending the nation by organizing and directing the principal warriors (*sma'knis*) of every district.

The overall organization of the nation remained decentralized for most purposes, however. Individual *saqmaw* continued to organize local harvesting activities and settle local disputes over personal injuries or encroachments on family lands. Matters were brought to the council only if the parties were intransigent, or the dispute crossed district boundaries. Justice was sought in compromise and settlement, mediated by the *saqmaw*, although in extreme cases of wrongdoing, a person could be banished to the edges of the allied world—many hundreds of miles.

For four centuries or longer, the midsummer gatherings have taken place at *Potlotek* on a tiny island (*mnikuk*) in the middle of Lake Bras d'Or, Nova Scotia. Ancient fire pits and dancing circles are visible everywhere. This is still the time and place for the Grand Council to discuss important problems, hear petitions, and address the people on moral, spiritual, and social concerns. As in years past, each extended family has its own camp in a traditional place, situated near related families. Days are spent in visiting and reaffirming kinship ties (Battiste 1977: 4).

The *Wapena'ki* Confederacy

The unification of the seven districts and the formation of the Grand Council from the thirteenth to the fifteenth centuries did not consolidate all of the neighboring peoples who spoke related languages. Farther south, along the Atlantic seacoast, were others who shared the same basic language and way of life: Mi'kmaq, Maliseet, Abenaki, Penobscot, Passamaquoddy, and Wowenock. These nations, who called themselves the "people of the dawn" (*Wapena'kikewak*), forged a strong social, economic, and military alliance. All of the seacoasts and seaways from Cape Cod to Labrador were *Wapena'ki* ("land of the dawn"), representing a vast ocean domain of safe travel and free trade. Wapena'ki trade also flowed up the Saint Lawrence River to the towns of the Huron (Wendat) Nation near present-day Toronto, and the **Iroquois** or Haudenosaunee **Confederacy** (*awisku'k*), with whom *Wapena'ki* always maintained peaceful relations.

The nations of the *Wapena'ki* maintained their connections through a protocol of annual visits and symbolic trade. Delegations from each member nation visited the principal villages of the others bearing the trade goods prescribed by tradition. Special visiting songs were sung, and **wampum** strings were delivered to the local *saqmaw* while the people feasted together. Stories were shared during games of *waltes*.[15] Goods were heaped up, displayed, and exchanged in commemoration and renewal of friendships. These celebrations were continued until the late nineteenth century, when greater restrictions were imposed upon travel and trade across the border between the United States and Canada. Efforts are currently under way to revive the *Wapena'ki* as a cross-border economic union.

There was a customary division of labor among the allies. While the Mi'kmaq possessed the greatest sea power, the southern allies had greater control of the western mountains and forests. Although it may not be that obvious today, *Wapena'ki* territory included many different ecological regions, including both boreal and temperate forests, which meant a diversity of wildlife, wild foods, and farming conditions. In some corners of the confederacy, maize and beans grew well; in others, the main products were moosemeat, salmon, or cranberries. Eels, which were highly prized for smoking and for stews, generally came from Cape Breton, while the southern allies supplied most tool materials.

The English settlement at Boston was located at the southern edge of *Wapena'ki* and rapidly grew in commercial importance during the seventeenth century. Meanwhile, the French had established their largest Atlantic naval station, Louisbourg, at Cape Breton in the heart of the Mi'kmaw district of *Unama'ki*. This north-south polarity did not undermine the *Wapena'ki* confederacy; the Penobscots subsequently managed all trade and diplomacy with the English, and the Mi'kmaq with the French, until French forces withdrew permanently from the region under the Treaty of Paris in 1763.

Diplomatic Relations

It is difficult to travel through Mi'kma'ki without appreciating the traditional importance of the sea, fishing, and trade. Mi'kma'ki is a region of islands, bays, and rivers. It is much easier to travel by water than over land, and until European commercial fishing fleets began to arrive in the fifteenth century, the productivity of the ocean was considerable (Martijn 1986). There are tales of trade missions as far away as the Gulf of Mexico.

As a nation of sailors and traders, Mi'kmaw were deeply conscious of the need for thoughtful diplomacy and far-ranging alliances. There were standard protocols for cementing alliances (*lekamanen*) with other peoples and for recording these ties in wampum (*l'napskuk*).[16] One of the three principal officers of the Grand Council, the *Putu's*, had the function of keeping records of treaties (*anku'kamkewel*).[17] One day of the midsummer gathering each year was devoted to a reading of all the treaties by the *Putu's*, which was witnessed by every man old enough to have killed his first moose. Adult men were likely to travel often to hunt, fish, and trade, and they needed to understand how to behave properly in the territories of other nations. In this way, they were annually reminded of their obligations to friends and allies.

One of the most important alliances was concluded with the *Kwetej* (Mohawks) after the great war, and it has been faithfully observed, on both sides, to this day. Speck (1922:107) saw the wampum or *l'napskuk* recording this treaty at Eskasoni, the capital of the Grand Council on Cape Breton Island since the eighteenth century. It appears subsequently to have been confiscated or destroyed, like many of the wampum belts that had been kept by the Haudenosaunee.

Mi'kmaq were quick to adapt to European diplomatic protocols, but never completely abandoned their own ideas of international relations. Like other indigenous Americans, Mi'kmaq thought of alliances in terms of kinship. In forming the alliance, nations became kin, individually and collectively. A treaty created extended families, connecting

both peoples at every level, imposing reciprocal filial duties on everyone. Consistent with this, treaties were usually accompanied (and followed) by marriages. There continue to be many marriage ties between
Mi'kmaq and Mohawk families, for example, and many Mi'kmaq families trace back to seventeenth century strategic marriages with French
and Basque merchants. An alliance is thus more than a business contract. It is a way of permanently enlarging the family.

Church and Crown

After the baptism of *Kji'saqmaw* Membretou in 1610, the nation was
allied with the Holy See. There is a belt of wampum showing the seven
hills, the sacred things of the Grand Council, and a *saqmaw* and priest
holding hands. Under the terms of this treaty (or concordat, in canon
law), the church was to enjoy complete liberty of movement and freedom to teach throughout Mi'kma'ki, while the Grand Council itself assumed the spiritual responsibilities of the Catholic priesthood.
Thereafter the Grand Council became *Sante' Mawio'mi*, or Holy Council, from *saint* in French or *sanctus* in Latin.

Since the early eighteenth century, the Mi'kmaw midsummer gathering has become associated with the Feast Day of St. Anne. At first, the
French priests who had baptized *Kji'saqmaw* Membretou were warned
to stay away from *Potlotek* and to build their churches elsewhere. One
summer, the priests claimed that a rock had rolled from the sea, and
this rock was meant to be the foundation of the Mi'kmaw mother
church. They brought the seaweed-covered rock by canoe to *Potlotek*,
where, to the chagrin of the Grand Council, it was rolled into the middle
of the great fire of the nation, where it can still be seen today. The mother
church was built nearby in 1721.[18]

There were more critical alliances to be made with the newcomers.
In 1725, the Penobscots and Passamaquoddies brokered an alliance
with the British at Boston following several years of naval warfare on
the Maine coast. British military operations against the combined
French and Mi'kmaq forces continued in the north, however, until the
British-Mi'kmaq Treaty of Halifax in 1752. This brought the entire *Wapena'ki* confederacy under the British Crown without any relinquish-
ment of its member nations' rights and privileges. The Grand Council
referred to this treaty as *Eleke'wa'ki* ("the King's homeland"). When
British and Mi'kmaw leaders renewed this treaty in a formal ceremony
at Halifax in 1761, they buried swords and hatchets beneath a "pillar
of peace." It was later said that the hatchets were buried lowest, since
the Mi'kmaq would only go to war if the British dug up their weapons
first.

On July 16, 1776, *Wapena'ki* representatives met with the leaders of
Boston's revolutionary council at the written invitation of George Wash-

ington. After reading a copy of the Declaration of Independence, the *Wapena'ki* agreed to recognize the United States as a sovereign and independent state and to help defend the United States from British forces. They obviously believed that the 1752 Halifax Treaty left the *Wapena'ki* as equals, rather than subjects, of the British Crown.

The Future

The Mi'kmaw constitution has always been flexible and continues to evolve in practice. Relations with the church were strained in the twentieth century by the abuse of Mi'kmaw children in Catholic residential schools (Knockwood 1992), for example, and the Grand Council responded in part by seeking restitution and the establishment of an independent Mi'kmaw diocese in accordance with the 1610 concordat. Since 1951, the Indian Act had prescribed the election of "band councils" for each one of the twenty-seven Mi'kmaw communities in Atlantic Canada, potentially eroding the political unity of the nation. By the 1980s, however, an informal separation of powers had been achieved leaving national-level concerns such as treaties, fisheries, and territorial integrity in the hands of the Grand Council. More recently, the "bands" and the Grand Council have collaborated in building new regional administrative bodies, including a Mi'kmaq Education Authority (a national school board),[19] and Mi'kmaw Fish and Wildlife Commission. The establishment of a Mi'kmaw House of Assembly in Nova Scotia is currently under consideration.

These developments reinforce the underlying logic of the original unification of the people centuries ago. Mi'kmaw is about the family, kinship, language, cooperation, and mutual respect, under the guidance of *Niskam*. Mi'kma'ki is not a "state" in the European sense, although it has a very ancient national government and the will to persist as a single, distinct, and irreducible society. Adaptation, compromise, and accommodation are possible because the identity and extended kinship of Mi'kmaq people continue to be a shared experience, more intimate, real, and sustaining than the material wealth and power of Europeans. After five centuries of trade and conflict with Europeans, Mi'kma'ki exists still, and it will continue to exist as long as the people share food, love, and children as they have since *Naku'set* first came down to them from the Milky Way.

NOTES

1. From *wikuom* comes the English term "wigwam."
2. Districts may also be referred to as *maqimikal* or "lands," from the word for "land" or "Earth" (*maqimikew*). In Mi'kmaw orthography, the ɨ symbol (the letter i with a line through it) stands for a schwa.
3. *Saqmaq* is the term from which early English explorers derived "saga-

more," the term applied to all New England and maritime "chiefs" until the early nineteenth century.

4. Or *kjiniskam*, the "greatest" spirit or power.

5. Or, alternatively, *maw-mijisultimk*.

6. These practices are currently in the process of renewal after an interruption caused by aggressive efforts by Canadian officials to assimilate Mi'kmaq beginning in the 1940s.

7. This term literally means the place of one's origin.

8. The localization of relationships is reflected in the fact that the names of many animals vary in different parts of Mi'kma'ki. The term for "rabbit," for example, is *apli'kmuj* in the core Mi'kmaw districts of Nova Scotia and *wapus* elsewhere. Some species are notably missing from particular districts, for instance, porcupines from Cape Breton.

9. Originally a conception of customary Mi'kmaw law, *netuklimkewe'l* was proclaimed and published as Mi'kmaq legislation by the late Kjisaqmaw, Donald Marshall, on Treaty Day (October 1), 1986.

10. In a much-publicized 1929 case, the late Kjisaqmaw Gabriel Sylliboy was convicted by a Nova Scotia county court of taking muskrats out of season. In fact, he was charged just four days prior to the opening of the Nova Scotia muskrat-trapping season, but the county court was not told that he was probably using the traditional season of *wikewikus* as his guide rather than the Gregorian calendar.

11. From *capitaine*, the term French explorers and merchants applied to all Mi'kmaw leaders, including *saqmaw* and *sa'ya*. *Capitaine* in French does not have quite so restrictive a meaning as the parallel English term "captain" and can be applied with propriety to the leader or chief of any organization.

12. This probably referred to the profound changes in the land created by the last glaciation some 10,000–12,000 years ago, which the people witnessed.

13. According to the same observer, women not only practiced medicine, but made conscious birth-spacing decisions (Diereville 1710: 164, 191).

14. Other references to bride services and women's conjugal rights are Lescarbot (1606: 216), LeClercq (1691: 238), and Denys (1672: 407).

15. A complex dice game, related to the Haudenosaunee peach stone bowl game, in which the stakes could range from furs to wives or captives.

16. It is appropriate to translate *l'napskuk* as "covenant" because the exchange of wampum belts was more solemn and permanent a relationship than a European paper treaty, for which *wi'katikn* is commonly used.

17. *Anku'kamkewel* ("treaties") connotes "joining together" or "adding on" in Mi'kmaw, Bernie Francis explains.

18. It was at about this time that the Grand Council adopted its flag, consisting of a Christian-style cross, sun, and moon in red on a white field. It has been in use ever since that time.

19. Negotiations with Canada's federal government are continuing, with the aim of enabling the Mi'kmaw Kinamasuti (as the Mi'kmaq Education Authority is now known) to assume complete responsibility for Mi'kmaw schooling in Nova Scotia.

FURTHER READING

Barsh, Russel L. "Indigenous Peoples' Perspectives on Population and Development." *Boston College Environmental Affairs Law Review* 21 (1994): 257–270.

Battiste, Marie. "Cultural Transmission and Survival in Contemporary Micmac Society." *Indian Historian* 10:4 (1977): 3–13.

"A History of the Grand Council to 1800." In *Mikmaq Grand Council, State Papers (Foreign Affairs) 1977–1984*, ed. Russel Barsh, Sakej Henderson, and Bernie Francis. Mikmaq Grand Council: 1977–1984, 3–9.

Biard, Pierre. *Nouvelle France, des ses Terres, Naturel du Pays, de ses Habitans, &c.* 1616. Reprinted in *Relations des Jesuites, contenant ce qui s'est passe de plus remarkable dans les missions des Peres de la Compagnie de Jesus dans la Nouvelle France.* Quebec [City]: Government of Canada, 1858.

Biggar, H. P., ed. *The Voyages of Jacques Cartier.* Ottawa: F. A. Acland, 1924.

Denys, Nicolas. *Description Geographique et Historique des Costes de l'Amerique Septentrionale, avec l'Histoire Naturelle du Pais.* Paris: Louis Billaine, 1672. English trans. by W. F. Ganong. Toronto: Champlain Society, 1908.

Diereville, Le Sieur de. *Relation du Voyage du Port Royal de l'Acadie ou de la Nouvelle France.* Amsterdam: Pierre Humbert, 1710.

Dorey, Dwight A. *Aboriginal Self Government for the Mi'kma'ki People of Nova Scotia.* Truro: Native Council of Nova Scotia, 1994.

Knockwood, Isabelle. *Out of the Depths.* Lockeport, Nova Scotia: Roseway Publishing, 1992.

LeClercq, Chretien. *Nouvelle Relation de la Gaspesie.* Paris: Amable Auroy, 1691. English trans. by W. F. Ganong. Toronto: Champlain Society, 1910.

Lescarbot, Marc. *Histoire de la Nouvelle France.* [History of New France]. Paris: Jean Milot, 1611. English trans. by W. L. Grant. Toronto: Champlain Society, 1907–1914.

Maillard, Antoine. *An Account of the Customs of the Micmakis and Maricheets Savage Nations.* London: Hooper & Morley, 1758.

Marshall, Murdena. "Mi'kmawi'skwaq Influence in Aboriginal Government: Complementary Organization or Electoral Equality?" Report to the Social Sciences and Humanities Research Council of Canada, 1996.

Martijn, Charles. "Voyages des Micmacs dans la vallee du Saint-Laurent, sur la Cote-Nord et a Terre-Neuve." In *Les Micmacs et la Mer*, ed. Charles Martijn, 197–223. Quebec [City]: Recherches amérindiennes au Québec, 1986.

The Mi'kmaq Treaty Handbook. Sydney and Truro: Native Communications Society of Nova Scotia, 1987.

Nietfield, P. *Determinants of Aboriginal Micmac Political Structure.* Ann Arbor, MI: University Microfilms, 1981.

Parsons, Elsie Clews. "Micmac Folklore." *Journal of American Folklore* 38 (1926): 55–133.

Rand, Silas T. "Glooscap, Cuhkw, and Coolpurjot." *American Antiquarian* 12 (1890): 283–286.

———. "The Legends of the Micmacs." *American Antiquarian* 12 (1890): 3–14.

———. *A Short Statement of Facts Relating to the History, Manners, Customs, Language, and Literature of the Micmac Tribe of Indians in Nova-Scotia and P. E. Island.* Halifax: James Bowes, 1850.

Speck, Frank G. *Beothuk and Micmac.* Indian Notes and Monographs. New York: Heye Foundation, 1922.

Thwaites, Reuben Gold, ed. *The Jesuit Relations and Allied Documents.* New York: Pageant Books, 1959.

RUSSEL LAWRENCE BARSH and JOE B. MARSHALL

MOE V. CONFEDERATED SALISH AND KOOTENAI TRIBES 425 U.S. 463 (1976)

A state may impose a tax on cigarettes sold to non-Indians from reservation lands, according to the Supreme Court ruling in *Moe v. Confederated Salish and Kootenai Tribes.* The Indian seller is required by this decision to collect the sales tax and turn it over to the state. This ruling has been virtually ignored by many Indian smoke-shop operators, who object that it is an illegal state intrusion into **Indian Country**.

Reservation sale of cigarettes has been a particularly volatile issue in western Washington, where several small reservations sell cigarettes near the large urban areas of Puget Sound. Cigarette sales also have been a major political issue in Canada, where the federal government has sought to discourage smoking by raising taxes on tobacco products to several times the level in the United States. The difference in price has produced a lively smuggling trade, particularly through the Akwesasne Mohawk (St. Regis) Reservation that straddles the border in northern New York State. By the mid-1990s, Iroquois at Grand River, Ontario, were manufacturing their own cigarettes and selling them (tax-free) on several native reserves across Canada.

While *Moe v. Confederated Salish and Kootenai Tribes* upheld the state sales tax on cigarette sales by Indians to non-Indians, it also struck down the state's attempt to impose other taxes on members of Native American nations. The **Treaty of Hell Gate** (1855) reserved 1.25 million acres in northwestern Montana for the Salish and Kootenai. Over the years, the reservation drew considerable numbers of non-Indians because of its rich farmland and scenic mountains. The reservation was allotted in the late nineteenth century, and by the time this case was adjudicated, more than half the land was owned by non-Indians, who comprised 81 percent of the residents.

FURTHER READING

Johansen, Bruce E. *Life and Death in Mohawk Country.* Golden, CO: North American Press/Fulcrum, 1993.

Wilkinson, Charles F. *American Indians, Time, and the Law: Native Societies in a Modern Constitutional Democracy.* New Haven, CT: Yale University Press, 1987.

MONTANA V. UNITED STATES 450 U.S. 544 (1981)

Aboriginal Crow land was awarded to Montana without compensation in the Supreme Court ruling in *Montana v. United States,* which held that the bed of the Bighorn River was owned by the state despite a treaty signed in 1868 that reserved the land for the Crows. The case arose after the Crows asserted a right to close its reservation to hunting and fishing by non-Indians.

In *Montana v. United States*, the Supreme Court held that the federal government's right to own lands under navigable rivers supersedes precedents indicating that treaties are to be construed in favor of Indians, and that treaties are grants of rights *from* Indians, not *to* them. This ruling also maintained that an Indian government cannot regulate hunting and fishing by non-Indians on reservation land that is owned by non-Indians. At the same time, the Court pointed out that this case did not threaten the Native American government's civil jurisdiction:

To be sure, Indian tribes retain inherent sovereign power to exercise some forms of civil jurisdiction over non-Indians on their reservations, even on non-Indian fee lands. A tribe may regulate, through taxation, licensing or other means, the activities of non-members who enter consensual relationships with the tribe or its members, through commercial dealing, contracts, or other arrangements. A tribe may also retain inherent power to exercise civil authority over the conduct of non-Indians on fee lands within its reservation when that conduct threatens or has some direct effect on the political integrity, the economic security, or the health or welfare of the tribe.

In this case, however, the Court ruled that the Crows' economic security, health, or welfare had *not* been compromised by non-Indian hunting and fishing. Therefore, the Court found that "exercise of tribal power beyond that necessary to protect tribal self-government or to control internal relations is inconsistent with the dependent status of the tribes, and so cannot survive without express congressional delegation."

MONTEZUMA, CARLOS (WASAJAH, WASAGAH, WASSAJA) (Yavapai) (c. 1867–1923)

Carlos Montezuma was a leading advocate of legal changes that would benefit Native Americans, principally through the **Society of American Indians**. He was born in the Superstition Mountains of central Arizona about 1867 of Yavapai Indian parents. His father was called Cocuyevah, but there is no record of his mother's name. At the age of five (about 1871), a group of Pima Indians seized him during a raid. Among the Yavapai, he was known as Wassaja, meaning "let my people go."

For a brief period, he resided with the Pimas on the Gila River, but a photographer-prospector by the name of Carlos Gentile bought him for about $30. At about this time, his mother, defying the Indian agent's admonitions not to leave her reservation, went out to search for her son, but she was shot by an Indian scout in the nearby mountains. In the meantime, Gentile took the young Wassaja to the East, where he was baptized as a Christian and given the name Carlos Montezuma. Young Carlos received a good education in Chicago and then went to Carlisle Indian School. When Montezuma was about twenty-five, Carlos Gentile's photography venture failed, and his depressed adopted father took his own life in 1893. Before his death, Gentile gave the boy to a Baptist missionary, George W. Ingalls, who soon turned him over to the Reverend W. H. Stedman of Urbana, Illinois.

For two years, Montezuma received private tutoring and then entered a prep school for the University of Illinois; after completing one year of prep school, he enrolled at the University of Illinois. In 1884, he received a bachelor of science degree (cum laude). Subsequently, he went to the Chicago Medical College at Northwestern University with a partial scholarship and also worked as a pharmacist. In 1889, he received his medical degree.

Montezuma briefly tried private practice in Chicago, but soon took a one-year appointment at the Fort Stevenson Indian School in North Dakota as physician and surgeon. After this appointment, he worked at Indian agencies in Washington and Nevada. In 1894, he accepted an appointment at the Carlisle Indian School in Pennsylvania and became a good friend of the head of Carlisle, Colonel Richard Henry Pratt. He also befriended Zitkala-sa—Gertrude Simmons Bonnin—a Sioux woman who was a famous writer and Indian-rights activist.

Montezuma returned to Chicago in 1896 and started a very successful private practice. He specialized in gastrointestinal disorders and was invited to teach at the College of Physicians and Surgeons as well as in the Postgraduate Medical School. Throughout his adult life, Montezuma opposed the reservation system and its administration by the Bureau of Indian Affairs. He remembered the humiliation of his mother having to ask the Indian agent's permission to leave her homeland to hunt for her son. Governmental caprice and insensitivity to American Indians fueled Montezuma's fight for Indian rights. Montezuma considered it an insult that African Americans were made U.S. citizens after the Civil War while America's Native American inhabitants were still legally regarded as aliens. Although he encouraged citizenship and **assimilation**, he also advocated pride in being an American Indian. He authored *Let My People Go* (1914) and two other books on Indian affairs. He also established the Indian-rights magazine *Wassaja* in 1916. In 1906, President Theodore Roosevelt offered him the post of commissioner of Indian affairs, but he refused. In 1917, he was jailed for opposing the drafting of American Indians in World War I. President Woodrow Wilson released him and then, as Theodore Roosevelt had done, offered him the position as head of the Bureau of Indian Affairs.

Once again, he declined, knowing that it would compromise his crusade for Indian rights and the abolition of the BIA.

Montezuma became a Mason in the latter part of his life and achieved the rank of Master Mason. Montezuma's first wife was a Romanian woman, and his second wife was Marie Keller. Due to his taxing Indian-rights activities and complications as a result of diabetes and tuberculosis, he returned to Arizona in 1922 with his second wife. On January 23, 1923, he died at the Fort McDowell Reservation and was buried in the Fort McDowell Indian Cemetery in Arizona. By then, *Wassaja* had ceased publication, but the name was revived by Rupert Costo and Jeannette Henry in 1972 to honor Carlos Montezuma's Indian-rights activities.

FURTHER READING

Iverson, Peter. *Carlos Montezuma and the Changing World of American Indians.* Albuquerque: University of New Mexico Press, 1982.

DONALD A. GRINDE, JR.

MORTON V. MANCARI 417 U.S. 535 (1974)

In *Morton v. Mancari*, the U.S. Supreme Court upheld Indian preference policies in hiring for the Bureau of Indian Affairs, finding that such policies do not constitute racial discrimination. Instead, the Court found Indian preference in hiring to be a political decision based on Native Americans' government-to-government relationship with the United States.

In this case, non-Indian employees of the BIA were challenging the Indian preference clause of the **Indian Reorganization Act**, charging that the clause constituted illegal racial discrimination that violated equal-protection and due-process guarantees in the U.S. Constitution. The Supreme Court found that the BIA's hiring preferences were based not on racial discrimination, but on Indians' membership in semisovereign nations. The relationship between these nations and the federal government was said to be of a political nature, an area into which the courts have been reluctant to intrude under the Political Question Doctrine, which holds that BIA employment is a political question, not a racial one. The majority held as follows:

Contrary to the characterization made by appellees, this preference does not constitute "racial discrimination." Indeed, it is not even a "racial" preference. ... The preference is not directed towards a "racial" group consisting of "Indians"; instead, it applies only to members of "federally recognized" tribes. This operates to exclude many individuals who are racially to be classified as "Indians." In this sense, the preference is political rather than racial in nature.

As long as the special treatment can be tied rationally to the fulfillment of Congress' unique obligation toward the Indians, such legislative judgements will not be disturbed. Here, where the preference is reasonable and rationally designed to further Indian self-government, we cannot say that Congress' classification violates due process.

Morton v. Mancari is regarded as a landmark case in American Indian law. Attorney Alvin J. Ziontz has written:

Not only did it apply a constitutional test to Indian legislation, it also defined the relationship between the tribes and the federal government in a new way. It is no accident that following *Mancari* the Interior Department began describing the relationship between the tribes and the United States as "government to government."

FURTHER READING

Ziontz, Alvin J. "Indian Litigation." In *The Aggressions of Civilization: Federal Indian Policy since the 1880s*, ed. Sandra L. Cadwallader and Vine Deloria, Jr. Philadelphia: Temple University Press, 1984.

N

NATCHEZ LEGAL AND POLITICAL TRADITIONS

The Natchez, an atypical example of a temple-mound people who survived into the period of sustained contact with Europeans along the lower Mississippi River, were ruled by a man called the Great Sun, whose decisions regarding individuals were absolute and despotic. In decisions regarding the nation, however, he was subject to the consensus of a council of respected elders. Unlike the **Pueblos**, whose houses were nearly equal in size, the Natchez afforded their ruler a palace. The Great Sun lived in a large house, twenty-five by forty-five feet, built atop a flat-topped earthen mound eight to ten feet high.

The Great Sun was an absolute ruler in every sense. A French observer said shortly after European colonization began in the area about 1700 that when the Great Sun

gives the leavings [of his meal] to his brothers or any of his relatives, he pushes the dishes to them with his feet. . . . The submissiveness of the savages to their chief, who commands them with the most despotic power, is extreme. . . . If he demands the life of any one of them he comes himself to present his head. (Maxwell 1978: 76)

Nearby, on another mound, stood a large building with two carved birds at either end of its roof—the temple in which reposed the bones of earlier Great Suns. Only the Great Sun (who was also head priest as well as king) and a few assistants were allowed to enter the temple.

The sons and daughters of the Great Sun were called Little Suns, the younger members of the royal family. Below the royal family in status was a class of nobles, and below them, a class of Honored Men. The rest of the people comprised the lower orders—the Stinkards. The term was not used in the presence of Stinkards themselves because they considered it offensive. In this hierarchical society, the Natchez sanctioned marriage customs that introduced some (usually downward) class mobility. A Great Sun had to marry from among the Stinkards. The male children of Great Suns became Nobles, who were also obliged to marry Stinkards. The male children of Honored Men became Stinkards. Descent was followed in the female line, and children of female Suns became Suns themselves. The system was matrilineal, but in the household the man's word was law. In the 1700s, this system broke down under the burdens of imported diseases and French colonial policies.

FURTHER READING

Maxwell, James A., ed. *America's Fascinating Indian Heritage.* Pleasantville, NY: Reader's Digest, 1978.

NATIONAL AMERICAN INDIAN COURT JUDGES ASSOCIATION

The National American Indian Court Judges Association (NAICJA) provides training for judges and attorneys who practice in Native American courts. In 1974, the group published several important studies related to law enforcement and jurisdiction on Indian reservations. The NAICJA, which developed from Arrow, Inc. (founded as an affiliate of the **National Congress of American Indians** in 1949), educated several hundred Native American judges in law and jurisprudence. This group also works to improve the quality of legal services on reservations.

FURTHER READING

National American Indian Court Judges Association. *Indian Courts and the Future.* Ed. David Getches. Washington, DC: NAICJA, 1978.
———. *Justice and the American Indian.* 5 vols. Washington, DC: NAICJA, 1974.

NATIONAL CONGRESS OF AMERICAN INDIANS

World War II altered American Indians' cultural and social status in the United States. Even before the war ended, Native Americans responded to this change in status by organizing a national Indian organization, the National Congress of American Indians (NCAI), in 1944. NCAI was an outgrowth of the Indian New Deal; its constitution was modeled along **Indian Reorganization Act** (IRA) lines, and most of the founders were Indians who had worked for the Bureau of Indian Affairs. With the formation of the NCAI, American Indian politics entered a new era as American Indian leaders in NCAI developed into adept lobbyists and politically savvy advocates for Indian policies and issues at the national and occasionally the international level.

Even though many of its founders had worked in the BIA, and its constitution mimicked the guidelines of IRA governments, the NCAI was anxious to become autonomous from the BIA. The NCAI rejected the idea that all Indian groups and Indian people had to support the Indian New Deal to be a part of NCAI. The proposed constitution stated that people of "Indian ancestry . . . or any Indian tribe, band, or community, may become a member." NCAI was especially anxious to advance Indian viewpoints on legislation in Washington and registered as a lobby. NCAI also formed an affiliate, Arrow, Inc., which was involved with fund-raising and field operations.

The founders of NCAI tried to create an organization that encompassed all political stances—New Dealers as well as those who had opposed the Indian New Deal throughout the previous decade. They wanted to secure civil rights for American Indians and educate non-Indians about the nature of American Indian people. They also wanted to "preserve rights under Indian treaties" and "promote the common welfare of American Indians."

Despite the NCAI's efforts to distance itself from the BIA, the American Indian Federation criticized the organization for being a government puppet. On April 29, 1945, the AIF resolved that NCAI

was sponsored and promoted by . . . John Collier and his satellites, meeting in Denver, Colorado, on November 16th, 1944, having as one of its objects and purposes the destruction of the American Indian Federation, which has heretofore opposed the communistic efforts of the said John Collier and his organization.

The BIA had, in fact, paid most of the travel costs of the founding members of NCAI for its planning meetings. Although the formation of NCAI in 1944 was significant, it did not gain widespread support within the Native American community until the early 1950s, when it became the center of organized opposition to the termination of American Indian treaty rights.

In a very real sense, NCAI was different from earlier pan-Indian groups such as the **Society of American Indians** in that it maintained its focus as a national lobby and advocate for Indian issues in Washington, D.C. At first, NCAI membership was only for persons "of Indian ancestry," but it did allow both Native American governments as well as individuals to join. Hence NCAI was both a federated body of Indian governments and an individual membership organization. From the 1950s until the present, NCAI has continued to be the single most important pan-Indian group in the United States. In the 1960s, the NCAI often was criticized by younger activist groups, such as the **National**

Indian Youth Council and the American Indian Movement, as being too representative of non-Indian ways and too imitative of the "establishment." The common ground in NCAI is not often evoked in racial terms. Instead, leaders of NCAI talk of "Indian people" and/or "Indian culture." NCAI leaders walk a tightrope representing not only the common interests of "Indian people" in general but also the multifaceted interests of various Native American governments.

FURTHER READING

Bernstein, Alison R. *American Indians and World War II*. Norman: University of Oklahoma Press, 1991.

Champagne, Duane. *American Indian Societies*. Cambridge. MA: Cultural Survival, 1989.

Collier, John. "The Indian in a Wartime Nation." *Annals of the American Academy of Political and Social Science* 223 (September 1942).

Nash, Gerald. *The American West Transformed*. Bloomington: Indiana University Press, 1985.

Parman, Donald. *Indians and the American West in the Twentieth Century*. Bloomington: Indiana University Press, 1994.

U.S. Senate Select Committee on Interior and Insular Affairs. "American Indian Federation, Resolution." 83rd Cong., National Archives. Record Group 46, Box 21, 83A–F9.

Witt, Shirley Hill. "Nationalistic Trends of the American Indian." In *The American Indian Today*, ed. Stuart Levine and Nancy O. Lurie. Baltimore: Penguin Books, 1972.

NATIONAL FARMERS UNION INSURANCE CO. V. CROW TRIBE
105 S. Ct. 2447 (1985)

An Indian child attending school on state land within reservation boundaries was injured in an accident, after which the child's guardian sued the school district in tribal court. The court issued a default judgment against the school district (which was insured by National Farmers Union Insurance); the school district then filed suit in federal court to have the judgment vacated.

The U.S. Supreme Court used this case to establish a precedent for primary legal authority in Native American courts over incidents occurring in **Indian Country**, as it ruled that the Native American court retained authority over this case. "We believe that examination should be conducted in the first instance in the Tribal Court itself," the Supreme Court ruled. "Until petitioners have exhausted the remedies available to them in the Tribal Court system . . . it would be premature for a federal court to consider any relief." This doctrine was refined two years later in *Iowa Mutual Insurance Co. v. LaPlante*. Legal scholar Frank Pommersheim commented, "Beneath the geologic holdings of the *National Farmers Union* and the *Iowa Mutual* cases, the tectonics of the

Supreme Court seem to be slowly bringing together the separate continents of federal and tribal courts" (1995: 95).

FURTHER READING

Pommersheim, Frank. *Braid of Feathers: American Indian Law and Contemporary Tribal Life.* Berkeley: University of California Press, 1995.

NATIONAL INDIAN YOUTH COUNCIL

The National Indian Youth Council (NIYC) was one of the first native-rights advocacy groups to grow out of the movement toward Native American **self-determination** that began in the early 1960s. The group, which took major initiatives in treaty-rights conflicts, was formed by people who began planning at the 1961 Chicago Indian Conference organized by anthropologist Sol Tax at the behest of President John F. Kennedy.

The organizers of NIYC, including John Redhouse, Clyde Warrior, Mel Thom, and Herb Blatchford, broke with older groups such as the **National Congress of American Indians**, believing them to be too imitative of non-Indian ways. The founders of NIYC, who were from a number of different native nations, brought a coordinated sense of pan-Indianism to native-rights advocacy. By the middle 1960s, the NIYC was assisting in organization of some of the first "fish-ins" in the Pacific Northwest, cooperating with a wide spectrum of Indian and minority-advocacy groups in that area. The efforts of the NIYC in this and other parts of the United States were notable for their multiethnic quality. For example, some of the earliest fish-ins were carried out with Latino, Afro-American, and Anglo-American (as well as Native American) support from organizations such as the Survival of American Indians Association and Seattle's El Centro de la Raza. The NIYC also was involved in a number of treaty-related lawsuits, voter-registration drives, and presentations before the United Nations on indigenous peoples' rights.

In the late 1970s, some of NIYC's major efforts were directed at stopping the construction of large coal strip-mining operations and coal-gasification plants on the Navajo reservation, on grounds that their pollution (particularly airborne lead, mercury, and boron) would make traditional Navajo agrarian life impossible. The NIYC also fought for cleanup of nuclear wastes on the reservation. In the late 1970s, NIYC also sought legal action to close several bars on the borders of the Navajo Nation. The NIYC sought a reservation economy that would be environmentally safe, economically productive, and respectful of traditional Navajo values. The group's 1976 *Annual Report* said:

In every sense of the word, we are engaged in a life and death duel. We have no other choice but to carry on with this struggle so that someday our children

[and] their children, and generations yet unborn will in their own time all walk in beauty.

FURTHER READING

Johansen, Bruce, and Roberto Maestas. *Wasi'chu: The Continuing Indian Wars.* New York: Monthly Review Press, 1979.

NATIVE AMERICAN BAR ASSOCIATION

The Native American Bar Association (NABA) joined other groups, including the Hispanic National Bar Association and the National Asian Pacific-American Bar Association, in providing opportunities for professional development among people who often have felt isolated in a professional legal setting. In 1993, the group established an electronic message center to allow instant communication between Native American attorneys nationwide.

Kirke Kickingbird, who received his J.D. degree from the University of Oklahoma in 1989, was elected to lead the NABA in 1996. Kickingbird heads the Native American Legal Resource Center at Oklahoma City University. The NABA has made legal services for Indians who cannot afford them a priority and has been active in developing peacemaker traditions as an alternative to the Anglo-American adversarial justice system. The group also emphasizes issues relevant to Native American **sovereignty** and treaty rights. In 1996, the NABA had about 275 dues-paying members out of roughly 1,500 Native American attorneys practicing in the United States.

NATIVE AMERICAN CHURCH V. NAVAJO TRIBAL COUNCIL 272 F.2d 131 (10th Cir. 1959)

In *Native American Church v. Navajo Tribal Council*, the provisions of the First Amendment regarding separation of church and state were found not to apply in **Indian Country**. The Tenth Circuit Court of Appeals held that "Indian tribes are not states. They have a status higher than that of states."

At issue in *Native American Church v. Navajo Tribal Council* was the right of the Navajo Council to prohibit the use of peyote in religious services and rituals on the Navajo reservation. The Native American Church asserted that the Navajo Council was bound by the First Amendment guarantee of freedom of religious expression. Ironically, this decision became a double-edged sword because a native government blocked arguments that would have favored its members' freedom of religion. The court held that

Indian tribes are not states. They have a status higher than that of states. They are subordinate and dependent nations possessed of all powers as such, only to the extent that they have expressly been required to surrender them by the supreme law of the land.

NATIVE AMERICAN EQUAL OPPORTUNITY ACT H.R. 13329, 95th Cong., 2d Sess. (1978)

The Native American Equal Opportunity Act was sponsored by state interests who used "equal opportunity" as a rationale for abrogating what they regarded as "special rights" allowed Native Americans by treaties. According to the ideology of those who wished to extend state jurisdiction over **Indian Country**, the treaties were said to make Indians **supercitizens**. This line of argument became prominent in the 1970s in such states as Washington, where State Attorney General Slade Gorton utilized it against Indian assertions of fishing rights that were vindicated in *United States v. Washington* (1974).

The Native American Equal Opportunity Act, which did not pass Congress, would have abrogated all treaties, ended federal supervision of Indian property, and subjected Indians to state law. No compensation was provided for lost rights or property. The measure has been characterized by Professor Robert N. Clinton as "only a stalking horse for the assimilationists' real demands—wholesale abrogation and appropriation of Indian property rights" (1981: 1018).

FURTHER READING

Ball, Milnar. "Constitution, Court, Indian Tribes." *American Bar Foundation Research Journal*, no. 1 (Winter 1987): 1–140.
Clinton, Robert N. "Indian Autonomy." *Stanford Law Review* 33 (1981): 1018.
Lowman, Bill. *220 Million Custers*. Anacortes, WA: Anacortes Printing, 1978.

NATIVE AMERICAN GRAVES PROTECTION AND REPATRIATION ACT 25 U.S.C.A. §§ 30001–30013 (1990)

The Native American Graves Protection and Repatriation Act includes several measures that outlaw the sale of Native American human remains and burial artifacts. This act also directed museums and other historical associations and societies to inventory their holdings of Native American remains and burial objects and to return them, when possible, to the native nations from which they were originally taken.

This act requires the secretary of the interior to establish a committee to monitor the return of human remains and objects buried with them. The secretary is also allowed to appropriate money, in the form of grants, to help museums and other historical repositories return remains. The act also imposes penalties for disturbance of burial sites, including unauthorized excavation, removal, damage, or destruction.

As early as 1976, California passed laws prohibiting individuals and private agencies from causing irreparable damage to any Indian religious site on public land (many are also grave sites), except for a "clear and convincing showing that the public interest and necessity so require" (Cal. Pub. Res. § 5097.9). Several states also have passed legislation requiring the return of Native American remains and burial objects. The first state to do so was Nebraska, following an intense controversy in which the State Historical Society at first refused to return its large inventory of Native American burial remains and objects.

FURTHER READING

"Symposium: The Native American Graves Protection and Repatriation Act of 1990 and State Repatriation-related Legislation." *Arizona State Law Review* 24 (1992): 1–562.

NATIVE AMERICAN RIGHTS FUND
The oldest and largest national Indian-interest law firm in the United States, the Native American Rights Fund (NARF) was started in 1970 as a project of California Indian Legal Services. The NARF does not retain individual clients like most law firms, but chooses cases on an issue-oriented basis, favoring those that will have the greatest impact on Native American people and American Indian law. In an average year, NARF provides advice to about a hundred Native American nations and bands. The fund supports two offices (one in Boulder, Colorado, and another in Washington, D.C.) through a combination of grants, contracts, and donations.

The NARF lists among its priorities legal education and the protection of Native American governments' independence, as well as the integrity of Indian lands, water, and other resources. It also seeks to protect human rights in **Indian Country** and to ensure that treaties and other federal laws affecting Native Americans are fairly enforced.

NATURAL LAW, NATURAL RIGHTS
During the 170 years between the first enduring English settlement in North America and the American Revolution, the colonists' perceptions of their Native American neighbors evolved from the Puritans' devil-man through the autonomous Noble Savage to a belief that the native peoples lived in confederations governed by natural law so subtle, so nearly invisible, that it was widely believed to be an attractive alternative to monarchy's overbearing hand. The Europeans' perceptions of Indian societies evolved as they became more dissatisfied with the European status quo. Increasingly, the native societies came to serve the transplanted Europeans, including some of the most influential founders of the United States, as a counterpoint to the European order. They found in existing native polities the values that the seminal European documents of the time celebrated in theoretical abstraction—life, lib-

erty, happiness, and a model of government by **consensus**, under natural rights, with relative equality of property. The fact that native peoples in America were able to govern themselves in this way provided advocates of alternatives to monarchy with practical ammunition for a philosophy of government based on the rights of the individual, which they believed had worked, did work, and would work for them in America.

This is not to say that the colonists sought to replicate Native American polities among societies in America descended from Europeans. The new Americans were too practical to believe that a society steeped in European cultural traditions could be turned on its head so swiftly and easily. They chose instead to borrow, to shape what they had with what they saw before them, and to create a new order that included aspects of both worlds.

The colonists' lives were pervaded by contact with native peoples to a degree that contemporary scholars sometimes find difficult to comprehend. Especially in its early years, colonization was limited to a few isolated pockets of land, widely dispersed, on a thin ribbon along the eastern seaboard. In the mid-eighteenth century, the frontier ran from a few miles west of Boston through Albany to Lancaster, Pennsylvania, or roughly to the western edge of today's eastern urban areas. The new Americans looked inland across a continent they already knew to be many times the size of England, France, and Holland combined. They did not know with any certainty just how far their new homeland extended. Maps of the time did not comprehend accurately the distances between the Atlantic and Pacific oceans. A few Spanish and French trappers and explorers had left their footprints in this vast expanse of land, but at that time at least 90 percent of North America was still the homeland of many hundreds of native peoples.

Through the seventeenth century, observers sometimes called native leaders "kings," then tended to contradict themselves by observing that leaders in native confederacies did not rule by fiat and cherished peace. Even before coming to America, William Penn wrote a letter to the **Iroquois** reinforcing Quaker and Iroquois ideas of "peace and justice that we may live friendly together as becomes the workmanship of the great God." In 1683, Penn commented in his letter to the Society of Free Traders on the Indians he knew:

Every king hath his council, and that consists of all the old and wise men of his nation. . . . nothing is undertaken, be it war, peace, the selling of land or traffick, without advising with them; and which is more, with the young men also. . . . The kings . . . move by the breath of their people. . . . It is the Indian custom to deliberate. . . . I have never seen more natural sagacity. (Dunn 261)

Why, for example, if colonial Americans were so infatuated with Europe, did they go to the trouble of a revolution to establish not only their own nation, but also their own identity? And why revolt in the name of "natural rights" exported in the books of European savants, when they had the European philosophers' original source material before their own eyes? The character of American democracy evolved importantly (although, of course, not solely) from the examples provided by American Indian confederacies that ringed the land borders of the British colonies. These examples provided a reality, as well as exercise for the imagination—and it is imagination, above all, that foments revolutions.

America's revolution emerged in both events and ideas: life, liberty, happiness; government by reason and consent rather than coercion; religious toleration (and ultimately religious acceptance) instead of a state church; checks and balances; federalism; and relative equality of property, equal rights before the law, and the thorny problem of creating a government that can rule equitably across a broad geographic expanse. Native America had a substantial role in shaping all these ideas, as well as the events that turned colonies into a nation of states. In a way that may be difficult to understand from the vantage point of the late twentieth century, Native Americans were present at the conception of the United States. We owe part of our national soul to those who came before us on this soil.

FURTHER READING

Dunn, Richard S., and Mary M. Dunn, eds. *The Papers of William Penn*. Vol. 2. Philadelphia: University of Pennsylvania Press, 1981–1987.

NATURAL MAN (AND WOMAN)

The Native American reference for the concepts of natural law, natural man, and natural rights stems from the Native American view of a maternal universe. David Cusick's *A Tale of the Foundation of the Great Island (Now North America), The Two Infants Born, and the Creation of the Universe* (1848) describes the **Iroquois** (Tuscarora) view, as our Native American example of the native peoples north of Mexico, of the understanding of natural law, that the universe comes from the Mother, simply referred to as the woman who conceives. Cusick's account tells of how she falls into a dark watery world of monsters who procure earth for her, which, when "varnished" on the back of a turtle, gradually increases to "a considerable island of earth" that breaks her fall into the dark watery world and allows her to give birth. A struggle within her womb, however, between the twins, Enigorio, the good-minded brother, and Enigonhahetgea, the bad-minded brother, over the manner of their birth, Enigorio, of "gentle disposition," being born in the natural way, and Enigonhahetgea, possessed of "an insolence of character," desiring to be born "under the side of the parent's arm," takes her life. After her death, Enigorio, favoring light, creates the universe, the sun, and the moon from his mother's head and body, and creeks, rivers, the forest, animals, fish, rain, and male and female from the dust in his own likeness, into whom he breathes life and calls them Ea-gwe-howe, "a real people." Contrary to Enigorio's efforts, Enigonhahetgea, wishing things to remain in darkness, as though he had no mother, confines the animals in the earth, creates "high mountains and falls of water, great steeps and reptiles injurious to mankind." Enigorio frees the animals and traces their likenesses on the rocks near the caves where they were confined. The two brothers then struggle over the universe. Enigorio defeats Enigonhahetgea with deer horns and confines him in the earth, but Enigonhahetgea, before "sinking down to Eternal doom" to become the Evil Spirit, declares that he "will have equal power over the souls of mankind after death."

The Senecas call the woman who conceives Falling Sky Woman and refer to the maternal Universe as Goyunaguna, "the Great Mother" (Peter Jemison, Seneca, conversation spring 1996), the Mohawk term being Istakowa (Eva Fadden, Six Nations Indian Museum, conversation, spring 1996). The Mohawks refer to the brothers in this myth as Ranikonriyo and Ranikonraksen. All agree, in our Iroquois example, that the universe is considered maternal and good, that moral aberrance is male, and that native freedom derives from mother honoring, through which Enigorio exhibits his goodness—"good-mindedness"—as life-giving and life enhancing, while Enigonhahetgea's moral turpitude or "bad-mindedness" exhibits itself as mother dishonoring in his desire to injure her and to confine animals.

The Mohawk term *kariwiyo*, "natural righteousness" or "natural goodness," meaning "it is right to love and wrong to hate," describes Enigorio's behavior as life-enhancing because he is born from his mother, his morality being based not on belief, but on experience and knowledge. *Kanontsitiio*, the Mohawk term for intelligence, therefore, defines intelligence as right male conduct, from the feminine *kanon* for mind, *ka* referring to the naturally flowing water of the Earth Mother, which accords with the masculine root *nikon* of Mohawk *ranikonriyo* designating "the proper or good mind," which renders *kanontsitiio* or intelligence as "He does things in the correct, good, or proper way" (Fadden, conversation, August 1994).

Orihwaienteritshera, the term that describes Mohawk education, contains spiritual and empirical knowledge that informs *kanontsitiio* or intelligence as meaning "He does things in the correct, good, or proper way," as just noted. *Orihwa*, like Seneca *orenda*, is spiritual knowledge, as in the opening address of the Iroquois Condolence Ceremony, which speaks to the mother, the earth, and says that everything comes from her body and spirit, implicitly and explicitly.

The *waienwa* element continues adherence to the spirit of the female in a cosmological sense as it refers to the additional knowledge, or tricks, for the survival and evolution of humans. The spiritual understanding is that humans are here for the short time and so they should not "mess it up," and that humanity's sole reason for being on earth is to prevent injustice, not to mete it out. Equity comes in because men cannot live alone.

The *shera* element is the empirical part of knowledge, what relates to skills and knowledge to do the tasks and to repeat them until they work. The basic understanding is that things evolve of themselves and that humans are not supposed to push them. The people's role is to work with the inventors to keep natural harmony. The result of *orihwaienteritshera* is *tsatonhkwis*, "to act like a human being" (Ron LaFrance, Mohawk educator, conversation, September 15, 1995).

Ga, for ground, the material earth signifier (as *ka* signifies water), informs *Gayanereh*, the Law of Peace of the Five Nations Wampum, meaning "to walk the good path according to Gaia" (or Goyunaguna, the Great Mother), "men walking the path of life with women," symbolically, "the man (*an*) flowing (or walking) with the mother (*ga*), as in two streams of water (*y*) coming together on the earth (*er*)." The understanding is that since men cannot live alone, equity coming from the human mother, male government is a trust from the mother to protect, to provide, and to work for peace. According to nature, as Iroquois law observes the mother's central place in government (government, the English-language ground, cognate of *Gayanereh*, meaning law founded from Gaia's ovum), the men accordingly draw their authority from the clan mothers who appoint their sons or male relatives and subject them to clan approval. Male appointees are required to be husbands and fathers (Tom Porter, Cornell University Bicentennial Conference, 1987), who legislate on everyone's behalf, according to men's duties and responsibilities to women and the community. The authority of the *Rotiyaner*, or Pathfinders, consequently, floats upward from the people (Louis Hall, Secretary, Ganienkeh Council Fire, letter).

As the natural man through *kariwiyo*, or natural goodness, adheres to nature through the mother in this way, Iroquois government seeks to imitate the natural authority and goodness of the mother, which, in the very deepest sense, is government according to natural law in the native world. In the deepest way, then, as feelings and intelligence connect government to nature, love and responsibility are the founding natural principles of Iroquois government that make the man free.

For example, in deeply human terms, where the quality of human life is finally evaluated, the breaking of ocean waves on the shore fills a human being with a sense of completeness, even when the waves are quite quiet. The rhythmic sound of water lapping at the shore or bank, in the breeze over the water, in water gently falling, or in the soundless liquid play of sunlight over moving water—these water sounds and the rhythm found in a steady gait of human feet on fall leaves, in the corresponding sounds of birds and animals during day and night. The rhythm of the seasons is the heartbeat of the earth that seeks, through the mother's choice that defines natural rights, human completeness in love, the squeeze and release of the muscles in loving and in the pulse of the mother's heartbeat pushing her blood to the fetus in her womb that culminates in the painful contractions of childbirth. Such maternal rhythms identify the mother with the human's sense of nature—hence the metaphor earth-mother or mother-earth or the earth, our mother.

Thus, love seeks to duplicate the same sense of completeness that humans experience in their own formation within the mother. Love is the table of being from the egg in humans being conceived of it and in their desiring it, men of women, women of men, the necessity of gender balance that results in happy children being fundamental to humans according to nature and the mother. Being human, therefore, among various native peoples, is the *hu*, or way of man, that evenness derived of even water of the mother—*ha, na*, and *wa*, as well as *ka* and *kwa*, evenness coming in the human comprehension of strong and gentle feelings expressed by a smile, song, or the drum, the contemplation of which gives rise to the human sense of well-being that allows for the trust that makes humans humane, which every culture must of nature's necessity, in some way, express—the highest expressions of this being the fair laws of government.

FURTHER READING

Colden, Cadwallader. *The History of the Five Indian Nations Depending on the Province of New-York in America*. 1727 and 1747. Binghamton: Cornell University Press, 4th printing, 1973.

Cusick, David. *A Tale of the Foundation of the Great Island (Now North America), The Two Infants Born, and the Creation of the Universe*. Lockport: NY: Turner and McCollum, Printers, 1848.

Erodes, R., and Alfonso Ortiz, eds. *American Indian Myths and Legends*. New York: Random House, 1984.

The Great Law of Peace of the Longhouse People. Rooseveltown, NY: Akwesasne Notes, 1971.

Hale, Horatio. *The Iroquois Book of Rites*. 1883. New York: Ams Press, 1969.

Morgan, Lewis H. *League of the Iroquois*. 1851. Secaucus, NJ: Citadel Press, 1972.

Parker, Arthur Caswell. "The League of the Five Nations." *Livingston County Historical Society Proceedings* (N.D.): 24–41.

BRUCE A. BURTON

NEW MEXICO V. MESCALERO APACHE TRIBE 462 U.S. 324 (1983)

The U.S. Supreme Court ruled in 1983 that the state of New Mexico could not enforce its hunting and fishing laws against anyone, Indian or not, within the Mescalero Apache reservation. The Court cited special circumstances to differentiate this case from others, such as the well-organized nature of the Mescaleros' government and the fact that nearly all of the reservation was owned by Native Americans. The Court held that state jurisdiction is preempted if it is compatible with and outweighed by federal and Native American interests. In other words, state jurisdiction is generally preempted if it conflicts with federal and Native American interests as reflected in federal law.

A Native American nation also may exclude nonmembers from its territory, according to *New Mexico v. Mescalero*. The court held that "a tribe's power to exclude non-members entirely or to condition their presence on the reservation . . . is well-established."

NORTHWEST COAST CULTURE AREA, POLITICAL AND LEGAL SYSTEMS

The peoples of the Northwest Coast departed from the general Native American reliance on a **consensus** model of law and government. This departure was not slight: their system was entirely different, being status-driven, caste-bound, and, compared to those of many native peoples, very aggressive, even among peoples who shared cultures very similar to their own. From the Chickliset in the north to the Makah in coastal Washington, down the coast to northwestern California, a large group of different peoples shared attributes of social organization based on hierarchy and the accumulation of wealth.

When English and Spanish explorers first encountered them in the late eighteenth century, European diseases were just beginning to devastate Northwest Coast peoples who had built a dense population network of relatively large villages among the fjords of western Vancouver Island. Skillful use of abundant fish runs and timber resources encouraged a density of population known in only a few areas of North America outside of the areas dominated by the Aztecs and Mayas. Each year, millions of salmon migrated past Northwest Coast villages on their way from the ocean to their spawning grounds at the headwaters of hundreds of rivers and streams. Northwest Coast villages usually did not communicate with one another on a regular basis (they often were separated by nearly impassible mountains). While the villages evolved distinct languages, their cultures shared many characteristics. Occasionally, nearby villages (which often communicated by sea) were grouped in loose confederacies, but no political authority existed that united all the Northwest Coast peoples.

The Northwest Coast culture stretched from the Alaska Panhandle to the northwest coast of present-day California. Members of Northwest Coast nations built large, substantial houses for extended families from massive beams taken from the tall timber of the coast. The lodges averaged roughly fifteen yards by forty yards in floor area; some were larger. Rank and status permeated nearly every facet of their lives, even dictating what portion of a house a given person occupied. The class system was hereditary as well. While many native peoples (especially in the eastern portions of North America) took steps to prevent accumulation of wealth or the carrying of power to the grave, the Northwest Coast peoples did the opposite. The class structure was fixed in time, handed down in temporal lockstep by the rules of primogeniture, the passage of rights and property to the firstborn son.

Northwest Coast peoples recognized three classes that seemed as imperishable as the red cedar from which they constructed their lodges: nobility, commoners, and slaves. The nobility comprised chiefs and their closest relatives; the eldest son was the family head. He, his family, and a few associates lived in the rear right-hand corner of the house, abutted by people of lower status. These people were said to be "under the arm" of the chief. The next-highest-ranking chief, usually a younger brother of the head chief, invariably occupied the rear left-hand corner of the house, with his family. He, too, had a number of people "under the arm." The other two corners were occupied by lesser chiefs' families. The space between the corners, along the walls, was used by commoners' families and a few very junior-ranking nobility. They were called "tenants," while the nobility in the corners reserved the right to ownership of the house. Commoners could move from one house to another at will, and since they often performed arduous but necessary skilled labor (such as carpentry or whaling), chiefs competed to retain the best workers. The most successful chiefs were affectionate and generous toward the common families who chose to live in their lodges. Slaves had no designated lodgings or rights; they were captured in raids on other peoples along the coast and were sometimes traded for other slaves or goods. A noble in one village could be captured and sold into slavery in another. The captive's relatives might then mount a counter-raid to free him. A person also could fall into slavery because of accumulated unpaid debts.

Economic, political, and ceremonial power was highly prized and unequally distributed among the Northwest Coast peoples. Like few other native peoples, they paid intense attention to private property. Such wealth was often inherited. A chief might own a lodge, salvage rights for foodstuffs in nearby forests, and even fishing rights along a portion of coastline for miles offshore. Chiefs also owned salmon spawning streams and the right to fish in them. A chief might also own important ceremonial property, such as dances and songs, as well as the right to present certain rituals. Lesser chiefs owned less valuable resources; all land that had an economic use was owned by some member of the nobility. A chief could create power networks under his aegis by allowing lesser chiefs' families or commoners access to his lands and waters, usually for a second harvest.

Because the chief controlled the access of people in lower orders to food, shelter, and even spiritual sustenance, the Northwest Coast societies were more hierarchical than even the Aztecs or the monarchical societies of Europe during the period of first contacts with native America. There were no councils to exercise restraint on the chiefs. As noted, however, a "good chief" did gather power by being generous to those "under the arm." The ceremonial potlatch was an expression of this ethic: on one level, it was a display of wealth by the chief or chiefs hosting it; on another level, the intricate gift giving of the ritual bespoke an inherent—but, like all other aspects of Northwest Coast native life, tightly controlled—distribution of that same wealth. The potlatch thus consolidated the power and authority of its hosts by reminding lesser nobles and commoners that the high chiefs controlled every aspect of village life.

Among the Northwest Coast peoples, the potlatch was not usually concerned so much with the economic motives of getting and giving as with enhancing social status, honoring ancestors, and sealing marriages. According to Duane Champagne, the ritual "should be understood from within its own cultural and institutional framework, and not be too easily compared with self-interested materialism" (210). Similarly, the emphasis on rank in Northwest Coast societies was not simply an imitation of Western hierarchical societies. Instead, the Tlingit concept of rank was integrated into that peoples' belief that proper behavior in the present (such as contributing to potlatches, fulfilling one's clan obligations, and submitting to the collective will of the house group) could cause one to be reborn into a more aristocratic lineage.

The speakers and war chiefs of a village usually were raised from youth through inheritance among the children who had a small quantum of royal blood. They tended to be administrative officers who carried out the will of the chiefs. Although most war chiefs were selected by the high chiefs from their families, one of the few ways in which a commoner family could advance in the village class structure was to have its eldest son receive such an office. Once a common family had been raised in this way, the title of war chief remained with it as a right of inheritance. Otherwise, the caste system of the Northwest Coast peoples was inviolate. People nearly always married others of similar rank; marriages out of rank were severely discouraged. One of the few rights that a Northwest Coast chief did not own was that of marrying a woman out of his class. To do so would risk reprimand by everyone in the village as an assault on a lineage system that the people involved believed had been the same since creation.

Unlike some of the more democratic native peoples elsewhere on the continent, the Northwest Coast peoples generally did not have an elaborate kinship system. The existence of clans tends to create affinity structures independent of class structures; the Northwest Coast peoples defined themselves, above all, by rank. Notions of status also seemed to be the major method of controlling interpersonal conflict. Should a verbal disagreement explode into a fistfight, members of each participant's family would urge him to cease or risk bringing shame on them. The two combatants might then relapse into a vigorous verbal battle, throwing the worst imaginable insults at each other, as relatives continued to pacify them: "Don't think about him anymore. It's not right to fight. You have a good name. Don't bring it down. Don't think about it—just let it go." In some cases, people who engaged in fisticuffs might be upbraided before the community and abjectly humiliated at public occasions. Outside of this, the Northwest Coast peoples, unlike the **Cheyenne, Wyandot** (Huron), **Mandan**, and **Iroquois**, had no formal methods of social control within their communities. The Northwest Coast peoples' use of sorcery was infrequent and mild compared to that of peoples who were less class conscious.

Class consciousness pervaded the mechanisms of justice among the Tlingit, one of the Northwest Coast peoples. The concept of crime against an individual did not exist. The loss of life (as in murder) or of property (as in theft) was taken to be an offense against the family. If, for example, a man of low status murdered a man of high status, the offender usually was not called upon to atone for the crime individually. Instead, the offending family would be compelled by custom to deliver for execution a person of equal status to that of the victim. The individual offender of low status might be sold into slavery. The penalty for offenses short of murder, such as assault or accidental death, was usually payment in goods to the offended family. After settlement of a dispute, the matter was closed with a ceremonial "peace dance" involving the entire community, the object being to restore social and spiritual harmony that had been disrupted by the crime.

While chiefs worked to maintain peace in their own villages and with allies, raids on other settlements were frequent and often very bloody. While they may have shared cultural attributes, there was no "Northwest Coast confederacy," and no law, as with the Iroquois, enforced peace between groups. Raids were minutely planned and rehearsed, from the initial landing, usually by canoe, on a moonless night to the swift capture or beheading of sleeping opponents, the burning of their canoes to prevent counterattack, and the seizure of booty. As with just about every other aspect of Northwest Coast life, the high chiefs planned and controlled every facet of planning and executing a raid.

FURTHER READING

Champagne, Duane. *American Indian Societies: Strategies and Conditions of Political and Cultural Survival.* Cambridge, MA: Cultural Survival, 1989.
Drucker, Philip. *Cultures of the North Pacific Coast.* San Francisco: Chandler, 1965.
————. *The Northern and Central Nootkan Tribes.* Bureau of American Ethnology Bulletin no. 144. Washington, DC: Smithsonian Institution, 1951.
Oberg, K. "Crime and Punishment in Tlingit Society." *American Anthropologist* 36 (1934): 145–156.
Stevenson, I. "Seven Cases Suggestive of Reincarnation among the Tlingit Indians of Southeastern Alaska." *Proceedings of the American Society for Psychical Research* 26 (1966): 231–234.

NORTHWEST ORDINANCE (1787)

The Northwest Ordinance of 1787 provided for gradual statehood of western lands north of the Ohio River and west to the Mississippi River. The ordinance was written to allow the eventual formation of between three and five states that could be admitted to the United States on terms equal to those of the original thirteen states. It provided a mechanism to bring western territories into the Union without a long period as colonies in an inferior (and exploitable) political position.

The Northwest Ordinance also outlined procedures for racial relations in the western lands. The ordinance stated that "the utmost good faith" should attend dealings with the Indians, and that their property "shall never be taken from them without their consent." The ordinance decreed that Indians "shall never be invaded or disturbed, unless in just and lawful wars authorized by Congress."

The Northwest Ordinance was passed by the **Articles of Confederation** government as the **Constitution** was being framed, and it is generally recognized that Charles Thomson (adopted Delaware and secretary to Congress) was the major author of this legislation. While this critical piece of legislation was in progress, Thomson traveled to Philadelphia to consult with his friends at the Constitutional Convention. Thomson was a Pennsylvanian and, of course, was close to James Wilson and **Benjamin Franklin**. Thomson also knew most of the other convention delegates who had served previously in the Continental Congress and the confederation government.

The Northwest Ordinance also contained an extensive Bill of Rights, a distinctly American idea. The **Iroquois** Great Law of Peace is very sensitive to the rights of individuals and the potential abuses of the state. Most European governments were still either divine-right monarchies or commercial oligarchies controlled by the middle and upper classes. The Articles of Confederation placed a great deal of emphasis on local rights and autonomy at the expense of defense and the regulation of commerce. But as the Northwest Ordinance was clearing Congress in July 1787 in New York, a convention was meeting in Philadelphia to draft a blueprint for the government that would replace the Articles of Confederation. No one has ever examined the agenda that the Northwest Ordinance and its Bill of Rights established in the ratification process.

O

OKIMAW OHCI HEALING LODGE

The Okimaw Ohci Healing Lodge (in Saskatchewan, Canada) is North America's first prison exclusively for Native American inmates. The prison utilizes Native American cultural practices to reform inmates' behavior, and many judges and prosecutors have said that it is more effective and less expensive than other methods of incarceration. Studies show an 80 percent reduction in repeat offenses when inmates of Okimaw Ohci are compared to prisoners who have served time in conventional Canadian prisons.

Okimaw Ohci (meaning "Hills of Thunder") was being operated only for women inmates in the middle 1990s. It was described in a *Los Angeles Times* account as "a collection of brightly painted wood-frame buildings set on a hillside near Maple Creek, a farm town in Southwestern Saskatchewan" (May 12, 1996: 11–A). Norma Green, the warden, is educated in social work rather than penal administration and is often called "Kikawaw," Cree for "our mother," by inmates. Staff (most of whom are Native American) and inmates mix freely and often eat meals together. Inmates live in townhouse-style dormitories. Prisoners are told that they are being healed, as well as serving a sentence for a crime.

Inmates are often referred to Okimaw Ohci by a "sentencing circle" from the defendant's peers made up of community leaders, the defendant, the victim of the crime, and members of both families. Sentences are arrived at by consensus after discussion that may extend for several hours.

FURTHER READING

"Canadians Open Indian Prison in Tryout of Cultural Justice." *Los Angeles Times* wire report in *Omaha World-Herald*, May 12, 1996, p. 11–A.

OLIPHANT V. SUQUAMISH INDIAN TRIBE 435 U.S. 191 (1978)

The U.S. Supreme Court's ruling in *Oliphant v. Suquamish Indian Tribe* denied Indians jurisdiction over crimes committed by non-Indians on their land. By extension, the Supreme Court found that Native American courts have no general criminal jurisdiction in cases involving non-Indians. In this Washington State case, the Court held that such criminal jurisdiction would violate the native nations' status as domestic dependent nations. It thus terminated the Suquamish tribe's attempt to become the first Native American nation in modern times to assert criminal jurisdiction over non-Indians.

The specific question at issue in *Oliphant v. Suquamish* was whether a native nation possessed criminal jurisdiction over non-Indians as an attribute of its inherent sovereign powers. The Supreme Court ruled 7–2 that it did not. The majority opinion was delivered by Justice William Rehnquist. His opinion held that Native American nations' **sovereignty** had been diminished by their incorporation into the United States.

American Indian criminal jurisdiction has been complicated by the frequent sale of formerly allotted land to non-Indians inside the 7,276-acre Port Madison Reservation's boundaries. This is a frequent problem on reservations where allotment was pursued vigorously, leading to a **checkerboard pattern** of landownership. The Suquamish reservation was unusual in that of 3,000 people living within its boundaries, only about 150 (roughly a quarter of a total of 550 Suquamish) were Suquamish when Mark Oliphant was brought before its court on a charge of disorderly conduct, as well as punching a tribal police officer who was arresting him.

The *Oliphant* case arose following the arrest of several non-Indians for rowdiness at the Suquamish reservation's annual Chief Seattle Days on the Port Madison Reservation across Puget Sound west of the city of Seattle. At the time, 127 Native American courts were operating in the United States, and 33 of them had claimed jurisdiction over non-Indian offenders. The Supreme Court held that such assertion required an affirmative declaration of power by Congress.

The *Oliphant* case is also remarkable for the fact that both a federal district court and the Ninth Circuit Court of Appeals used Chief Justice **John Marshall**'s opinions to uphold Suquamish jurisdiction, while the U.S. Supreme Court later cited the same case law to deny jurisdiction.

The Ninth Circuit emphasized the opinions of Marshall that stress Indian nations' separateness and residual sovereignty. Rehnquist's ruling
that Indian sovereignty has "inherent limitations" has been widely criticized by Native American legal experts as a legal invention against a
backdrop indicating that Indians retain sovereign powers not relinquished by treaty or extinguished by act of Congress. Attorney Alvin J.
Ziontz, who took an active role in this case, commented:

The Supreme Court refused to follow the residual sovereignty analysis. Instead,
it created a new gloss on the doctrine. Indian tribes, said the court, not only lost
powers by express congressional action, but they were also proscribed from
exercising powers "inconsistent with their status." The Supreme Court viewed
tribal punishment of whites as fundamentally incompatible with federal
sovereignty. (Interview, 1979)

The Supreme Court's ruling in *Oliphant v. Suquamish* also was based
in part on an earlier ruling in **United States v. McBratney** (1882), involving the murder of one non-Indian man by another on the Ute reservation in Colorado. The Court held that the state had jurisdiction over
crimes by non-Indians on reservation lands.

According to legal scholar Charles F. Wilkinson, the *Oliphant* decision "marked the historic low ebb of the doctrine of tribal sovereignty
and the Marshall-Cohen view of the field." Historic low ebbs can be
transitory, however. Wilkinson noted with some irony that "just sixteen
days after deciding *Oliphant*, the court rendered an endorsement of
tribal sovereignty" in **United States v. Wheeler**, in which Justice Stewart's majority opinion cited both Cohen and Marshall approvingly.

The Court held in *Oliphant* that "from the formation of the Union
and the adoption of the Bill of Rights, the United States has manifested
. . . great solicitude that its citizens be protected by the United States
from unwarranted intrusions on their personal liberty." This statement
evoked from legal scholar Milnar S. Ball the following reaction:

One is reminded of Richard Slotkin's observation that the mythology of rescuing
whites from their Indian captors was a recurrent pretext for making war upon
Indians and a means of gaining public support for it. Custer, for example, was
represented as the "rescuer and avenger of captive white women, the hero who
stands between white civilization and the exterminating fury of the savages."
(1987: 125)

FURTHER READING

Ball, Milnar. "Constitution, Court, Indian Tribes." *American Bar Foundation
    Research Journal*, no. 1 (Winter 1987): 1–140.
Slotkin, Richard. *The Fatal Environment*. New York: Atheneum, 1985.
Wilkinson, Charles F. *American Indians, Time, and the Law: Native Societies
    in a Modern Constitutional Democracy*. New Haven, CT: Yale University
    Press, 1987.

OMAHA (U'MA'HA) POLITICAL AND LEGAL TRADITIONS

The Omahas maintained a central council of seven chiefs who held the title for life, given good behavior, following the achievement of merit in their personal lives. Two of these chiefs were ranked preeminent, based on their records as leaders. The council had jurisdiction over political and legal (including judicial) affairs that affected the well-being of the nation. Its members refrained purposefully from interfering with the private lives of others unless their behavior threatened social cohesion.

The central council reached its decisions by **consensus**, deciding matters related to war and peace, the timing of collective hunts, and guilt or innocence in cases of major crimes, such as murder. The council was empowered by custom to order the death of an Omaha whose behavior endangered the well-being of the people. Usually, the offender was first warned by a slaughter of his horses. Murder was punished by **banishment** during which the murderer's family was allowed to give him provisions. The banishment ended at the discretion of the offended family.

The Omahas' Sacred Legend describes how the Council of Seven was assembled to "hold the people together," according to Alice Fletcher and Francis LaFlesche's *The Omaha Tribe* (1911). The legend tells of old (wise) men meeting to uphold peace within the nation and to limit incidences that might lead to accidental hostilities with other peoples.

Many centuries ago, the Omaha Council of Seven was made up of hereditary chiefs, but by the early reservation period a meritocracy developed for bestowing chieftainship, according to Fletcher and La-Flesche. An Omaha man could be admitted to one of two classes of chieftainship by performance of good and heroic deeds, as well as presentation of gifts to those who had achieved the status. The types of gifts required a great deal of personal sacrifice and bravery, as well as ingenuity. The requirement that gifts be given was a test of the applicant's generosity and skill at acquiring material possessions that he could then give away. An aspirant to the office of a chief who had died or resigned because of infirmity might be ordered to give eagles, eagle war bonnets, quivers (with bows and arrows), otter skins, buffalo robes, and ornamented shirts and leggings. With the coming of trade between Omahas and European Americans, such implements as copper kettles, guns, horses, and blankets often were required. "A lazy fellow or an impulsive, improvident man could not acquire the property represented by these gifts," commented Fletcher and LaFlesche (206). In addition, a candidate's character was considered; no number of gifts could win office for someone whom the sitting chiefs thought was unqualified by reason of his temperament. "A maxim was," wrote Fletcher and La-Flesche, " 'A chief must be a man who can govern himself' " (206).

Once the council had decided to elevate an aspirant to office, a delegation was sent to his lodge bearing the Omahas' two Sacred Pipes. The candidate was then given one last chance to decline the responsibilities of office. If he accepted, the pipes were smoked in his lodge as an initiation to chieftainship.

The Council of Seven was the Omahas' only governing body. There were no subchiefs of bands, and families did not carry a political role as did the clans among the **Iroquois**. The idea was to subordinate all contentions to a single body. When the council met, five other people were allowed to attend on an ex officio basis: the keeper of the Sacred Pole, the keeper of the Sacred Buffalo Hide, the keeper of the two Sacred Pipes (as well as the keeper of the ritual used to fill them), and the keeper of the Sacred Tent of War. The chiefs sat in order of their "counts" (accumulated honors). A member would introduce a proposal, which would be passed around the circle, with discussion on the first pass. The proposal would then be sent around the circle a second time, during which the chiefs would strive to reach consensus. A decision was made only when the chiefs could speak with one voice, a process that could consume many hours of intricate discussion. Sometimes rulings were delayed for days (or even weeks or months) so that leaders could confer with other members to consider the ramifications of a decision.

The Council of Seven functioned as a court as well as as a legislative body; it also appointed "soldiers" to announce and, when necessary, to enforce its decisions. Some of these police regulated the annual buffalo hunt, during which anyone who began the hunt early without permission was flogged for a first offense. On a second offense, the illegal hunter's tent was destroyed, his horses and other property were confiscated, and his family was reduced to begging. A staff of ironwood with a jagged edge was kept in the Sacred Tent of War for use against anyone whom the Council of Seven had decided must die to preserve peace within the nation. The jagged edge of the ironwood staff was dipped into poison (often from rattlesnakes) and rammed into the offender, usually in a crowd. Such punishment could be authorized for crimes as minor as making light of the council, according to Fletcher and La-Flesche.

Thievery was uncommon among the Omahas; the only punishment was restitution. Assaults also were not frequent and were usually dealt with by family members. Adultery was severely punished; a man guilty of it might have his property confiscated. A woman guilty of adultery usually was flogged. A woman who was jealous of another woman's attentions to her husband might attack the interloper with a knife. Such an attack was not generally considered a crime in Omaha society. Murder was punished by banishment, as outlined earlier.

With the coming of traders and widespread European-American settlement in the Omahas' territory during the first half of the nineteenth century, the old order of chiefs lost much of its authority. Some Omahas were made "treaty chiefs" by U.S. negotiators, while others of questionable character were enriched by trade. The elaborate system of accumulating honors to earn status began to disintegrate with the creation of new power centers in the society beholden to outside influences.

FURTHER READING

Dorsey, J. O. "Omaha Sociology." *Bureau of American Ethnology Bulletin* 3 (1884): 211–370.
Fletcher, Alice, and Francis LaFlesche. *The Omaha Tribe*. Bureau of American Ethnology Bulletin 27 (1911). Reprint. New York: Johnson Reprint Corp., 1970.
Lowie, Robert H. *Primitive Society*. New York: Boni and Liveright, 1920.
Tate, Michael. *The Upstream People: An Annotated Research Bibliography of the Omaha Tribe*. Metuchen, NJ: Scarecrow Press, 1991.

ONEIDA, COUNTY OF, V. ONEIDA INDIAN NATION 470 U.S. 226 (1985)

When the United States prohibited the sale of Indian land without federal approval by passing the **Trade and Intercourse Acts** (beginning in 1790), many states and individuals ignored the laws and bought or seized Native American land anyway. Nearly two centuries later, these laws were brought back into court to argue that land had been illegally seized. In *County of Oneida v. Oneida Indian Nation*, the Oneida people won rights to 100,000 acres of land transferred to New York State in 1795, while George Washington was president of the United States.

The case was filed in 1970 and was originally dismissed in federal courts for lack of jurisdiction. The case was contested in the courts until the Supreme Court reversed the lower-court decisions during its 1985 session. The Court held that the Oneidas had a right to sue under common law, and that the right had not been diminished by the passage of time because it was not limited by a statute of limitations or any other form of abatement. The Court also said that the Oneidas had an "unquestioned right" to their lands, and that the Indians' right of occupancy was "as sacred as the fee simple of the whites." The Court's decision was split 5–4, and the case was bitterly contested because it denied the property rights of some owners who had held title for as long as 175 years.

OPINIONS OF THE SOLICITOR

Opinions of the solicitor are issued by the Solicitor's Office of the Interior Department on points of American Indian law. These opinions are requested by administrators in the department in lieu of taking a matter to court to get a decision. The opinion defines the issue at hand and gives an indication of the laws that apply to it and how a judge might rule. There exist, of course, no guarantees that all judges will agree with the opinion. In the middle 1970s, the Interior Department published a collection of opinions of the solicitor running from 1917 to 1974. The collection is contained in two volumes and runs to about 2,200 pages.

P

PAWNEE POLITICAL AND LEGAL TRADITIONS
Prior to their 1875 confinement on a reservation in north central **Indian Territory**, the Pawnee were divided into four bands that occupied the central region of the Great Plains. As Caddoan-speaking people, their confederacy was loosely united by language, social custom, religious ceremony, trading partnerships, military alliances, and, later, intermarriage. The Chaui (Grand), Kitkahahki (Republican), and Pitahawirata (Tappage) bands always maintained a close relationship, but generally considered the Skidi (Wolf), or northernmost band, to be somewhat different. Because the Skidi had separated themselves from the other Pawnees during the early migrations to join the Arikara, and because they always wished to maintain a tradition of uniqueness, some resentment and internal conflict periodically emerged. Not until non-Indian pressures began to mount against them in the mid-nineteenth century did the four bands attempt to work as a more unified entity. Even today, Pawnee humor perpetuates sarcastic remarks by one band about another.

Although the Pawnee had long occupied the Great Plains, the zenith of their power occurred during the mid-eighteenth century when they combined three economic pursuits into a complementary whole. As always, they built their earth-lodge villages along the rivers and streams of the eastern Plains, where they engaged in diverse agriculture. They raised corn, squash, beans, and pumpkins, as well as gathered wild fruits and vegetables to maintain an adequate diet. But with the widespread availability of horses beginning in the early eighteenth century, they developed a more extensive buffalo-hunting culture. The horse provided mobility to follow the buffalo herds further out into the semiarid regions where their tipis and buffalo ceremonies came to distinguish them as Plains Indians. At about the same time, the Pawnees initiated a third enterprise by placing themselves in an important middleman position as traders between native nations. By acquiring French and Spanish manufactured goods, as well as horses, they exchanged goods far and wide across the Plains and all the way to the Santa Fe trade fair.

Economic prosperity brought a new power and increased numbers. By 1800, the combined population had risen to possibly 11,000 people. A series of smallpox epidemics began to reach their area within the following decades, and the virulent epidemic of 1837–1838 may have killed as many as 2,000 people. By 1840, the first official population count taken by missionaries recorded only 6,200 Pawnees. This was also a particularly difficult time because the Pawnee found increased trading and raiding pressures from other native groups, most notably the populous western Sioux, who were unrelenting in their attacks.

Kinship played a key role in the identity of each Pawnee and determined his or her relationship with all members of the immediate village. Each person in the village traced descent from a recognized (though often mythical) common ancestress. Kinship lines were matrilineal, and the place of residence by a newly married couple was with the wife's mother. Kinship terminology differed to indicate whether a person was speaking of a relative on the mother's or father's side of the family. The Pawnee also had a polygamous marriage system that permitted men of rank and respect to have more than one wife. Although the practice was not widespread within the general ranks of society, it allowed a man to look after the well-being of a widowed sister of his first wife. This kept kinship lines and children's birthrights intact, while recognizing the reality of a high degree of mortality in the population.

Although the southern bands of Chaui, Kitkahahki, and Pitahawirata have not been thoroughly studied by scholars, the Skidi have been the subject of much investigation. The Skidi provide our model for discussion of Pawnee political life, but readers should recognize that variations existed among the other bands, and no single model was followed by all.

A hereditary chief presided over each Skidi village, and a sacred bundle served as a symbol of unity for the villagers; it also represented the chief's authority to make decisions. Despite the matrilineal orientation of kinship, chieftainship (and many priestly duties) passed through a line of males. Generally the chief transferred authority to his eldest son, but approval had to come from the chief's council. If the eldest son was incapable of assuming the role, a younger son or another close male relative would likely be chosen by the council. Thirty-one men composed the council and were chosen from the most accomplished warriors and leaders among the Skidi. These nonhereditary chiefs rose to the position by merit and generally held the position for a lifetime unless they disgraced themselves and their families.

During council meetings, the nonhereditary chiefs stood out. They were entitled to wear the eagle feather in their hair and to specially decorate their clothing or buffalo robe with powerful symbols or depiction of their past bravery. Likewise, they could paint their faces red and place the special blue line and powerful image of the Turkey's Foot constellation across their foreheads.

The idea of **consensus** dominated every aspect of Pawnee decision making. Both the hereditary chief and his council were entrusted with maintaining harmony among the people. Sometimes they made decisions applicable to all village members regarding such matters as the movement of camps, the establishment of alliances with outsiders, and when to begin the buffalo hunt. At other times, they used their prestige and influence to settle disputes among the people. This might involve their personal intercession into a family feud, providing sage advice, or even distributing some of their own personal wealth to aggrieved individuals to placate them. Concord was the prime objective of all forms of political leadership, and a chief enhanced his credibility by selflessly risking his own fame and fortune to preserve this harmony.

The idea of punishment also followed the consensus formula. Rather than creating a long list of crimes and their requisite punishments, the Pawnees preferred to lead by example. Shame was a more compelling means of producing acceptable behavior than was physical retribution. Bad behavior led to counseling by one's kinsmen and perhaps representatives of the council. Only repeated violations of social custom produced severe retribution, and the entire family indirectly suffered from the stigma. To avoid this calamity, families not only policed their own members, but also exchanged presents or paid wealth to aggrieved parties so that further contentiousness could be avoided. Heinous crimes such as murder and rape of a tribal member could lead to blood revenge or total exile from the village. To be so ostracized must have seemed like the ultimate punishment to the small numbers who faced it because this act separated them from the social safety net that strong kinship lines readily provided.

Although hereditary village chiefs and their councils exercised enormous influence, their power was far from absolute. They did not have the authority to represent all members of the village or to speak with one voice regarding treaties or transfer of communal lands. Their decisions also could be challenged by religious leaders within the group, or even by a significant proportion of the rank-and-file villagers. Consensus ideology did not operate on the basis of simple majority rule, but rather on the strength of near unanimity. If sizable segments of the village population stood in opposition to an impending decision, then speeches and persuasion continued until one side or the other changed its position or withdrew from the debate. This method of decision making was very deliberate and often so slow that outsiders ridiculed the system. Yet it worked well among the Pawnee until the advent of the reservation system, which imposed a more dictatorial form of government over the people.

Governance of Pawnee society was manifested not only in the form of hereditary and nonhereditary chiefs, but also in men with spiritual power. Every Pawnee recognized the interconnection of all things and the supreme power of the Great Spirit known as Tirawahut. Guiding the people through the mystical understanding were holy men who supervised the ceremonies and protected the sacred medicine bundles. According to tradition, the sacred bundles were gifts from particular stars or were created under the supervision of a star. Each of the six medicine bundles preserved the unity and prosperity of the thirteen confederated Skidi communities. One of the towns, Center Village, also hosted the Evening Star bundle that contained the greatest of powers. While holy men perpetuated the rituals and passed the knowledge to a close relative, hereditary chiefs oversaw the physical care of the actual bundles. Each was also in the care of a woman who had special knowledge of that bundle, but she could not participate directly in the ceremonies associated with its power. Such was the esteem of holy men that they could overrule the hereditary chiefs and council on special matters, although this seems to have been a rare occurrence.

A second array of spiritual powers belonged to shamans who possessed special healing abilities. Each shaman's power came from an animal that, in turn, had acquired that power from a specific star. The healer could receive his power directly from the animal or through instruction from a proven shaman. These men participated in their own societies and performed some of the seasonal rituals such as those associated with the first thunder in spring. More often, however, they provided healing ceremonies and advice to individual patients seeking their aid.

Profound changes in the Pawnee governance system came during the late nineteenth and early twentieth centuries as life shifted to the reservations. Old ceremonies predicated on the buffalo hunt disappeared or underwent severe modification. Hereditary chiefs and councils no longer had any powers unless the agent approved them. Only compliant leaders were entrusted with authority by federal representatives, missionaries, and reformers who were committed to breaking the patterns of traditionalism. A legacy of dependency, high unemployment, cultural decay, and economic morass plagued the people throughout these decades.

The present Pawnee government owes its origins to a provision within the 1934 Oklahoma Indian Welfare Act. This act provided for incorporation and creation of a charter establishing two eight-member governing bodies. While the Nasharo Council is represented by chiefs from the four bands, the Business Council is elected at large by enrolled adult members. These two governmental bodies oversee economic development programs and daily management of national affairs, as well as negotiations with the Bureau of Indian Affairs and other organs of the federal government. At times, the two Pawnee groups have opposed each other on specific policies and philosophies of governing such as distribution plans for **Indian Claims Commission** monies, but overall the two have found common ground for preserving the consensus ideal that their ancestors so highly valued.

FURTHER READING

Blaine, Martha Royce. *Pawnee Passage, 1870–1875*. Norman: University of Oklahoma Press, 1990.

Dorsey, George A. *The Pawnee: Mythology*. Part 1. Washington, DC: Carnegie Institute, 1906.

Grinnell, George B. *Pawnee Hero Stories and Folk-Tales with Notes on the Origins, Customs, and Character of the Pawnee People*. New York: Forest and Stream Publishing Co., 1893. Reprint. Lincoln: University of Nebraska Press, 1961.

Horr, David Agee, ed. *Pawnee and Kansa (Kaw) Indians*. New York: Garland Press, 1974.

Hyde, George E. *Pawnee Indians*. Denver: University of Denver Press, 1951. Reprint. Norman: University of Oklahoma Press, 1973.

Murie, James R. *Ceremonies of the Pawnee*. Vols. 1 and 2. Ed. Douglas R. Parks. Smithsonian Institution Contributions to Anthropology, no. 27. Washington, DC: Smithsonian Institution Press, 1981.

Riding In, James. "Keepers of Tirawahut's Covenant: The Development and Destruction of Pawnee Culture." Ph.D. dissertation, University of California, Los Angeles, 1991.

Wedel, Waldo R. *An Introduction to Pawnee Archeology*. U.S. Bureau of American Ethnology, Bulletin 112. Washington, DC: Smithsonian Institution for the Bureau of American Ethnology, 1936.

Weltfish, Gene. *The Lost Universe, with a Closing Chapter on "The Universe Regained."* New York: Basic Books, 1965. Reprinted as *The Lost Universe: Pawnee Life and Culture*. Lincoln: University of Nebraska Press, 1977.

Wishart, David J. *An Unspeakable Sadness: The Dispossession of the Nebraska Indians*. Lincoln: University of Nebraska Press, 1994.

MICHAEL L. TATE

PEACEMAKER COURT (NAVAJO)

Since 1982, the Navajo Nation's court system has maintained a peace-maker system as an alternative to the Anglo-American adversarial system of justice. Each of twenty-five chapter houses (community meeting centers) on the Navajo Nation has designated a peacemaker who works to resolve disputes in that district. The number of disputes handled by such courts increased from about 150 a year in the early 1980s to almost 3,000 in 1996.

Most court sessions begin with a prayer and a request from the peace-maker for mutual respect. After that, investigation begins to identify the root of the conflict. "We don't point the finger in peacemaking," says Philmer Bluehouse, a Navajo peacemaker. "We talk about the problem. It's like peeling an onion. . . . After we discover that, we close [the onion] back up and repair the individual with good information, knowledge, and empowerment" (Thorpe 1996:54).

FURTHER READING

Thorpe, Dagmar. "The Ceremony of Making Peace: The Navajo Peacemakers Court." *Native Americas* 13:3 (Fall 1996): 54–57.

PLENARY POWER

Courts in the United States have generally held that the U.S. Congress holds unilateral power to exercise legislative control over Indian affairs. That is, the Congress may enact limits on Native American **sovereignty** without the consent of the involved Native American nations. While some legal decisions have endorsed a broad concept of Native American sovereignty in theory, the Congress has enacted (and authorized the Bureau of Indian Affairs to administer) a broad web of restrictions on Native American sovereignty that controls most reservation Indians' daily lives. This federal legislation defines how land may be bought and sold, how crimes are punished, traffic in liquor, and provision of social programs, among other matters.

In some of its opinions, such as *Lone Wolf v. Hitchcock* (1903) and *United States v. Kagama* (1886), the U.S. Supreme Court has upheld the plenary power of Congress. Other cases, such as *United States v. Wheeler* (1978), seem to indicate that Native American sovereignty does not fall completely under congressional hegemony. Regardless of the judicial context, Congress's plenary power has often been exercised and has become a major bone of contention for Indian-rights advocates. According to legal scholar Charles F. Wilkinson:

They consider outrageous a doctrine that justifies, among other things, strong-arm rules such as the doctrine of discovery that transmutes Indian fee title into a "right of occupancy" not protected by the Fifth Amendment . . . [and] the idea that Indian tribes are domestic dependent governments lacking direct access to

the international community, [as well as] the rule that Congress can order the
divestiture of tribal land and and then transfer it to tribal members in the form
of allotments, a "mere change in the form of investment" that in fact has cost
Indians tens of millions of acres of land. (1987: 79)

FURTHER READING

Wilkinson, Charles F. *American Indians, Time, and the Law: Native Societies
in a Modern Constitutional Democracy.* New Haven, CT: Yale University
Press, 1987.

PLENTY HORSES (Oglala Lakota) (fl. 1890s)

After five years at Carlisle Indian School, Plenty Horses returned to
the Pine Ridge Indian Reservation angry and alienated, just in time to
witness the 1890 massacre at Wounded Knee. A few days after the massacre, on January 7, 1891, he shot army officer Lt. Edward W. Casey in
the back, hoping to be hung for his bravery. Plenty Horses' wife, Roan
Horse, was killed in the ensuing melee. After his arrest, Plenty Horses
said that he killed Casey because

I am an Indian. Five years I attended Carlisle and was educated in the ways of
the white man. When I returned to my people, I was an outcast among them. I
was no longer an Indian. I was not a white man. I was lonely. I shot the
lieutenant so I might make a place for myself among my people. I am now one
of them. I shall be hung, and the Indians will bury me as a warrior. They will
be proud of me. I am satisfied. (Johansen and Grinde 1997: 293)

Plenty Horses was jailed at Fort Meade and tried in Sioux Falls, South
Dakota. Instead of convicting Plenty Horses and sentencing him to hang,
a judge threw the case out because he said that a state of war had existed
on the Pine Ridge Reservation—the same state of war that the army was
using as a reason not to prosecute the soldiers who had taken part in
the massacre. Instead, the army awarded them medals of honor. Plenty
Horses was sent home to Rosebud, still a very confused and alienated
young man. He died at Pine Ridge in the 1930s.

FURTHER READING

Jensen, Richard E., R. Eli Paul, and John E. Carter. *Eyewitness at Wounded Knee.*
Lincoln: University of Nebraska Press, 1991.
Johansen, Bruce E., and Donald A. Grinde, Jr. *The Encyclopedia of Native Amer-
ican Biography.* New York: Henry Holt, 1997.

PONCA POLITICAL AND LEGAL TRADITIONS

The Ponca are of the Degiha division of the Siouan language family,
which also includes the **Omaha**, Osage, Kansa, and Quapaw and is further related to the Chiwere division that includes the Iowa, Oto, and

Missouri (Howard 1965: 4). In language and custom, the Ponca are mostly akin to the Omaha (Dorsey 1884: 211), from whom they separated sometime between 1390 and 1700 after moving into present-day northeast Nebraska from southern Ohio (Dorsey 1884, 1886; Connelley 1918: 449). The closeness with the Omaha presents a major problem in identifying traditions specific to the Ponca because "of all the (D) Thegiha tribes the Omaha are best known ethnographically . . . and the Omaha have sometimes been accepted as representative of the group" (Fletcher 1909: 256). Because of the "particularly close historical connection between the Omaha and the Ponca, it was apparently considered appropriate to concentrate on the former and virtually ignore the latter except for incidental allusions and comparisons" (Jablow 1974: 37–38). Since many political and legal traditions labeled as Ponca in past literature may actually be Omaha, a careful review of past literature is necessary to identify what truly are Ponca political and legal traditions.

Another factor in the study of Ponca traditions was the removal of the Ponca from Nebraska by the U.S. government to Oklahoma in the summer of 1877 and the return of clan head **Standing Bear** and sixty-six fellow Ponca to Nebraska during the winter of 1877–1878, where they were arrested and incarcerated in Omaha, Nebraska, by General George Crook. This act led to the famous *Standing Bear v. Crook* case and Judge **Elmer Dundy**'s "landmark ruling in American jurisprudence, holding that an Indian is a person the same as a White man and similarly entitled to the protection of the Constitution" (Howard 1965: 37). Consequently, since that time there have been two Ponca tribes, the southern Ponca in Oklahoma and the northern Ponca in Nebraska, both adjusting and assimilating to their geographic and cultural surroundings. Due to these factors, the following discussion will concentrate on both tribal and clan political and legal traditions prior to the 1877 removal, especially those that differ from the Omaha.

The Ponca possessed a strict set of moral and social rules. Ponca elder Peter Le Claire (1965) offered the following moral laws as told to him by both northern and southern Ponca elders: (1) Have one god; (2) do not kill one another; (3) do not steal from one another; (4) be kind to one another; (5) do not talk about each other; (6) do not be stingy; and (7) have respect for the Sacred Pipe (Le Claire 1947). Almost all government and law were based on family relations or kinship, where family clans were central in Ponca governance. Social rules were both tribal and clan based (Yerington Paiute Tribe 1985: 20). Individual violations of specific laws of the Ponca often were enforced by the victim or his or her relatives, as was common among Plains native nations. The punishment of an adulterer was left to the injured husband, who might kill, scalp, or cut off the hair of a man whom he caught with his wife. A wife could kill another woman with whom her husband eloped (Skinner 1915: 800–801). Occasionally, Ponca women also went to war and became braves, whereas Omaha women did not (Skinner 1915: 794; Jablow 1974: 60). Killing as a form of capital punishment or in warfare was not considered murder. When murder was committed, retaliation was left to the relatives of the murdered individual and was often swift due to the belief that "the spirit of a murdered person will haunt the people, and when the tribe is on the hunt, will cause the wind to blow in such a direction as to betray the hunters" (Fletcher and La Flesche 1911: 216). Religious sanctions acted as a powerful deterrent to illegal acts. The murderer "can never satisfy his hunger, though he eat much food" (Dorsey 1894: 420).

Ponca law required that property belonged to either families, individuals, or the nation as a whole. Community buildings and land belonged to the nation. Individual property might include a man's gun and clothes. People had to ask to use one's individual property, and stealing was not tolerated. Families owned the tent or house. If a family member left, he lost his rights to the house. If a man left his wife, she kept the tipi. If she ran off with another man, he kept it (Le Claire 1965: 96). Divorce was simple in Ponca society. "If a man and wife didn't get along, or weren't satisfied, they just split up" (Le Claire 1965: 148). The children might go with their mother, her mother, or their father's mother. Should the father be unwilling, the wife could not take the children with her. Each could remarry (Dorsey 1884: 262).

In terms of clan politics and law, each clan was responsible for a certain duty. One clan might take care of military matters, another of religious duties, while another took charge of hunting or the harvest (Yerington Paiute Tribe 1985: 20–21). The political structure of the Ponca clans was hereditary and patrilineal. An individual's position in Ponca society depended upon his or her position in the family, the family's position in the clan, and the clan's position in the nation. Certain clans outranked certain others socially and had special rights and prerogatives not possessed by others (Howard 1965: 81). The terms "clan," "band," and "gente" have been used synonymously throughout past literature. The Ponca, like the Omaha, were divided into two moieties or half-nations, the earth and sky (Fletcher and La Flesche 1911: 140). The Ponca had seven clans until the mid-1800s, when the Wageziga or whitemen's sons clan became the eighth clan (Ponca Census 1860: 1).

A traditional Ponca camp is called Hu-thu-gah and is round with the entrance in the east. Each of the bands has duties in the camp (Ponca Census 1860; Skinner 1915; Le Claire 1965). From the entrance, the bands are arranged left to right, beginning with the Wazaze (Skinner 1915: 799) or Wahja-ta (Le Claire 1965) (snake or Osage), who guard the entrance and are expert trackers, and to whom touching snakes is taboo. The Nikapasna (skull or bald head) know all about the human head and how it should be dressed. The Dixida (Skinner 1915: 799) (blood) or Te-xa-da (Le Claire 1965) performed magic. When the camp was getting short of meats, they would get their bows and arrows out and make believe they were shooting animals, saying, "I'll shoot this fat one." The band in the center is the Wasabe, Washabe, or Wahshaba. The principal chief of the Poncas was always selected from this clan, and its members were forbidden to touch the head of an animal because they were of the head clan. The Maka or Miki (medicine) knew all about medicines and contained the best herbalists among the Poncas. The Nuxe or Nuxa (ice) knew everything about water and ice. The Hisada or He-sah-da (stretch-ing of a bird's leg when running) were the Poncas' rainmakers. The Wageziga (white men's sons), which originated in the 1850s, had been founded to accommodate the sons of Anglo-American traders who had taken Ponca wives. This clan had a similar taboo to that of the Dixida in that they could not touch mice (Skinner 1915: 799). Ponca subagency records identify that members of the Wageziga often were interpreters between the Ponca and the non-Indians. Some clans had one or two subclans or subgentes who also had specific clan duties and rules.

Although the principal chief of the Ponca came from the Wasabe, there were seven chiefs of the first order who were older chiefs, and a number of second-order chiefs, ranging from five to twelve. First- and second-order chiefs could be hereditary, could be chosen on the basis of bravery or trustworthiness to the people, or could buy their position based on acts of bravery in war, usually the number of times they counted coup (touched an enemy) in battle. Seven first-order chiefs, who included the principal chief, met in council to decide upon most matters. A third class of chiefs has been mentioned in past literature but was most likely a class of younger warriors who had demonstrated that they were "not just interested in themselves, but in the tribe as a whole" (Howard 1965: 92). Each clan also had a hereditary clan head or chief and a group of subchiefs, who were appointed by the clan head. A chief of the first, second, or third order might also be a clan head (Howard 1965: 92). In most cases, clan heads and subchiefs were se-lected by heredity (son of clan head), which was the norm with the Omaha. But among the Ponca a clan head could choose his successor or subchiefs based on trustworthiness or bravery in battle (Skinner 1915: 795). Thus Ponca chieftainships, unlike those of the Omaha, were both autocratic and democratic in nature (Jablow 1974: 55–58).

The clan heads and their subchiefs enforced the laws of the clan and settled conflicts within the clan. Conflicts between members of different

clans often were settled by the council of seven, which was made up of
the first-order chiefs and the principal chief (Howard 1965: 92–93). In-
tragroup loyalty and cooperation required that even the clan heads must
follow Ponca law. Clan heads and subchiefs must (1) be good to the old;
(2) be good to orphans; and (3) be good to the needy. Any violation
could mean shame to the clan and removal as clan head (Le Claire 1965:
98). Although the Ponca have had no female chiefs during the time they
have been known to historians writing in English, Ponca oral history
indicates that women were not barred from becoming chiefs. Often they
were women with great supernatural power, medicine women (Le
Claire 1965: 93), to whom the Poncas looked for leadership in times of
uncertainty due to unknown causes, such as an extended drought.

The summer buffalo hunt was one instance in which Ponca law pre-
dominated because all the clans were together for an extended period
of time and a successful hunt was essential to survival of the nation.
The Wasabe and the Maka clans "were given charge of the communal
buffalo hunt—the direction of the journey, the making of the camp, and
preservation of order. From these two camps the two main chiefs must
come" (Fletcher and LaFlesche 1911: 48). The Omaha had one hunt
leader rather than two, and the Nikapasna were responsible for the "supervision of all hunting of deer" (Fletcher and LaFlesche 1911: 44–45).
The leaders were in complete charge of the hunt and maintained discipline through the hunt police or Buffalo-police. Those selected to be
hunt police were the bravest warriors of some clan but not the whole
tribe; the bravest of some other clan served at another time. The hunt
police "were chosen from those who had the right to wear the 'Crow',
a decoration possessed by those men who more than once had achieved
war honors of the first three grades" (Fletcher and LaFlesche 1911: 441;
Skinner 1915: 794–795). Fletcher and LaFlesche (1911: 439–440) identified the Ponca six grades of honor: (1) to strike an unwounded man;
(2) the first to strike a fallen enemy; (3) the second to strike a fallen
enemy; (4) to kill a man; (5) to take a scalp; (6) capturing horses from
the enemy (Fletcher and LaFlesche 1911: 440). When the Ponca were
not on the hunt, responsibility and rules continued to be enforced by
one or two Buffalo-police appointed by the head of each clan. These
Buffalo-police did not have to achieve the war honors necessary to wear
the "Crow," but personal leadership and character were important factors in becoming Buffalo-police. The Buffalo-police could be very severe in their punishment, even to the point of killing the offender. Ponca
justice was directed more at preserving order than social revenge. Conformity, not revenge, was sought, and immediately after a promise to
conform was secured from the perpetrator, steps were taken to reincor-
porate him or her into the society once more (Province 1937: 350). For
example, after the Buffalo-police had whipped a man for violating the

rule against individual hunting during the communal bison hunt, they would give him gifts so that "his heart would not be bad" (Howard 1965: 96). The main functions of the Buffalo-police were (1) to regulate the communal hunt; (2) to regulate ceremonies; (3) to settle disputes, punish offenders, and preserve order in the camp; and (4) to regulate war parties and restrain such at inopportune times (Province 1937: 351; Howard 1965: 95). Being a clan head, subchief, or Buffalo-police in a small, highly interrelated nation such as the Ponca was not easy, for right or wrong, the actions of these political and legal leaders were liable to earn the ill will of not only the persons directly involved, but the clansmen of all those persons as well. In conclusion, the well-being of the group was always a major influence on the implementation of the political and legal traditions of the Ponca. A Ponca elder reported in 1979: "Not like the white people who put their laws in large, heavy books and forget them. We Ponca carry our laws in our hearts, where we never live a day without them."

FURTHER READING

Bureau of Indian Affairs. Census Roll of the Poncas Tribe Taken at the Poncas Camp, July 6, 1860, by I. Shaw Gregory, U.S. Special Agent. Niobrara, Nebraska. National Archives Microfilm Publications, Ponca Agency Documents, 1859–1863. Microcopy No. 234, Roll No. 670.

Connelley, William E. "Notes on the Early Indian Occupancy of the Great Plains." *Collections* (Kansas State Historical Society) 14 (1915–1918): 438–470.

Dorsey, J. O. "Migrations of the Siouan Tribes." *American Naturalist* 20:3 (1886): 221–222.

———. "Omaha Sociology." In *Third Annual Report of the Bureau of American Ethnology.* Washington, DC: Smithsonian Institution, Bureau of Ethnology. 1884, pp. 205–370.

———. "Siouan Sociology." 1893–1894. *Fifteenth Annual Report of the Bureau of American Ethnology.* 1897. Washington, DC: Smithsonian Institution, 1897.

———. "A Study of Siouan Cults." 1889–1890. *Eleventh Annual Report of the Bureau of American Ethnology.* Washington, DC: Smithsonian Institution, 1894, pp. 361–422.

Fletcher, Alice C. "Tribal Structure: A Study of the Omaha and Cognate Tribes." In *Putnam Anniversary Volume: Anthropological Essays.* New York, 1909.

Fletcher, Alice C., and Francis LaFlesche. "The Omaha Tribe." In *Twenty-Seventh Annual Report of the Bureau of Ethnology.* Washington, DC: Smithsonian Institution, 1911.

Howard, James H. Letter of August 26, 1947 appearing in *The Ponca Tribe.* Smithsonian Institution Bureau of American Ethnology, Bulletin 195. Washington, D.C.: U.S. Government Printing Office, 1965.

Jablow, Joseph. Ponca Indians: *Ethnohistory of the Ponca: Commission Find-*

ings. A Report for the Department of Justice, Lands Division, Indian Claims Section. New York: Garland Publishing, 1974.

Laravie, Ben. Oral interview. Stubben's Discount Store, Niobrara, Nebraska, 1979.

Le Claire, Peter. *Ponca History.* "Letter Written on Tribal History by Ponca Indian." August 26, 1947. Niobrara, Nebraska, 1965. In *The Ponca Tribe,* by J. H. Howard. Oral interview with tribal elder Peter Le Claire.

Province J. H. "The Underlying Sanctions of Plains Indian Culture." In *Social Anthropology of North American Tribes,* ed. Fred Eggan. Chicago: University of Chicago Press, 1937, pp. 341–374.

Yerington Paiute Tribe. *Introduction to Tribal Government.* Yerington, NV: Yerington Paiute Tribe, 1985.

Skinner, Alanson B. "Ponca Societies and Dances." *Anthropological Papers of the American Museum of Natural History.* Vol. XI. Washington, D.C.: American Museum of Natural History.

JERRY STUBBEN

PORTER V. HALL 34 Ariz. 308 (1928)

In 1928, during the first presidential election after passage of the Indian Citizenship Act in 1924, two Pima Indians tried to register to vote in Arizona. The local registrar denied the request, contending that the two Indians were under the guardianship of the United States and were not legal residents of Arizona. The Indians took the case to court, contending that the Arizona Enabling Act barred discrimination based on race, color, or condition of previous servitude. The Arizona Supreme Court denied the Indians' position, citing the state constitution, which denies voting rights to persons under guardianship.

POWHATAN (OPECHANCANOUGH) (c. 1545–1644)

In the early 1600s, Opechancanough as head of the Pamunkey band of Powhatans opposed the land expansion and attempted controls of the Jamestown colonists. In 1607, Opechancanough pursued and attacked Captain John Smith's forces with 300 Native American men. Smith was the only Caucasian to escape death during the battle. Opechancanough captured and took Smith to his brother's village on the York River, where Pocahontas (as local lore would have it) allegedly spared Smith's life. Released in 1608, Smith retaliated by leading his men to Opechancanough's village and seizing him as a hostage. The Powhatans regained Opechancanough from Smith by ransoming him with food.

Opechancanough died in 1618. Due to the profitability of tobacco, the English tricked the Indians into ceding huge tracts of land, which ruined the Indian economy. This frustrated and angered the Powhatans, but Opechancanough was uncertain whether his men could defeat the treacherous colonists. After some thought, he ordered a surprise military assault on March 22, 1622. Despite a warning by an Indian informer, 347 men, women, and children out of about 1,400 Euro-Americans were killed. The English started military operations against the Powhatans, burning crops and dwellings and forcing the Indians further into the interior. Intermittent warfare continued for many years.

In 1632, a peace treaty was finally signed to end the conflict. On April 18, 1644, Opechancanough ordered another military strike when he was over one hundred years old. His men killed almost 500 Anglo-Americans. Soon after, the Virginians launched a counterattack. Governor William Berkeley seized Opechancanough and brought the aged leader to Jamestown. Taunted by the Virginians as he entered the city, he was shot and killed by one of his guards in 1644 while incarcerated.

DONALD A. GRINDE, JR.

POWHATAN EMPIRE

Although they spoke an Algonquian language similar to those of the peoples of many confederacies in eastern North America, the governmental and legal systems of the Indians who met the first English colonists in Virginia were autocratic, not democratic. The Powhatan empire was the creation principally of one leader, whom the English called **Powhatan**, a personal title of chieftainship taken after the chief's birthplace, a village near the falls of the James River. Called Opechancanough as a private person, the Powhatan had assembled most of an empire of about thirty vassal villages during his lifetime. Helen C. Rountree called this political aggregation "a paramount chieftainship, not a confederacy."

While Powhatan sat atop a political hierarchy, he was constrained both by the necessary consent of his closest advisors (many of them members of his extended family) and custom. Powhatan and his tributary chiefs possessed a political and legal authority across the coastal plain of present-day Virginia that was uncommon among native peoples in eastern North America. When the English colonists made landfall in 1607, Powhatan's political influence extended over roughly 14,000 Indians, a number probably considerably reduced by smallpox and other diseases that reached the coast from European fishing fleets and traders before colonization.

A hierarchy of political leaders (*weroances*) and priests functioned as judiciary as well as executive in the Powhatan empire. Many of them became nearly autonomous as Powhatan aged. They were known for meting out beatings for even the most trivial of offenses, such as jostling an English visitor in their presence. Several offenses were punishable by death, including large-scale theft, murder, infanticide, and being an accessory to any of these crimes. A person found guilty of murder was brought to the ruler's house, was beaten until most of his major bones were broken, and then was burned alive. In some cases, simple insubordination was punished by clubbing the offender to death.

FURTHER READING

Rountree, Helen C. *The Powhatan Indians of Virginia: Their Traditional Culture.* Norman: University of Oklahoma Press, 1989.

PROCLAMATION OF 1763 (English)

The term **Indian Country** as a legal construct was first employed in the Proclamation of 1763, by which the English government attempted to stop non-Indian incursion at the spine of the Appalachian Mountains. The proclamation, by King George III, prohibited European-American land transactions and settlement west of the boundary. It read, in part:

And whereas it is just and reasonable, and essential to our interest, and the security of our colonies, that the several nations or tribes of Indians, with whom we are connected, and who live under our protection, should not be molested or disturbed in the possession of such parts of our dominions and territories as, not having been ceded to, or purchased by us, are reserved to them or any of them, as their hunting grounds; we do, therefore . . . declare it to be our royal will and pleasure that no governor do presume, upon any pretense whatever, to grant warrants of survey, or pass any patents for lands beyond the bounds of their respective governments, . . . or upon any lands whatever, which not having been ceded to, or purchased by us, as aforesaid, are reserved to the said Indians, or any of them. (Shortt and Doughty 1918: 163–168)

The British military was unable to stem the flow of illegal traders and squatters across the mountains along such a long border. The Proclamation of 1763 also became a source of tension between Britain and insurgent colonists in the American Revolution.

FURTHER READING

Shortt, Adam, and Arthur G. Doughty, eds. *Documents Relative to the Constitutional History of Canada, 1759–1791.* Ottawa: J. de la Taché, 1918.

PROPERTY, NATIVE AMERICAN CONCEPTS OF

In *Brave Are My People*, Frank Waters described a "purchase" by Puritan Miles Standish and two companions of a tract of land fourteen miles square near Bridgewater for seven coats, eight hoes, nine hatchets, ten yards of cotton cloth, twenty knives, and four moose skins. When native people continued to hunt on the land after it was "purchased" and were arrested by the Pilgrims, the Wampanoag sachem Massasoit protested:

What is this you call property? It cannot be the earth. For the land is our mother, nourishing all her children, beasts, birds, fish, and all men. The woods, the streams, everything on it belongs to everybody and is for the use of all. How can one man say it belongs to him only? (Waters 1993: 28)

While Standish and his companions thought that they had carried away an English-style deed, Massasoit argued that their goods had paid only for use of the land in common with everyone.

Differences in attitudes toward the land vis-à-vis European cultures recur time and again in the statements of Native American leaders recorded by Euro-American observers in many areas of North America. Tecumseh, rallying Native American allies with an appeal for alliance about 1805, said, "Let us unite as brothers, as sons of one Mother Earth. . . . Sell our land? Why not sell the air. . . . Land cannot be sold" (Waters 62–63). In 1971, the **Hopis** objected to the sale of their lands through the **Indian Claims Commission**:

This land was granted to the Hopis by a power greater than man can explain. Title is invested in the whole makeup of Hopi life. Everything is dependent on it. The land is sacred, and if the land is abused, the sacredness of Hopi life will disappear and all other life as well.

To us, it is unthinkable to give up control of our sacred lands to non-Hopis. We have no way to express exchange of sacred lands for money. It is alien to our ways. The Hopis never gave authority and never will give authority to anyone to dispose of our lands and heritage and religion for any price. We received these lands from the Great Spirit, and we must hold them for him, as a steward, a caretaker, until he returns. (Toelken 1976: 14)

Often, assumptions that Indians had no concept of landownership have served two contrary purposes in European eyes. This vastly oversimplified conception could suit the stereotype of the Noble Savage and, at the same time, salve the conscience of Europeans actively expropriating the land for their own uses. Some early New England colonists assumed that native people had no land-tenure ethic because they did not fence land or raise domestic animals on it. Native Americans did not issue deeds or trade in real estate, but they did use the land. Historian William Cronon reminded us to consider the differences between individual ownership of land, which most Native Americans did not practice, and collective sovereignty:

European property systems were much like Indian ones in expressing the ecological purposes to which a people intended to put their land; it is crucial that they not be oversimplified if their contributions to ecological history are to be understood. The popular idea that Europeans had private property, while the Indians did not distorts European notions of property as much as it does Indian ones. (1983: 68–69)

According to Cronon, both European and Native American property systems involved distinctions between individual ownership and community property. Both "dealt in bundles of culturally defined rights that determined what could and could not be done with land and personal property." Customs of land tenure varied greatly in detail across New England (and the rest of North America); generally, however, Native Americans owned the implements of their work, their clothing, and other items used in their daily lives. The extended family that occupied a lodging usually exercised a sense of ownership. Land, however, was usually held collectively. America was not a "Virgin Land" (in the words of George Bancroft) (Grinde and Johansen 1995: 37) when Europeans arrived. Large tracts were under intensive management for hunting and agriculture by Native Americans. Because Indians often did not farm or raise domestic animals in European patterns, nonnative observers often missed this.

Because attitudes toward land tenure varied, negotiations that Europeans took to involve acquisition of land from Native American people often involved a high degree of intercultural misunderstanding. When the English colonists of New England thought that they were buying land, Native Americans often took the same agreements to mean that they were agreeing to share it.

FURTHER READING

Coulter, Robert T., and Steven M. Tullberg. "Indian Land Rights." In *The Aggressions of Civilization: Federal Indian Policy since the 1880s*, ed. Sandra L. Cadwalader and Vine Deloria, Jr. Philadelphia: Temple University Press, 1984.

Cronon, William. *Changes in the Land: Indians, Colonists, and the Ecology of New England*. New York: Hill & Wang, 1983.

Grinde, Donald A., Jr., and Bruce E. Johansen. *Ecocide of Native America: Environmental Destruction of Native Lands and Peoples*. Santa Fe, NM: Clear Light, 1995.

Toelken, Barre. "Seeing with a Native Eye: How Many Sheep Will It Hold?" in *Seeing with a Native Eye: Essays on Native American Religion*, ed. Walter Holden Capps. New York: Harper Forum Books, 1976.

Waters, Frank. *Brave Are My People: Indian Heroes Not Forgotten*. Santa Fe, NM: Clear Light, 1993.

PUBLIC LAW 280 18 U.S.C. §§ 1161, 1162; 25 U.S.C. §§ 1321–1322; 28 U.S.C. § 1360 (1953)

Public Law 280 allowed some states to assume civil and/or criminal jurisdiction on Indian lands within their borders, subject to certain limitations. This law immediately extended state civil and criminal jurisdiction to **Indian Country** in California, most reservations in Minnesota, Nebraska, most reservations in Oregon, and Wisconsin. Alaska was added at statehood in 1958. Public Law 280 provided that other states could assume jurisdiction by state law or constitutional amendment at the state level. Between 1958 and 1968, total or partial jurisdiction was assumed by Arizona, Florida, Idaho, Montana, Nevada, Oklahoma, North Dakota, Utah, and Washington. Constitutional amendments were required in states with constitutions that prohibited assumption of state responsibility in Indian affairs.

According to legal scholar William Canby, Jr., the implementation of Public Law 280 "ran directly counter to **John Marshall**'s original characterization of Indian Country as territory in which the laws of the state (in *Worcester v. Georgia*, 1832), 'can have no force.' " Indeed, wrote Canby, "it went much further, for it not only gave state laws and courts force in Indian Country, it gave them power over Indians themselves" (Canby 1981: 178).

Before passage of P.L. 280 in 1953, several states had been granted various measures of jurisdiction over Indian reservations through specific legislation by Congress. In 1946, North Dakota was granted criminal jurisdiction over the Devils Lake Reservation; in 1948, Iowa gained criminal jurisdiction over the Sac and Fox reservation. A year later, a similar measure granted California criminal jurisdiction over the Agua Caliente Reservation near Palm Springs, California. In 1948, New York State was granted criminal jurisdiction over all Indian lands within its borders, a move that was hotly contested by members of the **Iroquois Confederacy**, who have long maintained their **sovereignty**.

Public Law 280 was part of a surge in legislation during the 1950s aimed at "terminating" Indian nations and reservations. Under the law, states assumed functions that had been controlled jointly by the federal government and the Native American governments. The assumption of jurisdiction by states often placed native peoples at the legal mercy of state officials and agencies that had bitterly opposed them on resource issues, such as fishing rights.

Public Law 280 and other pieces of **termination** legislation were opposed by most Indian groups because they eroded sovereignty, **treaty** rights, and **self-determination**. In 1958, **National Congress of American Indians** President Joseph Garry characterized termination (including P.L. 280) as the worst federal policy since the beginning of the twentieth century. Public Law 280 was designed as part of the process by which reservations would be broken apart and Native Americans would be assimilated into "mainstream" society. The effect of Public Law 280 on Native American governments has been characterized by **Vine Deloria, Jr.**, as "devastating":

Tribal court authority and law enforcement on the reservations involved were eliminated and replaced by state authority. Whereas the federal encroachments into Indian control over reservation crimes had been significant [under the

Major Crimes Act, 1885], under P.L. 280, state displacement of tribal authority
was even more complete. (Deloria and Lytle 1983: 176)

Under P.L. 280, states were prohibited from assuming jurisdiction in
certain areas, such as water rights. States were not allowed to infringe
on protected trust property. Nor were the states allowed to tax or otherwise restrict reservation economic activity. Rights granted by treaty
(usually governing hunting and fishing) were not compromised. Laws
to be enforced comprised those of general application. Local laws, such
as zoning ordinances, were not changed. Public Law 280 superseded
the Major Crimes Act (1885) and later modifications as the standard for
deciding which court retained jurisdiction.

With the collapse of termination efforts, assumption of jurisdiction
by the states was stopped in 1968. After that date, the consent of native
governments was required for assumption of jurisdiction, a requirement
that virtually halted its adoption. Senator Sam Ervin said at the time
that "subjecting a reservation to state, criminal or civil jurisdiction
without its consent runs counter to that basic tenet of our democracy
that governmental power is derived from the consent of the governed"
(Barsh and Henderson 1980: 133).

The legislation passed in 1968 allowed states to request retrocession
of jurisdiction under P.L. 280, and a few states, including Utah and
Nebraska, offered to do so. The law as revised in 1968 did not, however,
allow Native American nations to request retrocession; nor does it allow
a native government to review a state request for retrocession, which is
approved or disapproved by the secretary of the interior.

Because some states assumed jurisdiction over certain types of crimes
(and others had taken no such action by 1968), native-state relations
today vary widely state by state. Amendments to the law provided, however, that only states could ask for an end to civil or criminal jurisdiction over Native Americans, and that the Department of the Interior
would decide whether to accept the retrocession. Native governments
were still given no voice.

Public Law 280 has been one of the most criticized measures in U.S.
Indian law. In cases in which the states assumed jurisdiction, they only
rarely provided funds for law enforcement, especially because most Indian reservations are in rural areas that are difficult and expensive to
police. By the 1980s, some states were requesting Indians to assume
jurisdiction (or to arrange joint policing) because sole state jurisdiction
had proved politically ineffective, expensive, and unpopular with both
Indians and non-Indians.

FURTHER READING

Barsh, Russel, and James Henderson. *The Road: Indian Tribes and Political
    Liberty*. Berkeley: University of California Press, 1980.

Canby, William C., Jr. *American Indian Law in a Nutshell*. St. Paul, MN: West Publishing, 1981.

Deloria, Vine, Jr., and Clifford Lytle. *American Indians, American Justice*. Austin: University of Texas Press, 1983.

Goldberg, Carole E. "Public Law 280: The Limits of State Jurisdiction over Reservation Indians." *UCLA Law Review* 22 (1975): 535–594.

———. *Public Law 280: State Jurisdiction over Reservation Indians*. Los Angeles: UCLA American Indian Studies Center, 1975.

PUEBLO LANDS ACT Public Law 253 (1924)

The Public Lands Act required that non-Indian residents on Pueblo lands be required to prove their title. The congressional legislation was meant to quiet title to Pueblo lands after a flood of claims by non-Pueblos. The Pueblo Lands Act was passed after the **Bursum Bill** was proposed in Congress, but not passed. The Bursum Bill would have required Pueblos to prove title to their lands in U.S. courts, something that often would have been very difficult because the Pueblos' land rights stemmed from aboriginal title and Spanish grants made before the U.S. occupation of New Mexico during the Mexican-American War (1846).

The legislation included a special counsel who aided Pueblos in preparing cases. The original act was amended in 1933 to require that Pueblos receive fair market value for their lands, and to provide that aboriginal water rights were included. By 1938, about three thousand non-Indian squatters had been removed from Pueblo lands under this act. However, concluded Pueblo historian Joe Sando, "The Pueblo Indians came out losers" (1992: 120), in large part because of negligence by Herbert J. Hagerman, a former territorial governor of New Mexico who was appointed to represent them on the Pueblo Lands Board, which was charged with determining ownership and adjudicating conflicting claims.

FURTHER READING

Sando, Joe. *Pueblo Nations: Eight Centuries of Pueblo Indian History*. Santa Fe, NM: Clear Light, 1992.

PUEBLO PEOPLES, POLITICAL AND LEGAL TRADITIONS

While the Pueblos used similar architecture, spoke related languages, and observed a similar ceremonial cycle, each village was autonomous in government and law, although most have communicated with each other through an All Pueblo Council for several centuries. Governing structures of the various Pueblos are similar, a mixture of precontact systems and structures imposed by the Spanish beginning in 1598.

While few Native American cultures observed the separation between church and state that distinguishes U.S. law, the Pueblos are especially notable in meshing religious and secular life. According to legal scholar Sharon O'Brien, "Pueblo spiritual life was not just a part of life, but was life itself." In the Pueblo belief system, the spirit of nature infuses everything. As O'Brien describes it:

Nature and God are one. Humankind's task is to maintain a harmonious relationship with nature. An intricate system of dances and celebrations reinforces the Pueblos' quest for this oneness with God and Nature. The Pueblos give thanks and prayer for all aspects of their lives; the rain that falls, the crops that grow, the game they hunt, their good life, and their fellow human beings. (1989: 27)

Pueblo societies tend to be close-knit, with a strong emphasis on community life and welfare of the group. In most Pueblo communities, a person is a member of a clan and one or two moieties that govern daily life. The clans are responsible for maintaining interpersonal harmony. Most children are initiated into kachina or kiva societies. In addition, most Pueblos also include specialized societies for curing (medicine), hunting, and war. The Clowns, who have important roles in many ceremonies, also have their own society.

Most Pueblos are governed by one or two priests (if two, each serves half the year, alternating). In some Pueblos, the position is hereditary, whereas in others the leader is selected by a council of elders. The leadership position is a lifetime appointment. The priest is the head, in title, of all the societies in the community, but he can only counsel, not compel, obedience. He is charged with guiding the community toward decision by **consensus** and with affirming the decision once it is made. Traditionally, a community provides for the leaders' daily needs so that their attention may be directed toward spirituality and governance.

In several Pueblos, the leader is also assisted by a civil assistant and two war captains who look after the day-to-day practical needs of the people, including the care of livestock, the planting cycle, irrigation-system maintenance, and construction. These positions are made by annual appointment by the priest (who is sometimes called a "cacique," after Spanish usage). The appointees are expected to serve without monetary compensation as a service to their people. The assistants also often adjudicate disputes between individuals and, when necessary, provide for the defense of the Pueblo from outside attack. The council of elders in most Pueblos also assists the priest in adjudicating disputes, addressing antisocial behavior, and making law for the community. Usually, the elders debate a measure until consensus is reached.

Many Pueblos also have a position of governor, instituted during Spanish colonization. According to Pueblo historian Joe S. Sando,

The office of pueblo governor . . . shows the unique character of this great people. This office, originally designed for Spanish domination, was converted by the Pueblos into an effective bulwark against intrusion by foreigners. The governor, in effect, protected the spiritual leaders. Thus were their human values preserved. The governor is responsible, under the cacique, for all tribal business of the modern world. He is the liaison with the outside business and economic world. (14)

In the twentieth century, the Pueblos' traditional governance system also has adapted to the requirements of U.S. Indian policy. By 1990, six Pueblos (Isleta, Pojoaque, Santa Clara, Zuni, Laguna, and San Ildefonso) selected their governors and councils by secret ballot.

FURTHER READING

O'Brien, Sharon. *American Indian Tribal Governments*. Norman: University of
  Oklahoma Press, 1989.
Sando, Joe S., *Pueblo Nations: Eight Centuries of Pueblo Indian History*. Santa
  Fe, NM: Clear Light, 1992.

PUYALLUP V. DEPARTMENT OF GAME (I) 391 U.S. 392 (1968)

The Supreme Court in *Puyallup v. Department of Game* allowed some state regulation of Indian fishing rights under treaty in the interests of conservation, "provided the regulation meets appropriate standards and does not discriminate against the Indians." This case arose in the context of fishing by several Native American nations and bands in the Puget Sound area that the state contended was illegal, but that the Indians asserted was protected under the **Treaty of Medicine Creek**, signed in 1854. The state's attempts to close down Indian fishing with arrests and confiscation of boats, nets, and other gear had drawn protests by the Indians beginning in the early 1960s. These protests were among the first of the modern **self-determination** movement, presaging others, such as the efforts to end police brutality against Indians in Minneapolis that gave rise to the American Indian Movement in 1968, and the occupation of **Alcatraz Island** in 1969.

Justice William O. Douglas, speaking for the Supreme Court in *Puyallup v. Department of Game*, narrowed the case to a clause in the Treaty of Medicine Creek that reserved for the Indians who signed the treaty "[t]he right of taking fish at all usual and accustomed grounds and stations." Having established that the Indians had a treaty-guaranteed right to take fish, the Court then turned to contentions by the state that the means by which Indians caught most of their fish (nets set at the mouths of streams) was a violation of state conservation regulations. Justice Douglas wrote that "[t]he treaty is silent on the . . . modes of fishing that are guaranteed." Douglas reasoned that the state may regulate Indian fishing, but that it may not discriminate against it. The legal issues involved with "conservation" as it related to fishing with nets were refined further in a case popularly called "*Puyallup* II" (*Department of Game v. Puyallup Tribe*, 414 U.S. 44 [1973]), on which the Supreme Court ruled five years later. The Court found that a state ban on net fishing for steelhead (one of several types of salmon) was discriminatory.

The Supreme Court's ruling in *Puyallup v. Department of Game* did little to stanch the conflict regarding Indian fishing rights in western Washington. The Indians continued to fish with nets, and the state continued to arrest them and confiscate their gear in the name of "conservation." A more definitive solution of the problem was achieved in **United States v. Washington** (1974), popularly called the "Boldt decision," six years later.

Puyallup was much criticized by treaty supporters because it allowed state regulation in a situation that they contended was controlled by a treaty between the United States and signatory Indians, "the supreme law of the land," according to the U.S. **Constitution**. Legal scholar Ralph W. Johnson wrote:

No valid basis for the existence of such state power can be found. The Constitution of the United States provides that treaties are the "supreme law of the land." Because agreements with the Indians are treaties, the Indians are not subject to state regulation unless the treaty so provides or unless Congress so legislates. The treaties with the Indians do not provide for state regulation and Congress has never authorized such legislation. (1972: 207–208)

FURTHER READING

Brown, Bruce. *Mountain in the Clouds*. New York: Simon & Schuster, 1982.
Johnson, Ralph W. "The State versus Indian Off-Reservation Fishing: A United States Supreme Court Error." *Washington Law Review* 47 (1972): 207–208.

PYRAMID LAKE PAIUTE TRIBE V. MORTON 354 F. Supp. 252 (D.D.C. 1972)

In *Pyramid Lake Paiute Tribe v. Morton*, a Washington, D.C., district court enjoined the Interior Department from diverting water from Pyramid Lake to a federal project. The diversion diminished the quality and quantity of water for the Pyramid Lake Paiute downstream, who sued on grounds that the federal government had violated its **trust** responsibility. The court agreed, ruling that the executive branch of the government can be sued for breach of trust by an Indian nation or band.

Q

QUECHAN TRIBE V. ROWE 531 F.2d 408 (9th Cir. 1976)

Legal doctrine as developed by U.S. courts only rarely grants Indian nations jurisdiction over non-Indians. Native American nations may regulate on-reservation transactions by non-Indian-owned businesses with reservation residents (as in **United States v. Mazurie)**. In *Quechan Tribe v. Rowe*, the Ninth Circuit Court of Appeals framed another exception to the general doctrine: Indian nations may regulate hunting and fishing activities by non-Indians on their reservations. Furthermore, non-Indians may be legally barred from a reservation. The court held this right to be an inherent attribute of Native American **sovereignty**.

R

RECOGNITION, FEDERAL

An American Indian nation whose land is held in **trust** under the "guardianship" of the United States is said to be "recognized" for the purposes of federal programs. A native nation must be "recognized" to be eligible for federal grant money. The number of "recognized" Native American groups fell during the 1950s when several, including the Klamaths and **Menominees**, were "terminated." With reassertion of Native American **sovereignty** in the 1980s and 1990s, several Indian groups were recognized for the first time. One example is the **Poncas**, who were forcibly removed from their land along the Niobrara River in northern Nebraska during the 1870s after the United States mistakenly allocated their land to their traditional enemies, the **Sioux**, in the **Fort Laramie Treaty** of 1868. The Poncas reestablished their homeland and were recognized by the federal government in 1993. Even with the rise in recognition, several hundred Indian bands and nations remained without federal recognition and, many times, without land base.

RELIGIOUS FREEDOM, NATIVE AMERICAN: LEGAL AND PHILOSOPHICAL CONTEXT

Europeans established their legal rights to the lands of the "New World" chiefly through the **Doctrine of Discovery**, which was derived from theological and legal justifications for the Crusades launched by medieval Christian Europe against "the infidels." This Doctrine or Law of Discovery legitimated the territorial rights of Christian sovereigns and their representatives and denied those same rights to "infidels," who were characterized as peoples with false religion, such as Muslims, or peoples with no religion, which was the customary claim made regarding the indigenous peoples of the Americas. Thus the Europeans justified their conquests by virtue of possessing Christian religion, and they legally dispossessed Native American peoples on the grounds of their lack of religion.

A serious refutation of the Discovery Doctrine was undertaken by English colonists in America following the British **Proclamation of 1763**, which prohibited the colonists from further dispossessing the native peoples of Native American lands to the west of the extant colonies and which attempted to establish a political boundary between the colonists and the native peoples of those lands. Once the king's territorial rights of conquest under the Discovery Doctrine were seen to be protecting the Indian lands, colonial theorists turned to John Locke's claim that it is not the king's right as a Christian sovereign that gives true title to property, but it is natural law that justifies possession of property by those who secure it through their labor, which is what the colonists saw themselves as having done. **Thomas Jefferson** wrote a pamphlet in 1774 that rejected the prerogatives of the British Crown as a legitimating authority, instead identifying the colonists with ancestral Saxons as the ones who had initiated the struggle for natural-law rights to freedom. Jefferson concluded that the king, who represented the feudal rights of the Normans over against the Saxons, "has no right to grant lands of himself" (Williams 1990: 271).

The **Articles of Confederation**, which were ratified in early 1781, left the issue of rights to Indian lands undetermined. Thomas Paine described these lands in 1781 as the "vacant western territory of America," completely ignoring the issue of Indian rights to the lands, and he claimed that the sovereign discovery rights of the British Crown had been transferred to the new central government of the United States. Samuel Wharton, desirous of maintaining the legitimacy of private purchase of land from Indian peoples, wrote in that same year of 1781 that Indian peoples had natural rights to their lands through occupying them, and therefore "no European prince could derive a title to the soil of America from discovery, because that . . . can give a right only to lands which have either never been owned or possessed." In contrast to the Discovery Doctrine, Wharton asserted that

the pervading liberal influence of philosophy, reason, and truth, has since given us better notions of the rights of mankind, as well as of the obligations of morality and justice, which certainly are not confined to particular modes of faith, but extend universally to Jews and Gentiles, to Christians and infidels. (Williams 300)

Wharton's advocacy of Indian natural rights lost out in the making of the new republic, which reaffirmed the Doctrine of Discovery. This archaic piece of European feudalism received its clearest validation as the law of the land through the opinion of Chief Justice **John Marshall** in **Johnson v. McIntosh** in 1823. Marshall stated that the principle of discovery was the origin of title to lands by the United States according to the European-derived law of nations, and that this principle denied to indigenous peoples "their power to dispose of the soil at their own will." Marshall's opinion acknowledged the religious judgment inherent in this "principle of discovery," noting that "the character and religion of its [North America's] inhabitants afforded an apology for considering them as a people over whom the superior genius of Europe might claim an ascendancy." Robert Williams aptly characterized the meaning of *Johnson v. McIntosh*:

The Doctrine of Discovery's underlying medievally derived ideology—that normatively divergent "savage" peoples could be denied rights and status equal to those accorded to the civilized nations of Europe—had become an integral part of the fabric of United States federal Indian law. (317)

Williams concluded that Marshall's articulation of the Doctrine of Discovery brought it "to readability in a modern form that spoke with reassuring continuity to a nation that was about to embark on its own colonizing crusade against the American Indians who remained on the North American continent" (317).

In one way or another, the taking of Native American lands continued and was nearly completed by 1871. In that year, Congress acted to formally end all **treaty** making between the United States and Indian nations. While the treaty system had been an institutionalized form of dispossessing Indian peoples of their lands prior to 1871, what followed was, according to John R. Wunder, a "new colonialism" that attacked treaty rights and assaulted "every aspect of Native American life—religion, speech, political freedoms, economic liberty, and cultural diversity" (1994: 17). On December 2, 1882, Secretary of the Interior Henry M. Teller wrote a letter to the commissioner of Indian affairs in which he stated:

I desire to call your attention to what I regard as a great hindrance to the civilization of the Indian, *viz.* the continuance of the old heathenish dances, such as the sun-dance, scalp-dance, &c. These dances, or feasts, as they are sometimes called, ought, in my judgment, to be discontinued, and if the Indians now supported by the Government are not willing to discontinue them, the agents should be instructed to compel such discontinuance. (Prucha 1975: 60)

What followed in 1883 was the creation of the **court of Indian offenses**, staffed largely by Indian police, to enforce a ban on traditional religious practices, such as the sun dance and the sweat-lodge ritual. Indian agents, often religious appointees, became the instruments of the "new colonialism" of enforced acculturation by way of a coerced deculturation. This policy continued until Secretary of the Interior Harold C. Ickes in 1934 approved the order of **John Collier**, the commissioner of Indian affairs, which was dispatched to Indian Agencies as Circular 2970 under the title "Indian Religious Freedom and Indian Culture." This order stated that "no interference with Indian religious life or ceremonial expression will hereafter be tolerated." It marked the first U.S. government acknowledgment of rights to religious freedom for Native American peoples.

Despite the relatively benign acculturation policies of the New Deal era, the pervasive cultural presumption regarding Native American peoples was the stereotype of the "vanishing Indian," which absolved non-Indians of any responsibility for reconsidering the issues of Native American rights since there would cease to be any Indians in the next generation or so. A more assertive acculturation program was instituted in the 1950s to hasten the "vanishing" process by a policy of relocation and **termination** of distinct status as Native Americans. However, in the 1960s, a fundamental shift in the perception of Native American peoples and their rights began to appear, which was first clearly signaled in a speech to Congress by President Lyndon Johnson on March 6, 1968. The speech was titled "The Forgotten American," and in it Johnson called for a new policy of Indian **self-determination**, requesting Congress to implement legislation to bring it about. In that same year, a legislative process that had been under way for several years under the guidance of Senator Sam Ervin came to fruition when Congress enacted an "Indian Bill of Rights," representing Titles II–VII of the Civil Rights Act of 1968. This action reversed *Talton v. Mayes*, by which the U.S. Supreme Court in 1896 had denied the application of the Bill of Rights to Native American governments or courts. The "Indian Bill of Rights" of 1968 provided selected guarantees from the First, Fourth, Fifth, Sixth, and Eighth amendments to the **Constitution**. It omitted the establishment of religion clause of the First Amendment, as well as Second, Third, Seventh, Ninth, Tenth, and Fifteenth amendment rights. The "Indian Bill of Rights" was perceived as a progressive step in extending fundamental legal freedoms to Native American peoples, and it was a definite step away from either the old colonialism of the Discovery Doctrine or the new colonialism aimed at making Native American peoples vanish, both of which entailed the denial of rights to Native American peoples. Nevertheless, the judicial application of the 1968 act in the months and years immediately following resulted in serious erosion of Native American self-determination.

The true moment of governmental acknowledgment of Indian self-determination is represented by a congressional statement declaring protection for the religious freedom of Native American peoples. This happened when Congress passed the American Indian Religious Freedom Act in 1978. This act acknowledged that federal policy had often resulted in "the abridgement of religious freedom for traditional American Indians," and it declared:

That henceforth it shall be the policy of the United States to protect and preserve for American Indians their inherent right of freedom to believe, express, and exercise the traditional religions of the American Indian, Eskimo, Aleut, and Native Hawaiians, including but not limited to access to sites, use and possession of sacred objects, and the freedom to worship through ceremonials and traditional rites.

The rhetoric of this 1978 act is extraordinary, particularly in light of the negative history on this issue during the first two centuries of the United States, and it represents a stunning reversal of past policy. However, the grandness and power of its rhetoric proved to be of little practical value in affecting the judicial decisions played out in subsequent years. It was a statement of policy with no enforcement provisions.

The legal impotence of the American Indian Religious Freedom Act became brutally clear with the 1988 decision of the U.S. Supreme Court in *Lyng v. Northwest Indian Cemetery Protective Association*. In this case, three northern California native bands were opposing a U.S. Forest Service plan to construct a road through a sacred area to improve access to timber and recreational resources. Lower courts had applied an accepted protocol that required the government to demonstrate a "compelling state interest" in order to override freedom of religion rights, but the Supreme Court reversed the lower courts, rejecting the "compelling state interest" test. Furthermore, the Court held that the plaintiffs must show specific government intent to infringe upon a religion or show that the government's action would coerce individuals to act contrary to their beliefs in order to claim protection under the free exercise of religion clause of the First Amendment. The Court's decision specifically rejected the American Indian Religious Freedom Act as being merely a policy statement without legal significance.

The hostile stance taken by the Supreme Court toward the religious rights of Native American peoples in its 1988 decision was reinforced in 1990 when the Court reversed a ruling of the Oregon Supreme Court and denied unemployment compensation to Alfred L. Smith because he violated Oregon laws against peyote use during his participation in Native American Church rituals. The Oregon court had found that the "outright prohibition of good-faith religious use of peyote by adult members of the Native American Church would violate the First Amendment directly as interpreted by Congress," claiming that the

American Indian Religious Freedom Act was specifically intended to protect the religious use of peyote. Supreme Court Justice Antonin Scalia's ruling opinion held that America's religious diversity made the "compelling state interest" test no longer practicable as a rule for protecting the free exercise of religion.

The Native American Church had struggled for a full century against legal assaults on its members' sacramental use of peyote. As early as 1888, a federal agent on the Kiowa-Comanche Reservation had posted an order forbidding peyote use, and the Oklahoma Territorial Legislature in 1899 enacted a statute against the use of peyote, though mistakenly identifying it as "mescal bean." Other states also criminalized peyote use, but attempts to pass federal legislation failed. The Supreme Court of California in *People v. Woody* in 1964 exempted religious use of peyote from state laws outlawing peyote use, claiming that the state was unable to show a "compelling state interest." In 1973 the Arizona Supreme Court in *State of Arizona v. Whittingham* also found that the state's arguments failed the "compelling state interest" test, noting that "the uncontroverted evidence on the record is that peyote is not a narcotic substance and is not habit forming."

The rejection of the "compelling state interest" test by the U.S. Supreme Court in the *Lyng* and *Smith* decisions alarmed representatives of virtually all religious groups in the country, and a coalition was formed to seek legislation to restore the "compelling state interest" test in the protection of the free exercise of religion. This coalition preferred to make its case generic, and no special reference was made to the religious rights of Native American peoples, to sacred sites, or to peyote use. The coalition worked successfully with Congress, and President Bill Clinton signed the Religious Freedom Restoration Act into law on November 16, 1993. However, in the summer of 1997 the Supreme Court struck down this act as unconstitutional in *City of Boerne v. Flores*, a case not directly related to Native American religious freedom.

The Native American Religious Freedom Coalition was formed in response to the *Lyng* and *Smith* decisions of the Supreme Court. It aimed its efforts at seeking specific protections for Native American religious practices through congressional legislation. In May 1993, Senator Daniel Inouye of Hawaii, chairman of the Senate Committee on Indian Affairs, introduced Senate Bill 1021, which intended to extend legal protections for (1) preservation of and access to Native American sacred sites, (2) the use of peyote by Indians in Native American Church rituals, (3) the acquisition and use of eagle feathers and other plant and animal parts by Indian religious practitioners, and (4) the religious rights of Native American prisoners, including specifically the rights to wear long hair and to have access to sweat-lodge rituals and Native American religious leaders. The restoration of the "compelling state interest" test as the legal standard for protecting Native American religious freedom was also an original part of the bill. In July 1994, Senator Inouye introduced Senate Bill 2269 as a new and improved version of his 1993 bill. One part of Inouye's bill was enacted by Congress in the form of H.R. 4230, introduced by Representative Bill Richardson of New Mexico, chairman of the Native American Affairs Subcommittee of the House's Natural Resources Committee, and was signed by President Clinton on October 6, 1994, as the American Indian Religious Freedom Act Amendments of 1994. This act declares: "Notwithstanding any other provision of law, the use, possession, or transportation of peyote by an Indian for bona fide traditional ceremonial purposes in connection with the practice of a traditional Indian religion is lawful, and shall not be prohibited by the United States, or any State."

The Republican-controlled 104th Congress has not enacted any further parts of Senator Inouye's proposed amendments to the American Indian Religious Freedom Act, instead offering various measures to diminish the free exercise of traditional Native American religion. However, some elements represented by Senator Inouye's legislative formulation have been put in force by executive actions of President Clinton's administration. At President Clinton's White House meeting with Native American leaders on April 29, 1994, he signed a "Memorandum for the Heads of Executive Departments and Agencies" that directs that "agencies shall take steps to improve their collection and transfer of eagle carcasses and eagle body parts for Native American religious purposes." In the late spring of 1996, President Clinton signed an executive order requiring federal agencies to "accommodate access to and ceremonial use of Indian sacred sites by Indian religious practitioners," to "avoid adversely affecting the physical integrity of such sacred sites," and to "promptly implement procedures" to carry out the order. This executive order affects Devils Tower National Monument in Wyoming, Sweetgrass Hills in Montana, and Mount Graham in Arizona, along with approximately fifty other sacred sites.

The provisions of Senator Inouye's bill would have required federal agencies such as the U.S. Forest Service, the Bureau of Land Management, and the U.S. Fish and Wildlife Service to follow the directives of the American Indian Religious Freedom Act of 1978 by facilitating Native American religious practices and by consulting with Native American religious practitioners. However, these directives were defined in Senator Inouye's bill as governmental protection of Native American religion by virtue of the federal government's **trust** responsibility for the welfare of Native American peoples rather than as a protection of First Amendment rights, so that constraints of the establishment clause of the First Amendment would not apply. Whereas the land-management agencies of the government had traditionally administered federal lands chiefly in the interest of mining, timber, and grazing usage and had been indifferent or hostile to Native American religious interests, they would have been redirected by Senator Inouye's legislation to give full and equal concern to protecting Native American religious sites. Because neither the First Amendment right to religious freedom nor the American Indian Religious Freedom Act have proven to be effective in protecting sacred sites, Native American practitioners have been bringing forward their claims under cultural resource protection laws, such as the National Historic Preservation Act, the National Environmental Policy Act, and the Archaeological Resources Act.

One important dimension of Native American religious freedom had reached congressional enactment well before Senator Inouye presented his bill mandating specific protections. In late 1989, the National Museum of the American Indian Act became law. This act directed the Smithsonian Institution to establish a program for the **repatriation** of human remains of Native American peoples along with related funerary objects. Previously, Smithsonian repatriation rules permitted return of remains only to those identifiable as direct descendants. The new act broadened this to include groups culturally affiliated with the human remains. The Smithsonian was instructed to inventory its collection, identify cultural affiliations, notify the affiliated Native American peoples, and return all remains to these groups upon request.

The **Pawnee** people had been engaged during the 1980s in efforts to repatriate and rebury ancestral remains in Kansas and Nebraska. The Kansas Historical Society had assisted their efforts, while the Nebraska State Historical Society had stoutly resisted the Pawnee request. Attorneys for the **Native American Rights Fund** actively assisted the Pawnees' legal negotiations, including a request to the Smithsonian for repatriation of Pawnee ancestral remains in 1988. In 1989, Pawnee negotiations with the Smithsonian led to the "Smithsonian Agreement," which based repatriation on cultural affiliation. This "agreement" was incorporated into the congressional bill and subsequently enacted into law.

The 1989 act mandating a liberal policy for repatriation of Native American ancestral remains by the Smithsonian Institution represented the formal demise of the "vanishing Indian" presumption that had dominated nineteenth- and twentieth-century cultural attitudes and governmental policy in America. When Indians were thought to be "vanishing," there was no need to be accountable to anyone regarding treatment of their ancestral remains. In 1989, the Congress by its legislation acknowledged that Native American peoples of the United States presently have, and will continue to have in the foreseeable future, a distinct cultural identity, and that their dead and their burial customs deserve legal and religious respect.

On November 16, 1990, President George Bush signed the **Native American Graves Protection and Repatriation Act**. This act expanded the categories liable to repatriation beyond Native American "human remains" and "funerary objects," as required of the Smithsonian in the 1989 act, by including also "sacred objects" and "objects of cultural patrimony." This 1990 act applied to all federal agencies and public institutions and to all institutions in any way supported by federal funding, excepting the Smithsonian Institution and Native American museums not federally supported. The Smithsonian's National Museum of Natural History subsequently adopted the provisions of the 1990 act as its own policy. Section 13 of the 1990 act required the secretary of the interior to publish regulations carrying out the provisions of the act, and the Final Rule establishing these regulations took effect January 3, 1996. The 1990 act, like its 1989 predecessor, directed repatriation on the basis of "cultural affiliation," and its rules of compliance included both current institutional collections and future discoveries of Native American human remains and culturally connected objects.

Enactment of the American Indian Religious Freedom Act in 1978 served as a clear indicator that the cultural perception of Native American peoples by the American culture at large had significantly shifted from viewing them as either "savages" or "vanishing." However, the American Indian Religious Freedom Act had only symbolic weight, and federal agencies and federal courts continued to apply old patterns of perception and policy for the most part. Indeed, the Supreme Court under Chief Justice William Rehnquist took a decidedly hostile course regarding the American Indian Religious Freedom Act, reversing lower-court rulings honoring the act and even reversing the long-accepted protocol requiring the "compelling state interest" test in cases concerning freedom of religion. Nevertheless, the American Indian Religious Freedom Act is being gradually transformed from symbolism into the law of the land by way of the congressional legislation enacted in 1989, 1990, and 1994 affecting various aspects of Native American religious freedom. Specific congressional legislation is finally bringing the First Amendment right of freedom of religion into effect for Native American peoples. Treatment of the dead and of ancestral objects as well as the sacramental use of peyote have gained federal protection. The guarantee of religious freedom remains to be legislatively extended to the religious rights of Native American prisoners, the Native American use of eagle feathers and other animal parts as sacred materials, and the protection of and access to the sacred sites of Native American peoples.

FURTHER READING

Bray, Tamara L., and Thomas W. Killion, eds. *Reckoning with the Dead: The*

Larsen Bay Repatriation and the Smithsonian Institution. Washington, DC: Smithsonian Institution Press, 1994.

Echo Hawk, Walter. *Study of Native American Prisoner Issues.* Washington, DC: National Indian Policy Center, 1996.

Horse Capture, George P., ed. *The Concept of Sacred Materials and Their Place in the World.* Cody, WY: Buffalo Bill Historical Center, 1988.

Prucha, Francis Paul. *Documents of United States Indian Policy.* Lincoln: University of Nebraska Press, 1975.

Smith, Huston, and Reuben Snake, eds. *One Nation under God: The Triumph of the Native American Church.* Santa Fe, NM: Clear Light, 1996.

Vecsey, Christopher, ed. *Handbook of American Indian Religious Freedom.* New York: Crossroad, 1991.

Williams, Robert A., Jr. *The American Indian in Western Legal Thought: The Discourses of Conquest.* New York: Oxford University Press, 1990.

Wunder, John R. *"Retained by the People": A History of American Indians and the Bill of Rights.* New York: Oxford University Press, 1994.

DALE STOVER

RELOCATION PROGRAM (1950s)

By the 1950s, the economic rationale of allotment had become obsolete. The fancied myth of the yeoman farmer had dissolved into the reality of large-scale growing units in a global network of agribusiness. Most Americans now lived and worked in cities. Advocates of **termination** and relocation saw themselves generally as modernists and realists, promoting the eradication of native land, identity, and lifeways for the Indians' own good, to ease their transition into a modern industrial economy—the benign, all-knowing hand forever shaping the soft underside of conquest.

Between 1954 and 1966, Congress passed legislation terminating federal recognition and services to 109 Native American nations and bands. Some of them disappeared as organized communities. Their residents moved to other places, particularly cities, where the Bureau of Indian Affairs (BIA), through its "relocation" program, was busily building a wing of the urban proletariat that would come back to haunt it as the **self-determination** generation of the 1960s and 1970s—a crisp contradiction of the belief that the hand of BIA paternalism would stir the last of Indian identity into the vast American urban melting pot.

Many opponents of termination were Native American traditionalists who asserted that distinct cultures and land bases should be maintained. During the renaissance of native activism in the 1960s, they were joined in this effort by the young, urbanized children of an earlier generation that had made its own long marches, one by one or family by family, from their homelands to the cities at the behest of the BIA. Between 1953 and 1972, more than 100,000 Native Americans moved to urban areas. By 1980, about half of the Native Americans in the United States lived in urban areas. Young Native Americans raised in urban areas in the 1960s began to reverse relocation's effects. Sometimes college educated, sometimes veterans of the Vietnam War or of terms in state prisons, the young urban Indians by the 1970s were returning to the reservations.

REMOVAL ACT OF 1830 4 Stat. 411

Provisions for "removal"—the relocation of entire Indian nations from areas about to be settled by non-Indians—were first laid down in the 1817 **Treaty between the Cherokee Nation and the United States** (7 Stat. 156–160). By 1830, the federal government had passed general removal legislation aimed at the Five Civilized Tribes—the **Cherokee, Choctaw, Chickasaw, Creek**, and Seminole—because of the intensive efforts they had made in adopting lifeways and political institutions resembling those of European Americans. Many other Native American nations (such as the Osage and **Poncas**) also were removed to **Indian Territory** (later Oklahoma) during the nineteenth century. By 1883, twenty-five Indian reservations occupied by a total of thirty-seven nations had been established in **Indian Country**.

Passage of the Removal Act of 1830 climaxed a two-decade-long struggle over the issue. The Creeks, for example, had become concerned about non-Indian usurpation of their lands by 1818, when the Muscogee (Creek) Nation passed a law against the sale of any Native American land without council approval, with a penalty of death. In 1825, federal treaty commissioners bribed William McIntosh, leader of the Creek Lower Towns, to sign a land-cession treaty, the **Treaty of Indian Springs**, along with a few of his close associates. The National Council declared McIntosh to be a traitor and on May 1, 1825, sent a delegation to torch his house. When McIntosh appeared at the door of his burning home, his body was riddled with bullets.

Removals for specific Indian nations usually were negotiated by treaties (frequently under duress), in which the Indians surrendered what remained to them of their aboriginal homelands in exchange for lands west of the Mississippi River, most of it in Indian Territory. Although some small bands (and a few members of larger nations) had been moving westward since the War of 1812, the Removal Act forced the wholesale removal of entire Indian nations, notably the Five Civilized Tribes on the **Trails of Tears**.

As the federal government prepared to remove entire nations of native people west of the Mississippi River, little thought was given to the fact that Indians, European Americans, and African Americans had been intermarrying among the local settlements and the Five Civilized Tribes for nearly a century. Many of the families that were forced to abandon their homes were nearly as European American genetically as their non-reservation neighbors.

These complications meant little to President **Andrew Jackson**, who had earned his national reputation as a general in the U.S. Army whose primary business was subjugating Indians. In one instance, Jackson led his troops into Florida (which was claimed by Spain at the time) in pursuit of Seminoles who later carried on a protracted war with the army in the Everglades. When he ran for president, Jackson sought frontier votes by favoring removal. Once in office, Jackson considered the Removal Act of 1830 to be the fulfillment of a campaign promise. Others felt less sanguine; even with extensive lobbying from the White House, the House of Representatives passed the Removal Act by only 6 votes (103–97). Representative William Ellsworth of Connecticut opposed removal in a passionate speech delivered on the House floor, saying, in part:

We must be just and faithful to our treaties. There is no occasion for collision. We shall not stand justified before the world in taking any step which shall lead to oppression. The eyes of the world, as well as of this nation, are upon us. I conjure this House not to stain the page of our history with national shame, cruelty, and perfidy.

FURTHER READING

Deloria, Vine, Jr. ed. *American Indian Policy in the Twentieth Century.* Norman: University of Oklahoma Press, 1985.
Washburn, Wilcomb E., comp. *The American Indian and the United States: A Documentary History.* 4 vols. New York: Random House, 1973.

REPATRIATION

The controversy over the reburial of American Indian human remains has been a volatile issue in the United States because by the 1980s the remains or burial offerings of two million American Indians were being stored in museums, state historical societies, universities, National Park Service offices, warehouses, and curio shops. Usually, the remains were classified as "resources" or were said to be part of an archaeological "data base." In most instances, they were not called "human remains." Typically, archaeologists and physical anthropologists used them in "scientific" experiments, or they were displayed as part of entertainment or "educational" programs.

Native American people have long resented the retention of such human remains on religious, humanitarian, ethical, and legal grounds. However, until the initial legislation was introduced to create the Smithsonian's new National Museum of the American Indian during the late 1980s, the issue did not have much national visibility outside of Native American communities. When the U.S. Congress began to hold hearings and consult with American Indian groups to facilitate Native American community opinion to develop the museum, it became clear that American Indian cooperation with the Smithsonian to create the new Indian museum would not be forthcoming until some equitable solution was devised to salve Indian objections about the Smithsonian's policies on the retention of American Indian human remains.

The argument by American Indians for the return of human skeletal remains and related funerary objects is based on several assertions. First, many, but not all, American Indian religions hold that the souls of the deceased do not find rest unless the remains are properly interred. Associated with this religious argument is the question of how to implement **religious freedom** for American Indians on this matter. Also, there is the question of whether religious freedom can be mitigated. Can you declare that some burials are to be protected and others are not to be protected, or is the right to assert one's religious freedom on such an issue absolute?

Second, American Indians in the past have not been viewed fully as human beings, so all aspects of American Indian culture were not accorded respect and equality under the law. The argument states that American Indians were brutal savages who lacked essential qualities for civilization and often, by their very nature, would find it difficult, if not impossible, to acquire civilization. In essence, civilized people were naturally masters, and savages were, by their very nature, subhuman. However, modern American Indians argue that contemporary civil-rights laws and the Thirteenth, Fourteenth, and Fifteenth amendments to the U.S. **Constitution** have legally erased these arguments. It is significant that Native Americans are distinct in their treatment since they alone have been the exclusive property of a group of scholars to the extent that even the bones of American Indian dead can be displayed and disinterred. These remains are featured in museums and used in speculative scientific experiments. This is the humanitarian argument for reburial of American Indian remains.

The **Native American Rights Fund** contends that retention of American Indian human remains violates the Fourteenth Amendment (equal protection) and constitutional guarantees of religious freedom. The legal argument asserts that claims of academic freedom and exclusive rights of possession and scientific inquiry do not take precedence over federal and state laws, especially when such laws were not enforced equally in the past with regard to American Indian remains. Every state has well-defined laws to protect the human remains of non-Indians, but Indians have not been accorded equal protection under the law. Just because an American Indian burial predates the U.S. Constitution does not mean that it should not be protected by federal and state laws, it is argued. Federal and state laws presently protect historic sites, natural wonders, and the like that clearly predate the Constitution. In most cases, federal and state governments regulate access, use, and scientific inquiry with regard to these sites and objects. American Indians are distinct once again, although in their assertions concerning the right to be protected they have had to "prove" their religious beliefs.

Additionally, many American Indians do not believe that the collection and maintenance of human remains constitutes a science. Most Indian intellectuals are unimpressed by the alleged scientific argument. Native Americans also question why American Indian burials must remain aboveground conveniently shelved in museum collections for future use. When the remains of members of the armed forces who had died in captivity, pilots, and other Vietnam veterans were returned to the United States, no one stated that these bones should be studied to give us some answers about the perils and treatment of Agent Orange and other dangers of war. Instead, the remains were respectfully reinterred with appropriate dignity and ceremony. There is a deep and abiding need to reverently bury one's dead in all cultures. American Indians have been deprived of that right.

On the other side of the reburial argument, anthropologists, archaeologists, state historical society personnel, and groups such as the Society for American Archaeology oppose the reburial of Indian human remains and funerary objects. These groups utilize a variety of arguments. The most vocal group in opposition to American Indian reburial in California is the American Committee for the Preservation of Archaeological Collections.

In 1978, the California Department of Parks and Recreation developed a policy for reinterring Indian human remains excavated in the 1930s in Cuyamaca State Park in San Diego County, California. In 1981, the remains were reinterred according to the new state policy. Partly in response to this precedent-setting move, southern California archaeologists formed the American Committee for the Preservation of Archaeological Collections (ACPAC). This organization opposed all reburials of American Indian human remains and associated objects. ACPAC is a group of educated, professional people who make judgments from a Western "scientific" viewpoint on this issue. ACPAC's chief argument is that reburial will destroy "scientific data." It also assumes that all prehistoric remains belong to the "public," notably excluding Native Americans themselves. The ACPAC believes that "scientific data" are so important that native remains should be preserved at all costs, and that the religious, legal, and ethical concerns of American Indians in the controversy are secondary to that consideration.

The arguments in favor of retaining American Indian remains in museums and other non-Indian institutions are focused on the nature of scientific inquiry, academic freedom, and the statements and activities of alleged "political" Indians who oppose the retention of American Indian remains by museums. Certainly, ACPAC's is the most extreme position arguing for the retention of American Indian human remains in museum collections. First and foremost, ACPAC believes that attempts by "political" Indians seeking to "destroy" collections through reburial are not sincere. Moreover, ACPAC asserts that Indian claimants to skeletal collections are not concerned with "time depth" or the fact that many remains can be dated back thousands of years. ACPAC claims that demands to rebury ancient Indian remains without direct genealogical ancestry have become a political power issue for many Indians.

Second, ACPAC believes that scholars or granting agencies that excavate Indian human remains "own" them, and thus giving them back to Indians raises serious "property" questions. Third, donors who gave remains to museums did so thinking that they would be preserved, so when museums return such items, they may be blocked by the "owners," who demand they be returned to the original "donor" or his descendants. Fourth, ACPAC asserts that "property owners," who often are also donors, have a claim to materials found on their property and thus might be unwilling to give future items if human remains were returned to Indians. Fifth, ACPAC alleges that agencies that sponsor archaeological research are technically "owners" of the remains. In the case of the California Department of Parks and Recreation reburying Indian remains in 1981, the federal government pointed out to the State Indian Museum staff that under the Federal Antiquities Act, the state of California could not rebury its collections because many were acquired on federal land. Sixth, ACPAC and others argue that they had a right to study Indian human remains through the doctrine of academic freedom and the necessity for objective analysis in scientific experimentation. ACPAC claims that scientific inquiry must take precedence over religious, ethical, and legal considerations.

In the midst of this controversy, the Smithsonian Institution decided in 1991 that because of federal legislation it would offer to return almost 20,000 American Indian human remains in its collection. The secretary (chief executive officer) of the Smithsonian, Robert M. Adams, said that American Indians, like all people, have a fundamental right to bury their dead. He believes that this fundamental right overrides any "scientific" considerations.

By 1991, twenty-two states had passed laws protecting Indian burial sites. One of the first states to pass such a law was Nebraska, where the return of remains brought opposition from James Hanson, director of the Nebraska State Historical Society. Hanson called a state law mandating return of Native American skeletons and burial artifacts "censorship." "The work of a generation of scholars will be lost," Hanson told an annual meeting of the historical society in Kearney, Nebraska. "For the first time in my professional career, a state government has decided to dictate."

The "dictator," to Hanson, was Nebraska State Senator Ernie Chambers, who sponsored the act mandating return of remains and burial objects that passed the state's unicameral legislature 30–16 in May 1989. Within three months, agreements along similar lines opened much larger collections to Indian nations at Stanford University, the University of Minnesota, the Peabody Museum of Boston, and the Smithsonian Institution.

Chambers was no novice to initiating nationwide controversy. Chambers, who represents North Omaha, Nebraska's only sizable black community, sponsored legislation that made Nebraska the first state government to divest its financial interests in South Africa during the middle 1980s. He has recently figured in national controversy over proposals that college athletes be paid for their services, a measure Chambers has introduced for several years in the Nebraska legislature without success.

Until passage of the Nebraska law, most governmental bodies and academic institutions would release skeletons and artifacts only to Indians who could prove familial relations to the deceased. Such relationships are usually nearly impossible to prove, since very few of the remains have names attached to them. The Nebraska measure (and others negotiated later in the year) allows claims of remains by Native American nations, something that is much easier to document than family relationships.

Like Hanson, the American Anthropological Association (AAA) asserts that return of bones and artifacts to Indian nations will destroy scholarship. The subject was a focus of intense controversy at the AAA's annual meeting in Washington, D.C., during November 1989. **Vine Deloria, Jr.**, whose books, such as *Custer Died for Your Sins* and *God Is Red* helped initiate Indian **self-determination** efforts two decades ago, leveled a stinging address at the anthropologists, saying that even today, most of them regard Indians not as living human beings, but as artifacts whose remains should be owned by the state.

Chambers's major ally in the effort to return remains and artifacts was the **Pawnee** Indian Tribe, which had carried on a three-year campaign against the State Historical Society. The measure was drafted with the aid of the **Native American Rights Fund** of Boulder, Colorado.

The Pawnees were active on a nationwide scale in demanding the reburial of Native American remains, mainly through the efforts of Walter and John Echo Hawk, both Pawnees. They were particularly galled by a farmer who had unearthed 146 Indian skeletons on his property and created a tourist attraction out of them near Salina, Kansas. The exhibit lasted more than fifty years before it became the center of a growing controversy over the uses, and misuses, of Native American remains and burial objects. By 1990, Kansas had passed the Kansas Unmarked Burial Sites Preservation Act and appropriated $90,000 to buy and close the Salina burial pit.

Robert Peregoy, an attorney with the Native American Rights Fund, defended Chambers against Hanson's charge that he had engaged in "censorship." "When duly elected lawmakers decide on a policy and enact it into law, my understanding is that it's called representative government," Peregoy told the Associated Press. During the fall of 1990, the Nebraska State Historical Society prepared, reluctantly, to return about 37,000 artifacts to the Pawnees. These included not only items manufactured by Pawnees, but also spurs, bits, and buckles worn by Spanish conquistadors, a French medal, thousands of trade beads, and the bones of now-extinct animals such as the Great Plains grizzly bear and the ivory-billed woodpecker. The Nebraska State Historical Society also returned the remains of 398 people to the Pawnees. More than 100 of the skeletons were taken from a village site near present-day Genoa, Nebraska, where a Pawnee village was devastated by disease about 1750. Some of the remains dated to about 1600, when the Pawnees moved into Nebraska from Kansas. For a century before that, a great drought is believed to have rendered Nebraska uninhabitable.

The debate ranges beyond bones to such things as the **wampum** belts used to preserve memories of the Iroquois Great Law of Peace, which, scholars now assert, provided a precedent for **Benjamin Franklin**'s drafts of the **Articles of Confederation**. The wampum belts have been held by New York State for almost a century. Three months after Nebraska passed its law, New York agreed to return twelve of the belts to the Onondagas, who tend the central council fire of the **Iroquois Confederacy**. "These belts are our archives. That's why we have been trying to get them back," said Raymond Gonyea, an Onondaga who specializes in Native American affairs at the New York State Museum.

The changes in policy across the country also benefitted the **Omaha** Indian Tribe. About 280 artifacts were returned to the Omahas in late August 1990 from Boston's Peabody Museum, which is affiliated with Harvard University. The Peabody had held them for more than 100 years. The Smithsonian Institution returned an albino buffalo hide and a ceremonial pipe to the Omahas in 1991, after having held them since 1898. The two objects, believed to be at least 300 years old, were being housed at the University of Nebraska's Lincoln campus until the Omahas completed a historical and cultural museum at Macy, the largest town on their present-day reservation. Near Macy, the Omahas also buried the remains of 92 skeletons returned to them by the University of Nebraska. While the skeletons were reburied, artifacts were kept aboveground for exhibit and further study. The Omahas also planned to send their artifacts on tour around Nebraska, on the theory that they belong to everyone, not just to the Omaha Nation.

The artifacts returned from the Peabody Museum included the Omahas' sacred pole, which was used for centuries as the life force that unified and renewed the Omahas. Until it was made part of the Peabody's collection in 1888, the cottonwood and ash pole was carried by the Omahas in their travels. People told their troubles to it. The return of remains and artifacts spurred additional study of the Omahas, who once held sway over the area that now forms the eastern half of Nebraska, where they were the dominant military and cultural force. For a time during the early contact period, a substantial-sized town named Tonwantoga (near present-day Homer, Nebraska) functioned as a trading center (primarily for buffalo hides) between native people to the west and Euro-American settlements to the east of the Missouri River.

Dennis Hastings, Omaha historian, said that the Omahas hope to build a small museum to house the artifacts within ten years. The artifacts were returned to the Omahas at their annual powwow in Macy, Nebraska, as about 650 people watched. Omaha elders later recalled, some with tears in their eyes, how non-Indian police officers along the route had removed their hats and bowed their heads in respect as the remains passed.

The agreement to allow Native American nations to claim skeletons and artifacts from the Smithsonian, which has the world's largest collection, was part of negotiations to build an Indian museum within the Smithsonian complex, next to the National Air and Space Museum on the Mall. The Smithsonian is under pressure to make living Indians an important part of the new museum's board and management.

"Basically, we want dead Indians out, and live Indians in," Susan Shown Harjo, executive director of the National Congress of American Indians, said. "It's a victory for America to solve a disgraceful situation where Indians are an archaeological resource, [and] our relatives are U.S. property—not quite human" (Johansen 1989: 15–16).

The Smithsonian established a "repatriation office" in 1991 to determine how to return 18,000 "sets" of Native American remains that had been collected by the National Museum of Natural History during the previous century and a half. This is the largest single collection of Native American remains, thought to comprise about 100,000 "sets" at that time. Most of the Smithsonian's collection was boxed and stacked in hallways amidst offices on the fifth floor of the museum, an area closed to the public, which some employees call "the mortuary." By 1996, the Smithsonian had returned about 2,500 of its 18,000 "sets" of remains, according to Thomas Killion, director of the Smithsonian's repatriation office. The pace of returns was being slowed by the complicated process of verifying the national origins of the remains, and by the small number of people (five) assigned to the job by the government.

FURTHER READING

Deloria, Vine, Jr. "A Simple Question of Humanity: The Moral Dimensions of the Reburial Issue." *Native American Rights Fund Legal Review* 14:4 (Fall 1989).

Echo Hawk, Walter. "Who Owns the Past? How Native American Indian Lawyers Fight for Their Ancestors' Remains and Memories." *Human Rights* 16:3 (1989): 24–29, 53–55.

Gonyea, Raymond. Interview. July 3, 1992.

Johansen, Bruce E. "Dead Indians Out, Live Indians In." *The Progressive* (December 1989): 15–16.

"Policy Regarding the Repatriation of Native American Ceremonial Objects and Human Remains." Adopted by the Council of the American Association of Museums, January 15, 1989. Reprinted in *Northeast Indian Quarterly* 7:1 (Spring 1990): 45–46.

Raymond, Chris. "Reburial of Indian Remains Stimulates Studies, Friction among Scholars." *Chronicle of Higher Education*, October 3, 1990.

"Return of Indian Bones No Small Task." [*Baltimore Sun*]. Reprinted in *Omaha World-Herald*, September 14, 1996, 10.

DONALD A. GRINDE, JR., and BRUCE E. JOHANSEN

RESERVED RIGHTS DOCTRINE

The Reserved Rights Doctrine, first enunciated by the U.S. Supreme Court in **United States v. Winans** (1905), held that "a treaty is not a grant of rights to Indians, but a grant of rights from them—a reservation of those not granted." Three years later, the Supreme Court handed down the classic water-rights case **Winters v. United States**, in which the Reserved Rights Doctrine was used to give, in effect, Indians first preference for water supplies.

The *Winans* case referred to a treaty signed by the Yakimas in 1859 in which they retained the right to fish off-reservation at "the usual and accustomed places, in common with citizens of the Territory." In 1896, the federal government filed suit on behalf of the Yakimas to prevent European Americans from obstructing the Indians' fishing rights. Non-Indian commercial fishermen were using large "fish wheels" that emptied streams of their salmon runs before Indians could harvest their fair share. A lower federal court held that the Indians' treaty rights were no broader than those of the non-Indian immigrants, so the fish wheels were allowed to continue operation. The Supreme Court reversed that ruling, finding in favor of the Yakimas. The Reserved Rights Doctrine is based on the fact that before European-American settlement, Indians enjoyed extensive control over their lands and resources.

ROSEBUD SIOUX TRIBE V. KNEIP 430 U.S. 584 (1977)

The U.S. Supreme Court upheld congressional acts that diminished the Rosebud Sioux reservation, even though the acts in question made no mention of changing boundaries. The Court fell back on geopolitical circumstances and its interpretation of prior legislation to support the ruling.

The Court found that Congress had intended to disestablish **Indian Country** in all or part of four South Dakota counties over which the Rosebud Sioux had asserted jurisdiction. The ruling was split, with Justice Thurgood Marshall in dissent. He said, in part, that "ultimately, what the legislative body demonstrates, as co-counsel for the State has aptly concluded, is that Congress demonstrated an 'almost complete lack of . . . concern with the boundary issue.' " This decision, which placed two thousand Rosebud Sioux and seven towns outside the reservation boundaries, has been criticized for its sparse support in prior legislation.

ROSS, JOHN (COOWESCOOWE OR "THE EGRET") (Cherokee) 1790–1866)

Born along the Coosa River at Tahnoovayah, Georgia (near Lookout Mountain), John Ross, who would become the founder of a constitutional government among the **Cherokees**, was the third of nine children. His father was Daniel Ross, a Scot, and his mother, Mary (Molly) McDonald, was a Scot-Cherokee woman. As a youth, he was called Tsan-usdi or "Little John."

Although Ross was brought up with other Cherokees, he was educated at home by non-Indian tutors and then continued his education at Kingston Academy in Tennessee. Although he was about one-eighth Cherokee, Ross always identified himself as Cherokee and was married in 1813 to "Quatie" or Elizabeth Brown Henley, a full-blooded Cherokee. They had five children.

Ross began his political career in 1809 when he went on a mission to the Arkansas Cherokees. By 1811, he was serving as a member of the Standing Committee of the Cherokee Council. In 1813–1814, he was an adjutant in a Cherokee regiment under the command of General **Andrew Jackson** and saw action with other Cherokees at Horseshoe Bend in 1813 against the Red Sticks commanded by "Red Eagle" or William Weatherford. Ross led a contingent of Cherokee warriors in a diversionary tactic and thus was an important factor in Jackson's success at Horseshoe Bend.

In 1814, shortly after his marriage, Ross set up a ferry service and trading post at Ross's Landing. In 1817, he became a member of the Cherokee National Council; he served as president of the National Council from 1819 to 1826. In 1820, a republican form of government was instituted by the Cherokee people, similar in structure to that of the United States. As an advocate of education among his people, Ross thought that the Cherokees might become a state in the Union with its own constitution. When New Echota became the Cherokee national capital in 1826, he moved there with his family. In 1827, he became president of the Cherokee constitutional convention that drafted a new constitution. From 1828 to 1839, Ross served as principal chief of the Cherokee Nation under this new constitution.

During Ross's years as chief, he opposed federal and state encroachments on Cherokee lands. He resisted Georgia's contention that the Cherokees were mere tenants on state lands. When Georgia stripped the Cherokees of their civil rights between 1828 and 1831, Ross took their case to the Supreme Court and won, but President Andrew Jackson violated his oath of office by defying the Supreme Court when he refused to enforce the decision. With the discovery of gold near Dahlonega, Georgia, Georgia state officials pressed for the relocation westward of the Cherokees along with other eastern American Indians. Jackson also signed the Indian **Removal Act of 1830**, which provided for the relocation of eastern Indian nations west of the Mississippi in an area that would become **Indian Territory**.

Although Ross continued to resist removal policies as principal chief of the Cherokees, a dispirited minority of Cherokee leaders called the Treaty Party, including Major Ridge, John Ridge, Elias Boudinot, and Stand Watie, in 1835 consented to removal by signing the **Treaty of New Echota**. Ross and a majority of the Cherokees sought to have the treaty reversed and sent a letter to Congress in 1836 asking for an investigation into its legality.

Although Ross continued to protest removal for three more years, the state of Georgia started to coerce the Cherokees into selling their lands for a fraction of their real value. Marauding European Americans plundered Cherokee homes and possessions and destroyed the *Cherokee Phoenix*'s printing press because it opposed removal. The army forced Cherokee families into internment camps to prepare for the arduous trek westward. As a result of unhealthy and crowded conditions in these hastily constructed stockades, many Cherokees died even before the **Trail of Tears** began. Although Ross failed in his efforts to stop removal, he managed to gain additional federal funds for his people.

During the internment of the Cherokees in Georgia and the two disastrous trips along the Trail of Tears, over four thousand Cherokees died of exposure, disease, and starvation—about a quarter of the total Cherokee population. Quatie, Ross's wife, was among the victims of this forced emigration. After removal, the miserable conditions did not cease because many Cherokees died after they arrived in Indian Territory as epidemics and food shortages plagued the new settlements.

Upon his arrival in Indian Territory, Ross joined the Western Cherokees who had moved several years earlier. He aided in the drafting of the constitution for the United Cherokees and served as its head from 1839 until his death in 1866. In 1839, with the assassination of the Ridges and Boudinot in retaliation for their role in signing the removal treaty, Cherokee factions became polarized, and some of the proponents of the Treaty Party claimed that Ross had a role in the assassinations, but they never produced any evidence. Sequoyah, the originator of the Cherokee alphabet, and other peacemakers sought to reconcile the factions within the Cherokees. In 1844, Ross married a Quaker woman named Mary Bryan Stapler, and they had three children. Between 1839 and 1856, he went to Washington five times seeking justice for his people.

Although Ross was a large slaveholder when the Civil War began, he opposed a Cherokee alliance with the Confederacy. Instead, he advocated Cherokee neutrality. Many of Ross's supporters were nonslaveholding Cherokees. By the summer of 1861, many influential leaders, including Stand Watie, favored joining the Confederacy. Ross convened a national conference and was overruled by the pro-Confederacy forces. By 1862, federal troops had regained control over most of Indian Territory, so Ross moved his wife and family to Kansas. As a result, Ross was deposed from office, and the Cherokees repudiated their ties to the Confederacy in 1863. But the Southern Cherokees under Stand Watie formed a separate government that still allied with the Confederacy. Faced with such tragic divisions, Ross went to Washington to tell President Abraham Lincoln about the rebellious Southern Cherokees.

At the end of the Civil War, the Cherokees were deeply split. Ross, at seventy-five and in bad health, journeyed to Washington as the head of the Northern Cherokees for new treaty negotiations that sought to protect the Cherokees and their constitution. He died while in Washington on August 1, 1866, during negotiations. His body was returned to Indian Territory, and he was buried at Park Hill, Oklahoma.

DONALD A. GRINDE, JR.

RUSSELL TRIBUNAL (FOURTH) (1980)

The Fourth Russell Tribunal met November 24–30, 1980, in Rotterdam, the Netherlands, to consider violations of international law and human-rights standards against native peoples of the Americas. Heretofore, the Russell Tribunal had investigated war crimes, particularly in Europe.

Of forty-five cases submitted to the tribunal from both North and South America, fourteen were selected for examination through witnesses and documentation. Cases involving native peoples within the United States included the St. Regis (Akwesasne) Mohawks of New

York State, the **Hopis**, the Dine (Navajos), and the Shoshones. All of these cases involved land taken in violation of international protocols as well as treaties signed with the United States.

The Fourth Russell Tribunal concluded that

the most severe persecution in human history, lasting for almost 500 years, has been mounted against the native peoples of the Americas. We refer to the wars of conquest, the fatal contagions brought to the Americas as part of European contact; the enslavement and forced-labor systems; integration by violent means into a colonialist economic system incompatible with their community organization of production and way of life, and inconsistent with their self-determination; and the prohibition of their religions and the use of their languages.

The tribunal described a long history of oppression, including the following actions:

- "The usurping character of the governmental bodies which are supposedly dedicated to the protection of the native people"
- Mass killings of native people, particularly in Guatemala
- Expulsion of native peoples from their homelands, often to make way for exploitation of natural resources
- Violations of religious and civil rights
- Violations of treaties and other agreements

The Russell Tribunal is not a court of law and has no enforcement powers. Instead, it relies on publicity of human-rights abuses to address them.

FURTHER READING

Russell Tribunal. *Report of the Fourth Russell Tribunal on the Rights of the Indians of the Americas.* Nottingham, England: Russell Tribunal, 1980.

S

SANTA CLARA PUEBLO V. MARTINEZ 436 U.S. 49 (1978)

In *Santa Clara Pueblo v. Martinez*, the U.S. Supreme Court held that the **Indian Civil Rights Act** of 1968 did not abrogate a Native American nation's sovereign immunity. More precisely, the court held that section 1302 of the civil rights act, which brings Indian nations under the Bill of Rights, does not authorize a private civil cause of action in any federal court.

The case was brought by a woman member of the Santa Clara Pueblo who, with her daughter, challenged a **Pueblo** law that denied membership to the children of female (but not male) members. They contended that this ordinance violated the equal-protection clause and was therefore illegal.

The Court did not rule on the validity of the case, but denied that federal courts had jurisdiction over the case, a move widely interpreted as supportive of Native American self-government nationwide. Such unnecessary intrusion into Native American affairs by federal courts was held to threaten a native nation's ability to "maintain itself as a culturally and politically distinct entity." While the Court's ruling in *Santa Clara* was strongly supportive of Native American sovereignty in the facts of this case, this opinion also reminded Indian nations that "Congress has plenary authority to limit, modify, or eliminate the powers of self-government which the tribes otherwise possess."

FURTHER READING

Ziontz, Alvin J. "After Martinez: Civil Rights under Tribal Government." *University of California Davis Law Review* 12:1 (March 1979): 1–35.

SELF-DETERMINATION, AS CONCEPT

In 1961, voices of protest were raised at the American Indian Chicago Conference, which brought together more than five hundred native people from more than sixty groups. The conference was organized by Sol Tax, professor of anthropology at the University of Chicago, at the behest of President John F. Kennedy, as a forum to enable native people to express their views regarding their own futures.

New, more politically active native organizations emerged during the 1960s. In 1961, a group of young, college-educated American Indians formed the **National Indian Youth Council** (NIYC). This organization had deep roots in impoverished, traditional Indian communities. By 1964, the first modern civil disobedience by Native Americans was taking place on Puget Sound salmon streams as Indian "fish-ins" dramatized native assertion of treaty rights to harvest fish that state authorities had long ignored. American Indian activism and nationalism were transformed by the occupation of the former federal penitentiary at **Alcatraz** on November 19, 1969. The resulting media attention provided a national platform for discussion of American Indian issues relating to self-determination. On December 16, 1969, the occupants said:

We are issuing this call in an attempt to unify our Indian brothers behind a common cause. . . . We are not getting anywhere fast by working alone as individual tribes. If we can get together as brothers and come to a common agreement, we feel that we can be much more effective, doing things for ourselves, instead of having someone else doing it, telling us what is good for us. So we must start somewhere. We feel that if we are going to succeed, we must hold on to the old ways. *This is the first and most important reason we went to Alcatraz Island.* (Leaflet, author's files)

American Indian militant movements also were springing up in other cities as well. In 1968, the American Indian Movement (AIM) was formed in Minneapolis to combat police brutality and the selective law-enforcement policies of the Minneapolis police. Initially, an "Indian patrol" was established to follow the police as they traveled through Native American neighborhoods. Arrest rates of Native Americans fell to the general average of the city in just nine months after the AIM patrols were introduced.

Militant nationalist activities became more frequent in the early 1970s. During the spring of 1972, AIM leaders openly castigated the Chippewa council for allowing non-Indians to exploit reservation resources (especially fishing rights). For a few days at the Cass Lake Convention Center (Minnesota), AIM leaders blocked traffic and demanded that Native American leaders reassert treaty fishing rights (the non-Indians, afraid of AIM's tactics, reluctantly accepted Native American control of resources as a result of this confrontation). At the same time, AIM led one thousand American Indian people into Gordon, Nebraska, to protest the murder of Raymond Yellow Thunder by five Euro-Americans. Protests over the death of Richard Oakes (a leader of the Alcatraz occupation) at the hands of a prison guard in California also flared up in 1972.

Traditional people on the Pine Ridge Reservation had rallied around AIM. Some people detested the brutality of the reservation police, while others wanted help in settling fractionalized heirship problems that inhibited ranching and agriculture on the reservation. Local issues at Pine Ridge laid the basis for the national attention given AIM as it occupied the small village of Wounded Knee early in 1973.

On March 11, 1973, AIM members declared their independence as the Oglala Sioux Nation, defining its boundaries according to the **Fort Laramie Treaty** (1868). At one point, federal officials considered an armed attack on the camp at Wounded Knee, but the plan was ultimately discarded. The occupation by AIM lasted seventy-two days. Dennis Banks and Russell Means, AIM leaders, stated that they would hold out until the Senate Foreign Relations Committee had reviewed all broken treaties and the corruption of the Bureau of Indian Affairs had been exposed to the world. After much gunfire and negotiation, AIM's occupation of Wounded Knee ended on May 7, 1973.

FURTHER READING

Barsh, Russel L. "The Challenge of Indigenous Self-Determination." *University of Michigan Journal of Law Reform* 26(1993): 277.

SELF-DETERMINATION, LEGAL ASPECTS
In 1975, Congress passed the Indian Self-Determination and Education Assistance Act (P.L. 93-638, 25 U.S.C. §§ 450 *et seq.*), which strengthened Native American governments' control over federal programs administered on reservations. Self-determination as a concept had been embraced as federal policy under President Richard Nixon in the early 1970s. In 1970, Nixon had addressed Congress on Indian affairs and had announced an end to policies of **termination**. Nixon urged protection of Native American land base and resources.

SEMINOLE NATION OF INDIANS V. UNITED STATES 316 U.S. 286 (1942)
The U.S. Supreme Court upheld the federal government's **trust** responsibility toward Native American peoples on legal and moral

grounds in *Seminole Nation v. United States*, a case brought after the Seminoles filed suit alleging that the government had mismanaged money due them under a treaty signed in 1856. The Supreme Court held that the government assumes a distinctive trust obligation when dealing with "these dependent and sometimes exploited people." Furthermore, the government also carries "moral obligations of the highest responsibility and trust," which must be carried out according to the "most exacting fiduciary standards."

SEMINOLE TRIBE OF FLORIDA, INC. V. FLORIDA 11 F.3d 1016 (11th Cir. 1996)

The Seminoles, who started the first commercial gaming operation in **Indian Country** by opening a bingo parlor in 1979, filed suit in 1991 alleging that the state had failed to negotiate "in good faith" a compact required by the **Indian Gaming Regulatory Act** of 1988 to allow the installation of casino games such as slot machines and roulette wheels. Florida contended that casino gambling violated its state constitution.

In *Seminole v. Florida*, the U.S. Supreme Court struck down a provision in the Indian Gaming Regulatory Act that allowed Native American governments to sue a state if it failed to negotiate in good faith on compacts allowing casino gambling. In a majority opinion by Chief Justice William Rehnquist, the court ruled that the law's requirement violated the Eleventh Amendment, which grants states immunity from federal lawsuits.

Following the 5–4 Supreme Court decision, attorneys and legal scholars debated its scope and impact. Bruce Rogow, of Fort Lauderdale, an attorney for the Seminoles, speculated that the ruling might negate the requirement for any agreement with the state, allowing the Seminoles to negotiate casino gambling directly with the Department of the Interior. Florida governor Lawton Chiles called the ruling "a significant victory" that would strengthen "our hand in the effort to defend our communities from casino gambling." At the time the ruling was issued, the Seminoles operated bingo, low-stakes poker, and pull-tab gaming in Hillsborough, Broward, and Collier counties of southern Florida, all games that were allowed in nonreservation areas of the state. In 1994, Florida voters had voted by a large margin to prohibit casino-style gambling.

Concern was raised that the ruling might interfere with native nations' attempts to obtain redress in the court system on questions other than gambling, such as environmental protection and land claims. Justice John Paul Stevens, in dissent, wrote that the ruling could threaten the federal government's authority over the states in many legal areas, including environmental regulation, copyright law, patent law, and bankruptcy. Timothy Wapato of the National Indian Gaming Association argued that the Court meant to limit the effect of the case to the matter at hand. "It's important to note that the high court surgically removed the lawsuit provision of the IGRA and left the rest intact. The result, therefore, is that the case returns Native American nations to pre-IGRA time where the Interior Secretary is responsible for completing gaming agreements with tribes," Wapato told *Native American News.*

In *Seminole v. Florida*, the Supreme Court overturned a prior decision in *Pennsylvania v. Union Gas* (1991), holding that the interstate commerce clause of the U.S. **Constitution** granted Congress the right to abrogate state sovereign immunity. The Seminoles had rested their argument on this case, contending that the Indian commerce clause should be treated similarly.

FURTHER READING

Ewen, Alex. "A Supreme Court Question of Power: High Court Paves Legal Road to States' Supremacy." *Native Americas* 13:2 (Summer 1996): 26–29.
"Seminole: Tribe May No Longer Sue States in Federal Court." *Native American News*, Sample Issue, 1996.

SEMINOLE TRIBE V. BUTTERWORTH 658 F.2d 310 (5th Cir. 1981), *cert. denied*, 455 U.S. 1020 (1982)

The recent history of reservation gambling began in 1979, when the Seminoles became the first Indian nation to enter the bingo industry when they opened a bingo hall on their reservation. The state of Florida, which had assumed **Public Law 280** criminal jurisdiction, challenged the legality of the games, only to have the Fifth Circuit Court of Appeals rule that Seminole bingo could continue because the federal government had never transferred to Florida jurisdiction that would have allowed the state to enforce its civil laws on Indian lands.

To show how complicated Indian law can get, the Seminole decision hinged on a finding of the court that Indian bingo in Florida fell under civil jurisdiction, not criminal law. If the Fifth Circuit had ruled that the bingo games fell under criminal law, the state's jurisdiction would have applied because Florida is a P.L. 280 state. Federal P.L. 280 allowed states to extend criminal jurisdiction over Indian reservations. In 1968, the law was amended to require Native American consent before the state could assume jurisdiction. After 1968, the assumption of criminal jurisdiction by states effectively stopped. The states that had taken jurisdiction before 1968 were allowed to keep it, however.

According to the *Christian Science Monitor* (March 25, 1985), by early 1985, 75 to 80 of the 300 recognized Indian nations and bands in the United States were conducting some sort of game of chance. The proliferation of gambling on native reservations came at a time when gambling was moving from a few enclaves, such as Reno and Las Vegas,

Nevada, to become a more broadly accepted feature on the social land-scape across the United States. Reservations, many of them within an hour's drive of major metropolitan areas, became small islands where many state prohibitions on gambling did not apply. By the fall of 1988, the Congressional Research Service estimated that more than 100 Indian nations and bands were participating in some form of gambling, which grossed as much as $255 million a year. By 1996, the gross income exceeded $1 billion.

FURTHER READING

Johansen, Bruce E. *Life and Death in Mohawk Country*. Golden, CO: North American Press, 1993.

SEMINOLES, TRADITIONAL

The Seminoles' ancestors were chased by an army under the command of **Andrew Jackson** from present-day Georgia into Florida during the early nineteenth century, when the area was still claimed by Spain. The Seminoles hid in the Everglades for nearly half a century, resisting re-peated attempts at subjugation by the U.S. Army as Jackson's presidency came and went, and as the other four of the Five Civilized Tribes (**Cher-okees, Chickasaws, Choctaws** and **Creeks**) were removed to **Indian Ter-ritory**, now Oklahoma.

Until the mid-twentieth century, some of the Seminoles lived nearly isolated in the Everglades. When Seminole land claims were settled, the traditional Seminoles refused to take part, insisting that land cannot be bought and sold under the Creator's law. They insisted on their right to occupy the land that had belonged to their ancestors under natural law, not U.S. civil law. The traditional Seminoles are, wrote Catherine Caufield in the magazine *South Florida*, "the true descendants of the 'unconquered Seminoles' of Florida schoolbook cliche" (Caufield 1994: 64).

The distance between schoolbook cliché and present-day reality can be measured in time (a century and a half) and in space (several million acres). In 1996, the assimilative weapon of choice against one small village of surviving traditional Seminole community, down to its last five acres of land (to which the villagers did not even hold title), was a county electrical and plumbing code. Collier County, which includes Naples, Florida, had been attempting to disperse one of the last surviv-ing traditional Seminole settlements because their chickee dwellings (which are designed with four cypress poles and a thatched roof of palmetto fronds) did not conform to late-twentieth-century Anglo-American regulations for plumbing and electrical wiring. At least two children recently had been removed from traditional Seminole villages by county officials on grounds that their parents' homes were "substan-dard." The traditional Seminoles have been living on their present site for the last twelve years; many of them wonder where they would go if they were evicted from their five-acre settlement.

For nearly a hundred years after the Seminole wars ended in the mid-nineteenth century, the surviving Seminoles were left more or less alone because immigrants regarded the Everglades as hostile and nearly impenetrable. In the mid-twentieth century, however, roads and canals with picturesque names like Alligator Alley began to pierce the "wild" Everglades. Many of the Seminoles settled a land claim stemming from 1842 by agreeing to move to designated reservations. One such group (there are five Seminole reservations) became known as the Seminole Tribe of Florida, Inc., a body known to patrons of Everglades "Jungle" tours, alligator wrestling, and gambling. This "recognized" Seminole tribe opened the first Indian bingo halls in the late 1970s and has since figured in several major lawsuits defining the legal status of Indian gaming.

The traditional Seminoles point to an 1842 agreement signed by President James Polk as evidence that, as traditional Seminole leader Bobby Billie puts it, "we have a right to live on this land, same as everyone else" (Johansen 1996: 44). In the middle 1950s, however, as the federal government pressed the Seminoles to accept reservation land in exchange for extinguishment claims to five million acres of southwest Florida, the traditionals refused to participate because, said Billie, "We don't sell the land; we don't buy the land, and we don't say a person can own the land, because it doesn't belong to man. It belongs to the Creator."

For many years, the traditional Seminoles had lived largely from hunting and trading, almost unknown to other Floridians, wishing to be left alone. As long as their land was held to be without value as defined by mainstream capitalism, the traditional Seminoles were allowed to live outside the dominant culture. As the twentieth century passed its midpoint, however, the tendrils of asphalt, the wakes of power boats, and the attention of county government breached their cherished solitude.

When the federal government prepared to pay off Seminole land claims with $16 million in the late 1970s and early 1980s, the traditionals engaged legal help from the **Indian Law Resource Center** to make sure they would not get any of it. The request was lodged by Guy Osceola, a descendant of the famous Seminole chief of the same name who led resistance during conflicts with the U.S. Army in the early nineteenth century. The ILRC persuaded Congress to overrule the state of Florida and regard the traditional Seminoles as a separate group.

The traditional Seminoles also detest attempts to memorialize their ancestors in Anglo-American fashion. In 1995, a number of traditional Seminoles protested the unveiling of a life-size, bronze statue of Seminole medicine man Sam Jones, who also fought in the Seminole wars, at Florida's Tree Tops Park. Bobby Billie told the *Fort Lauderdale Sun-Sentinel* that a statue of a holy man is sacrilegious. The Seminole Tribe of Florida, Inc., had paid $15,000 of the statue's $60,000 cost.

The villages of the traditional Seminole contrast sharply with the garish development that characterizes the Seminole Tribe, Inc.,'s reservation near Hollywood, Florida, which straddles State Route 441 amidst discount smoke shops, a tourist attraction called the Magical Indian Village, and the facade of the original Seminole Bingo. Tribal chairman James Billie operates his own tourist attraction, Camp Billie Safari, where, according to an article in the magazine *South Florida*, "Tourists looking for an Everglades experience can spend the night in a chickee and ride in a swamp buggy." An alligator-wrestling arena with a wet bar has been added recently to the camp. It was Billie who came up with the idea of bingo in the 1970s. He calls it "the best thing that ever happened to the Seminoles," and "sweet revenge" on the Seminoles' conquerors. The money is all the sweeter, says Billie, because the federal and state governments cannot tax it. With Billie in the lead, the Seminole Tribe of Florida, Inc., also has negotiated a royalty on the sales of sports clothing marketed by Florida State University. Instead of rejecting the Seminole mascot as a stereotype, Billie decided to get in on the fiscal action (Caufield 64–97).

Since bingo was introduced in 1979, the Seminoles' annual income has risen from $1 million to $40 million a year. The state of Florida refuses to negotiate the necessary compacts required by the federal **Indian Gaming Regulatory Act** to permit casino gambling by the Seminoles of Hollywood. With only bingo, enrolled Seminoles each receive monthly per capita checks of about $1,000. Most recently, the Seminole Tribe of Florida went to court against the state of Florida on grounds that the state was not negotiating a gambling compact "in good faith." The U.S. Supreme Court ruled 5–4 that a state cannot be sued by an Indian nation under the Indian Gaming Regulatory Act.

As one group of Seminoles joined the cash economy, the traditionals continued to live in small villages of traditional chickee huts. Because they had refused to deal with the federal government, the traditional Seminoles had no treaty, no reservation status, and no protection from the body of federal law that defines Native American communities' semisovereign status. Because the traditional Seminoles had held to their traditional law, the U.S. legal system had defined them out of existence. The present-day traditional Seminoles' villagers live on land owned by Pacific Land Company, which is leased to them at $1 a year. Many of the Seminoles work in the vast agricultural fields that surround their settlement.

Bobby Billie reacted to the eviction threat by becoming one of the

main organizers of a 750-mile environmental protest walk from the Everglades to Florida's state capital, Tallahassee. Along the way, the walkers visited with Mexican farm workers who are constantly exposed to
pesticides in central Florida, poor people who live near large phosphate
mines, and others who are fighting development of a major landfill near
Newberry. They made a point of visiting burning sugar-cane fields and
pulp mills, as well as portions of the Ocala National Forest that serve
as a bombing range for the U.S. Navy. About thirty people walked all
or most of the 750 miles as others came and went. The statewide walk
was organized by the Florida Coalition for Peace and Justice, based in
Gainesville. Walkers included local residents, a number of traditional
Seminoles, and other people from such countries as Venezuela, Mexico,
and Belgium. Walkers averaged eighteen miles on foot a day, with an
occasional day off to rest. Along the way, Billie and his cowalkers held
press conferences and issued statements summarizing the environmental destruction they had been witnessing:

You cannot overpower the Creator's law. You are part of the creation. I'm telling
you to stop destroying his creation. You are part of the creation, and you are
destroying yourselves—which means your [children, and their] kids, and their
grandkids beyond the future. You are not thinking about them. . . . I know you
white people who look like a human being. I am asking you to act like human
beings and do the right thing for generations yet to come. . . . [Y]ou call
yourselves human beings, but I don't think so. (Johansen 44)

During the nearly two months that the Walk for the Earth traversed
Florida, the Seminoles' situation provided a unifying issue for environ-
mentalists in Florida, many of whom admit that they are fragmented,
outlobbied, and shamelessly outspent by the allies of development in
state politics. Still, despite numbers that ranged up to two hundred
people at a time, the marchers for the earth met a lonely welcome at the
end of their walk.

Julie Hauserman, columnist for the *Tallahassee Democrat*, wrote that
"no cheering crowds greeted Bobby Billie as he walked up Monroe
Street toward the Old Capitol." Billie and two hundred others who took
part in the Walk for the Earth seemed hardly noticed by the thousands
of people who milled along the street in mid-April as part of the annual
Springtime Tallahassee celebration. Legislators in the Florida state-
house, where Billie had arrived with a petition for the governor, seemed
even less concerned. The petition called for an end to pollution, unrestrained development, and corporate control of resources, especially in
Florida wilderness areas. It pointed out that the greatest impact of pollution falls on the poor, many of whom, like the traditional Seminoles,
are members of minority groups.

Bobby Billie arrived home again after the Walk for the Earth to his family's hamlet of chickee huts near Immokalee, in the Everglades roughly thirty miles northeast of Naples, to catch up on the battle of the building code. Contrary to the impressions of some people who have never lived in them, the Seminoles' traditional houses are quite sturdy; many of them are said by their occupants to have withstood hurricanes.

As they defend their right to live in chickees, the traditional Seminoles have adopted other aspects of late-twentieth-century U.S. society, economy, and culture. Many of the chickees now have electricity; some have computers, telephones, and fax machines, all now enlisted in the effort to maintain their small island of personal and communal sovereignty. They are adamant that change should be accommodated on their own terms. English is spoken side by side with Seminole in the settlements; some Seminoles drive trucks and drink soft drinks, but they also maintain schools in their villages in a conscious effort to maintain language and culture. While the best-known traditional village is Bobby Billie's settlement of about thirty people on five acres near Immokalee, other traditional settlements nestle in the Everglades near Naples and Tampa, as well as along the Tamiami Trail across the Everglades. "They are trying to take the last things that are part of our lifestyle," said Danny Billie of the struggle to retain traditional chickee dwellings. "What's happening to us is a continuation of what happened five hundred years ago when Europeans arrived," Billie told the *Fort Lauderdale Sun-Sentinel*.

In early September 1996, eying a growing chorus of protest from Indians and non-Indians across the United States, the Collier County Commission relented and allowed the traditional Seminoles to live in their own chickee huts without harassment. In addition to gathering substantial public and media support, the Seminoles had gained legal support as well from two lawsuits designed to protect their religious rights. In addition, the Pacific Land Company had given the land to its original owners, including the Seminoles, who now had an ownership stake for the first time.

FURTHER READING

Caufield, Catherine. "When Worlds Collide." *South Florida* (June 1994): 64–97.
Johansen, Bruce E. "The Right to One's Own Home: The Seminole Chickee Sustains Despite County Codes." *Native Americas* 13:3 (Fall 1996): 44.

SEQUOYAH STATEHOOD DRIVE

After their "removal" west to **Indian Territory** (roughly present-day Oklahoma) in the 1830s, the **Choctaws, Chickasaws, Creeks, Cherokees,** and Seminoles gradually rebuilt their lives, only to watch them dismantled anew in 1887 during the massive cultural, political, and economic dislocations caused by the Dawes Severalty Act (*see* **Allot-**

ment Act, General), a land grab disguised as the newest method of "civilizing the Indians." In the interests of self-protection against further depredations by Euro-Americans cashing in on the Dawes "land boom," the Choctaws, Chickasaws, Creeks, Cherokees, and Seminoles joined together in an "Indian" statehood drive. Their plan was to incorporate Indian Territory as a state separate from the Euro-dominated Oklahoma Territory by petitioning the U.S. Congress for admission as the State of Sequoyah before its counterpart, the Oklahoma statehood drive, could subsume Indian Territory.

The concept of self-protection against aggression by creating one's own ethnic state was a common theme of the nationalist nineteenth century, animating many besieged ethnic groups. (Theodore Herzl, for instance, conceived of Zionism as the Jews' best hope for safety from European abuses.) Rennard Strickland traced the Sequoyah petition back to **Thomas Jefferson**'s advice "to become civilized," words "listened to" by the "five civilized tribes" (as the Choctaws, Chickasaws, Creeks, Cherokees, and Seminoles were patronizingly termed) (Strickland 1980:49). While Jefferson's words were remembered, Native Americans hardly needed European advice to form smoothly functioning governments. Before contact, all Native Americans lived within their own well-defined territories, many of which were intricately structured democracies. Native polities were always referred to as "nations" by European colonial powers.

The concept of a native state in the prospective United States was first broached in 1778, during the American Revolution. The hard-pressed Continental Congress offered to reward the "Moravian" Delaware Mohicans of Ohio with statehood should they refrain from joining their Haudenosaunee (**Iroquois**) League sponsors in an alliance with Great Britain against the American colonists (Heckewelder 1958: 151). Native American statehood is, therefore, an idea with which the Western Door Seneca and **Wyandot**, league mentors of the "Moravian" Delaware Mohicans, were quite familiar. They carried the knowledge of it west with them into Oklahoma during their own removal, during the 1840s. In addition, according to Martin Delaney's presentation of the slave oral tradition of the 1822 Denmark Vesey Revolt (*Blake*), the Choctaws and Chickasaws were invited, and agreed, to join in Vesey's plan to create a separate African state in the south central region of North America. The Creeks and Seminoles were likewise aware of Vesey's plan, but opted to work on their own to create a free, joint Native-African territory in southern Georgia and northern Florida in the same period (Delaney 1970: 85–87). Thus by 1887, the concept of self-protection through statehood was an old idea to at least the Choctaws, Chickasaws, Creeks, and Seminoles, while the highly sophisticated Cherokee could hardly have been unaware of it.

By 1900 in Indian Territory, the murderous Dawes-era land grab was well under way. The situation was dire for native peoples sitting on land clearly desired by Euro-Americans. The **Four Mothers**, a joint resistance league, zeroed in on statehood as the best bet for Native American safety and security under the circumstances (Senate Report 1: 89–93). Accordingly, the Keetoowahs and Nighthawks of the Cherokee joined the Creeks, Choctaws, Chickasaws, and Seminoles to prepare a statehood petition for Indian Territory, the land still remaining under Native American control. The poet laureate of the Creek Nation, Alexander Lawrence Posey, suggested that they call their new state Sequoyah in honor of the great Cherokee Sikwayi who invented the Cherokee syllabary between 1809 and 1821.

The Cherokee, Creek, Seminole, Choctaw, and Chickasaw counsellors knew that they would have to act before March 4, 1906, the date on which the U.S. government had unilaterally decided to abolish all Native American governments in Indian Territory, placing it under the control of Euro-Americans. Euro-Oklahomans were to open their own Oklahoma statehood convention that same day. Realizing that the feeding frenzy on what was left of "allotted" Native American lands would only worsen once this happened, Native American counsellors hurried to put together their own Sequoyah Statehood Convention. A preliminary Sequoyah Constitutional Convention of native nations held on February 1, 1904, fizzled when the Chickasaws declined to participate. Their political leader, Douglas H. Johnston, favored a joint statehood petition with Euro-Oklahoma. While there was a significant minority in the other native nations that sympathized with this point of view, the Choctaws, Seminoles, Cherokees, and Creeks decided to go ahead with the Sequoyah petition.

By July 1905, a second, stronger Sequoyah initiative had gathered speed, legal documentation, and enthusiasm. James Norman, Cherokee, garnered the support of Pleasant Porter, Creek; Green McCurtain, Choctaw; and John F. Brown, Seminole. The joint Sequoyah Convention of all Native American groups met at Muskogee in August and September 1905 to hammer out its statehood initiative. Meantime and thereafter, Norman, Porter, McCurtain, and Brown were to work within their own councils to procure the four separate councilmanic go-aheads necessary for the confederated councils to put the Sequoyah Constitution up for a general vote on the November ballot.

Although the U.S. government would have allowed the several national councils to continue meeting officially until March 4, 1906, the counsellors decided that their respective national councils would all meet for the last time in October 1905, so that each of their own councils would have ample time to present and, hopefully, ratify the joint Sequoyah petition. Hamlin Garland unwittingly witnessed the proposal being shepherded through the Creek Council by Chief Pleasant Porter on October 10, 1905, recording the momentous event he little understood in his manuscript, "The Final Council of the Creek Nation." Ted Byron Hall, son of a Choctaw counsellor, more cognizantly recorded his father's efforts in *Oklahoma Indian Territory*.

Even though some of those working on the Sequoyah statehood petition were, like the Creek resistance leader Chitto Harjo, not literate in English, the final referendum was well written and researched and, moreover, was perfectly legal under U.S. law. The Sequoyah State Constitution issue was placed on the November 1905 ballot. In an election that included Euro-American as well as Native American voters, the initiative passed by a wide margin of 56,279 yeas to 9,073 nays (Hall 1971: 65).

Under the U.S. **Constitution**, Congress was required to recognize, and was supposed to act, on the Sequoyah referendum. Hall stated that "a bill was perfunctorily introduced in each house of Congress for admission of the State of Sequoyah, but no hearings were ever held on the bill" (Hall 65–66). As Angie Debo noted, "There was never the slightest chance that Congress would consent to the admission of two states, Sequoyah and Oklahoma. There was never even a final bill" (1940: 164). Neither Debo nor Hall looked beyond pure politics for the reason. Congress was overwhelmingly Republican in 1905. Should both Sequoyah and Oklahoma be admitted, there would have been four new senators who would certainly have voted Democratic.

Nevertheless, there is also a more disturbing dimension to the disdain with which the Sequoyah petition was snubbed. This was the age of eugenics. The Ku Klux Klan was soon to be reorganized (1915) and would eventually claim one-third of congressmen as members. By 1905–1907, the overwhelming majority of congressional leaders were sympathetic to the fashionable eugenic point of view. Congress had no intention of admitting a "red" state to the Union; only a "white" state would do. This is why Congress quickly passed the Oklahoma Enabling Act, signed into law by President Theodore Roosevelt, on June 16, 1906. The act combined the Indian Territory that was Sequoyah with the Euro-Oklahoma Territory to facilitate the admission of Oklahoma as a "white" state.

In November 1906 through January 1907, Congress did finally hold hearings—on the Oklahoma statehood petition. To the astonishment, frustration, and, not infrequently, outright hostility of the Select Committee members holding these hearings, the Four Mothers sent protest delegates, demanding to know what had become of the earlier, and entirely legal, Sequoyah statehood petition since (theoretically anyway) Congress could not act on Oklahoma statehood before addressing the Sequoyah petition. The two volumes of these hearings (Senate Report

5013, parts 1 and 2, of the Fifty-Ninth Congress) are composed largely of speeches by Four Mothers delegates that make for interesting reading today, but that had little impact on the Select Committee, whose recommendation to admit Oklahoma as the forty-sixth state of the Union in 1907 was a foregone conclusion.

FURTHER READING

Debo, Angie. *And Still the Waters Run*. Princeton: Princeton University Press, 1940.
Delaney, Martin R. *Blake, or, The Huts of America*. 1861–1862. Boston: Beacon Press, 1970.
Garland, Hamlin. "The Final Council of the Creek Nation." In *Hamlin Garland's Observations on the American Indian, 1895–1905*, Ed. Lonnie E. Underhill and Daniel F. Littlefield, Jr., 184–192. Tucson: University of Arizona Press, 1976.
Hall, Ted Byron. *Oklahoma, Indian Territory*. Fort Worth, TX: American Reference Publishers, 1971.
Heckewelder, John. *Thirty Thousand Miles with John Heckewelder*. Ed. Paul A. W. Wallace. Pittsburgh: University of Pittsburgh Press, 1958.
Maxwell, Amos D. *The Sequoyah Constitutional Convention*. Boston: Meador Publishing Company, 1953.
Strickland, Rennard. *The Indians in Oklahoma*. Norman: University of Oklahoma Press, 1980.
U.S. Congress. Senate. *Report of the Select Committee to Investigate Matters Connected with Affairs in the Indian Territory with Hearings, November 11, 1906–January 9, 1907*. 59th Cong., 2nd sess. S. Rept. 5013, pts. 1 and 2. 2 vols. Washington, DC: U.S. Government Printing Office, 1907.

BARBARA A. MANN

SIOUX POLITICAL AND LEGAL TRADITIONS

The word "Sioux" was derived from an archaic French Canadian slang term that meant "snake" or, by derivation, "enemy." The people whom the French called "Sioux" called themselves Lakota (Teton Sioux), Nakota (Yankton), and Dakota (Santee). The Sioux were organized politically as a loose **confederacy** on several levels. The Lakota Nation was comprised of seven bands, according to author Sharon O'Brien, called the Oglala (meaning Scatter One's Own), the Sicangu (Burnt Thighs), the Minneconjou (Those Who Plant by the Stream), the Hunkpapa (Those Who Camp by the Entrance), the Itazipico (Without Bows), the Sihasapa (Blackfeet), and the Oohinunpa (Two Kettles).

The Lakota Nation by the time of pervasive contact with Europeans (in the middle nineteenth century) was made up of many bands of roving hunters. The *tiyospáye*, small groups of related families within a band, were the basic unit of Lakota political and legal society. Each such group of roughly thirty tipis (families) was led by a headman who was selected for the role based on his personal attributes. As with many Native Americans who governed themselves through confederations, the Sioux generally distrusted authority obtained by force. Instead, leadership was bestowed by popular opinion on people thought worthy of it. For a man, this meant personifying the virtues of bravery, honesty, generosity, and fortitude. For a woman, the same values applied, along with industry, hospitality, and chastity. Sioux leaders were chosen by **consensus** and retained their positions only as long as public opinion supported them. The primary criterion for continued leadership was whether a given person was perceived to have kept the group's welfare in mind at all times.

Authority in traditional Sioux society was widely diffused, not only by the number of roles available within a given group, but also by the fact that Sioux society was organized in small, stable bands. The bands met a few times a year at sun dances and other formal occasions, when headmen from the different bands met to consider issues that involved all of their people. At such informal councils, agreement also was reached by consensus.

Most Lakota societies included fraternal societies that performed policing and judicial functions. The police societies, or *akicitas*, recruited into their membership the brightest young men by invitation. Members of the *akicitas* maintained order during the frequent occasions when camps were moved, as well as during buffalo hunts. The hunts were carried on under a strict social protocol. Anyone who went on the hunt before the group was ready might be disciplined severely. Another type of fraternal society, the *nacas*, consisted of older men, usually those who had distinguished themselves as community leaders, hunters, warriors, and medicine men. The senior *naca*, the Naca Ominica, served as a national council.

A number of the members of the Naca Ominica were appointed by the rest to form an executive committee that enforced the decisions of the council. This executive committee was headed by as many as four *wica'sa*, or "shirt wearers." These men might act as ambassadors to other nations, negotiate treaties, and adjudicate conflicts within the nation. The council also appointed as many as four *wakincuzas*, or "pipe carriers," who performed certain policing functions (such as assigning each family a place to camp), as well as religious ceremonies involving the Sacred Pipe, which symbolized the unity and harmony of the universe.

Each summer, the seven bands of the Lakota Nation met to perform the sun dance, renew acquaintances, feast, and decide matters that affected everyone. At this time, the *nacas* of each nation or band combined to form a national Lakota council. Out of their number were appointed four of the most esteemed statesmen to enact policies com-

mon to all the bands and to sit in judgment of offenses or conflicts that
threatened the peace of the Lakota.

FURTHER READING

O'Brien, Sharon. *American Indian Tribal Governments*. Norman: University of
    Oklahoma Press, 1989.

SLOAN, THOMAS (Omaha) (c. 1860–c. 1925)

Thomas Sloan was one of the first Native Americans to be admitted
to practice before a state bar. The mixed-blood Sloan (who was of
Omaha and French ancestry) was admitted to the bar in Nebraska after
having studied law. He practiced in Omaha. Even as a teenager, it was
said, Sloan worked to uncover Bureau of Indian Affairs fraud on the
Omaha reservation.

Sloan was one of the founders of the **Society of American Indians**
and served a term as its president beginning in 1919. He was an early
advocate of defending treaties through the legal system and a staunch
critic of ways in which the Bureau of Indian Affairs abused its **trust**
responsibilities over Indian lands. He delivered several speeches to
meetings of the Society of American Indians on subjects such as poverty
on the Blackfoot reservation. Sloan also pleaded the cause of Indian
veterans who had returned from World War I to find their land leased
by Indian agents.

Sloan, like many leading Omahas, was an advocate of the General
Allotment Act when it was passed. He delivered a speech praising the
Dawes Act at the Hampton Institute, which he had attended as a student, in 1887, the year it was enacted. By 1920, however, Sloan criticized the government's handling of heirships complicated by allotment.

FURTHER READING

Davis, Leicester Knickerbocker. "Thomas L. Sloan—American Indian." *Amer-
    ican Indian Magazine* 7 (August 1920): 39–40.
Iverson, Peter. *Carlos Montezuma and the Changing World of American Indi-
    ans*. Albuquerque: University of New Mexico Press, 1982.
Sloan, Thomas L. "Law and the American Indians." *American Indian Magazine*
    2 (April–June 1913): 166–182.
Tate, Michael. *The Upstream People: An Annotated Research Bibliography of
    the Omaha Tribe*. Metuchen, NJ: Scarecrow Press, 1991.

SOCIETY OF AMERICAN INDIANS

Founded in 1912, the Society of American Indians was composed of
Native Americans who had achieved a measure of success in the non-
Indian world and who had an interest in legal and legislative reform.
As a group, the Society of American Indians lasted until the early 1930s,
when the group split over the issue of how much control the Bureau of

Indian Affairs should have over Indians' property. See also **Montezuma, Carlos; Sloan, Thomas**.

FURTHER READING

Society of American Indians. *The Papers of the Society of American Indians.* Ed. John William Larner, Jr. Microfilm. Wilmington, DE: Scholarly Resources, 1986.

SOHAPPY, DAVID (Wanapam) (1925–1991)

The 1974 **Boldt** decision (*United States v. Washington*) restored recognition of treaty rights, at least regarding salmon fishing west of the Cascades. East of the Cascades, during the 1980s, the fishing-rights battle continued in a form that reminded many people of the "fish-ins" of the 1960s. Many Native American people along the Columbia River and its tributaries also fished for a livelihood long before Euro-Americans migrated to their land, but their right to do so had not been judicially recognized. For years, David Sohappy, his wife Myra, and their sons erected a riverbank shelter and fished in the traditional manner.

The Sohappys' name came from the Wanapam word *souiehappie*, meaning "shoving something under a ledge." David Sohappy's ancestors had traded fish with members of the Lewis and Clark expedition. The Wanapams never signed a treaty, wishing only to be left in peace to live as they had for hundreds, if not thousands, of years. By the early 1940s, Sohappy's family was pushed off its ancestral homeland at Priest Rapids and White Bluffs, which became part of the Hanford Nuclear Reservation, in the middle of a desert that Lewis and Clark characterized as the most barren piece of land that they saw between St. Louis and the Pacific Ocean. Still, David Sohappy fished, even as his father, Jim Sohappy, warned him that if he continued to live in the old ways, "The white man is going to put you in jail someday."

During the 1950s, development devastated the Celilo Falls, one of the richest Indian fishing grounds in North America. Most of the people who had fished there gave up their traditional livelihoods and moved to the nearby Yakima reservation or into urban areas. David Sohappy and his wife Myra moved to a sliver of federal land called Cook's Landing, just above the first of several dams along the Columbia and its tributaries. They built a small longhouse with a dirt floor. Sohappy built fishing traps from driftwood. As the "fish-ins" of the 1960s attracted nationwide publicity west of the Cascades, Sohappy fished in silence until state game and fishing officials raided his camp, beat family members, and, in 1968, put Sohappy in jail on charges of illegal fishing. He then brought legal action, and the case, *Sohappy v. Smith*, produced a landmark federal ruling that was supposed to prevent the states of

Washington and Oregon from interfering with Indian fishing, except for conservation purposes.

Washington State ignored the ruling and continued to harass Sohappy and his family. Usually under cover of darkness, state agents sank their boats and slashed their nets. In 1981 and 1982, the states of Washington and Oregon successfully (but quietly) lobbied into law a federal provision that made the interstate sale of fish taken in violation of state law a felony—an act aimed squarely at Sohappy. Eight months before the law was signed by President Reagan, the state enlisted federal undercover agents in a fish-buying sting that the press called "Salmonscam" to entrap Sohappy. He was later convicted in Los Angeles (the trial had been moved from the local jurisdiction because of racial prejudice against Indians) of taking 317 fish and was sentenced to five years in prison. During the trial, testimony about the Sohappys' religion and the practice of conservation were not allowed.

Sohappy became a symbol of Native American rights across the United States. Myra Sohappy sought support from the United Nations Commission on Human Rights to have her husband tried by a jury of his peers in the Yakima Nation's court. The new trial was arranged with the help of Senator Daniel Inouye, chairman of the Senate Select Committee on Indian Affairs. The Yakima court found that the federal prosecution had interfered with Sohappy's practice of his Seven Drum religion.

Released after twenty months in prison, Sohappy had aged rapidly. Confinement and the prison diet had sapped his strength. Sohappy suffered several strokes during the months in prison, when he was even denied the use of an eagle prayer feather for comfort (it was rejected as "contraband" by prison officials). Back at Cook's Landing, Sohappy found that vindictive federal officials had tacked an eviction notice to his small house. Sohappy took the eviction notice to court and beat the government for what turned out to be his last time. He died in a nursing home in Hood River, Oregon, on May 6, 1991.

A few days later Sohappy was buried as his Wanapam relatives gathered in an old graveyard. They sang old songs as they lowered his body into the earth, having wrapped it in a Pendleton blanket. He was placed so that the early morning sun would warm his head, facing west toward Mount Adams. Tom Keefe, Jr., an attorney who had been instrumental in securing Sohappy's release from prison, stood by the grave and remembered:

And while the sun chased a crescent moon across the Yakima Valley, I thanked David Sohappy for the time we had spent together, and I wondered how the salmon he had fought to protect would fare in his absence. Now he is gone, and the natural runs of Chinook that fed his family since time immemorial are headed for the Endangered Species Act list. "Be glad for my dad," David Sohappy, Jr. told the mourners. "He is free now, he doesn't need any tears."

FURTHER READING

Keefe, Tom, Jr. "A Tribute to David Sohappy." *Native Nations*, June/July 1991.

SONG DUEL, INUIT

Social tensions among the Inuit (Eskimo) often reach the boiling point when people are crowded in large numbers during the gruelling months of winter camp. Minor disagreements (most often between men, over women) can explode into verbal battles, fistfights, or even murder. Inuit sometimes resort to face-to-face fistfights when a conflict between two people cannot be managed by words alone. Such a public fight is usually concluded by the loser, when he has sustained enough punishment to end it.

In other cases, two people engaged in bitter discord take part in an elaborate "song duel," an adversary proceeding with harmony, in which the weapons are words—as one song puts it, "little, sharp words, like the wooden splinters which I hack off with my ax." Each of the two aggrieved parties composes a long song accusing his opponent of various problems and vices, from sexual impotence to laziness in the hunt. Each accuser tries to skewer his opponent's foibles and vulnerabilities. In West Greenland, the singer has the vocal backing of his household; the family rehearses the songs until its members can sing them in chorus.

On an appointed day, most of the people in a settlement convene in the communal house to hear the wives of the two men sing the songs as their husbands back them up on drums. The public performance is designed to provoke hilarity in the audience. While the audience does not act as a court, and no "verdict" of guilt or innocence is issued, the "winner" is the couple whose ridicule and satire are most enjoyed by the audience. Despite the virulence of the insults that people hurl at each other, outward showing of anger is considered bad form, and all parties are expected to display friendly relations after the contest.

Song duels may be used to work through all manner of grudges and other interpersonal disputes, even murder, if the aggrieved party is too old and weak to respond with a retaliatory killing. Singing is a highly prized talent among the Inuit; occasionally, participants will get so engrossed in the artistry of singing that they forget the grudge that motivated the contest. Among some Inuit in Greenland, a song duel can continue for years, but most are concluded within a single season.

Song duels do not suffice for the most serious problems of interpersonal relations in Inuit society. In the most extreme cases of antisocial behavior (such as a person who is aggressive and insane), Inuit extended kin can arrange to have the offender murdered. Other families within a settlement are informed secretly, beforehand, and the killing is carried out by a close relative to avoid revenge by members of other families. Such murders are rare, but they are sanctioned as a means of preserving community stability against irreconcilable violence by individuals.

FURTHER READING

Hoebel, E. Adamson. *The Law of Primitive Man*. Cambridge, MA: Harvard University Press, 1954.

SOUTH DAKOTA V. U.S. DEPARTMENT OF INTERIOR 69 F.3d 878 (8th Cir. 1995)

On November 7, 1995, the Eighth Circuit Court of Appeals ruled that section 5 of the **Indian Reorganization Act**, which governs mechanisms for placing land into **trust** for Indian nations, was unconstitutional. The court's opinion indicated that the secretary of the interior had been acquiring land and placing it in trust illegally during the previous six decades. In February 1996, the Eighth Circuit refused to rehear the case, a decision that was called a devastating blow by some Indian advocates.

The appeals court ruled that the secretary's authority under the existing IRA was too broad, according to an analysis in *Native American News*. "By its literal terms, the statute permits the secretary to purchase a factory, an office building, a residential subdivision, or a golf course in trust for an Indian tribe, thereby removing these properties from the tax rolls. . . . Indeed, it would permit the secretary to purchase the Empire State Building in trust for a tribal chief as a wedding present."

Between 1934 and 1985, Indian lands grew by about 8 million acres, mainly through provisions of the IRA that allow trust land to be added. The Eighth Circuit Court's ruling, if it stands, may stop that practice and, in some cases, even reverse it. The suit was filed by South Dakota after the Lower Brule Sioux Tribe bought 91 acres near Interstate 90 in the southern part of the state. The land was placed in trust by the Interior Department in 1992, taking it off of local and state tax rolls.

This case bore some similarities to others in litigation at about the same time. For example, the Mashantucket Pequot were attempting to put 240 acres in Ledyard, Connecticut, into trust. The land includes the largest Indian-run casino in the United States and would be a major source of local and state tax revenue if the Supreme Court sustains the Eighth Circuit Court in *South Dakota v. Department of Interior*.

Frank Pommersheim, professor of law at the University of South Dakota, said that if the Eighth Circuit Court is sustained and the ruling is found to be retroactive, "it will wreak unbelievable havoc" (Little Eagle 1996: A–1). He said that if native nations are to continue to be viable economically, they must have mechanisms to recover land alienated before the passage of the IRA.

FURTHER READING

Little Eagle, Avis. "Appeals Court Will Not Hear Trust Lands Case." *Indian Country Today*, February 15, 1996, A–1.
"U.S. Supreme Court Could Hear Eighth Circuit IRA Challenge." *Native American News*, Sample Issue, 1996.

SOVEREIGNTY, INDIAN, LEGAL BASIS

Sovereignty is the supreme power from which all other specific powers are derived. Because Native American nations possessed the elements of sovereignty before contact with large numbers of Europeans and their descendants, U.S. fundamental law, beginning with the **Constitution**, always has recognized that Indian nations possess a degree of sovereignty consistent with the negotiation of **treaties**, the instruments traditionally used in European diplomacy to seal agreements between sovereign nations.

The nature of Native American sovereignty and the relationship of that sovereignty to federal and state power have been central issues— perhaps *the* central issues—in the last two centuries of American Indian law. Surveying the opinions of the U.S. Supreme Court, one can find different justices with differing ideological orientations reacting to different facts. The result is a sense of contradiction and confusion. By 1961, according to the U.S. Civil Rights Commission, Indians had been the subject of two thousand federal court opinions and five thousand federal statutes, many of them defining issues of sovereignty and jurisdiction.

According to legal scholar **Felix Cohen** in ***The Handbook of Federal Indian Law*** (1942),

Perhaps the most basic principle of all Indian law, supported by a host of decisions . . . is the principle that *those powers which are lawfully vested in an Indian tribe are not, in general, delegated powers granted by express laws of Congress, but rather, inherent powers of a limited sovereignty which has never been extinguished.* (emphasis in original)

According to Cohen, "Each Indian tribe begins its relationship with the Federal Government as a sovereign power, subject to certain limitations by subsequent historical events." He continued:

The whole course of judicial decision on the nature of Indian tribal powers is marked by adherence to three fundamental principles: (1) An Indian tribe possesses, in the first instance, all the powers of any sovereign state. (2) Conquest renders the Indian tribe subject to the legislative power of the United States and, in substance, terminates the external powers of sovereignty of the tribe, e.g., its power to enter into treaties with foreign nations, but does not by itself affect the internal sovereignty of the tribe, e.g., its powers of local self-government. (3) These powers are subject to qualification by treaties and by express legislation of Congress, but, save as thus expressly qualified, full powers of internal sovereignty are vested in the Indian tribes and in their duly constituted organs of government. (528)

The nature of the limits placed on Indian sovereignty by the power of the United States, particularly the Congress and the judiciary, has been the major flintstone of conflict in American Indian law for two centuries. Such a relationship also predates the establishment of the United States as a political entity. In 1743, for example, the English Court of Commissioners ruled that the colonies could purchase land only from legitimate native representatives. The commissioners said:

The Indians, although living amongst the king's subjects in these countries, are a separate and distinct people from them, [and] they are treated with as such . . . [and] have a policy of their own[.] [T]hey make peace and war with any nation of Indians when they think fit, without control from the English.

Two decades later, King George III demarcated Indian sovereignty in America geographically with the **Proclamation of 1763**, which forbade agents of the Crown from purchasing lands or otherwise interfering with the affairs of Native Americans living west of the spine of the Appalachians. After the American Revolution, in which the **Cherokees** sided with the British, that nation demanded a separate treaty with the United States. The Cherokees refused to recognize the British surrender at Yorktown or the Treaty of Paris. Mutual demobilization was included in the **Treaty of Hopewell** (1785).

Indian treaties, signed under protocols of international law, were kept in State Department archives with the treaties concluded with European nations. Indeed, for the first two decades after the United States ratified its **Constitution**, treaties with Indians were the major business of the new nation's State Department. Indian visitors to Washington, D.C., were feted in the manner of international dignitaries until well into the nineteenth century. Some of the early treaties required passports of European Americans visiting designated Indian nations that were, for all intents and purposes, treated as semi-independent nations.

U.S. Supreme Court Chief Justice **John Marshall** delineated judicial limits on Indian sovereignty in the **Marshall Trilogy** of opinions handed down during the 1820s and 1830s. For four decades after that, Congress intruded only rarely into the type of micromanagement of Indian affairs that would become commonplace after affirmation of its **plenary power** at the turn of the century. The only major congressional action related to Indians between the 1830s and 1871 (when treaty making was abolished) was regulation of non-Indian traders on native lands.

Joyotpaul Chaudhuri, professor of government at New Mexico State University, characterized the state of law regarding Native American sovereignty:

[T]he actual case law on sovereignty constitutes a middle-eastern bazaar where practically anything is available to those who are eager and earnest and have the resources for persisting in an adversary system of justice. This has been the way from the beginning of constitutional law as shaped by John Marshall. (Deloria 1985: 23)

As construed by U.S. federal courts, Native American governments generally possess the following rights:

1. To make laws governing the conduct of persons, Indians and non-Indians, within reservation boundaries in such matters as tribal membership, marriage and divorce, other domestic relations, levying of taxes, and regulating use of property, inheritances, and the like (*see*, as one example, **Merrion v. Jicarilla Apache Tribe**, 455 U.S. 130 [1982])
2. To establish police and courts to enforce these laws (**Iron Crow v. Oglala Sioux Tribe**, 231 F.2d 89 [8th Cir. 1956])
3. To exclude nonmembers from Indian land (**Quechan Tribe v. Rowe**, 531 F.2d 408 [9th Cir. 1976])
4. To regulate fishing, hunting, and gathering on their lands (*Colville Tribe v. Washington*, 412 F. Supp. 651 [E. D. Wash. 1976])

Although Indian sovereignty has a long historical and legal record in U.S. (as well as Canadian) law, courts in each nation have qualified the concept. In the United States, most of the qualifications stem from court decisions written during the 1820s and 1830s by John Marshall, chief justice of the U.S. Supreme Court. These cases, including **Worcester v. Georgia** and **Cherokee Nation v. Georgia**, have defined various degrees of internal sovereignty for Indian nations while maintaining that they are "domestic" and "dependent" on the United States.

Many cases that define sovereignty issues also define limits of jurisdiction, the legal power or authority of a government to rule or govern its people or territory. As Native American nations have implemented **self-determination** efforts late in the twentieth century, jurisdictional disputes often have arisen with state interests over theoretical and practical matters that influence whether an Indian nation may assemble the kind of economic base that is usually a necessary prerequisite for political sovereignty. In which court, for example, will a non-Indian be tried for an offense committed on an Indian reservation? Several decisions of the Supreme Court (the best-known of which may be **Oliphant v. Suquamish**) largely abrogate Indian sovereignty over offenses by non-Indians, but maintain it for Native American reservation residents.

Ex parte Crow Dog is one of the best-known Supreme Court decisions that maintained native sovereignty over offenses by Indians against Indians.

U.S. courts have circumscribed Indian sovereignty in other ways, for example, by recognizing, since the early twentieth century, the plenary power of Congress to legislate Indian policy. A state held sovereign under international law would not be subject to the unilateral legislative authority of another sovereign state's legislature. The same would be held true of that other nation's legal system, but U.S. courts have been adjudicating the nature of sovereignty in **Indian Country** since the early nineteenth century. At the same time, these courts have recognized that Indian nations possess the authority to tax their members, as well as non-Indian corporations that mine minerals on their land. The Supreme Court has even endorsed the position that members of a native nation still possess some of their treaty rights even after their land base has been extinguished.

Under the rubric of "Indian protection," the United States in the nineteenth century created a colonial system that governed individual American Indians' lives in minuscule detail from cradle to grave. As ideas of sovereignty were asserted more often beginning in the 1960s, the pervasiveness of federal control was challenged. Even in the late twentieth century, federal control existed in an uneasy alliance with assertions of sovereignty. Every time a tribal government receives federal money, it also has to accept the many restrictions on its uses, a submission to federal jurisdiction.

Congress in many cases has micromanaged Indians' internal affairs through exercise of its plenary power. For example, in the middle 1980s, more than 110 federal statutes had been passed to govern the administration of Indian timber and mineral resources alone. The **American Indian Policy Review Commission** found that Indians often consider that the government's trust responsibility is being used in a paternal manner, to establish political control rather than to enhance Indian self-governance. Federal oversight too often is used "as a tool to deny them . . . control over their own lives, to inject federal bureaucracy where there should be self-government, to encourage paternalism where co-operation or independence should prevail." Indeed, said the AIPRC, the federal government often uses its "trust" responsibility to curtail Indian sovereignty rather than to enhance it. The trust responsibility often becomes a vehicle to micromanage the lives of individual Indians, as described by Edgar Cahn in *Our Brother's Keeper*:

Through the pervasiveness of the bureau's role, the exercise of power and administrative programs by the B.I.A. has come to ensure that every effort by Indians to achieve self-realization is frustrated and penalized, that the Indian is kept in a state of permanent dependency as his price of survival, and that alienation from his people and past is rewarded and encouraged. (1969: 13)

FURTHER READING

Cahn, Edgar. *Our Brother's Keeper: The Indian in White America*. New York: World Publishing Co., 1969.
Cohen, Felix. *Handbook of Federal Indian Law*. Washington, DC: Interior Department, 1942.
Deloria, Vine, Jr., ed. *American Indian Policy in the Twentieth Century*. Norman: University of Oklahoma Press, 1985.
Kickingbird, Kirke, Alexander Tallchief Skibine, and Lynn Kickingbird. *Indian Sovereignty*. Washington, DC: Institute for the Development of Indian Law, 1983.
Prucha, Francis Paul. *American Indian Policy in the Formative Years*. Cambridge, MA: Harvard University Press, 1962.
Wilkinson, Charles F. *American Indians, Time, and the Law: Native Societies in a Modern Constitutional Democracy*. New Haven, CT: Yale University Press, 1987.

STANDING BEAR (Ponca) (c. 1830–1908)

Standing Bear gained national notoriety in the late 1870s, during a time of forced removal for the **Ponca** and other Native American peoples on the Great Plains. He led some of the Poncas on a forty-day, five hundred-mile march from **Indian Territory** (now Oklahoma) back to their homeland along the Niobrara River in northern Nebraska. When the group reached Omaha, Standing Bear became engaged in the first court case to result in a declaration that American Indians are to be treated as human beings under U.S. law. Thus the army could not legally relocate Standing Bear's party by force without cause.

Before they were forcibly removed from their homeland, the Poncas had gone to great lengths to maintain friendly relationships with the United States. In 1858, they ceded part of their homeland along the Niobrara in exchange for a homeland in the same area that was then said to be theirs in perpetuity. Ten years later, the United States, in a classic example of sloppy bureaucracy, signed the Poncas' land over to the Sioux, the Poncas' traditional enemies, in the **Fort Laramie Treaty** of 1868. It took a dozen years for the United States to acknowledge its error, and in the meantime many of the Poncas had died in Oklahoma or on forced marches.

During 1877, federal troops removed 723 Poncas from three villages along the Niobrara River to Indian Territory. The Poncas were moved at bayonet point after eight of their leaders had inspected and refused to accept the arid land that the government wanted the Poncas to occupy in Oklahoma. During their march to Indian Territory, several of the Poncas died of starvation and disease.

A year after their removal, a third of the Poncas had died. One of the dead was a son of Standing Bear, who, determined to bury his bones in the lands of his ancestors, escaped northward, toward the Niobrara, with thirty other Poncas. Standing Bear recalled:

It was winter. We started for home on foot. We barely lived [un]til morning, it was so cold. We had nothing but our blankets. We took the ears of corn that had dried in the fields; we ate it raw. The soles of our moccasins wore out. We went barefoot in the snow. (Massey 1979: 8)

After two months of walking, including a ten-day stop among the Otoes, the group led by Standing Bear took shelter on land owned by the **Omahas**, their bloody feet leaving tracks in the snow.

The following spring, army troops under the command of General George Crook arrived at the Omaha camp and began to force the Poncas southward again. They camped for a time outside of Omaha, where local citizens obtained a writ of habeas corpus and brought the army into the federal court of Judge **Elmer Dundy**, who ruled, "An Indian is a person within the meaning of the law, and there is no law giving the Army authority to forcibly remove Indians from their lands." Further, Dundy ruled that the right of expatriation is "a natural and inherent right of all people, indispensable to the enjoyment of the rights of life, liberty, and the pursuit of happiness."

Ironically, the case was prepared with the help of General Crook, who was swayed by the manifest injustice of the Poncas' case. The harsh treatment of the Ponca also received publicity in Omaha newspapers that was wired to larger newspapers on the east coast, causing a storm of protest letters to Congress.

Shortly after Judge Dundy denied the army's presumed power to forcibly relocate Indians in the case of Standing Bear, his brother Big Snake tested the ruling by moving roughly one hundred miles in Indian Territory, from the Poncas' assigned reservation to one occupied by the Cheyennes. He was arrested by troops and returned. On October 31, 1879, Ponca Indian Agent William H. Whiteman called Big Snake a troublemaker and ordered a detail to imprison him. When Big Snake refused to surrender, contending that he had committed no crime, he was shot to death. Later, the U.S. Senate called for an investigation of the shooting and other aspects of the Poncas' tragedy. Following the Senate investigation, Standing Bear's band was allowed to go home. Standing Bear died in his homeland along the Niobrara in 1908.

In 1990, the Poncas were again recognized by an act of Congress, signed by President Bush, twenty-five years after their **termination** in 1965. Across the United States, several dozen Native American nations were following the same path. In 1992, the Poncas moved into new offices at Niobrara. During the restoration, a new generation of Poncas recalled how their elders had held a requiem for the old ways in 1962, standing above the Niobrara Valley near the unmarked grave of Standing Bear.

FURTHER READING

Massey, Rosemary, and American Indian Center of Omaha. *Footprints in Blood: Standing Bear's Struggle for Freedom and Human Dignity.* Omaha: American Indian Center of Omaha, 1979.
Nabokov, Peter, ed. *Native American Testimony.* New York: Viking, 1991.
Tibbles, Thomas Henry. *The Ponca Chiefs: An Account of the Trial of Standing Bear.* Lincoln: University of Nebraska Press, 1972.

STANTON, ELIZABETH CADY (1815–1902)

Feminist historian Sally Roesch Wagner asserted that "nineteenth-century radical feminist theoreticians, such as Elizabeth Cady Stanton and **Matilda Joslyn Gage**, looked to the Iroquois for their vision of a transformed world." Stanton quoted the memoirs of the Reverend Asher Wright, who wrote of Seneca home life:

Usually the females ruled the house. The stores were in common, but woe to the luckless husband or lover who was too shiftless to do his share of the providing. No matter how many children, or whatever goods he might have in the house, he might at any time be ordered to pick up his blanket and budge; and after such an order it would not be healthful for him to attempt to disobey. The house would be too hot for him, and unless saved by the intercession of some aunt or grandmother he must retreat to his own clan, or go and start a new matrimonial alliance with some other. (Stanton 1981:4)

According to Stanton, Wright also noted that Iroquois women alone could "knock off the horns" of a sachem who had abused his office, as well as make the original nominations for sachemships. In early treaty negotiations, representatives of the United States, all male, often found themselves face-to-face with **Iroquois** women. Many of the treaties negotiated before 1800 were signed by both male sachems and their female advisors.

In her 1891 speech before the National Council of Women, Stanton surveyed the research of Henry Lewis Morgan and others that indicated that "among the greater number of the American aborigines, the descent of property and children were in the female line. Women sat in the councils of war and peace and their opinions had equal weight on all questions." In this regard, she mentioned the Iroquois' councils specifically. After surveying aboriginal societies in other parts of the world as well, Stanton closed her speech with a case for sexual equality:

In closing, I would say that every woman present must have a new sense of dignity and self respect, feeling that our mothers, during long periods in the long past, have been the ruling power and that they used that power for the best interests of humanity. As history is said to repeat itself, we have every reason to believe that our turn will come again[.] It may not be for woman's supremacy, but for the as yet untried experiment of complete equality, when the united thought of man and woman will inaugurate a just government, a pure religion, a happy home, a civilization at last in which ignorance, poverty and crime will exist no more. Those who watch already behold the dawn of the new day. (7)

FURTHER READING

Allen, Paula Gunn. *The Sacred Hoop: Recovering the Feminine in American Indian Traditions*. Boston: Beacon Press, 1986.
Brown, Judith K. "Economic Organization and the Position of Women among the Iroquois." *Ethnohistory* 17:3–4 (Summer–Fall 1970): 151–167.
Carr, Lucien. *The Social and Political Position of Women among the Huron-Iroquois Tribes*. Salem, MA: Salem Press, 1884.
Gage, Matilda Joslyn. *Woman, Church, and State*. 1893. Watertown, MA: Persephone Press, 1980.
Stanton, Elizabeth Cady. "The Matriarchate or Mother-Age." *National Bulletin* (National Council of Women) 1:5 (February 1891).
Stanton, Elizabeth Cady, Susan B. Anthony, and Matilda Joslyn Gage. *History of Woman Suffrage*. Salem, NH: Ayer Co., 1985.
Wagner, Sally Roesch. "The Iroquois Confederacy: A Native American Model for Non-sexist Men." *Changing Men* (Spring–Summer 1988): 32–33.
———. *The Untold Story of the Iroquois Influence on Early Feminists*. Aberdeen, SD: Sky Carrier Press, 1996.

STEVENS, ISAAC INGALLS (1818–1862)

Washington became a territory of the United States on March 2, 1853. Isaac Stevens was appointed governor and superintendent of Indian affairs for the territory. As governor, Stevens wished to build the economic base of the territory; this required the attraction of a proposed transcontinental railroad, which, in turn, required peace with the Indians. Stevens worked with remarkable speed; in 1854 and 1855 alone, he negotiated five treaties with six thousand Indian people west of the Cascades.

Stevens was born in Andover, Massachusetts, and graduated from the U.S. Military Academy at West Point in 1839. He served in the U.S. Army as an engineering officer after graduating from West Point and during the war with Mexico (in 1846–1847) served on the staff of General Winfield Scott. After that, still an army officer, Stevens was named Indian agent for Washington Territory. His main charge at the time was to survey the area as a prospective route for a new transcontinental railroad. In 1853, President Franklin Pierce appointed Stevens governor of the territory.

After 1853, Governor Stevens acquired from the Indians the land area comprising most of the present-day states of Idaho and Washington. In all the treaties, Stevens drove an extremely tough bargain, but the Indians who had relied on fishing for a livelihood would not relent on their continued right to fish. Stevens said, "It was also thought necessary to allow them to fish at all accustomed places, since this would not in any manner interfere with the rights of citizens and was necessary for the Indians to obtain a subsistence." He said these words after emerging from the signing of the **Treaty of Medicine Creek** on December 26, 1854. The treaty, signed on a small island surrounded by salt marshes not far from the present-day state capital, Olympia, guaranteed the Indians the right to fish at their usual and accustomed places "in common with" citizens of the territory. By signing the treaty, the Indians ceded to the United States 2,240,000 acres of land, an immense sacrifice for the right to fish.

Many Native American peoples refused to sign Stevens's treaties, including Old Joseph, father of Chief Joseph. Other "nontreaty" Indians pointed to unlawful invasions of land set aside for Indians in the treaties by miners and settlers as they began armed resistance in the Yakima War of 1855 and 1856. At one point, an Indian force led by Leschi raided the frontier settlement of Seattle. Stevens was merciless in his suppression of the uprising, to the point of prosecuting European Americans whom he thought were aiding the insurgents. Leschi was hanged after his participation in the uprising.

While settlement of the coastal Northwest began in temporal tandem with California, accelerating about 1850, most of the people who traversed the continent along the Oregon Trail were not looking for gold or other quick riches. Most sought to set up farms (some planned utopian communes).

Stevens's militia arrested several settlers whom he suspected of aiding "renegade" Indians. The settlers asserted that they were taken from their land claims in Pierce County "without process of law, and without any complaint or affidavit being lodged against them." The men were escorted against their wills to Fort Steilacoom, near Tacoma, where they were held, at Stevens's request, on charges of treason. Following complaints by attorneys for the men, Stevens issued a martial-law declaration suspending civil liberties in Pierce County, and accused the arrested settlers of giving "aid and comfort to the enemy." A few days later, Stevens ordered the men back to Olympia, out of Pierce County, because a judge there had issued a writ of habeas corpus on their behalf.

Later, the case was taken up in the court of the Honorable Edward Lander, chief justice of the territory. When Judge Lander convened court to hear the case, a column of militiamen filed into his courtroom and arrested him, leading the judge and the clerk of the court from the bench. The arrests occurred on May 6; by May 9, the judge was released.

A few days later, Stevens extended martial law to Thurston County, including Olympia, the territorial capital.

A legal ballet ensued in which Governor Stevens refused to honor the writ of habeas corpus. Members of the militia stood outside the house in which Chief Justice Lander was holding court. "The marshal, being ordered to keep the room clear of armed men, was compelled to lock the door. . . . The counsel engaged inside could distinctly hear the men [outside] cocking their rifles" ("A Brief Notice . . ." 1856: 389), said a contemporary statement. An officer of the militia called on Judge Lander to surrender once again. He refused. Finally, the armed men barged into the courtroom, seized the judge and clerk, and transported them to the office of Governor Stevens. An observer said that the judge was "kidnapped." The judge was told that he would be freed if he stopped issuing orders contrary to the decree of martial law. The judge flatly refused, but was freed. Stevens had violated his oath of office by refusing to respect a writ of habeas corpus, an act that the U.S. **Constitution** says may be suspended only by Congress.

Stevens served as Washington's territorial delegate to Congress in 1857, then returned to active duty with the Union army during the Civil War. During that war, he was promoted to major general before he was killed at the Battle of Chantilly (Virginia) during 1862.

FURTHER READING

American Friends Service Committee, comp. *Uncommon Controversy: A Report on the Fishing Rights of the Muckleshoot, Puyallup, and Nisqually Indians.* Seattle: University of Washington Press, 1970.
"A Brief Notice of the Recent Outrages Committed by Isaac I. Stevens: May 17, 1856." In W. H. Wallace, "Martial Law in the Washington Territory," *The Annals of America*, 1856, pp. 3–16.
Brown, Bruce. *Mountain in the Clouds.* New York: Simon & Schuster, 1982.
Stevens, Hazard. *The Life of Isaac Ingalls Stevens.* 2 vols. Boston: Houghton, Mifflin, 1900.

SUPERCITIZENS

"Supercitizens" was a phrase coined in the 1970s by advocates of treaty abrogation to describe American Indians, on whom they believed the treaties bestowed special status ("supercitizenship") unavailable to other Americans. The phrase was often used by Washington State Attorney General (and later U.S. Senator) Slade Gorton in attempts to curtail Indian fishing rights in the Pacific Northwest. Indian fishing rights were vindicated in **United States v. Washington** (1974) and other rulings that comprise a judicial rebuke of the ideology of supercitizenship.

Using the rhetoric of supercitizenship, advocates of treaty abrogation in 1978 introduced into the U.S. House of Representatives the **Native**

American Equal Opportunity Act, a bill sponsored by state interests who used "equal opportunity" as a rationale for abrogating what they regarded as "special rights" endowed on Native Americans by treaties. Implicit in this line of reasoning is an assumption that Indian nations do not possess powers of **sovereignty** and that treaties with them do not represent government-to-government relationships.

In addition to abrogating treaties, the Native American Equal Opportunity Act, which did not pass Congress, would have ended federal supervision of Indian property and would have subjected Indians to state law. No compensation was provided for lost rights or property. The measure has been characterized by Professor Robert N. Clinton as "only a stalking horse for the assimilationists' real demands—wholesale abrogation and appropriation of Indian property rights."

FURTHER READING

Clinton, Robert N. "Isolated in Their Own Country: A Defence of Federal Protection of Indian Autonomy and Self-Government." *Stanford Law Review* 33 (1981): 979–1068.
Lowman, Bill. *220 Million Custers.* Anacortes, WA: Anacortes Printing, 1978.
Williams, C. Herb, and Walt Neubrech. *Indian Treaties: American Nightmare.* Seattle: Outdoor Empire Publishing, 1976.

SWAN (WANROW), YVONNE (Sinixt/Arrow Lakes Nation)

In 1972, a reputed child molester broke into the home of Yvonne Swan (then known as Yvonne Wanrow, by previous marriage) in Spokane, Washington. She killed him to protect her children and was later charged with murder by state prosecutors. After an initial conviction, the case was appealed to the state supreme court and later to the U.S. Supreme Court. In 1979, the U.S. Supreme Court used the case to frame the so-called Wanrow instruction, which expanded women's right to self-defense.

The Washington State Supreme Court overturned the initial conviction because it ruled that the trial judge had not adequately explained a woman's right of self-defense to the jury. The court ordered Wanrow retried, but she plea-bargained a guilty plea to a manslaughter charge rather than undergo another ordeal. She received a suspended sentence and was ordered to do community service, which grew into a career as a Native American and women's activist. The court case ended in 1984, a dozen years after the incident that spawned it. In the early 1990s, Swan was affiliated with the San Francisco office of the **International Indian Treaty Council**.

T

___

TALTON V. MAYES 163 U.S. 376 (1896)

Talton, a **Cherokee**, was convicted of murder by a Cherokee grand jury of five Cherokees. Talton then filed for a writ of habeas corpus against Mayes, the high sheriff of the Cherokee Nation. He asserted that the grand jury had been called in violation of the **Fifth Amendment** to the U.S. **Constitution**, a violation of due process because the grand jury had only five members, rather than six, as required under U.S. law. At issue was whether the Cherokee government was bound by the U.S. Constitution. At a time when allotment and other assimilative legislation was the order of the day, the Supreme Court surprised nearly everyone concerned by dismissing the writ of habeas corpus and affirming the sovereignty of the Cherokees:

[T]he powers of local self-government enjoyed by the Cherokee nation existed prior to the Constitution [and] they are not operated upon by the Fifth Amendment, which, as we have said, had for its sole object to control the powers conferred by the Constitution on the National government.

TEE-HIT-TON INDIANS V. UNITED STATES 348 U.S. 272 (1954)

The Supreme Court held that aboriginal lands may be taken without just compensation required by the **Fifth Amendment** to the U.S. **Constitution**. The Court ruled that the federal government is liable under the Fifth Amendment only for takings of land in which Indian title is "recognized" by treaty or statute.

This case has often been cited as an example of how the opinions of the Supreme Court can be influenced by the political climate in which they take place. As Congress was setting the legal machinery of **termination** into motion, the Court was reaffirming its ideological rationale:

After conquest [Indians] were permitted to occupy portions of territory over which they had previously exercised "sovereignty," as we use the term. This is not a property right, but amounts to a right of occupancy which the sovereign grants and protects against intrusion by third parties but which right of occupancy may be terminated and such lands fully disposed of by the sovereign itself without any legally enforceable obligation to compensate the Indians.

Legal scholar Milnar Ball commented on the contradictions of this decision:

Tee-Hit-Ton . . . said the original lands of the Indians, the lands on which they still live as they have from times immemorial (and to which it is said they have "aboriginal title") are not "property" for Fifth Amendment purposes! The United States had sold timber on the Alaskan lands of the Tlinget Tribe. As distinguished from the taking of property belonging to any other Americans, this taking was found not to be compensable under the Fifth Amendment. (1987: 114)

Thus the most ancient of property rights in America were demoted by the Supreme Court in *Tee-Hit-Ton* to a status inferior to that of non-Indian holdings. The Supreme Court added that "the position of the Indian has long been rationalized by the legal theory that discovery and conquest gave the conquerors sovereignty over and ownership of lands thus obtained." Further, the Court held, in one of the most ethnocentric passages to grace a Supreme Court opinion:

Every American schoolboy knows that the savage tribes of this continent were deprived of their ancestral ranges by force and that, even when the Indians ceded millions of acres by treaty in return for blankets, food, and trinkets, it was not a sale but the conquerors' will that deprived them of their land.

"*Tee-Hit-Ton* was widely criticized and may be disregarded as a precedent because it was tried on meagre, poorly presented evidence," wrote legal scholars Russel Barsh and James Henderson. "Nevertheless, it was a portent of things to come" (1980: 142). The Supreme Court argued in this case that unrecognized rights cannot be compensated and that (by implication) even recognized rights are privileges granted by Congress. The argument here revolved around one of the most significant disagreements in American Indian law regarding Native American sovereignty: by what legal right can U.S. courts circumscribe the powers of Indian governments that existed before the United States was established? "When a power is delegated for the time being, it can be revoked freely," wrote Barsh and Henderson. "The exercise of an original power is another matter. *Tee-Hit-Ton* implies that Native American nations with treaties enjoy mere privileges, an unsubstantiated historical hypothesis, and tribes without treaties have nothing. No tribe, therefore, could be safe from termination" (142–143).

FURTHER READING

Ball, Milnar. "Constitution, Court, Indian Tribes." *American Bar Foundation Research Journal*, no. 1 (Winter 1987): 1–140.
Barsh, Russel Lawrence, and James Youngblood Henderson. *The Road: Indian Tribes and Political Liberty.* Berkeley: University of California Press, 1980.

TEN BEAR V. REPSIS ET AL. 73 F.3d 982 (1995)

Thomas L. Ten Bear, a **Crow** Indian, was arrested by game warden Chuck Repsis of the Wyoming Fish and Game Department during 1989 for killing an elk in the Big Horn National Forest without a hunting license. Ten Bear claimed the right to take the elk because the Crows' 1868 treaty with the United States gave Crows the right to hunt on federally unoccupied lands, including national forests, which had earlier been ceded by the Crows. The Tenth Circuit Court of Appeals disagreed, finding that the area had been "occupied" after a national forest was established there in 1887. Before the 1868 treaty, the area had been Crow land.

In 1992 the Crows sued the State of Wyoming and various agencies of the state (as well as employees of the agencies) in federal district court, seeking a declaration upholding the Crows' rights to hunt and fish in areas guaranteed to them by treaty that had since passed out of native control. The state moved to dismiss the case on grounds of eleventh-amendment immunity. In 1993 the district court dismissed the case, after which the Crows requested a re-hearing before the circuit court.

The circuit court also ruled that the Crows' hunting rights on federally owned land ended when Wyoming became a state in 1890. The court held that "Indeed, the whole argument of the [Crows] rests on the assumption that there was a perpetual right conveyed by the treaty, when in fact the privilege given was temporary and precarious." This wording raised the legal question of what other treaty rights might be declared "temporary" by future court decisions.

FURTHER READING

Melmer, David. "Court Calls Treaty Rights 'Temporary.' " *Indian Country Today*, January 18, 1996, p. A-1.

TERMINATION

Passed as House Concurrent Resolution 108 (1953), termination legislation was aimed at dissolving remaining Indian lands and Indian communal relationships. The act was phrased in terms of equality, "to make the Indians . . . subject to the same laws and entitled to the same privileges as . . . other citizens of the United States." The Termination Act was designed to end Indians' status as wards of the United States. Between 1954 and 1966, 109 American Indian nations and bands were dissolved under the provisions of this legislation. Roughly 11,400 people lost their status as Indians belonging to "recognized" Native American governments; 1.5 million acres of land were removed from **trust** status. Most of the terminated groups were small bands, but two of them, the **Menominees** of Wisconsin (with 3,270 members at termination) and the Klamaths of Oregon (with 2,133 members) were substantial communities.

Under termination, land and resources were purchased from native nations and the proceeds distributed to individual members, who found themselves temporarily enriched in cash, but suddenly poor in land and community. Through various legal devices, much of the purchased land was then transferred into the private sector, often through lease for a specific purpose.

During the 1930s and early 1940s, **John Collier**'s policies as commissioner of Indian affairs had halted a general decline in Native American populations, economic conditions, and land base, but Indian people still remained desperately poor compared to middle-class mainstream standards. By the late 1940s, arguments began to win favor that advocated rapid assimilation and demanded forceful elimination of tribalism and native land bases. It was assumed that obliteration of "Indianness" would propel native peoples out of poverty and a dependence on government that earlier Bureau of Indian Affairs (BIA) policies had created. This consensus built in the late 1940s and reached the peak of its political expression in the wave of "terminations" enacted by the government in the 1950s. Conservative Republican Senator Arthur V. Watkins of Utah led congressional support for termination, convinced, wrote **Vine Deloria, Jr.**, and Clifford Lytle, "that if the Indians were freed from federal restrictions they would soon prosper by learning in the school of life those lessons that a cynical federal bureaucracy had not been able to instill in them" (1983: 18).

The **Indian Claims Commission** was linked with the emerging termination policy on Capitol Hill. Senator Watkins wrote three years after its passage: "[The] basic purpose of Congress in setting up the Indian Claims Commission was to clear the way toward complete freedom of the Indian by assuring final settlement of all obligations—real or purported—of the Federal government to the Indian tribes" (Deloria and Lytle, 18). Political momentum toward termination was accelerating when Dwight Eisenhower assumed the presidency in 1952. Eisenhower

appointed Glenn L. Emmons, a supporter of Watkins's termination legislation, as commissioner of Indian affairs.

After passage of the Termination Act, Congress sometimes held up
Indian Claims Commission payments until the native nation in question
also agreed to termination proceedings. In 1963, for example, the Indian
Claims Commission awarded the Kalispels $3 million, an award that
was held by Congress (under legislation passed at the behest of Idaho
Senator Frank Church) until they agreed to termination. The Klamaths,
holding title to a million acres of prime timber in Oregon, were enticed
into terminating after BIA agents promised them per capita payments
of $50,000. Only afterward did the Klamaths learn painfully that "going
private" can be expensive. They found themselves paying rent, utilities,
health-care costs, and taxes they had never faced before.

The Menominees of Wisconsin shared ownership of property valued
at $34 million when their termination bill was enacted in 1953. By 1961,
the federal government was out of Menominee Country, and each of the
Menominees' former members had become the owner of one hundred
shares of stock and a negotiable bond valued at $3,000, issued in the
name of Menominee Enterprises, Inc. (MEI), a private enterprise that
held the former nation's land and businesses. Governmentally, the Menominee Nation had become Menominee County, the smallest (in terms
of population) and poorest (in terms of cash income) in Wisconsin.

As a county, Menominee had to raise taxes to pay for its share of
services, including welfare, health services, utilities, and the like. The
only taxable property owner in the county was MEI, which was forced
to raise the funds to pay its tax bill by restructuring so that stockholders
had to buy their homes and the property on which they had been built.
Most of the Menominees had little savings except for their $3,000
bonds, which were then sold to MEI to make the required residential
purchases. Many Menominees faced private-sector health costs, property taxes, and other expenses with no more money than they had had
before termination. Unemployment rose to levels that most of the
United States knew only during the 1930s. By 1965, health indicators
in Menominee County sounded like a reprint of the **Meriam Report**
almost four decades earlier. Tuberculosis afflicted nearly 35 percent of
the population, and infant mortality was three times the national average. Termination, like allotment, had been an abject failure at anything other than alienating Indian land. The termination of the
Menominee was such an abysmal failure that in 1973 their federal trust
relationship was reestablished by Congress.

By the 1950s, the economic rationale of allotment had become obsolete. The fancied myth of the yeoman farmer had dissolved into the
reality of large-scale growing units in a global network of agribusiness.
Most Americans now lived and worked in cities. Advocates of termi-

nation and relocation saw themselves generally as modernists and realists, promoting the eradication of native land, identity, and lifeways for the Indians' own good, to ease their transition into a modern industrial economy—the benign, all-knowing hand forever shaping the soft underside of conquest. Termination was the twentieth-century equivalent of "Kill the Indian, save the man." An Indian agent at Colville, in northeastern Washington, reported the plain language with which the native people under his "**wardship**" looked at termination proposals: "They seem to feel that the program is a government means to move the Indians from the reservation in order to allow European-American operators to exploit the reservation and eventually force all the Indians from the reservation areas."

FURTHER READING

Deloria, Vine, Jr., and Clifford Lytle. *American Indians, American Justice*. Austin: University of Texas Press, 1983.

Hasse, Larry J. "Termination and Assimilation: Federal Indian Policy, 1943 to 1961." Ph.D. dissertation, Washington State University, 1974. Ann Arbor, MI: University Microfilms, 1974.

Vaughan, Arthur V. "Termination of Federal Supervision: The Removal of Restrictions over Indian Property and Persons." *Annals of the American Academy of Political and Social Science* 311 (May 1957): p 50.

TRADE AND INTERCOURSE ACTS (1790 and Later) 1 Stat. 137 (1790 Act); 25 U.S.C.A. 177 (1793 Act)

In 1789, in one of his first acts as president, George Washington asked Secretary of War Henry Knox to prepare a report on the status of Indian affairs. Knox prepared a lengthy report on Native Americans' rights and mechanisms for dealing with them under the new U.S. **Constitution**. His conclusions closely resembled Spanish and English interpretations of the **Doctrine of Discovery** since the time of **Francisco de Vitoria** in the early sixteenth century. Knox found that the Indians had a right to their lands, and that land could not be taken except by mutual consent (as in the signing of a treaty), or in a "just" war as defined by the European powers of the day. Knox determined that non-Indian squatters must be kept off Indian lands to keep the peace on the frontier.

Out of Knox's report came the first of several Trade and Intercourse Acts passed by Congress between 1790 and 1834. The first Congress to convene under the Constitution passed the first such act in 1790 (25 U.S.C.A. § 177). The act held that no sale of Indian lands was valid without the authority of the United States. This initial act was extended and amended several times, in 1793, 1796, 1802, 1817, 1822, and 1834. In addition to extending federal authority to land sales, many of the Trade and Intercourse Acts forbade European-American entry into Indian lands, regulated trade, and prohibited liquor. The Trade and Intercourse Act of 1802 contained this clause providing prosecution of non-Indians who trespassed on Indian land:

SEC. 2. *And be it further enacted*, that if any citizen, or other person resident in, the United States . . . shall cross over, or go within the said boundary line, to hunt, or in any wise destroy the game; or shall drive, or otherwise convey any stock of horses or cattle to range on any lands allotted or secured by treaty with the United States, to any Indian tribe, he shall forfeit a sum not exceeding one hundred dollars, or be imprisoned not exceeding six months.

Some of the Trade and Intercourse Acts made depredations by non-Indians against Indians a federal crime in protected areas and pledged monetary compensation to injured Indians if they did not seek revenge. The acts also set uniform standards for punishment of crimes by non-Indians against Indians (and vice versa) and enunciated a goal of "civilization and education" for U.S. Indian policy. Trade with Indians also came under federal regulation in the Trade and Intercourse Acts.

In a legal sense, the Trade and Intercourse Acts were a double-edged sword for Indian **sovereignty**. On the one hand, they were passed to protect Indians from land fraud; on the other, they were an extension of federal law over **Indian Country**. The later intercourse acts were drafted under the theory that "tribes should be considered foreign nations and that tribal lands protected by treaty, even though situated within the boundaries of a state, should be considered outside the limits of jurisdictions of states" (Act of June 30, 1834, 4 Stat. 729, 733).

Federal jurisdiction over trade and land sales concerning Indians had been an issue at least since the **Albany Plan of Union** (1754), when **Iroquois** delegates led by Tiyanoga (**Hendrick**) advised **Benjamin Franklin** and other colonial delegates to develop a single system for trade, land dealings, and diplomacy. The Albany Plan was rejected by the individual colonies, but the idea that the federal government retains authority over the states for dealing with Indians was written into the Constitution and has been central to American Indian law in the United States for more than two centuries.

The Trade and Intercourse Act of 1817 (3 Stat. 383) attempted the first systematic regulation of criminal jurisdiction regarding both Indians and non-Indians in Indian Country. The act held that anyone, Indian or not, who committed an offense in Indian Country would be subject to the same punishment as if the offense had occurred in the United States, except for offenses defined as domestic. This exception became an important influence on subsequent court decisions delimiting jurisdiction. This law became the source of opinions that defined the powers of Indian courts; generally, a non-Indian accused of a crime on Indian land has been held to be under the jurisdiction of the United States, while an Indian charged with an offense against another Indian is tried in a Native American court.

FURTHER READING

Canby, William C., Jr. *American Indian Law in a Nutshell*. St. Paul, MN: West Publishing, 1981.
O'Brien, Sharon. *American Indian Tribal Governments*. Norman: University of Oklahoma Press, 1989.

TRAIL OF BROKEN TREATIES (1972)

During the summer of 1972, a number of Indian activist groups met in Denver to plan a "Trail of Broken Treaties" caravan. Their hope was to marshal thousands of protesters across the nation to march on Washington, D.C., to dramatize the issue of American Indian **self-determination**. At Minneapolis, the group issued its Twenty Points, a document that sought to revive Native American **sovereignty**. Basically, the Twenty Points advocated the following:

1. The repeal of the 1871 federal statute that ended the treaty-making era

2. The restoration of treaty-making status to native governments

3. The establishment of a commission to review past treaty violations

4. The resubmission of unratified treaties to the Senate

5. That all Indians be governed by treaty relations

6. The elimination of all state jurisdiction over American Indian affairs

The Trail of Broken Treaties caravan began its trek across America at San Francisco and Seattle, visiting many reservations and gathering support. From St. Paul, Minnesota, the caravan continued to Washington, D.C., during the final weeks of the 1972 presidential campaign.

Nearly a thousand people arrived in Washington, D.C., on November 3, 1972. The protesters learned that there was not enough lodging, so they elected to stay in the Bureau of Indian Affairs (BIA) building for several hours until security guards sought to forcibly remove them. At that point, events turned violent. The protesters seized the building for six days as they asserted their demands that Native American sovereignty be restored and immunity be granted to all protesters. Files were seized and damage was done to the BIA building (American Indian Movement leaders claimed that federal agents had infiltrated the movement and had done most of the damage). On November 8, 1972, federal officials offered immunity and transportation home to the protesters. The offer was accepted the next day, and the immediate crisis was resolved.

TRAILS OF TEARS (1830s)

In 1829, gold was discovered on **Cherokee** land in the mountains of present-day northern Georgia. The Georgia state legislature quickly passed a law forbidding the Cherokee to prospect or mine gold on their own land as three thousand or more European Americans surged onto Cherokee territory, wrecking the farmsteads and villages that the Indians had so carefully built. When the Cherokee Nation indicted non-Indians for destruction of native life and property, Georgia courts, having asserted their jurisdiction over Cherokee lands and lives, dismissed all Cherokee testimony as incompetent.

By the time their homelands were dismembered by the **Removal Act** of 1830, many Native American peoples in the Southeast had taken up the European-American ways of life and had married into non-Indian families. The Cherokees, for example, owned 22,000 cattle, 2,000 spinning wheels, 700 looms, 31 grist mills, 10 sawmills, 8 cotton gins, and 1,300 slaves. The Cherokees also had a written constitution that emulated that of the United States, a written language, developed by Sequoyah, and a bilingual newspaper, the *Cherokee Phoenix.* **John Ross**, the Cherokees' best-known leader at this time, was only one-eighth Cherokee by blood. He lived in a plantation-style house and owned several slaves.

Because they no longer had federal protection from predatory state interests, Indian lands were thrown open to anyone, including dealers in alcohol, who had a heyday exchanging land and anything else they could get their hands on for strong whiskey and rum. Actions could be brought against Indians in state courts, and so their land and other belongings were often attached for debt. State laws were enacted barring courts from accepting an Indian's testimony against a European-American man in court. In practice, then, no claim by a European-American man, no matter how baseless, could be contested by Indians.

By about 1830, non-Indian squatters were swarming onto the lands of the Five Civilized Tribes. Many native people were dispossessed before the removals began. They had the choice of two untenable options: move or be pushed off the land anyway. When a well-known **Chickasaw** leader, Emubby, was killed by a European American named Jones, the incident made the papers only because Emubby had served several campaigns with General **Andrew Jackson**. Before their removal westward, the **Creeks** were driven into the forests and swamps by non-Indian squatters. Their homes were taken, and many starved. A newspaper of the time described their destitution:

To see a whole people destitute of food—the incessant cry of the emaciated creatures being *bread! bread!* is beyond description distressing. The existence of many of the Indians is prolonged by eating roots and the bark of trees. . . . nothing that can afford nourishment is rejected, however offensive it may be.

. . . They beg their food from door to door. . . . It is really painful to see the wretched creatures wandering about the streets, haggard and naked. (Brandon 1961: 27)

Land speculators were at the root of the starvation. One U.S. marshal said that they were "some of the most lawless and uncouth men I have ever seen." A special agent wrote to President Jackson: "A greater mass of corruption, perhaps, has never been congregated in any part of the world" (Brandon 227).

Following passage of the Removal Act in 1830, removals began with four thousand **Choctaws** in 1831, bound for western Arkansas. The winter was hard, but during the next few years the weather was often even worse. The cruelty of the removal was compounded by governmental mismanagement and by Indian agents who kept for themselves much of the money that the government had given them to feed the native people. In the summer of 1831, cholera spread through areas of the South, returning each summer until 1836. Only the Chickasaws managed to transport much of what they owned westward (agents complained about the bulk of their livestock and baggage). The rest of the people suffered cruelly. One native man was quoted as saying: "We were drove off like wolves . . . and our peoples' feet were bleeding with long marches. . . . We are men . . . we have women and children" (Brandon 224).

The Cherokee leader John Ross took part in a tenacious fight against removal. He was a key figure in arguments before the U.S. Supreme Court (in *Cherokee Nation v. Georgia*) in which Chief Justice **John Marshall** acknowledged a limited measure of Cherokee **sovereignty**. The ruling was ignored by President Andrew Jackson. President Jackson refused to enforce Indian treaties in the wake of southern states' resistance. When South Carolina nullified a federal tariff, however, Jackson sent troops into the state and a naval force to anchor off Charleston. He also vowed to execute John C. Calhoun, leader of the nullification movement, on a charge of high treason, along with any member of Congress from South Carolina who had taken part in the nullification proceedings. Even these threats turned out to be more bluster than substance. From President Jackson, however, the Indians got neither bluster nor substance to sustain treaties that had been drawn up to last forever, and that were being trampled within living memory of their signing.

The assertion of states' rights over native territory in the Southeast provided the legal grist for the 1832 Supreme Court decision in *Worcester v. Georgia* written by Chief Justice Marshall, which has defined the relationship of native and states' rights for more than a century and a half. The case began when three non-Indian missionaries living on Cherokee territory refused to swear an oath of allegiance to the state of

Georgia. They were arrested, chained to a wagon, and forced to walk more than twenty miles to jail. Two Methodist preachers who objected to the cruelty that accompanied the arrests were also chained and taken to jail. The three missionaries were tried, convicted, and sentenced to four years of hard labor at the Georgia state penitentiary. Justice Marshall wrote that native nations had

always been considered as distinct, independent political communities, retaining their original natural rights . . . and the settled doctrine of the law of nations, that a weaker power does not surrender its independence—its right to self-government—by associating with a stronger, and taking its protection. . . . The Cherokee nation, then, is a distinct community, occupying its own territory, with boundaries accurately described, in which the laws of Georgia can have no force, and which the citizens of Georgia have no right to enter, but with the assent of the Cherokees, or in conformity with treaties, and with the acts of Congress.

There has been some debate among historians regarding whether President Jackson actually said, "John Marshall has rendered his decision, now let him enforce it." In effect, however, Jackson refused to implement the law as determined by Marshall's opinion, no matter how he described his position on the issue.

In the meantime, Ross had been evicted from his mansion and was living in a dirt-floored cabin when John Howard Payne, the author of "Home Sweet Home," came to visit him at the cabin, just across the Georgia state line in Tennessee. The Georgia State Guard crossed the state line and kidnapped both men. Realizing that the federal government did not intend to protect the Cherokees, Ross and others reluctantly signed the **Treaty of New Echota** in 1835 and prepared, with heavy hearts, to leave their homes.

By 1838, the Cherokees had exhausted all their appeals. Before they were forced to leave their homes, the Cherokees passed a "memorial" that expressed the injustice of the forced relocation:

The title of the Cherokee people to their lands is the most ancient, pure, and absolute known to man; its date is beyond the reach of human record; its validity confirmed by possession and enjoyment antecedent to all pretense of claim by any portion of the human race.

The free consent of the Cherokee people is indispensable to a valid transfer of the Cherokee title. The Cherokee people have neither by themselves nor their representatives given such consent. It follows that the original title and ownership of lands still rests with the Cherokee Nation, unimpaired and absolute. The Cherokee people have existed as a distinct national community for a period extending into antiquity beyond the dates and records and memory of man. These attributes have never been relinquished by the Cherokee people, and cannot be dissolved by the expulsion of the Nation from its territory by the power of the United States Government. (O'Brien 1989: 57)

An observer in Kentucky described the Cherokees' mid-winter march to Arkansas: "Even aged females, apparently nearly ready to drop into the grave, were travelling with heavy burdens attached to their backs, sometimes on frozen ground, and sometimes on muddy streets, with no covering for their feet" (Collier 1947: 124). A U.S. Army private who witnessed the Cherokee removal wrote:

I saw the helpless Cherokee arrested and dragged from their homes, and driven by bayonet into the stockades. And in the chill of a drizzling rain on an October morning I saw them loaded like cattle or sheep into wagons and started toward the west. . . . Chief Ross led in prayer, and when the bugle sounded and wagons started rolling many of the children . . . waved their little hands goodbye to their mountain homes. (Worcester 1975: 67)

Indian agents who were infamous for their penny-pinching sometimes hired rotten boats to transport Indians across rivers. Many of the boats sank, with the loss of uncounted lives. To the agents, these were merely mouths that no longer had to be fed, creating even more profits.

Alexis de Tocqueville, author of *Democracy in America*, witnessed portions of the early removals. He wrote:

At the end of the year 1831, whilst I was on the left bank of the Mississippi, at a place named by the Europeans Memphis, there arrived a numerous band of Choctaws. These savages had left their country, and were endeavoring to gain the right bank of the Mississippi, where they hoped to find an asylum which had been promised them by the American government. It was in the middle of the winter, and the cold was unusually severe; the snow had frozen hard upon the ground, and the river was drifting huge masses of ice. The Indians had their families with them; and they brought in their train the wounded and the sick, with children newly born, and old men upon the verge of death. They possessed neither tents nor wagons, but only their arms and some provisions. I saw them embark to pass the mighty river, and never will that solemn spectacle fade from my remembrance. No cry, no sob was heard amongst the assembled crowd; all were silent. . . . The Indians had all stepped into the bark which was to carry them across, but their dogs remained upon the bank. As soon as these animals perceived that their masters were finally leaving the shore, they set up a dismal howl, and plunging all together into the icy waters of the Mississippi, swam after the boat. (Reeves 1898: 435–36, 448)

The many "trails of tears" during the 1830s and early 1840s resulted in immense suffering among the estimated 50,000 to 100,000 native people who were forced to move. As many as 8,000 Cherokees, between one-third and one-fourth of the people who were removed, died on the

Cherokees' Trail of Tears or shortly thereafter. The Cherokees' move involved the most human suffering, and their phrase for the long, brutal march (*nuna-daa-ut-sun'y*, "the trail where they cried") gave the removal policy its native name. At least one-fourth of the Cherokees who were removed died along the way. A few hundred Cherokees escaped to the mountains, where their descendants still live.

Despite the cruelty of the marches they were forced to undertake, and the death and disease that dogged their every step, the surviving members of the peoples who were removed to **Indian Territory** quickly set about rebuilding their communities. Much as they had in the Southeast, the Creeks, Cherokees, and others built prosperous farms and towns, passed laws, and set about rather self-consciously civilizing themselves once again. Within three generations, however, this land that in the 1830s had been set aside as Indian Territory forever was being sought for its oil and because the frontier had closed everywhere else. At the turn of the century, as a rush for "black gold" inundated Oklahoma, the **Allotment Act** (1887) was breaking up the native estate much as Georgia's state laws had done a little more than half a century earlier. There would be no trail of tears this time, however—at least not a collective one. Instead, the land would be alienated section by section. There was no virgin land left to which to send native peoples who stood in the way of European-style progress.

FURTHER READING

Brandon, William. *American Heritage Book of Indians*. New York: American Heritage Publishing Co., 1961.
Collier, John. *Indians of the Americas*. New York: W. W. Norton, 1947.
O'Brien, Sharon. *American Indian Tribal Governments*. Norman: University of Oklahoma Press, 1989.
Reeves, Henry, trans. *Alexis de Tocqueville: Democracy in America*. Cambridge, MA: Sever and Francis, 1898.
Thornton, Russell. "Cherokee Population Losses during the Trail of Tears: A New Perspective and a New Estimate." *Ethnohistory* 31:4 (1984): 289–300.
Worcester, Donald E., ed. *Forked Tongues and Broken Treaties*. Caldwell, ID: Caxton, 1975.

TREATIES, AS CONCEPT (with Indian Nations)

According to **Francisco de Vitoria**'s 1532 opinion that defined a **Doctrine of Discovery** for European nations, one of two ways in which European nations could legally gain title to land from Native American nations was by treaty, a consensual agreement of willing parties. The other was through "just" war. Treaties often were signed as an alternative to a war of attrition that would prove even more devastating to Native American nations than the cession of most of their land bases.

Provisions in the 371 treaties negotiated with Indian bands and nations varied widely, but most of them contained similar elements: a guarantee that both sides would keep the peace, a marking of boundaries between Indian and non-Indian land, a statement that the signatory Indians were placing themselves under the "protection" of the United States, and definition of Indian fishing and hunting rights (often applied to ceded land). Many treaties also regulated travel by non-Indians on Indian land, as well as containing provisions to punish non-Indians who committed crimes on Indian land and Indians who committed offenses against non-Indians.

The U.S. Supreme Court in **Washington v. Washington State Commercial Passenger Fishing Vessel Association** (1979) characterized a treaty between the federal government and a Native American government as "essentially a contract between two sovereign nations." The treaties have been generally held to reserve to Native American governments powers not relinquished to the United States, just as the Tenth Amendment reserves to the states powers not delegated to the U.S. government by the **Constitution**. According to legal scholars Russel Barsh and James Henderson, these agreements between Native American governments and the federal government are "something more than 'treaties' as they are understood in international law. They are political compacts irrevocably annexing tribes to the federal system in a status parallel to, but not identical with, that of the states" (1980: 270–271).

The U.S. Constitution (article VI, section 2) holds that "all Treaties made . . . shall be the Supreme Law of the Land." On that basis, the United States entered into more than 800 treaties with Native Americans between 1789 and 1871, when Congress halted formal treaty making. Only 371 of these treaties were ratified by the Senate. Even after 1871, commissions of the executive branch continued to sign treaties with Indian governments until 1914, when the last agreement of this type was signed with the Ute Mountain Utes. These instruments were called "agreements," not "treaties," when presented to Congress.

Treaties have been the most frequent sources of litigation in Indian law. According to legal scholar Charles F. Wilkinson, "These laws are unique in our jurisprudence, for they set aside territory within the United States for self-government, subject to federal supervision, by sovereigns that are both preconstitutional and extraconstitutional" (1987: 14).

Although the term "treaty" carries connotations of diplomatic solemnity and equality, many of the treaties were negotiated under less than agreeable conditions, especially after 1800, when, in the opinion of **Vine Deloria, Jr.**, "The treaty process was allowed to deteriorate from a sacred pledge of faith between nations to a series of quasi-fraudulent real-estate transactions" (1985: 110). Before 1800, the balance of power between immigrant Europeans and Native Americans acted as a check on abuses, although even during the early years of the British colonies and the United States, treaty records indicate that negotiations were liberally lubricated with liquor. Treaties were always written in English and presented to Indian people who did not understand the written language or the European protocol used to negotiate them.

The very concepts of landownership and centralized government regulation often were foreign to Indian leaders who negotiated treaties. Native Americans very often did not completely understand what they were signing, and even when they did, the Senate sometimes unilaterally changed treaty provisions before ratification. Treaties often were signed with Native American "leaders" who had been recruited by treaty commissioners who failed to realize that the treaties had little or no support among the people of the nation being represented as the contracting party. During negotiations for the 1851 **Treaty of Fort Laramie** (sometimes called the Horse Creek Treaty), the U.S. representatives insisted that the **Sioux** designate one leader to speak for all of them. The Sioux refused, after which the U.S. negotiators designated Conquering Bear as the Siouxs' leader without the consent of the people he was supposed to be leading. The problem was compounded three years later when Conquering Bear was killed by U.S. Army troops during the Grattan fight near Fort Laramie. The Sioux had a great deal of trouble comprehending why the army had killed the chief who had earlier been handpicked as the Siouxs' supposed "leader."

In some cases, errors of large magnitude were made during treaty negotiations. In 1868, for example, the Fort Laramie Treaty granted the Sioux land in northern present-day Nebraska that had long been occupied by the **Poncas**. The Sioux, traditional enemies of the Poncas, fully approved of the U.S. Army's intervention to force the Poncas off their land and into exile in **Indian Territory**, later called Oklahoma. This mistake in treaty negotiation gave rise to a long march homeward by **Standing Bear** and other Poncas that in turn created the conditions that caused a landmark case to be brought in Omaha during 1879 under which Standing Bear and his party were held to be human beings under U.S. law, able to legally return to their homeland. After several decades of bureaucratic battling, the Poncas finally reacquired some of the land taken from them by the error in the Fort Laramie Treaty.

Judge **George Boldt**, in *United States v. Washington* (1974), pointed out that treaty negotiations in the Pacific Northwest often were carried out in three languages—English, Chinook (a trade jargon with limited vocabulary), and a native language. The use of Chinook severely limited both parties' ability to communicate complex concepts. Because of the disadvantages at which treaty making often placed Indians, the Supreme Court has held that treaties should be construed as the Indians would have understood them (*Tulee v. Washington*, 315 U.S. 681, 684–85 [1942]). Treaties, according to Supreme Court rules of construction, are also to be interpreted to accomplish their protective purposes, according to legal scholar William S. Canby, Jr., "with ambiguities to be resolved in favor of the Indians [*Carpenter v. Shaw*, 280 U.S. 363 (1930)]" (1981: 80).

FURTHER READING

Barsh, Russel, and James Henderson. *The Road: Indian Tribes and Political Liberty.* Berkeley: University of California Press, 1980.
Canby, William C., Jr. *American Indian Law in a Nutshell.* St. Paul, MN: West Publishing, 1981.
Deloria, Vine, Jr. *Behind the Trail of Broken Treaties: An Indian Declaration of Independence.* 1974. Austin: University of Texas Press, 1985.
Prucha, Francis Paul. *American Indian Treaties: The History of a Political Anomaly.* Berkeley: University of California Press, 1994.
Wilkinson, Charles F. *American Indians, Time, and the Law: Native Societies in a Modern Constitutional Democracy.* New Haven, CT: Yale University Press, 1987.

TREATIES, SPECIFIC AGREEMENTS AND PROVISIONS

The following is a brief annotated tour of some of the major treaties with Indian nations. Each treaty is a story in and of itself; 371 of them were negotiated and ratified by the U.S. Senate before 1871.

Lancaster Treaty (1744)

The important Lancaster Treaty attempted to set boundaries between Indian and non-Indian settlements and required permission for non-Indians to visit **Indian Country** or vice versa. Both parties were granted the right to punish intruders under their own laws. The **Iroquois** negotiated this treaty with Pennsylvania, Maryland, and Virginia; it concerned lands within the present-day boundaries of West Virginia. At the Lancaster Treaty meeting, **Canassatego**, Tadadaho (speaker) of the Iroquois Confederacy, advised the colonists to unite on a federal model resembling the Iroquois system.

Treaty with the Delaware Tribe (1778) 7 Stat. 13–15

The first treaty signed by the United States as a national entity guaranteed the territory of the Delaware Nation and opened the possibility that it might join the Union as a state. Article IV of this treaty directed that neither party might punish citizens of the other party until "a fair and impartial trial can be had by judges and juries of both parties, as near as can be to the laws, customs, and usages of the contracting parties and natural justice." This idea of joint justice was terminated in 1885 by the **Major Crimes Act**.

Treaty with the Wyandots, Delaware, Chippewa, and Ottawa (1785) 7 Stat. 16–18

This treaty with the Wyandots contained a clause that forbade illegal non-Indian settlement on reserved lands and said that any person establishing such settlement "shall forfeit the protection of the United States, and the Indians may punish him as they please." The treaty also contained a clause saying that any Indian who "shall commit a robbery or murder on any citizen of the United States" would be delivered to the nearest U.S. Army post and dealt with under U.S. law.

Treaty of Hopewell (1785) 7 Stat. 18–21

The **Cherokees** sided with the British during the American Revolution, and after it that nation demanded a separate treaty with the United States. The Cherokees refused to recognize the British surrender at Yorktown or the Treaty of Paris. Mutual demobilization was included in the Treaty of Hopewell (1785).

The Hopewell Treaty also provided that illegal non-Indian squatters on Cherokee lands must move out within six months, or "such person will forfeit the protection of the United States and the Indians may punish him or not as they please." A year later, however, the Shawnee Treaty of 1786 (7 Stat. 26) required that Indians accused of crimes against non-Indians be delivered to the nearest army post. The same rule was applied to European Americans accused of wronging Indians.

The Cherokee treaty, like the one negotiated with the Delawares seven years earlier, opened the possibility of their admission to the United States: "That the Indians may have full confidence in the justice of the United States, respecting their interests, they shall have the right to send a deputy of their choice, whenever they think fit, to Congress."

Treaty of Holston (1791) 7 Stat. 39–42

Negotiated with the Cherokees after the Treaty of Hopewell (1785) was violated, the Holston Treaty forced them to relinquish much of the subsequently formed states of Kentucky and Tennessee in exchange for $1,500 worth of goods per year, or a fraction of a penny per acre.

Jay Treaty (1794) 7 Stat. 47–48

Among other provisions, the Jay Treaty allowed for free passage by Iroquois across the U.S.-Canadian border. In 1968, Mohawks at Akwesasne, which straddles the border, protested the denial of free passage by Canadian officials. Mohawks blockaded the Cornwall International

Bridge, and several were arrested, after which they pressed their treaty claims in Canadian courts until charges were dropped.

Treaty of Greenville (1795) 7 Stat. 49–54

The Treaty of Greenville involved the Miami Confederacy, Delawares, Shawnees, Wyandots, Chippewas, Potawatomis, and Ottawas and ceded much of present-day Ohio to the United States following the Indians' defeat by "Mad Anthony" Wayne at the Battle of Fallen Timbers. Prior to that defeat, the Indian alliance had inflicted more than eight hundred fatalities on army units commanded by Major General Anthony St. Clair, the largest battlefield defeat (in terms of deaths) in the history of westward expansion.

Treaty of Mount Dexter (1805) 7 Stat. 98–100

The Treaty of Mount Dexter, negotiated with the **Choctaws**, was notable for the penny-pinching amounts paid by the United States for 4.1 million acres of land in southern Mississippi and southwestern Alabama. The Choctaws were paid $3,000 for the land, or less than a penny an acre.

Treaty between the Cherokee Nation and the United States (1817) 7 Stat. 156–160

Provisions for "removal"—the relocation of entire Indian nations from areas about to be settled by non-Indians—were first laid down in an 1817 treaty between the United States and the Cherokee Nation. By 1830, the federal government had passed general removal legislation.

Treaty of Indian Springs (1825) 7 Stat. 237–240

The **Creeks** had become concerned about non-Indian usurpation of their lands by 1818, when the Muscogee (Creek) Nation passed a law against the sale of any Creek land without council approval, with a penalty of death. In 1825, federal treaty commissioners bribed William McIntosh, leader of the Creek Lower Towns, along with a few of his close associates, to sign a land-cession treaty, the Treaty of Indian Springs. The National Council declared McIntosh to be a traitor and on May 1, 1825, sent a delegation to torch his house. When McIntosh appeared at the door of his burning home, his body was riddled with bullets. The fraudulent treaty was annulled by the United States, but the Creeks were coerced into signing two other treaties (both commonly referred to as the Treaty of Washington) by which they were forced, in the 1830s, to cede their homelands and move, under the provisions of the **Removal Act of 1830**, to **Indian Territory**, later called Oklahoma.

Treaty at Prairie du Chien (1825) 7 Stat. 272–277

The Treaty at Prairie du Chien was negotiated between the United States and the **Menominee, Sioux**, Sac and Fox, Ottawa, and Chippewa, as well as the Iowa and Winnebago. A major object of the treaty was cessation of intertribal warfare.

Treaty with the Choctaws (1830) 7 Stat. 333–342

The Treaty with the Choctaws, negotiated at Dancing Rabbit Creek, was the first negotiated under the Removal Act of 1830. As in most of the removal treaties, the government assured the Indians that they would have wide-ranging control over territory and resources in their new homes. For example, the Treaty with the Choctaws (1830) pledged

jurisdiction and government of all persons and property that may be within their limits west, so that no Territory or State shall ever have the right to pass laws for the government of the Choctaw nation . . . and that no part of the land granted to them shall ever be embraced in any Territory or State.

Treaty of New Echota (1835) 7 Stat. 478–488

The Treaty of New Echota implemented the Removal Act of 1830 for the Cherokees. For more detail, see **Trails of Tears**.

Treaty of Guadalupe Hidalgo (1848) 9 Stat. 922–930

The Treaty of Guadalupe Hidalgo ended a three-month-long war between the United States and Mexico in 1846, after which Mexico was forced to cede almost half its land area, including all or part of the subsequently established states of California, New Mexico, Arizona, Nevada, Utah, Colorado, and Wyoming. Under this treaty, the United States acquired 334.4 million acres, or 552,568 square miles, of land area.

Article XIII of this treaty extended American citizenship to all residents of the area, including American Indians, a provision that conflicted with U.S. policy in the rest of the country at the time, as well as later court cases such as *Elk v. Wilkins*, which denied Indians citizenship, including voting rights.

Treaty of Fort Laramie (1851) 11 Stat. 749

More than 10,000 Plains Indians—among them Lakota, Arapaho, **Crow, Cheyenne**, Arikara, Assiniboine, Hidasta, and **Mandan**—took part in the largest treaty-related gathering in American history near Fort Laramie, Wyoming. In a conference lasting eighteen days, U.S. treaty commissioners and native leaders agreed to exchange $50,000 a year ($1 per year per person represented by the treaty) for fifty years to allow the United States to construct military posts and roads through the upper Midwest. When the treaty was ratified by the Senate, that body reduced the payment to $15,000 a year without the native nations' consent. The peace wrought by this treaty was short-lived, as by 1854 friction between Indians and European-American immigrants sparked the Plains Indian Wars.

Treaty of Fort Atkinson (1853) 10 Stat. 1013–1017

The Yamparika band of **Comanches**, the Kiowas, and the Kiowa-Apaches signed the Treaty of Fort Atkinson, which allowed the United States to build roads through their hunting grounds. The United States also was permitted under this treaty to build forts along the Santa Fe Trail and to protect non-Indians traveling the route. The Indians agreed to make restitution for injuries to U.S. citizens. The United States also promised to compensate injuries by its citizens to Indians who were party to the treaty.

Treaty with the Oto and Missouri Indians (1854) 10 Stat. 1130–1131; 11 Stat. 605–606

The Treaty with the Oto and Missouri Indians was one of several treaties negotiated with native peoples in the Kansas and Nebraska territories by Commissioner of Indian Affairs George W. Manypenny. These treaties were probably the first to contain clauses for allotment of land to individual Indians, a measure that was enacted nationwide in the General **Allotment Act** of 1887.

Treaty of Medicine Creek (1854) 10 Stat. 1132–1137

The Treaty of Medicine Creek ceded large parts of present-day western Washington. In exchange for relinquishing the land, native people in the area retained "the right of taking fish, at all usual and accustomed grounds and stations . . . in common with all citizens of the Territory." This treaty was the basis of Judge **George Boldt**'s holding in *United States v. Washington* (1974) that Indians of the area were entitled to a fair share of the catch, an amount later defined judicially as up to 50 percent.

The Treaty of Medicine Creek was one of many negotiated by territorial governor **Isaac Stevens** by which most of the Pacific Northwest was ceded. Most of the negotiations were exceptionally heavy-handed and hurried. Stevens's diplomatic indiscretions sparked the Yakima War, which reached across the Cascades westward to Seattle. On one occasion, in a treaty signed June 11, 1855, Stevens promised Indian signatories that lands guaranteed to them would not be invaded by non-Indians, and then announced them open for settlement only twelve days later.

Treaty of Hell Gate (1855) 12 Stat. 975–979

The Treaty of Hell Gate reserved 1.25 million acres in northwestern Montana for the Salish and Kootenai. Over the years, the reservation drew considerable numbers of non-Indians because of its rich farmland and scenic mountains. The reservation was allotted in the late nineteenth century, and by the time this case was adjudicated, more than half the land was owned by non-Indians, who later comprised 81 percent of the area's residents.

Treaty with the Creeks and Seminoles (1856) 11 Stat. 699–707

The 1856 Treaty with the Creeks and Seminoles pledged "secure and unrestricted self-government and full jurisdiction over persons and property, within their respective limits."

Treaty of Little Arkansas (1865) 14 Stat. 699–711

Signed by the United States with the Southern Cheyenne and Arapaho, the Treaty of Little Arkansas contained an apology for the Sand Creek Massacre against the two Indian nations on November 29, 1864, reading, "The United States, being desirous to express its condemnation of, and as far as may be, repudiate[s] the gross and wanton outrages perpetuated against certain bands of Cheyenne and Arapahoe Indians . . . while the said Indians were at peace by lawful authority."

Treaty with the Creeks (1866) 14 Stat. 785–792

Following the onset of the Civil War in 1861, the Creeks signed a treaty with the Confederate States of America. In 1866, following the end of that war, the Treaty with the Creeks was negotiated by the Seneca Ely S. Parker, who had been General U.S. Grant's secretary, and who wrote the articles of surrender ending the Civil War. The treaty of 1866 reestablished relations between the Creeks and the United States.

Treaty of Medicine Lodge (1867) 15 Stat. 581–587

The Treaty of Medicine Lodge with the Cheyennes and Arapahos contained among its provisions a pledge of compensation for victims of the Sand Creek Massacre. The payments were never made because the Department of the Army considered the attack a battle. At the same time, a House of Representatives investigating committee called the killings at Sand Creek a massacre.

Fort Laramie Treaty (1868) 15 Stat. 619–627, 635–647

The Fort Laramie Treaty of 1868 ended the Powder River War, during which Red Cloud and other Sioux leaders forced the United States to abandon its forts along the Bozeman Trail. In this treaty, the United States recognized the Great Sioux Nation as including most of the western half of present-day South Dakota. The treaty guaranteed that no unauthorized person "shall ever be permitted to pass over, settle upon, or reside in [this] country."

The **Black Hills**, called *paha sapa* ("hills that are black") by the Sioux, were included as reservation land under the Fort Laramie Treaty of 1868. An expedition led by George Armstrong Custer found rich deposits of gold and other minerals in the Black Hills during 1874 and sparked a rush of non-Indian settlement.

The Treaty of Fort Laramie validated land transfers only if they were approved by three-fourths of the adult men of the Sioux Nation. Treaty commissioners attempted to validate the cession of the Black Hills, but were able to get only 10 percent of the Sioux men to agree. Congress ratified the act in 1877 despite its contravention of the treaty.

In 1920, the Sioux brought a complaint before the U.S. Court of Claims, which upheld the 1877 act of Congress. After the **Indian Claims Commission** was founded in 1946, the Sioux sought to reintroduce the claim, but it was barred because of the earlier review as a matter of *res judicata*. In 1978, the Sioux obtained passage of a special act of Congress that allowed them to bring the case to the Court of Claims again to be argued on its merits despite the earlier judgment of *res judicata*. In *United States v. Sioux Nation*, the Supreme Court held that the United States had acted in bad faith in the matter, vindicating the Sioux' decades of legal perseverance.

The Fort Laramie Treaty of 1868 also mistakenly gave the Sioux land that was occupied by the **Poncas**, their traditional enemies. To enforce the treaty, the U.S. Army forced the Poncas to march to Oklahoma from their homelands along the Niobrara River in northern Nebraska during 1877. Following the death of his son, Ponca chief **Standing Bear** decided to march back to his homeland for the burial; a number of Poncas joined him. This march gave rise to a suit heard in Omaha during 1879 in which District Court judge **Elmer S. Dundy** held that Indians were subject to the English common-law practice of habeas corpus. Therefore, the army could not compel their return to Oklahoma.

Treaty with the Nez Perce (1871) 15 Stat. 693–695

The Treaty with the Nez Perce was the last treaty with an Indian nation ratified by the Senate.

FURTHER READING

Hosen, Frederick E., comp. *Rifle, Blanket, and Kettle: Selected Indian Treaties and Laws.* Jefferson, NC: McFarland, 1985.

Prucha, Francis Paul. *American Indian Treaties: The History of a Political Anomaly.* Berkeley: University of California Press, 1994.

TRIBAL COURTS, HISTORY OF

Courts in **Indian Country** do not find their origins in any specific statutory authorization, but rather in the early administrative practice of the Bureau of Indian Affairs and in the subsequent and implicit authorization suggested by the **Indian Reorganization Act** of 1934. This view, of course, does not consider the existence of Native American adjudicatory mechanisms that may have preexisted or existed in tandem with formally identified Native American courts. Such concerns are, however, often critical in examining issues of legitimacy.

The "need" for some sort of Native American court system emanated from the perceptions of local and national non-Indian administrators in Indian Country that some formal device was necessary to regulate law and order on reservations. Prior to the authorization by the secretary of the interior in 1883 to establish **courts of Indian offenses**, local Indian agents on the reservations resorted to a variety of expedients. The most common solution was for the agent himself to act as judge or to delegate the duty to one of his other subordinates or to a "trusted" Indian. This practice, though not statutorily authorized, was in line with the course of action suggested several times by earlier commissioners of Indian affairs and secretaries of the interior, who envisioned the local agents as justices of the peace.

Despite these ad hoc practices throughout Indian Country, the specific impetus for courts of Indian offenses seemed to come from the reform impulse of Secretary of the Interior H. M. Teller, who was appointed in 1882. Indian Affairs Commissioner Hiram Price compiled a set of rules for courts of Indian offenses, which were approved on April 10, 1883, by Secretary Teller and circulated to the agents. These rules provided guidelines for court organization and procedure and an abbreviated criminal and civil code. The only express qualification for prospective jurists was that they not be polygamists. The range of jurisdictional authority was thought to be modeled after that of a justice of the peace in the state or territory where such a court was located.

It was recognized from the first that there was, at best, a shaky legal foundation for these tribunals. There was no federal statutory authorization for the establishment of such courts, only the generally acknowledged authority of the Department of the Interior to supervise Indian affairs. Because no authorizing legislation defined the jurisdiction of the courts of Indian offenses, the courts and police were often challenged. The usual reaction of the commissioner of Indian affairs in the face of a jurisdictional challenge was to try to avoid a showdown. In this regard, there was unblemished success: no successful legal challenges were brought against the courts of Indian offenses. Tribal courts remained fragile and potentially volatile forums for all concerned.

The tasks of the courts of Indian offenses became vastly more complicated when the ravages of the allotment process and the sale of "surplus" Native American lands brought substantial numbers of non-Indians as permanent residents to the reservation. The bright line that had separated European-American and Indian communities was obliterated; jurisdictional dilemmas became apparent. Various questions arose: What courts had (or would accept) jurisdiction over non-Indians, over Indian allottees, or over mixed-bloods? How would these courts be financed? These dilemmas are still not fully resolved today, more than one hundred years later. Despite the principal claim that the courts of Indian offenses were necessary to maintain law and order on the reservation, other motives were at work. For example, the 1892 revision provided that "if an Indian refuses or neglects to adopt habits of industry, or to engage in civilized pursuits or employments, but habitually spends his time in idleness and loafing, he shall be deemed a vagrant" and punished accordingly. The "need" for law and order often meant a "need" for acculturation and **assimilation**. This notion of reform often sought to impose or instill "proper virtues" in Indians; it was particularly characteristic of federal policy during the period 1871–1928.

A court of Indian offenses was established on a particular reservation when its Indian agent and the commissioner of Indian affairs concluded that it was practicable and desirable; thus such courts were established for all Indians with the exception of the Five Civilized Tribes, the Indians of New York, the Osage, the **Pueblos**, and the eastern **Cherokees**, all of whom had recognized Native American governments and courts. The peak of their activity was reached around 1900, when about two-thirds of the agencies had their own courts. Some agencies never established a court, and others experimented with them only briefly. Congress's penurious appropriations for the courts limited the number that could function at any time. The commissioner of Indian affairs determined where the courts would be located. In 1891, an acting commissioner expressed this selection process and its unbounded discretion by noting that courts would be established "as it may appear the good of the Indian Service requires." Today only about twenty-five courts of Indian offenses continue to function. They are popularly referred to as "CFR" courts because most of their governing regulations are found in volume 25 of the *Code of Federal Regulations*. Most other Native American nations have established courts pursuant to their constitutions.

Finally, the wheels of reform began to turn in Indian Country. The late 1920s saw renewed public concern for the conditions on Indian reservations. Reports appeared that criticized Anglo-controlled land-tenure patterns, growing poverty, and administrative abuse in Indian Country. The 1928 **Meriam Report** initiated by Secretary of the Interior Hubert Work is the best-known of these, but it made no recommendations on the subject of law and Native American courts. The report argued that the situation varied too greatly among the various Native American nations.

The Indian Reorganization Act of 1934 was the culmination of this reform movement. One of the sweeping changes it sought to accomplish was in the matter of law and order on Indian reservations. **John Collier**, commissioner of Indian affairs, proposed a sweeping reform bill that dealt with four major areas: self-government, special education for Indians, Indian lands, and a court of Indian affairs. The Collier proposal envisioned a dual system of Native American courts. The first level was to be organized under the self-government title of the proposed act. Native American nations would be able to retain their local courts either as courts of Indian offenses or as courts created through specific authorization in a native nation's constitution adopted pursuant to the Indian Reorganization Act. At the same time, a national court of Indian affairs would be staffed with seven judges appointed by the president and subject to confirmation by the Senate. The court would always be in session and would be held in a number of different circuits. Each judge would be responsible for a particular region.

The jurisdiction of this special court of Indian affairs was set out in section 3 of the proposed legislation. The court would assume responsibility over the following matters: major criminal cases; cases where an Indian community was a party; cases involving questions of commerce where one litigant was an Indian and the other a non-Indian; civil and criminal cases involving an ordinance where a party was not a member of the Indian community; questions involving Indian allotments where the rights of an Indian were involved; and cases involving the determination of heirs and the settlement of such things as estates, land partitions, and guardianships.

According to some commentators, a number of provisions in the court of Indian affairs title would have changed the traditional concept of Indian justice rather significantly. All federal guarantees to criminal defendants and the federal rules of evidence would apply. In essence, the court would duplicate the system of procedure and appeal that prevailed in the federal court system. No Indian thinking or input was considered in the drafting of the bill. If things were not going well on the reservation, improvement lay in ratcheting up of applicable federal standards.

Despite these familiar difficulties, the Collier Bill did go a long way in attempting to improve the system of justice in Indian Country. In addition to the powers already discussed, the proposed court could have removed cases from Native American and state courts and heard appeals from local Indian courts. The secretary of the interior also was authorized to appoint ten special attorneys to provide legal advice and representation to both native governments and individual Indians before the court. Not unexpectedly, as with much of the proposed Collier Bill, this title generated a great deal of controversy during legislative hearings. The final enactment of the bill, which became known as the Indian Reorganization Act of 1934, or the Wheeler-Howard Act, bore faint resemblance to the original proposal. The title dealing with the court of Indian offenses disappeared entirely.

Under the IRA, Native American nations and bands were to draft their own constitutions, adopt their own laws, and set up their own court systems. Regardless of the statutory provisions, most Native American constitutions were drafted by the Bureau of Indian Affairs without Indian consultation and consequently reflected little, if any, direct local concern. As a result, there was no opportunity to formally reinstitute traditional law on the reservation, even if it existed at the time. These BIA constitutions did not provide for any separation of powers and did not specifically create any court system. Most constitutions, rather facilely, it seems, recognized the power of a council—an elected legislative body—to "promulgate and enforce ordinances providing for the maintenance of law and order and the administration of justice by establishing a reservation court and defining its duties and powers." Most legislation also required the approval of the Bureau of Indian Affairs. In recent years, a number of Indian nations have amended their constitutions to remove the approval power of the Bureau of Indian Affairs. It is important to note, however, that the exercise of these constitutional powers (whether by an IRA government or not) is not to be considered the exercise of federally delegated powers but rather the exercise of a sovereign authority that predates the U.S. **Constitution**.

Most current Native American judicial codes that serve to elucidate the framework of Indian court activity are a combination of unique Native American law and adapted state and federal law principles. Apparent in the newer codes is a decided commitment to develop increased Native American statutory, including customary, law and an organized and reported body of Indian decisional law.

FURTHER READING

Hagan, William. *Indian Police and Judges: Experiments in Acculturation and Control.* Lincoln: University of Nebraska Press, 1980.

Llewellyn, Karl, and E. Adamson Hoebel. *The Cheyenne Way: Conflict and Case Law in Primitive Jurisprudence.* Norman: University of Oklahoma Press, 1941.

Pommersheim, Frank. *Braid of Feathers: American Indian Law and Contemporary Tribal Life.* Berkeley: University of California Press, 1995.
Zion, James W. "The Navaho Peacemaker Court: Deference to the Old and Accommodation to the New." *American Indian Law Review* 11 (1983): 89.
                                                                FRANK POMMERSHEIM

TRIBE, LEGAL DEFINITION

A "tribe" or "nation," as a community of Native American people, is the basic unit of Indian law, according to legal scholar Charles F. Wilkinson. **Treaties** were signed with nations, each of which has its own legal system, governmental structure, language or dialect, and lifeways and other customs. In the middle 1990s, roughly 550 Native American governments were recognized by the U.S. federal government, and perhaps 300 more functioned with some degree of legal and political coherence without such recognition.

According to legal scholar William C. Canby, Jr., "At the most general level, a tribe is . . . a group of Indians that is recognized as constituting a distinct and historically continuous political entity for at least some governmental purposes" (1981: 4). For the purposes of U.S. law and colonial administration, "recognition" usually comes from the government, principally through treaties or other instruments negotiated with the approval of Congress. Under U.S. law, a "tribe" can be created by "acknowledgment" of its existence through the Department of the Interior; several Native American governments have been recognized or rerecognized since criteria for this procedure were published in 1978.

"The precise legal definition of Indian tribes remains a source of confusion," wrote Russel Barsh and James Henderson. "Fundamental to this confusion is the basic fact of the survival of the tribes as the only consensual government of Indian people—a fact that defies the anticipated disintegration of the tribes and submersion of tribal Indians in white society" (1980: vii). During the nineteenth century, the entire body of U.S. law concerning Indian nations operated under an assumption that they and their members would be dissolved into "civilized" non-Indian society. "Although Indian tribes have survived, notwithstanding a century of coercive government intervention," Barsh and Henderson continued, "the legal system appears content to quibble over the details of the old rules rather than abandon them" (vii).

FURTHER READING

Barsh, Russel, and James Henderson. *The Road: Indian Tribes and Political Liberty.* Berkeley: University of California Press, 1980.
Canby, William. *American Indian Law in a Nutshell.* St. Paul, MN: West Publishing Co., 1981.
Wilkinson, Charles F. *American Indians, Time, and the Law: Native Societies*

in a Modern Constitutional Democracy. New Haven, CT: Yale University Press, 1987.

TRUST, DOCTRINE OF

Since the nineteenth century, the U.S. government has considered itself to have a trust relationship with Native American nations within its borders. The trust relationship has been defined as the legal obligation of the United States to protect Native American lands and resources, as well as Indians' rights to self-government. In theory, this trust relationship is supposed to protect Indian interests; in practice, it has sometimes been a political and legal "cover" for exploitation of land and resources, as well as Indian people (*see* **Sovereignty; Wardship**).

The doctrine of a fiduciary or trust relationship toward Native Americans is said to have grown out of court decisions, the best-known of which is ***Cherokee Nation v. Georgia***, in which U.S. Supreme Court Chief Justice **John Marshall** held that Indian nations stood in U.S. law as wards to their federal guardian. In theory, according to Kiowa attorney Kirke Kickingbird (1983:6), trust responsibilities have been held to fall into three areas:

1. Protection of Indian trust property
2. Protection of the Indian right of self-government
3. Provision of social, medical, and educational services necessary for survival of individual members

Legal scholar Frank Pommersheim wrote that "it was in this soil of expansion and exploitation that federal Indian law developed and took root. This was a soil without constitutional loam. . . . The theory of the trust responsibility with the U.S. government as owner and trustee of Indian land, natural resources, and (trust) provider of many services is in direct conflict with any meaningful theory of tribal sovereignty" (1995: 38, 45). In other words, as the courts talk a measured sense of sovereignty for reservation residents, the government walks a potent form of colonialism through the "trust" doctrine.

Equally rootless in the loam of the **Constitution**, and equally inconsistent with any meaningful theory of Native American sovereignty, is the **plenary power** of Congress over Indian affairs, which evolved out of the Supreme Court's 1903 decision in ***Lone Wolf v. Hitchcock***. Because of its plenary power, U.S. courts in the twentieth century have held that Congress is the ultimate trustee in this relationship and has sole power to change it. The pervasive network of rules and regulations promulgated by Congress and administered by the Bureau of Indian Affairs and other agencies for the "protection" of Indians often has had an effect that diminishes the day-to-day operation of Native American sovereignty by subjecting nearly every move made by individual Indians to federal government approval. The nature of "protection" has always been defined by the government vis-à-vis its own interests with minimal native consultation. During the late 1880s, for example, the **Allotment Act** (or Dawes Act) was advanced as a means to "protect" (i.e., "civilize") American Indians. This form of "protection" cost Indians two-thirds of their collective land base over the next half-century.

Robert C. Coulter, executive director of the **Indian Law Resource Center**, and Steven B. Tullberg, a senior staff attorney at the center, have argued that "trust" status, as practiced by the U.S. government, has often been less than trustworthy:

Advocates of the trust theory have forgotten or overlooked the fact that the federal government itself initiated the destructive policies of Indian removal, allotment, termination and other wholesale denials of Indian rights. Through these policies and a host of other federal acts, the federal government has confiscated massive areas of Indian lands for its own use and that of its non-Indian citizenry. One looks in vain through the historical record for actions by the Supreme Court to protect Indians from these confiscatory actions. (1984: 188)

Legal scholar Felix S. Cohen reflected on the rather unusual status of Indian "trusts" in Anglo-American law:

In the white man's business world, a "trust" is likely to be a property of great value; the trustee is required to protect the trust property and to turn over all the profits of the enterprise to the beneficiaries of the trust. The trustee has no control over the beneficiaries' person. In the Indian's world, the same principles should apply; there is no legal basis for the common view that the Indian bureau may deal with Indian trust property as if it were the owner thereof, or use such power over lands to control Indian lives and thoughts. Unfortunately, administrators often find it convenient to forget their duties, which are lumped under the legal term "trusteeship," and to concentrate on their powers, which go by the name of "guardianship." (Cohen and Cohen 1960: 333)

Questions about governmental conduct toward Native American trust assets have continued. In 1995, an audit of funds being held in trust for Indians by the BIA could not account for $2.4 billion the BIA was supposed to be holding. The auditing firm, Arthur Andersen and Co., spent five years on its study and found trust accounts to be "a total mess." Of the 2,000 accounts the BIA was maintaining at the time, paperwork for 15 percent was found to be missing, leaving little or no trace of the money in them. These 2,000 accounts represent only money held by Indian groups (such as BIA-recognized Native American governments), not the 300,000 individual accounts maintained by the BIA, of which a complete audit would be prohibitively expensive.

FURTHER READING

"BIA Missing Money." *Native Americas* 13:1 (Spring 1996): 4.

Cohen, Felix, and Lucy Kramer Cohen. *The Legal Conscience: Selected Papers of Felix S. Cohen.* New Haven: Yale University Press, 1960.

Coulter, Robert C., and Steven B. Tullberg. "Indian Land Rights." In *The Aggressions of Civilization: Federal Indian Policy since the 1880s,* ed. Sandra L. Cadwalader and Vine Deloria, Jr. Philadelphia: Temple University Press, 1984.

Hall, G. *The Federal-Indian Trust Relationship.* Washington, DC: Institute for the Development of Indian Law, 1981.

Kickingbird, Kirke, Alexander Tallchief Skibine, and Lynn Kickingbird. *Indian Jurisdiction.* Washington, D.C.: Institute for the Development of Indian Law, 1983.

Pommersheim, Frank. *Braid of Feathers: American Indian Law and Contemporary Tribal Life.* Berkeley: University of California Press, 1995.

U

UNITED STATES EX REL. STANDING BEAR V. CROOK 25 F. Cas.
695 (C.C. Nebr. 1879) (No. 14,891)

United States ex rel. Standing Bear v. Crook was the first case to
establish that Indians had the rights of human beings under U.S. law
(with roots in English common law). For more description of the case
and the circumstances giving rise to it, see **Dundy, Elmer S.**, and
Standing Bear.

Judge Dundy wrote that he had "searched in vain for the semblance
of any authority justifying the commissioner [of Indian Affairs] in attempting to remove by force any Indians. . . . No fact exists, and nothing
has occurred. . . . to make it necessary or lawful to exercise such authority over them." Judge Dundy held:

1. That an Indian is a "person" within the meaning of the laws of the United
States and has, therefore, the rights to sue out a writ of *habeas corpus* in a federal
court, or before a federal judge, in all cases where he may be confined or in
custody under color of authority of the United States, or where he is restrained
of liberty in violation of the constitution or laws of the United States. . . .

2. That General George Crook . . . has custody of the relators. . . .

3. That no rightful authority exists for removing by force any of the relators
to the Indian Territory, as the respondent has been directed to do.

4. That the Indians possess the inherent right of expatriation, as well as the
more fortunate white race, and have the inalienable right to "life, liberty, and
the pursuit of happiness," so long as they obey the laws.

FURTHER READING

Prucha, Francis Paul, ed. *Documents of United States Indian Policy.* Lincoln: University of Nebraska Press, 1975.

UNITED STATES V. ADAIR 723 F.2d Cir. 1394 (1983), *cert. denied* 467 U.S. 1252 (1984)

Native American water rights, like hunting and fishing rights, survive the termination of a native land base, according to the federal courts in *United States v. Adair.* The question arose on the lands occupied by the Klamath reservation in Oregon. Most of the Klamaths' land was acquired by the U.S. Forest Service under the Klamath Termination Act, but individual Klamaths retained the right to hunt and fish in the area.

The Second Circuit Court of Appeals ruled that the Klamaths' water rights were recognized in a treaty signed in 1864 as carrying "a priority date of time immemorial." Therefore, the court ruled, the Klamaths continued to be entitled to "the amount of water necessary to support its hunting and fishing rights as currently exercised to maintain the livelihood of tribal members, not as these rights were exercised by the Tribe in 1864." Thus, while water rights remain after the termination of a Native American land base, they are diminished compared to rights under the Winters Doctrine (*see* **Winters v. United States**), which entitles Indians to water to suit present and potential uses.

UNITED STATES V. CREEK NATION 295 U.S. 103 (1935)

The U.S. Supreme Court ruled that treaty lands taken from the Creeks and later sold by the U.S. government due to a surveying error were an illegal "taking" without compensation under the **Fifth Amendment**. The error and resulting sale of land also were held to be a violation of the government's **trust** responsibility.

UNITED STATES V. KAGAMA 118 U.S. 375 (1886)

The Supreme Court enunciated a "superior position" of the federal government vis-à-vis Indian nations (*see* **plenary power**) as it upheld the **Major Crimes Act** (1885). The Court was upholding the federal **trust** responsibility against erosion by the states. The Court said that "the people of the states . . . are often [the Indians'] deadliest enemies." This case was the first Supreme Court decision to directly address the legality of federal jurisdiction over both Indians and non-Indians in **Indian Country**.

A year after the Major Crimes Act was passed, attorneys for Kagama argued that it was unconstitutional. The Supreme Court ruled that the commerce clause of the **Constitution** did not authorize the Congress to regulate the internal affairs of Indian nations and their members. However, the Court held that since the states had no legal authority over Indians living on reservations, the role of sovereign must be played by the United States. Native American conceptions of **sovereignty** were omitted from this legal formulation.

The facts of the case concerned two Indians, Kagama and Mahawaha, who killed another Indian on the Hupa reservation in California. They were arrested, tried, and convicted in federal court on grounds that the commerce clause of the Constitution gave the government jurisdiction on the Hupa reservation. The U.S. Supreme Court, following **John Marshall**'s opinions in *Cherokee Nation v. Georgia* and *Worcester v. Georgia*, held that Indian lands did not comprise foreign nations. "These Indian tribes *are* the wards of the nation," ruled the Court. "They are communities dependent on the United States. . . . From their very weaknesses and helplessness, so largely due to the course of dealing of the federal government with them and the treaties in which it has been promised, there arises the duty of protection, and with it the power." The Court also held that "[t]he Indians owe no allegiance to a state within which their reservation may be established, and the state gives them no protection." Justice Samuel Miller, writing for the Court majority, said that the government had always regarded native nations as semisovereign entities, "not as states, not as nations, but as separate people, with power of regulating their internal relations and thus not brought into the laws of the Union or the States within whose limits they resided." Kiowa attorney Kirke Kickingbird provided the following evaluation of *Kagama*'s legal legacy:

The decision in *Kagama* and the line of cases which flowed from it led to an overly broad and often destructive exercise of federal power in Indian affairs. In these decisions, the courts have placed no legally enforceable standards or criteria on the trustee. Instead, they have designated Congressional power in Indian affairs as "plenary," or almost absolute. (1983:20)

FURTHER READING

Kickingbird, Kirke, Alexander Tallchief Skibine, and Lynn Kickingbird. *Indian Jurisdiction*. Washington, DC: Institute for the Development of Indian Law, 1983.

UNITED STATES V. MAZURIE 419 U.S. 544 (1975)

In *United States v. Mazurie*, Indian **sovereignty** was tested by a non-Indian who operated a bar on Indian land in the face of a Native American liquor-licensing law that held his business to be illegal. The Supreme Court in this decision affirmed native nations' sovereign powers over both their members and their territory. Because of the Congress's **plenary power** regarding Indian legislation, the Court held that it could legally delegate its powers to regulate distribution of alcoholic beverages to a Native American government.

The Mazuries owned and operated the Blue Bull Bar on a ten-acre tract of privately owned (fee) land on the Wind River Reservation at Fort Washakie. About 20 percent of the reservation is owned in fee, giving it a characteristic **checkerboard** ownership pattern that results in problems with legal enforcement and jurisdiction. The federal law at issue here prohibited the sale of liquor in **Indian Country**, which is defined by this law as "all land within the limits of any Indian reservation under the jurisdiction of the United States government, notwithstanding the issuance of any patent . . . [except on] fee-patented lands in non-Indian communities." The Mazuries contended that the phrase "non-Indian communities" was unconstitutionally vague. The statute did not specify what percentage of population comprised a "non-Indian community." The Supreme Court upheld the Wind River Reservation's authority to license liquor traders within the reservation, regardless of their race.

In this decision, Indian nations were described as "unique aggregations possessing attributes of sovereignty over both their members and their territory." Furthermore, the Court held that Indian governments have "independent authority over matters that affect . . . internal and social relations of tribal life," including the distribution of alcoholic beverages.

While the Supreme Court has often denied Indian jurisdiction over non-Indians (most notably three years later in *Oliphant v. Suquamish*), the majority opinion in this case held that an Indian government had a right to close a non-Indian's bar. The opinion cited *Williams v. Lee* as precedent indicating that Indian governments may regulate the activities of non-Indians "insofar as concern[s] their transactions on a reservation with Indians."

UNITED STATES V. MCBRATNEY 104 U.S. 621 (1882)

The Supreme Court held that Colorado, not the federal government, had jurisdiction over the murder of a non-Indian by another non-Indian on the Ute reservation. Thus state law applied to a crime by a non-Indian against another non-Indian on a reservation; the Native American courts were denied jurisdiction. According to legal scholar William C. Canby, Jr., "The *McBratney* decision is subject to severe criticism on a number of grounds, not the least of which is that it seems utterly inconsistent in principle with *Worcester v. Georgia* (1832)" (1981: 101). In that case, Chief Justice **John Marshall** held that state law had no effect in **Indian Country**. Despite its contradiction with precedent, the *McBratney* doctrine was upheld in *Draper v. United States*,

164 U.S. 240 (1896), and was further developed in ***Oliphant v. Suqua-mish*** (1978).

McBratney, a European American, killed Thomas Casey, another Caucasian, on the Ute reservation. McBratney was arrested and convicted in federal court before he moved to have the judgment dismissed on the grounds that the court lacked jurisdiction. The Supreme Court supported McBratney's petition, basing its judgment in part on the Ute Treaty of 1868, which had described the reservation on which the murder took place as having been set aside for the Utes' "absolute and undisturbed" use.

The Court then examined the legal instruments that created Colorado as a territory, which excluded state jurisdiction over Indian lands unless their occupants gave permission. Finally, the Supreme Court examined the Colorado Statehood Act, which contained no language excluding Indian lands. The Court's opinion followed the statehood act's provisions, holding that the lack of an exclusion for Indian lands meant that the Ute reservation was within the state in cases related to its non-Indian citizens.

The *McBratney* ruling is regarded as pivotal because it marked the first time the Supreme Court had approved the use of state law in Indian Country. Additionally, this decision was pronounced in a vacuum of legal support; the Indian Country Crimes Act had prescribed federal jurisdiction in such a case.

FURTHER READING

Canby, William. *American Indian Law in a Nutshell.* Sr. Paul, MN: West Publishing Co., 1981.

UNITED STATES V. MCGOWAN 302 U.S. 535 (1938)

In *United States v. McGowan*, the Supreme Court elaborated on ***United States v. Sandoval*** (1913), which created a legal basis for recognition of American Indian communities that had not been sanctioned by **treaty** with the United States. This case held that the Reno Indian colony in Nevada was **Indian Country** because it was located on land set aside by the federal government for Indian occupancy. The Court held that the Reno Indians had been "afforded the same protection by the government as that given other Indians in other settlements known as 'reservations.' "

In this case, automobiles had been seized in accordance with a law that allowed confiscation of personal property used to bring liquor into Indian Country. In the majority opinion, Justice Hugo Black said that no legal distinctions existed between an "Indian colony" such as Reno, which had been purchased beginning in 1917, and "Indian Country."

The liquor law was held to apply at Reno, and the automobiles remained impounded.

UNITED STATES V. NICE 241 U.S. 591 (1916)

When allotted land began to be granted in fee simple early in the twentieth century, legal questions arose as to whether state or federal law applied on lands that were no longer classified as being in **trust** status. In *United States v. Nice*, the U.S. Supreme Court held that state jurisdiction applied, but that it was "to be taken with some implied limitations, and not literally." The Supreme Court also ruled in *United States v. Nice* that Indian citizenship was not incompatible with the integrity of Native American governments or earlier U.S. rulings establishing federal protection for Indian lands and peoples.

UNITED STATES V. ROGERS 45 U.S. (4 How.) 567 (1846)

United States v. Rogers was an early test of Indian jurisdiction in which Rogers, a Caucasian, was accused of murdering another European American on **Cherokee** territory. Both men were members of the Cherokee Nation by adoption. This case was later cited in *United States v. Kagama* as the Supreme Court defined what became known as the Political Question Doctrine. Under this doctrine, certain actions of Congress are held to be political rather than legal in nature and thus not questionable under judicial review. The Political Question Doctrine has often been applied to the presumed **plenary power** of Congress to legislate Indian affairs. Because it has been held to be a political rather than a judicial doctrine, plenary power has never been challenged by the courts.

At issue in *United States v. Rogers* was whether federal jurisdiction applied in the aforementioned murder case. The Supreme Court ruled that it did. The Supreme Court claimed that non-Indians who had been adopted into an Indian nation (and who carried dual citizenship) fell under the jurisdiction of the federal courts. In its finding, the Court gave no legal justification, but simply asserted the Political Question Doctrine:

It would be useless at this date to inquire whether the principle adopted [the Political Question Doctrine] is just or not, or to speak of the manner in which the power claimed was in many instances exercised. . . . But, had it been otherwise, and were the right and propriety of exercising this power now open to question, yet, it is a question for the law-making and political departments of the government, and not for the judicial. It is our duty to expound and execute the law as we find it.

FURTHER READING

Kickingbird, Kirke, Alexander Tallchief Skibine, and Lynn Kickingbird. *Indian*

Jurisdiction. Washington, DC: Institute for the Development of Indian Law, 1983.

UNITED STATES V. SANDOVAL 231 U.S. 28 (1913)

The U.S. Supreme Court legally superimposed U.S. Indian law on the New Mexico **Pueblos**, who had held their lands in fee simple from Spanish land grants before the United States assumed authority in the area. Thus the Indians' title had not been heretofore "recognized" under U.S. legal authority. Specifically, the Court upheld a ban on liquor in the Pueblos, defining them as part of **Indian Country** for U.S. legal authority. In so doing, the Supreme Court declared that the United States now had a "**trust** responsibility" for the Pueblos and that federal laws regarding Indians generally would be enforceable on Pueblo land. The Supreme Court's rationale for extending U.S. Indian law to the Pueblos was couched in ethnocentric language that reflected popular assumptions about American Indians at the time:

The people of the Pueblos, although sedentary rather than nomadic in their inclinations and disposed to peace and industry, are nevertheless Indians in race, culture, and domestic government . . . adhering to primitive modes of life, largely influenced by superstition and fetishism, and chiefly governed according to the crude customs inherited from their ancestors. They are essentially a simple, uninformed, and inferior people.

UNITED STATES V. SHOSHONE TRIBE 304 U.S. 111 (1938)

In *United States v. Shoshone Tribe*, the U.S. Supreme Court ruled that an Indian nation's right of occupancy includes timber and mineral resources if the landholding is "recognized" by the federal government. Therefore, the illegal taking of such rights must be compensated under the **Fifth Amendment**. This case clarified issues raised earlier in *United States v. Creek Nation* (1935).

This case arose after the U.S. government relocated an Arapaho band on Shoshone land in violation of a treaty with the Shoshone. The government agreed to compensation for the land, but argued that it should not have to pay for timber and minerals. The issue before the Court was whether a native nation's right of occupancy included minerals and timber. The Court held that "[T]he right of occupancy [is] as sacred as the fee." For the government to give away or otherwise mismanage the land "would be not an exercise of guardianship or management, but confiscation."

UNITED STATES V. SIOUX NATION 100 S. Ct. 2716 (1980)

The Supreme Court ruled that an act of Congress passed in 1877 asserting U.S. title to the **Black Hills** region of South Dakota was an illegal expropriation within the meaning of the **Fifth Amendment**. The Court also ruled that the **Sioux** were due compensation of $17.5 million for the seizure of the 7.3 million acres of land, plus roughly $100 million interest, a figure that had risen to more than $300 million by the middle 1990s. The Court held that

the 1877 Act effected a taking of tribal property, property which had been set aside for the exclusive occupation of the Sioux by the Fort Laramie Treaty of 1868. That taking implied an obligation on the part of the government to make just compensation to the Sioux Nation, and that obligation, including an award of interest, must now, at last, be paid.

The Black Hills, called *paha sapa* ("hills that are black") by the Sioux, were included as reservation land under the **Fort Laramie Treaty** of 1868. An expedition led by George Armstrong Custer found rich deposits of gold and other minerals in the Black Hills during 1874 and sparked a rush of non-Indian settlement. The 1877 act of Congress virtually confiscated the area, contravening the treaty. In 1920, the Sioux brought a complaint before the U.S. Court of Claims, which upheld the 1877 act of Congress. After the **Indian Claims Commission** was founded in 1946, the Sioux sought to reintroduce the claim, but it was barred because of the earlier review as a matter of *res judicata*. In 1978, the Sioux obtained passage of a special act of Congress that allowed them to bring the case to the Court of Claims again to be argued on its merits despite the earlier judgment of *res judicata*. In *United States v. Sioux Nation*, the Supreme Court held that the United States had acted in bad faith in the matter, vindicating the Siouxs' decades of legal perseverance.

Following the ruling in *United States v. Sioux Nation*, a sharp debate continued among the Sioux nations as to whether to accept the monetary settlement or to continue to press for return of land in the Black Hills, which are widely held by Sioux to be sacred. Although they now include a mountain-sized sculpture of four U.S. presidents and a major national park, the Black Hills have never been legally ceded to the United States.

FURTHER READING

Lazarus, Edward. *Black Hills, White Justice: The Sioux Nation versus the United States, 1775 to the Present*. New York: HarperCollins, 1991.

UNITED STATES V. WASHINGTON 384 F. Supp. 312 (1974), 520 F.2d 676 (9th Cir. 1975), *cert. denied* 423 U.S. 1086 (1976)

On February 12, 1974, U.S. District Court Judge **George Boldt** ruled that Indians were entitled to an opportunity to catch as many as half the fish returning to off-reservation sites that had been the "usual and accustomed places" when treaties were signed with Puget Sound Indian nations in the 1850s. The case became an object of major controversy between Indians and commercial and sports fishermen.

After intense study of the treaties and their historical milieu, Judge Boldt interpreted the guarantee in the **Treaty of Medicine Creek** of 1854 that Indians could fish "in common with all citizens of the territory" to mean that the catch could be equally shared. Fish caught at reservation sites, on which Indians have an exclusive right to fish, were not to be counted in this apportionment. The state's right to regulate off-reservation fishing by Indians at their "usual and accustomed places" was limited by Judge Boldt to that which is "reasonable and necessary for conservation . . . the perpetuation of a run or species of fish."

Lost in the fray were a number of small, landless western Washington native communities that were not "recognized" by the federal government and therefore were not entitled to participate in the federally mandated solution. A few such communities, such as the Upper Skagit and Sauk-Suiattle, were recognized after the Boldt decision. A number of others remained in legal limbo with no fishing rights under federal law. While the commercial interests raged, the Indians were catching nothing close to the 50 percent allowed by the Boldt ruling; in 1974 they caught between 7 and 8 percent, in 1975 between 11 and 12 percent, in 1976 between 13 and 25 percent, and in 1977, 17 percent, depending on who did the counting, the Indians or the state.

Among state officials during the middle and late 1970s, a backlash to Indian rights formed that became the nucleus for a nationwide non-Indian campaign to abrogate the treaties. Washington State Attorney General (later U.S. Senator) Slade Gorton called Indians "**supercitizens**" with "special rights" and proposed that constitutional equilibrium be reestablished not by open state violation of the treaties (Boldt had outlawed that), but by purchasing the Indians' fishing rights. The Indians, who had been listening to offers of money for Indian resources for a century, flatly refused Gorton's offer. To them, the selling of fishing rights would have been tantamount to **termination**.

FURTHER READING

American Friends Service Committee, Comp. *Uncommon Controversy: A Report on Fishing Rights of the Muckleshoot, Puyallup, and Nisqually Indians.* Seattle: University of Washington Press, 1970.

Barsh, Russel L. *The Washington Fishing Rights Controversy: An Economic Critique.* Seattle: University of Washington School of Business Administration, 1977.

Brown, Bruce. *Mountain in the Clouds.* New York: Simon & Schuster, 1982.

Miller, Bruce J. "The Press, the Boldt Decision, and Indian-White Relations." *American Indian Culture and Research Journal* 17:2 (1993): 75–98.

UNITED STATES V. WHEELER 435 U.S. 313, 98 S. Ct. 1079, 55 L. Ed. 2d 303 (1978)

In *United States v. Wheeler*, the U.S. Supreme Court ruling held that a Native American nation has inherent jurisdiction over its own members, and that such jurisdiction does not derive from the federal government. Thus an Indian who was convicted of a crime in a federal court could also have been convicted in a Native American court of a lesser, but similar offense without violating the U.S. **Constitution**'s prohibition of double jeopardy because the federal government and native nations are separate sovereigns.

Justice Stewart's opinion in this case supported the concept of Native American **sovereignty** at great length, with considerable historical annotation. It distinguished Native American communities from states and local non-Indian governments, which derive their powers from the U.S. government. Stewart found that the Indian nations possess a third kind of sovereignty. Stewart's opinion resembled earlier reasoning in **Talton v. Mayes** (1896) and rejected the court's opinion in **United States v. Kagama** (1886) that only two kinds of sovereignty—federal and state—could be asserted in the United States.

UNITED STATES V. WINANS 198 U.S. 371 (1905)

In a case that was key to many treaty-rights struggles later in the twentieth century, the U.S. Supreme Court held that a treaty may reserve a Native American nation's right to hunt or fish in "usual and accustomed places" off reservation. The Court also defined a treaty not as a grant of rights to Indians, but as a grant from them, "a reservation of those [rights] not granted." This ruling was a key component, for example, of Judge **George H. Boldt**'s 1974 ruling in **United States v. Washington** that upheld fishing rights of several Native American nations in the Pacific Northwest.

UPLAND YUMAN POLITICAL AND LEGAL TRADITIONS

The Upland Yumans of Arizona are a prime example of how modern Native American political structures have obscured more traditional ones. Upland Yuman is a linguistic categorization, referring to peoples known today as Yavapais, Hualapais (Walapais), and Havasupais. The identification of three Upland Yuman "tribes" is misleading, for such tribal structures did not aboriginally exist.

Before 1870, Upland Yumans organized themselves into small local bands, perhaps twenty to thirty members each, structured around several interrelated extended families. Their combined traditional ranges covered almost 30,000 square miles in what is now northwestern and central Arizona, and estimates suggest a total population between 3,500 and 5,000. To best exploit their fluctuating desert environment, aboriginal Upland Yumans maintained a hunting and gathering economy, supplemented in places with small-scale agriculture. From late fall to early spring, local bands gathered and roasted agave and hunted wild game. During the remainder of the year, the bands split into even smaller gathering camps that relocated frequently as they followed the ripening sequence of wild plant foods.

The local band was the largest real social and political unit, but its structure and function were rather informal. Postmarital residence shifts, seasonal adjustments, and other factors brought frequent changes in band membership. Exogamy rules were kin based, not group based. Local territorial boundaries were more a function of use area than of discrete political units. Indeed, ties of kinship, affinity, and friendship, which allowed for much cooperation between local bands—in warfare, resource sharing, and ceremonials—had greater significance than strict band affiliations.

The broad Upland Yuman social field of interrelated local bands was interrupted by one fundamental reality: Yavapai-Pai enmity. At least in the eighteenth and nineteenth centuries, Upland Yuman bands in northwestern Arizona, collectively identified as Pai, generally were at odds with all other Upland Yumans, essentially those located further south and east now collectively known as Yavapai. This was not an enduring war between two peoples. Rather, it was a series of blood feuds between individual local bands. Neighboring Yavapais and Pais sometimes intermarried and shared resources; at other times, when friendship broke down, they staged raids and counterraids with the primary intent of killing each other. Oral traditions tell how a children's quarrel escalated into hostilities between adults and caused the Upland Yumans to separate into two peoples—Yavapai and Pai. Relations varied from band to band, but by the nineteenth century a buffer zone of unoccupied land stretched between Yavapai and Pai territories, Pais referred to Yavapais as *Jiwha'* (the enemy), and non-Indians entering the region identified the two as separate "tribes."

Yavapais and Pais did recognize territorial affiliations beyond the local band. Besides noting their local band membership, they could identify themselves according to larger geographical areas. For example, an individual from the Peach Springs region in Pai territory was Yi Kwat Pa'a (Peach Springs People), and someone from flat-topped Mingus Mountain in Yavapai lands was Walkeyanyanyepa (Pine Tableland People). Anthropologists have identified these geographical affiliations as regional bands, each consisting of several local bands, but they are best understood as regional categories. They denote residence in a region, but do not imply political or social structures. There were even broader categories, today sometimes called subtribes, but, again, without social or political function. Yavapais actually recognized themselves as four peoples: Yavapé, Wipukepa, Tolkepaya, and Kwevkepaya; they did not call each other Yavapai, which probably comes from the Yuman word *nyavkopai* (people living to the east).

Aboriginal Upland Yuman leadership was an informal affair. No enduring titles, authority, or territories were officially associated with Yavapai and Pai leaders. Rather, leaders were leaders because others chose to follow them, heeded their advice, and supported their decisions. A local band tended to coalesce around a single influential man noted for his bravery, wisdom, and speaking ability. This headman led through the force of his personality, his ability to forge **consensus** on communal issues, and the quality of his speeches. Headmen had no real power to exact allegiance, obedience, or tribute. Instead, they regularly delivered long and loud harangues to their local bands, dispensing advice on such matters as food production, work ethics, and selection of campsites. A headman also acted as spokesman for his band when dealing with outsiders, though other distinguished fighters could lead war parties. The role of headman was not a hereditary position, but a headman's son, if he possessed the necessary personality traits, usually had the inside track to succeed his father.

Traditionally, a headman's authority rarely extended beyond his immediate camp. When several local bands came together to exploit rich concentrations of wild food or in time of war, they may have recognized the preeminence of one headman, but after they broke up, that headman could hardly have maintained sway over the scattered population. Indeed, a headman's influence over his own local band must have temporarily diminished each year when the members dispersed into summer gathering camps. In the 1860s and 1870s, U.S. Army officers and Indian agents misidentified Upland Yuman headmen as "chiefs" and "head chiefs," at times presenting headmen with official papers identifying them as such. Certain headmen, such as the Pai leader Cherum and Kwevkepaya leader Delshe, gained prominence for their ability to negotiate with or direct war parties against U.S. forces, but their leadership still hung on personal influence. There were no head chiefs, subchiefs, or tribal councils with the formal authority to speak or sign treaties for large segments of the Yavapai or Pai populations.

Upland Yuman local bands, lacking formal political structures and institutions of coercive power, did not develop an extensive system of law and enforcement. Cultural taboos warned against certain practices considered dangerous or unhealthy, such as eating fish and marriage between close cousins. A third party, often a headman, might try to adjudicate a dispute between individuals, but had no power to enforce a settlement. Potentially divisive social issues—for example, control and use of land or the taking of human life—played out along the lines of kinship that defined Yavapai and Pai society.

Land was the source of life, and local bands claimed ownership, meaning exclusive use and occupancy, of local resource areas. They defined their territories by natural features such as hills and springs, placed rock cairns along boundaries, and drove out unauthorized trespassers. However, because children typically developed use rights in both of their parents' natal band areas and because intermarriage and friendship connected many families from different bands, most individuals had ties to most local bands. This meant that Pai families could hunt game and gather wild plants in almost all regions of Pai territory, although in some cases it was necessary to request permission beforehand. Similar arrangements developed within Yavapai lands. Farmland was a different matter. Some Yavapai and Pai families planted crops along springs and streams in late spring and returned in late summer to harvest. Fertile areas were few, and individual families often claimed the best garden spots for their own private use.

The taking of life also brought kin involvement. If an enemy or other foreigner killed an Upland Yuman, the victim's relatives were obligated to seek vengeance. This tradition helped perpetuate the many Yavapai-Pai blood feuds. Among nonenemies, similar obligations existed. If a Pai killed another Pai, or a Yavapai another Yavapai, even accidentally, the killer's relatives needed to offer a buckskin or other items to the victim's family to prevent retaliation. However, if a murderer became a repeat offender, relatives of the victims would request and typically receive permission from the murderer's family to kill him. In this way, local bands dealt with particularly vicious characters. Other offenses, including rape and theft, also required reparations to the victimized family to avoid retaliatory attacks or destruction of property. In marital conflicts it was best to leave an adulterous spouse; a man might get away with beating or disfiguring his disloyal wife, but killing a spouse would lead to a feud with his or her relatives and probably to retribution.

An invasion of non-Indians destroyed traditional Upland Yuman organization. In the 1860s, European-American miners and ranchers invaded Yavapai and Pai lands. The local bands resisted militarily for several years, but the U.S. Army eventually subdued and confined them at military posts. Devastated by warfare, hunger, disease, and dislocation, local band structures gradually disappeared. Traditional headmen continued to provide leadership, but found their authority undermined by U.S. Army officers and government agents, the new arbiters of power and justice.

In the 1880s, U.S. President Chester Arthur ordered the creation of two reservations in Pai lands. The Hualapai Reservation, misleadingly named for one Pai regional band, Mat Whala Pa'a (Pine Mountain People), was for the western Pais. They had fought U.S. soldiers, endured mass relocation to the Colorado River Indian Reservation in 1874, and fled back to their homelands the following spring. The Havasupai Reservation contained eastern Pais, primarily from the regional band Havsooa Pa'a (Blue Green Water People), who lived in and around what is now Grand Canyon National Park and had avoided most of the fighting with non-Indians. U.S. Army officers were in the habit of identifying two "tribes" of Pais, and the creation of separate reservations perpetuated this misunderstanding. In the 1930s, under the provisions of the **Indian Reorganization Act**, the two divisions of Pais accepted nontraditional forms of government. The Hualapai Tribe and Havasupai Tribe adopted separate constitutions, elected tribal councils, and gained official federal recognition.

In the late 1890s, Yavapais wandered back to traditional homelands, ending their long exile at the San Carlos Apache Reservation. They squatted near their old farmlands, performed wage labor for European-American farmers and mine owners, and eventually received scattered reservation lands from the federal government. As with the Pais, the reservation system and the Indian Reorganization Act created new political structures for the Yavapais. The Fort McDowell Reservation and the Prescott Yavapai Reservation each have a constitution and tribal council; the Camp Verde, Middle Verde, and Clarkdale reservations together elect a single council under their constitution.

Throughout the twentieth century, the Upland Yumans—now the Yavapais, Hualapais, and Havasupais—were embroiled in legal conflicts with the Arizona government and with private corporations. Besides winning large monetary settlements from the federal government in **Indian Claims Commission** cases, which sought payment for traditional lands unfairly and illegally taken by non-Indians, the tribes fought in court and in Congress to defend the integrity of their reservations. Since its creation in 1904, Yavapais at the Fort McDowell Reservation have resisted forced removal, struggled to secure water rights, and blocked the construction of Orme Dam, which would have left the reservation under water. In the 1990s, Yavapais faced politically motivated legal challenges to their gaming casinos at Fort McDowell and Prescott. The Havasupais lobbied successfully to have Congress, in 1975, restore 185,000 acres to their reservation and grant them exclusive use of an additional 95,300 acres in Grand Canyon National Park. In 1990, though, they lost their federal district court case that sought to prevent uranium mining on national forest lands they consider sacred though not a part of their reservation. Ironically, in a general push to destroy Native American traditions, the federal government encouraged the creation of nontraditional governments through which the Upland Yuman tribes, like many others, continue to defend their rights and interests.

FURTHER READING

Gifford, Edward W. "Northeastern and Western Yavapai." *University of California Publications in American Archaeology and Ethnology* 34:4 (1936): 247–354.

———. "The Southeastern Yavapai." *University of California Publications in American Archaeology and Ethnology* 29:3 (1932): 177–252.

Herr, David A., ed. *Yavapai Indians.* New York: Garland Publishing, 1974.

Kroeber, A. L., ed. *Walapai Ethnography.* Memoirs of the American Anthropological Association 42 (1935).

Martin, John F. "From Judgment to Land Restoration: The Havasupai Land Claims Case." In *Irredeemable America: The Indians' Estate and Land Claims,* ed. Imre Sutton, 271–300. Albuquerque: University of New Mexico Press, 1985.

———. "Havasupai Political Leadership and Structure." *Arizona State Anthropological Research Papers* (1987).

Spier, Leslie. "Havasupai Ethnography." *Anthropological Papers of the American Museum of Natural History* 39:3 (1928): 81–392.

TIMOTHY BRAATZ

V

VITORIA, FRANCISCO DE (1486–1546)

As one of the first European experts to advise the king of Spain on the nature of aboriginal title in the New World, the theologian Francisco de Vitoria in 1532 wrote in *De Indis et Juri Belli Relectiones* that "the aborigines undoubtedly had true dominion in both public and private matters . . . neither their princes nor private persons could be despoiled of their property on the ground of their not being true owners." Spain could not, therefore, simply assert ownership of lands occupied by aboriginal people; title by discovery could be justified only if the land was ownerless.

In Vitoria's opinion, Spain could legally acquire title to Native American land in the New World by conquest resulting from a "just" war, unless the Indians surrendered their title by "free and voluntary choice." A "just war" was precisely defined. War was not to be undertaken on a whim or solely to dispossess the aboriginal inhabitants. As **Felix Cohen** summarized Vitoria's opinions:

He concluded that the Spaniards' discovery of the Indians did not give the Spaniards any right to Indian property any more than the Indians' discovery of the Spaniards gave the Indians a right to Spanish property. And finally he reached the conclusion . . . a rather courageous conclusion for a professor of moral theology in the University of Salamanca to reach, that since the Pope's authority was purely spiritual . . . the Pope could not, even if he wanted to, bestow any title to land upon the Spanish crown. (1960: 163–164)

This doctrine, at least in theory, became the general definition of the **Doctrine of Discovery** by which the taking of aboriginal land would be justified for the next four centuries in both Spanish and U.S. legal practice. The **treaty**-making procedures of the U.S. government originally stemmed from Vitoria's 1532 opinion, at least in theory. In practice, treaties were sometimes fraudulent, and wars were undertaken for less than "just" cause.

FURTHER READING

Cohen, Felix, and Lucy Kramer Cohen. *The Legal Conscience: Selected Papers of Felix S. Cohen.* New Haven: Yale University Press, 1960.
Vitoria, Francisco de. *De Indis et Juri Belli Relectiones.* Trans. John Pawley Bate; ed. Ernest Nys. Washington, DC: Carnegie Institution, 1917. Reprint. Dobbs Ferry, NY: Oceana Press, 1964.

W

WAMPUM, LEGAL ROLE

Wampum are strings or patterns of quahog and periwinkle seashells, cut and formed into beads and strings, that were used by many American Indians in the Northeast to preserve accounts of history, to conduct diplomacy, and to complete some commercial transactions. Although the use of wampum as "money" has been emphasized by some historians, its other uses were probably more important in history. Nearly every important treaty negotiated in the eighteenth century was sealed with the presentation of wampum belts. The shells that comprised the belts were harvested and traded to inland Native American nations on the coast.

Peace among the formerly antagonistic **Iroquois** nations was procured and maintained through the Haudenosaunees' Great Law of Peace (*Kaianerekowa*), which was passed from generation to generation by use of wampum, a form of symbols (written communication) that outlined a complex system of checks and balances between nations and sexes. A complete oral recitation of the Great Law can take several days. The wampum belts, complex designs of purple (or sometimes black) and white shells, acted to prompt the memory of a speaker.

Under the Iroquois Great Law, the blood feud was outlawed and replaced by a Condolence Ceremony. Under the new law, when a person killed someone, the grieving family could forgo the option of exacting clan revenge (the taking of the life of the murderer or a member of the murderer's clan). Instead, the bereaved family could accept twenty strings of wampum from the slayer's family (ten for the dead person and ten for the life of the murderer himself). If a woman was killed, the price was thirty wampum strings. William Penn described some aspects of the Iroquois Condolence Ceremony. He noted that when someone killed a "woman they pay double" (the wampum) since "she breeds children which men cannot" (Dunn 2: 448, 452–453).

In 1612, John Smith of Virginia visited the Susquehannocks in the northern regions of the Chesapeake Bay. There he encountered the use of wampum and found hints of the existence of the Iroquois Confederacy. During the course of their meeting, the Susquehannocks implored Smith to defend them against the "Atquanahucke, Massawomecke and other people [that] inhabit the river of Cannida." The Susquehannocks draped "a chaine of white beads (waighing at least 6 or 7 pound) about" Smith's neck while reciting an "oration of love" (Barbour 1: 232).

The **Cherokees** used wampum in a ceremony meant to provide for the poor. During a special war dance, each warrior was called on to recount the taking of his first scalp. During the ceremony, anyone with something to spare, according to Henry Timberlake, "a string of wampum, piece of [silver] plate, wire, paint, lead" (Cameron 1967: 37–38), heaped the goods on a blanket or animal skin that had been placed on the ground. Afterwards, the collection was divided among the poor of the community, with a share reserved for the musicians who had provided entertainment during the ceremony.

FURTHER READING

Barbour, Philip L., ed. *The Complete Works of John Smith.* Vol. 1. Chapel Hill: University of North Carolina Press, 1986.

Barreiro, Jose. "Return of the Wampum." *Northeast Indian Quarterly* 7:1 (Spring 1990): 8–20.

Cameron, Kenneth W. *The Works of Samuel Peters of Hebron, Connecticut.* Hartford: Transcendental Books, 1967.

Dunn, Richard S., and Mary M. Dunn, eds. *The Papers of William Penn.* Vol. 2. Philadelphia: University of Pennsylvania Press, 1981–1987.

Hill, Richard. "Oral Memory of the Haudenosaunee: Views of the Two-Row Wampum." *Northeast Indian Quarterly* 7:1 (Spring 1990): 21–30.

Jacobs, Wilbur. "Wampum: The Protocol of Indian Diplomacy." *William and Mary Quarterly,* 3rd ser., 4:3 (October 1949): 596–604.

Jemison, G. Peter. "Sovereignty and Treaty Rights We Remember." *St. Thomas Law Review* 7 (1995).

Mann, Barbara. "The Fire at Onondaga: Wampum as Proto-writing." *Akwesasne Notes,* n.s. 1:1 (Spring 1995): 40–48.

Williams, Robert A., Jr. "Linking Arms Together: Multicultural Constitutionalism in a North American Indigenous Vision of Law and Peace." *California Law Review* 82 (1994).

WARDSHIP

"Wardship," in American Indian law and policy, refers to a legal doctrine, said to be based on opinions by U.S. Supreme Court Chief Justice **John Marshall**, that Native Americans live in "dependent domestic nations" and are therefore wards of the federal government. The Bureau of Indian Affairs was initially established to hold Indians' land and resources "in **trust**." Wardship status rationalized the establishment of Indian reservations and schools to assimilate Native Americans into mainstream U.S. culture.

The concept of wardship also lay behind the storage of thousands of Native American skeletal remains and burial artifacts in many federal and state research institutions (see **Repatriation**). The idea of Native American **sovereignty** in modern times has been developed in large part in opposition to wardship doctrines. Indians reacted to a social-control system that was so tight that in many cases (for example, if a will affected the status of allotted land) individual actions of Native American people were subject to approval by the secretary of the interior.

The assertion of states' rights over native territory in the Southeast provided the legal grist for a 1832 Supreme Court decision written by Chief Justice John Marshall. In *Worcester v. Georgia*, Justice Marshall wrote that inhabitants of native nations had assumed a relationship of "pupilage" (or wardship) in their relations with the United States. Using this doctrine, which has no constitutional basis, the executive branch of the U.S. government, principally through the Bureau of Indian Affairs, has created a superstructure of policies and programs that have had a vast impact on individual Native Americans and their governments. Through the use of the **plenary power** of Congress, such policies as allotment divested much of the Indian estate between 1854 and 1934.

A concept of wardship also has been used since the mid-nineteenth century to construct for American Indians a cradle-to-grave social-control system that was described during the mid-twentieth century by legal scholar **Felix Cohen**:

[T]he question of whether Indians are wards under federal guardianship has been squarely raised in a series of test cases, in which . . . the courts have held that Indians are not wards under guardianship, but on the contrary are full citizens of the United States. (1960: 328)

While Chief Justice Marshall's opinions have been used as a legal rationale for government policies that have treated American Indians as "wards," "[t]here is nothing," according to Robert T. Coulter, executive director of the **Indian Law Resource Center**, "in the rulings of the Marshall Court [that] even remotely suggested that the United States could unilaterally impose a guardian-ward relationship on Indians, that it held trust title to Indian lands, or that, as trustee, it could dispose of lands without Indian consent" (Coulter and Tullberg 1984: 199).

Wardship as historically practiced by the Bureau of Indian Affairs differs markedly from the legal status of non-Indian "wards." Under most conditions, wardship is viewed as a temporary condition, with established standards for cession. Civil guardianship and custody law must allow people who have been deprived of their civil rights means of regaining them in accordance with the due-process clause. As developed by the BIA, however, Indian "wardship" has no standard for cession and no ending date. An Indian is defined as a "ward" regardless of his or her accomplishments or other actions, as the object of a policy that may have misinterpreted Marshall's intent.

FURTHER READING

Barsh, Russel, and James Henderson. *The Road: Indian Tribes and Political Liberty*. Berkeley: University of California Press, 1980.

Cohen, Felix. *The Legal Conscience: Selected Papers of Felix S. Cohen*. Ed. Lucy Kramer Cohen. New Haven, CT: Yale University Press, 1960.

Coulter, Robert T., and Steven M. Tullberg. "Indian Land Rights." In *The Aggressions of Civilization*, ed. Sandra L. Cadwallader and Vine Deloria, Jr. Philadelphia: Temple University Press, 1984, pp. 185–214.

WASHINGTON CENTENNIAL ACCORD (1989)

After decades of costly and acrimonious litigation over fishing rights between the state of Washington and Indian communities within its borders, both parties in 1989 celebrated the state's centennial by signing the Washington Centennial Accord, which pledged respect for Native American **sovereignty**. Each state government agency in Washington is directed by this accord to develop a government-to-government relationship with Indian nations. The accord read, in part:

Each party to this accord respects the sovereignty of the other. The respective sovereignty of the state and each respective tribe provide paramount authority for that party to exist and to govern. The parties share in their relationship particular respect for the values and cultures represented by tribal governments. Further, the parties share a desire for a complete accord between the state of Washington and federally recognized tribes in Washington respecting a full government-to-government relationship and will work with all state and tribal governments to achieve such an Accord.

See also **Boldt, George;** *United States v. Washington* (1974); **Year of Reconciliation, South Dakota** (1990).

WASHINGTON V. CONFEDERATED TRIBES OF THE COLVILLE INDIAN RESERVATION 447 U.S. 134 (1980)

Washington v. Confederated Tribes of the Colville Indian Reservation set legal rights of states to tax sales on Indian reservations. According to this decision, only a sale from a resident of a reservation to another resident could not be taxed by the states. All other transactions, even Indian to Indian (if not resident of the reservation in question), were held to be taxable.

In this case, the Supreme Court held that the **Federal Preemption Doctrine** did not apply. The majority opinion said that although acts of Congress have maintained a concern with fostering Indian self-government, "none goes so far as to grant tribal enterprises, selling goods to non-members, an artificial competitive advantage over all other businesses in the state."

Washington State, which collects no individual income taxes, has enacted some of the highest tobacco and alcohol taxes in the United States. Since the 1960s, several Indian communities in the state had used their federal status to sell cigarettes without state taxes, particularly in the urbanized areas around Puget Sound.

WASHINGTON V. WASHINGTON STATE COMMERCIAL PASSENGER FISHING VESSEL ASSOCIATION 443 U.S. 658, 686 (1979)

Washington v. Washington State Commercial Passenger Fishing Vessel Association, an elaboration of **United States v. Washington** (1974), commonly called the **Boldt** decision, established that Indians are entitled to up to 50 percent of the anadromous fish harvest. The Supreme Court's ruling in this case held that the figure of 50 percent should be a "maximum and not a minimum allocation." The central premise of its decision, the Court said, is that Indians should be entitled to enough fish to provide them a livelihood, "that is to say, a moderate living."

The Court held that special benefits accorded Indians under treaties do not violate the equal-protection clause of the Fourteenth Amendment. Furthermore, the Court ruled that the treaties should be understood "in the sense in which they would naturally be understood by Indians." The words "in common with" and "right of taking fish" in the original treaties indicated to the Court's majority that the Indians who signed them were entitled to a share of the harvest, over and above an equal opportunity to fish. Indian fishing rights are reserved by a Native American community, not granted to it.

WATER RIGHTS . *See Winters v. United States* (1908); *Pyramid Lake Paiute Tribe v. Morton* (1972); *Arizona v. California* (1963); *Colville Confederated Tribes v. Walton* (1981); *United States v. Adair* (1984).

WILLIAMS, ROGER (1603–1683)

Today Roger Williams is known as the founder of Rhode Island. During his own life, Williams was excoriated as a spreader of intellectual infections. Afterwards, he was hailed as the first flower of Enlightenment's spring. Roger Williams was the first North American revolutionary, or at least the first of European extraction.

Although they were couched mainly in a religious context, Williams's ideas also engaged debates regarding political liberty that would fire the American Revolution more than a century later. Like many of the founders of the United States, Williams also often used his perceptions of American Indians and their societies as a reference point by which to hone his preexisting desires for an alternative to the European status quo. As the founder of Providence Plantations (Rhode Island), Williams tried to implement his ideas of "soul liberty," political freedom, and economic equality. His experiment presaged the later revolution of continental scope.

Within a few months of Williams's arrival in Puritan Boston during 1631, he was learning the Algonquian language. He would master the dialects of the Showatuck, Nipmuck, Narraganset, and others. Williams became friendly with Massasoit, a sachem among the Wampanoags (also called Pokanokets), a man described by William Bradford in 1621 as "lustie . . . in his best years, an able body grave of countenance, spare of speech, strong [and] tall" (Covey 1966: 125). Williams met Massasoit when the latter was about thirty years of age, and, in Williams's words, he became "great friends" with the sachem. Williams also became close to Canonicus, an elderly leader of the Narragansets. With both, Williams traveled in the forest for days at a time, learning what he could of their languages, societies, and opinions, drinking in experiences that, along with prior European experience, would provide the intellectual groundwork for the model commonwealth Williams sought to establish in Providence Plantations.

By January 1635, the Puritans' more orthodox magistrates had decided that Williams must be exiled to England, jailed if possible, and shut up, because he had preached that the Indians, not the Puritans, were the rightful owners of the property on which the colony had been built. The authorities opposed exiling Williams in the wilderness, fearing that he would begin his own settlement, from which his "infections" would leak back into Puritania. A summons was issued for Williams's arrest, but he stalled the authorities by contending that he was too ill to withstand an ocean voyage. At the same time, Williams and his associates were rushing ahead with plans for their new colony. Williams already had arranged with Canonicus for a tract of land large enough to support a colony.

Aware of his impending arrest, Williams had set out three days earlier during a blinding blizzard, walking south by west to the lodge of Massasoit, at Mount Hope. Walking eighty to ninety miles during the worst of a New England winter, Williams suffered immensely and likely would have died without Indian aid. Near the end of his trek, Williams lodged with Canonicus and his family.

During the ensuing months, Williams's family and friends filtered south from Plymouth and Salem. By spring, houses were being erected, and fields were being turned. The growing group also began to erect an experimental government very novel by European (or Puritan) standards of the time. For the first time among English-speaking people in America, they were trying to establish a social order based on liberty of conscience and other natural rights.

Very quickly, Williams's house became a transcultural meeting place. He lodged as many as fifty Indians at a time—travelers, traders, and sachems on their way to or from treaty conferences. If a Puritan needed to contact an Indian, or vice versa, he more than likely did so with Williams's aid. Among Indian nations at odds with each other, Williams became "a quencher of our fires" (Ernst 1932: 252). When citizens of Portsmouth needed an Indian agent, they approached Williams. The Dutch did the same thing after 1636. Williams often traveled with Canonicus, Massasoit, and their warriors, lodging with them in the forest. The Narragansets' council sometimes used Williams's house for its meetings.

Williams had collected material for an Indian grammar much of his adult life, but the press of events left him little time to write. It was not until 1643, on a solitary sea voyage to England, that Williams composed his *Key into the Language of America*, the first Indian grammar in English, as well as a small encyclopedia of his observations among Native Americans. In the *Key*, Williams also began to formulate a critique of European religion and politics that would be a subject of intense debate on both sides of the Atlantic for decades to come. Some of Williams's American lessons were offered in verse:

> I've known them to leave their house and mat
>   To lodge a friend or stranger
> When Jews and Christians oft have sent
>   Jesus Christ to the Manger.
>
> Oft have I heard these Indians say
>   These English will deliver us
> Of all that's ours, our lands and lives
>   In the end, they'll bereave us. (Rider 1904: 44)

In some ways, Williams found what Europeans called "Christian values" better embodied in Native American societies: "There are no beggars amongst them, nor fatherless children unprovided for" (Rider 29). The *Key* was not only a grammar. It also was a lesson in humility directed at the most pompous and ethnocentric of the English:

When Indians heare the horrid filths,
    Of Irish, English men
The horrid Oaths and Murthurs late
    Thus say these Indians then:

We weare no Cloathes, have many Gods,
    And yet our sinnes are lesse:
You are Barbarians, Pagans wild,
    Your land's the wildernesse. (Rider 9)

When some Puritans asked whether a society based on individual choice instead of coerced consent would degenerate into anarchy, Williams found the Indians' example instructive: "Although they have not so much to restraine them (both in respect of knowledge of God and lawes of Men) as the English have, yet a man shall never heare of such crimes amongst them [as] robberies, murthurs, adultries &c., as among the English" (Williams 1963: 225).

Among the colonists of Providence Plantations, as among the Indians he knew, Williams envisioned a society where "all men may walk as their consciences perswade them." Williams's ideal society also shared with the Native American societies he knew a relatively egalitarian distribution of property, with political rights based on natural law: "All civil liberty is founded in the consent of the People"; "Natural and civil Right and Privilege due . . . as a Man, a Subject, a Citizen" (Ernst 276–277).

Establishing such a utopian society was easier said than done. As Williams watched, some of his cosettlers set up land companies similar to those in other colonies in an attempt to hoard land set aside for future arrivals. The land had been set aside to prevent the growth of a landless underclass in the colony. In 1654, in a letter to the town of Providence, Williams showed how isolated he sometimes felt in his quest for a new way of life: "I have been charged with folly for that freedom and liberty which I have always stood for—I say, liberty and equality in both land and government" (Miller 1953: 221–222).

As Williams entered his sixties, his body grew old quickly. In 1663, he complained often of "old pains, lameness, so th't sometimes I have not been able to rise, nor goe, or stand." The mantle of leadership among the Wampanoag had fallen to Metacom, who was called King Philip by the English. Aged about twenty-five in 1662, Metacom distrusted nearly all European Americans, Williams being one of the few exceptions. Metacom grew more bitter by the day. He could see his nation being destroyed before his eyes. The devastation of alcohol and disease and the loss of land destroyed families and tradition. These were Metacom's thoughts as he prepared to go to war against the English.

When Indians painted for war appeared on the heights above Providence, Williams picked up his staff, climbed the bluffs, and told the war parties that if they attacked the town, England would send thousands of armed men to crush them. "Well," one of the sachems leading the attack told Williams, "Let them come. We are ready for them, but as for you, brother Williams, you are a good man. You have been kind to us for many years. Not a hair on your head shall be touched." Williams died March 15, 1683, in Providence.

FURTHER READING

Brockunier, Samuel H. *The Irrepressible Democrat: Roger Williams*. New York: Ronald Press, 1940.

Chupack, Henry. *Roger Williams*. New York: Twayne & Co., 1969.

Covey, Cyclone. *The Gentle Radical: A Biography of Roger Williams*. New York: Macmillan, 1966.

Davis, Jack L. "Roger Williams among the Narragansett Indians." *New England Quarterly* 43 (1970): 593–604.

Ernst, James. *Roger Williams: New England Firebrand*. New York: Macmillan, 1932.

Grinde, Donald A., Jr., and Bruce E. Johansen. *Exemplar of Liberty: Native America and the Evolution of Democracy*. Los Angeles: UCLA American Indian Studies Center, 1991.

Miller, Perry. *Roger Williams: His Contribution to the American Tradition*. Indianapolis: Bobbs-Merrill, 1953.

Parrington, Vernon Louis. *Main Currents in American Thought*. New York: Harcourt, Brace, & Co., 1927.

Rider, Sidney S. *The Lands of Rhode Island As They Were Known to Caunounicus and Miantunnomu When Roger Williams Came in 1636*. Providence, RI: The Author, 1904.

Savelle, Max. "Roger Williams: Minority of One." In *The American Story*, ed. Earl S. Miers. Great Neck, NY: Channel Press, 1956.

Slotkin, Richard, and James K. Folsom, eds. *So Dreadfull a Judgment: Puritan Responses to King Philip's War, 1676–1677*. Middletown, CT: Wesleyan University Press, 1978.

Vaughan, Alden T. *New England Frontier: Puritans and Indians, 1620–1675*. Boston: Little Brown, 1965.

Williams, Roger. *The Complete Works of Roger Williams*. Vol. 1. New York: Russell & Russell, 1963.

———. *A Key into the Language of America*. 1643. Providence, RI: Tercentenary Committee, 1936.

Winslow, Ola Elizabeth. *Master Roger Williams*. New York: Macmillan, 1957.

WILLIAMS V. LEE 358 U.S. 217 (1959)

In *Williams v. Lee*, the non-Indian owner of a trading post on the Navajo reservation brought a legal action in Apache County, Arizona, Superior Court to recover money owed by a Navajo who had purchased goods at the trading post on credit. The court held that the Navajo court, not the state, had jurisdiction over the matter because state jurisdiction in this matter would have undermined (or infringed) on a Native American community's ability to govern itself. In retrospect, this ruling's emphasis on Native American **sovereignty** is often said to have presaged developments in the 1960s. The case also established the "infringement test" of the **Federal Preemption Doctrine**. The Supreme Court held that

[t]here can be no question that to allow the exercise of state jurisdiction here would undermine the authority of the tribal court over reservation affairs and hence would infringe on the right of the Indians to govern themselves. It is immaterial that respondent is not an Indian. He was on the reservation and the transaction with an Indian took place there. The cases in this court have consistently guarded the authority of Indian governments over their reservations.

At first blush, this case seems overwhelmingly favorable to Indian sovereignty. The Court did hint, however, that states could assert civil jurisdiction in instances that did not interfere with Native American self-government, leaving the definition of the same to the future. Legal scholar Milnar Ball expressed the fears of many Native American legal advocates when he wrote:

According to [Justice Hugo] Black [author of the majority opinion in this case], the purpose of encouraging tribal self-government is not self-government. The goal is not tribes that can sustain themselves, but tribes fit for assimilation into the states. In the Black view, the tribes presently fail to meet the standards for consumption by the states. Self-government is encouraged so that the tribes can be found worthy of the states—calves fattened for the feast. (1987: 75)

FURTHER READING

Ball, Milnar S. "Constitution, Courts, Indian Tribes." *American Bar Foundation Research Journal*, no. 1 (Winter 1987): 1–140.

WINTERS DOCTRINE . *See Winters v. United States*.

WINTERS V. UNITED STATES 207 U.S. 564 (1908)

In *Winters v. United States*, the U.S. Supreme Court ruled that water should be reserved for present and future needs of Indians. This is an important case in arid parts of the U.S. West because it establishes who has first call on scarce water resources. The ruling holds that Indians in a watershed have first claim on enough water to carry on their lives in a productive fashion. These rights are not limited by prior appropriation or "actual beneficial use" that may be upheld in state laws. Water rights under *Winters* are not forfeited if they are not used.

Winters v. United States involved the Fort Belknap Reservation in Montana, which was created by an agreement ratified by Congress in 1888 from a much larger area that had been ceded. The agreement drew the reservation border down the middle of the Milk River, but contained no explicit provisions for water rights. Non-Indians not living on the reservation subsequently built dams that diverted enough water to interfere with the Indians' agriculture. After the Gros Ventres filed suit to stop this practice, the Supreme Court held that the 1888 agreement had reserved water rights by "necessary implication," because without such rights the Indians' land would be "practically valueless." "The Indians had command of the land and waters," the Court held; they "cannot be presumed to have given up all the water that made their land valuable." Therefore, the Court ruled, the state's prior appropriation doctrine did not allow the non-Indian settlers to claim priority for "beneficial use." *Winters v. United States* became the foundation of all Indian water law.

FURTHER READING

Burton, Lloyd. *American Indian Water Rights and the Limits of Law.* Lawrence: University Press of Kansas, 1991.
Canby, William C., Jr. *American Indian Law in a Nutshell.* St. Paul, MN: West Publishing, 1981.

WORCESTER V. GEORGIA 31 U.S. (6 Pet.) 515 (1832)

John Marshall, as chief justice of the U.S. Supreme Court, was the author of several decisions that still define Native American rights in the United States, most notably *Worcester v. Georgia*, which upheld limited **sovereignty** for the **Cherokee** Nation in 1832. President **Andrew Jackson**, surrendering to states' rights interests in the South, ignored the decision and proceeded with plans to remove the Cherokees to **Indian Territory** (later Oklahoma). Jackson's actions later resulted in the Cherokees' **Trail of Tears**.

In the Removal Act (1830) Jackson pressed for congressional action that would remove the Cherokees and other Indian nations of the Southeast to "Indian Territory." Jackson's actions ultimately comprised contempt of the Supreme Court (an impeachable offense under the **Constitution**). In the incendiary years before the Civil War, however, the political cost of following the Supreme Court's rulings upholding Cherokee sovereignty proved too great for Jackson's sense of political expediency.

The case began when European-American missionaries living on Cherokee territory refused to swear an oath of allegiance to the state of Georgia. They were arrested, chained to a wagon, and forced to walk more than twenty miles to jail. Two Methodist preachers who objected to the cruelty that accompanied the arrests also were chained and taken to jail. The three missionaries were tried, convicted, and sentenced to four years of hard labor at the Georgia state penitentiary. When the case reached the Supreme Court as *Worcester v. Georgia*, Justice Marshall wrote that native nations had

always been considered as distinct, independent political communities, retaining their original natural rights . . . and the settled doctrine of the law of nations, [which] is that a weaker power does not surrender its independence— its right to self-government—by associating with a stronger, and taking its protection. . . . The Cherokee nation, then, is a distinct community, occupying its own territory, with boundaries accurately described, in which the laws of Georgia can have no force, and which the citizens of Georgia have no right to enter, but with the assent of the Cherokees, or in conformity with treaties, and with the acts of Congress.

To this situation, Marshall applied the standing rule of international law: "[T]he settled doctrine of the law of nations is that a weaker power does not surrender its independence—its right to self-government—by associating with a stronger, and taking its protection."

At one turn, Marshall's opinion in this case acknowledged the real-politik of conquest: "[P]ower, war, [and] conquest give rights which, after possession, are conceded by the world; and which can never be controverted." On the other hand, Marshall questioned the morality of naked conquest, as had Bartolomé de Las Casas and **Roger Williams** before him:

The extravagant and absurd idea, that the feeble settlements made on the seacoast, or the companies under whom they were made, acquired legitimate power by them to govern the people, or occupy the lands from sea to sea, did not enter the mind of any man. They were well understood to convey the title which, according to the common law of European sovereigns respecting America, they might rightfully convey, and no more. . . . This was the exclusive right of purchasing such lands as the natives were willing to sell. The crown could not be understood to grant what the crown did not affect to claim; nor was it so understood.

Marshall concluded that

[Georgia's law] interfered forcibly with the relations between the United States and the Cherokee Nation, the regulation of which according to the settled principles of our constitution, are committed exclusively to the government of the United States.

While Chief Justice Marshall's opinion was ignored by President Jackson, it shaped the relationship of the United States to Native American nations within its borders to the end of the twentieth century. The 1934 **Indian Reorganization Act** and legislative efforts promoting **self-determination** after the 1960s were based on Marshall's opinion that the rights of "discovery" did not extinguish the original inhabitants' "legal as well as . . . just claim to retain possession [of their land] and to use it according to their own jurisdiction." Marshall defined Indian nations not as totally sovereign, nor as colonies, but as "domestic dependent nations."

Marshall had long-running political differences with President Jackson, and he agonized over the conflicts between states' rights and Native American sovereignty. In *Cherokee Nation v. Georgia*, Marshall was forced, based on precedent, to rule that the Cherokees had no standing at court to appeal the state of Georgia's seizure of their lands. This situation troubled Marshall so deeply that he said at one point that he thought of resigning from the Supreme Court.

Historians disagree over whether, after the *Worcester* and *Cherokee* rulings, President Jackson actually said, "John Marshall has made his decision, now let him enforce it." Whether Jackson expressed himself in those words may be a moot point; his implementation of removal flew in the face of the law as interpreted by Marshall.

Legal scholars Russel Barsh and James Henderson offered the following analysis of Marshall's opinion in *Worcester*: "*Worcester* overruled the court's characterization of tribes in *Cherokee Nation*, making it clear that tribes' relationship to the United States is governed by consent and the concept of dependency in international law, not by wardship or subordination arising out of Indians' nature or condition" (1980: 58). *Worcester v. Georgia* also was the source of an important legal doctrine that has had profound effects to the present time—the legal assumption that the language used in treaties should be construed as Indians of the time understood it. This doctrine played a large role in many cases, one of the most notable of which is *United States v. Washington* (1974), in which District Court Judge **George Boldt** interpreted mid-nineteenth-century treaties to indicate that Indians had a right to fish at their "usual and accustomed" places. The origin of this doctrine dates not to Marshall, but to his fellow justice John McLean's opinion in *Worcester v. Georgia*:

The language used in treaties with Indians should never be construed to their prejudice. If words be made use of which are susceptible of a more extended meaning than their plain import, as connected with the tenor of the treaty, they should be construed only as written in the latter sense. . . . How the words of the treaty were understood . . . rather than their critical meaning, should form the rule of construction.

FURTHER READING

Barsh, Russel, and James Henderson. *The Road: Indian Tribes and Political Liberty*. Berkeley: University of California Press, 1980.

Venables, Robert. "Revisiting 1984" (Review Essay). *Native Americas* 13:1
    (Spring 1996): 60–62.

WYANDOT CONFEDERACY, POLITICAL AND LEGAL TRADITIONS
The political and legal system of the Wyandots was remarkably similar
to that of their neighbors, the **Iroquois**. According to Bruce G. Trigger's
Children of Aataentsic: A History of the Huron People to 1660, the Wyandots' polity, like that of the Iroquois, was rooted in family structure.
Leaders of the various clans used public opinion and **consensus** to
shape decisions. Issues "were usually decided upon by majority vote
. . . [and] discussed until a general consensus was reached" (1976: 54).
No human being would be expected to be bound by a decision to which
he had not given his conscious consent.

The Wyandots (Ywendat) were called "Huron" (or "Hure") by French
sailors who remarked on their bristly, Mohawk-style hair. "Hure," in
French, actually means "prickly boar's hairs" and is considered a slur.

As among the Iroquois, the clans—Porcupine, Snake, Deer, Beaver,
Hawk, Turtle, Bear, and Wolf—created familial affinity across the
boundaries of the four confederated Wyandot clans. Clan mothers held
their own councils and ran local affairs, while men sat on the national
council. Members of each clan could trace their ancestry to a common
origin through the female line. In each village, clan members elected a
civil chief and a war chief. The titles were carried through the female
family line, but were bestowed on men, again resembling the Iroquois.
While the titles were hereditary in that sense, they did not pass from
head to head of a particular family, as in most European monarchies.
When the time came to choose a leader, members of each clan segment
in a particular village had a choice of several candidates, among whom,
according to Trigger, personal qualities counted most heavily: "intelligence, oratorical ability, reputation for generosity and, above all, performance as a warrior" (55).

If a village included more than one clan segment (most did, but not
all), the elected leaders of each segment formed a village council. The
council resolved issues through debate, leading to consensus, on purely
local issues. Each of the four nations, including several villages, held
councils that included all the village civil and war chiefs. The four
nations, the Attignawantan, Arendarhonon, Attigneenongahac, and Ta-
hontaeanrat, also held a central council, which, according to Trigger,
probably consisted of all the village chiefs, representing all the clans.

Compared to the Iroquois Grand Council, we know very little about
how this council operated once it met. The Wyandot council system
may have been a model for the Iroquois, since **Deganawidah** (the Peacemaker) came from Wyandot country. Some observers contend that the

Peacemaker's stutter (as heard by the Haudenosaunee) was actually a Wyandot dialect. It is likely that the Wyandot Confederacy central council met only once a year, usually for several weeks in the spring, although emergency meetings could be called at any time. The meeting of the central council was meant to bind the four clans and served as much as a social occasion as as a legislative session. Its proceedings were embellished with feasts to install new village headmen, reacquaintances between old friends, singing, dancing, and war feasts. The central council dealt with issues that affected all four clans, such as treaty negotiations and trade with Europeans.

When the central council met, the Attignawantan, by far the largest of the four clans, sat on one side of a ceremonial longhouse, with the representatives of the other three clans opposite them, across the council fire. The speaker, always an Attignawantan, presided over speeches of welcome and thanksgiving, followed by recitation of the agenda.

As each item of the agenda was taken up, representatives stated their opinions in turn, without interruption. Speaking in council called for a special oratorical style, according to Trigger, "full of metaphors, circumlocutions, and other rhetorical devices that were uncommon in everyday speech" (59). Members of the council were expected to retain their composure even during severe disagreement, guiding the debate toward eventual consensus on which all could vote in favor. We do not know whether the clans on each side of the council fire debated among each other before deliberating as a whole (as the Iroquois did). Nor do we have the detail of procedure regarding qualities for sachems or grounds for impeachment. Such provisions probably existed, but have been lost to history.

FURTHER READING

Trigger, Bruce G. *The Children of Aataentsic: A History of the Huron People to 1660*. Montreal: McGill-Queen's University Press, 1976.

Y

YAMASEE POLITICAL AND LEGAL TRADITIONS

The Altamahas (Yamasees) of Georgia are one of the surviving Indian peoples of the Southeast. This observation is based on William H. Gilbert's published census of Yamasees in *Surviving Indian Groups of the Eastern United States* (1948: 422). In 1959, James H. Howard examined some of the spiritual and cultural aspects of contemporary "Altamahas." In 1960, Howard identified contemporary Altamahas as Yamasees, and in 1962 Howard and a Yamasee elder (Stewart Shaffer) coauthored an article on surviving traditional customs. In 1995, Donald A. Grinde, Jr. (Yamasee) published a historical analysis of the Yamasee Nation entitled "Pre and Post-Columbian Native Ecology: The Yamasees" in Grinde and Bruce Johansen's *Ecocide of Native America*. These scholarly works document the continuing survival and existence of this federally nonrecognized American Indian nation in the American Southeast.

Historically, women have occupied a prominent place in Yamasee politics and culture. Hernando de Soto encountered a powerful female leader at Cuta Fichique (outside of present-day Augusta, Georgia) who offered him a string of pearls, her lands, and her people as well as other small gifts. In many ways, this sixteenth-century Native American ruler exemplified the political power of women among Muscogean-speaking peoples like the Yamasees. An examination of the spiritual traditions of Yamasees reveals that traditional stories about women defeating powerful giants like the evil Ocasta (the Creator's helper) also reinforced the spiritual and political power of women in Yamasee society.

For men, special powers for the hunt were passed down in the bowmen's societies. These bowmen's societies helped to initiate boys into adulthood when they joined such societies in their early teens. Essentially, young men gained leadership skills as they matured in these hunting or bowmen's societies. For Yamasee men, special powers for the hunt also came from the *sabia* bundle, which contained crystals derived from rose flowers as well as red paint and other power objects of medicinal value. Often, a man's Shadow Fighting Knife also was instrumental in dealing with life-threatening situations. According to Stewart Shaffer, the Shadow Fighting Knife was kept by a man "throughout his life, and . . . at the time of his death . . . the knife was burned so that he could use it on his journey to the afterworld."

Contemporary political and legal traditions of the Yamasee still reflect many of these traditional values. Yamasees still have a strong matrilineal tradition. The Yamasees of Yemassee, South Carolina, have an able contemporary elder in Rachel Sequoyah, who also has kinship ties with the Poarch Band of **Creeks** in Alabama. Today, Yamasees from South Carolina probably total about 150 people. Most studies of contemporary Yamasees focus on the Georgia communities at Shellbluff Landing, Statesboro, and Rocky Ford, Georgia. These Yamasee communities total about 600 people, and the family names associated with them are Woodrum, Deal, Beasley, Shaffer, Jones, Green, and Taylor. An extensive kinship network connects these families through their maternal as well as paternal sides. Yamasees in Georgia also have kinship ties with American Indian groups in South Carolina and North Carolina. Yamasee families maintain their Native American identities through a variety of matrifocal mechanisms such as family reunions, kinship patterns, traditional stories, Native American cooking, and traditional agricultural practices. Yamasees on both the South Carolina and Georgia sides of the Savannah River are emerging from their submerged identities that were fostered during the nineteenth century for survival and are currently striving to reassert their heritage and political traditions. In the past few years, the Georgia and South Carolina Yamasees have been seeking ways to reunite politically and culturally after years of separation and isolation.

FURTHER READING

Bourne, Edward G., ed. *Narratives of the Career of Hernando de Soto.* Vol. 1. New York: A. S. Barnes & Co., 1904.

Gilbert, William H. *Surviving Indian Groups of the Eastern United States.* Washington: Smithsonian Institution, 1948.

Grinde, Donald A., Jr., and Bruce E. Johansen. *Ecocide of Native America: Environmental Destruction of Indian Lands and Peoples*. Santa Fe, NM: Clear Light, 1995.

Howard, James. "Altamaha Cherokee Folklore and Customs." *Journal of American Folklore* 72: 248 (Spring 1959).

———. "The Yamasee: A Supposedly Extinct Southeastern Tribe Rediscovered." *American Anthropologist* 62:4 (August 1960): 681–683.

Shaffer, Stewart (Yamasee), and James H. Howard. "Medicine and Medicine Headdresses of the Yamasee." *American Indian Tradition* 8:3 (1962).

Spicer, Edward H. *The American Indians*. Cambridge, MA: Belknap Press of Harvard University Press, 1982.

DONALD A.GRINDE, JR.

YEAR OF RECONCILIATION (South Dakota, 1990)

A year after Washington State celebrated its centennial by signing the **Washington Centennial Accord** with federally recognized Indian communities within its borders, South Dakota's governor George Mickelson signed a Year of Reconciliation Proclamation in South Dakota. This proclamation also celebrated that state's centennial. The Year of Reconciliation also marked one hundred years since the assassination of Sitting Bull and the massacre at Wounded Knee, both of which occurred only thirteen months after South Dakota had become a state. This statement did not implement a government-to-government relationship between Native American communities and state, as did the Washington accord. It called on

our citizens, both Indian and non-Indian to look for every opportunity to lay aside our fears and mistrust, to build friendships, to join together and take part in shared cultural activities, to learn about one another, to have fun with one another, and to begin a process of mutual respect and understanding that will continue to grow into South Dakota's second one hundred years.

Selected Bibliography

Adams, John. *A Defence of the Constitutions of the Governments of the United States of America*. Philadelphia: Hall and Sellers, 1787.

Allen, Paula Gunn. *The Sacred Hoop: Recovering the Feminine in American Indian Traditions*. Boston: Beacon Press, 1986.

American Friends Service Committee, comp. *Uncommon Controversy: A Report on Fishing Rights of the Muckleshoot, Puyallup, and Nisqually Indians*. Seattle: University of Washington Press, 1970.

American Indian Policy Review Commission. *Report on Federal, State, and Tribal Jurisdiction: Final Report: Task Force Four*. Washington, DC: U.S. Government Printing Office, 1976.

Ball, Milnar. "Constitution, Court, Indian Tribes." *American Bar Foundation Research Journal*, no. 1 (Winter 1987): 1–140.

Barreiro, Jose. "Return of the Wampum." *Northeast Indian Quarterly* 7:1 (Spring 1990).

Barsh, Russel L. "Behind Land Claims: Rationalizing Dispossession in Anglo-American Law." *Law and Anthropology* 1 (1986): 15–50.

———. "The Challenge of Indigenous Self-Determination." *University of Michigan Journal of Law Reform* 26 (1993).

———. "Indian Land Claims Policy in the United States." *North Dakota Law Review* 58 (1982): 7–82.

———. "Indigenous North America and Contemporary International Law." *Oregon Law Review* 62 (1983): 73–125.

———. *The Washington Fishing Rights Controversy: An Economic Critique*. Seattle: University of Washington School of Business Administration, 1977.

Barsh, Russel L., and James Y. Henderson. *The Road: Indian Tribes and Political Liberty*. Berkeley: University of California Press, 1980.

Baudet, Henri. *Paradise on Earth: Some Thoughts on European Images of Non-European Man.* Trans. E. Wentholt. New Haven, CT: Yale University Press, 1965.

Bee, R. *The Politics of American Indian Policy.* Cambridge, MA: Schenkman, 1982.

Berkhofer, Robert F., Jr. *The White Man's Indian: Images of the American Indian from Columbus to the Present.* New York: Knopf, 1978.

Berman, H. "The Concept of Aboriginal Rights in the Early History of the United States." *Buffalo Law Review* 27 (1978): 637–667.

Blue Cloud, Peter. *Alcatraz Is Not an Island.* Berkeley, CA: Wingbow Press, 1972.

Bowers, Alfred W. *Mandan Social and Ceremonial Organization.* Chicago: University of Chicago Press, 1950.

Brakel, S. *American Indian Tribal Courts: The Costs of Separate Justice.* Chicago: American Bar Foundation, 1978.

Brandon, William. *The American Heritage Book of Indians.* New York: Dell, 1961.

Brown, Bruce. *Mountain in the Clouds.* New York: Simon & Schuster, 1982.

Burton, Jeffrey. *Indian Territory and the United States, 1866–1906.* Norman: University of Oklahoma Press, 1995.

Burton, Lloyd. *American Indian Water Rights and the Limits of Law.* Lawrence: University Press of Kansas, 1991.

Cadwallader, Sandra L., and Vine Deloria, Jr., eds. *The Aggressions of Civilization: Federal Indian Policy since the 1880s.* Philadelphia: Temple University Press, 1984.

Cahn, Edgar S. *Our Brother's Keeper: The Indian in White America.* New York: World Publishing Co., 1969.

Canby, William C., Jr. *American Indian Law in a Nutshell.* St. Paul, MN: West Publishing, 1981.

———. "The Status of Indian Tribes in American Law Today." *Washington Law Review* 62 (1987): 1–22.

Carr, Lucien. *The Social and Political Position of Women among the Huron-Iroquois Tribes.* Salem, MA: Salem Press, 1884.

Chamberlain, Alexander F. "The Contributions of the American Indian to Civilization." *Proceedings of the American Antiquarian Society* 16 (October 1903): 91–126.

Champagne, Duane. *American Indian Societies: Strategies and Conditions of Political and Cultural Survival.* Cambridge, MA: Cultural Survival, 1989.

Churchill, Ward. *Struggle for the Land.* Monroe, ME: Common Courage Press, 1993.

Churchill, Ward, and Jim Vander Wall. *Agents of Repression: The FBI's Secret Wars against the Black Panther Party and the American Indian Movement.* Boston: South End Press, 1988.

———. *The COINTELPRO Papers: Documents from the FBI's Secret Wars against Domestic Dissent.* Boston: South End Press, 1990.

Clark, Blue. *Lone Wolf v. Hitchcock: Treaty Rights and Indian Law at the End of the Nineteenth Century.* Lincoln: University of Nebraska Press, 1994.

Clinebell, J., and J. Thompson. "Sovereignty and Self-Determination: The Rights of Native Americans under International Law." *Buffalo Law Review* 27 (1978): 669–714.

Clinton, Robert N. "Criminal Jurisdiction over Indian Lands: The Historical Perspective." *Arizona Law Review* 18:3 (1976): 503–583.

———. "Isolated in Their Own Country: A Defense of Federal Protection of Indian Autonomy and Self-Government." *Stanford Law Review* 33 (1981): 979–1068.

Cohen, Felix S. "The Erosion of Indian Rights, 1950–1953: A Case Study in Bureaucracy." *Yale Law Journal* 62:3 (February 1953): 348–390.

———. *Handbook of Federal Indian Law.* Washington, DC: Interior Department, 1942.

Collier, John. *Indians of the Americas.* New York: W. W. Norton, 1947.

Combs, Jerald A. *The Jay Treaty: Political Battleground of the Founding Fathers.* Berkeley: University of California Press, 1970.

Corkran, David H. *The Cherokee Frontier: Conflict and Survival, 1740–62.* Norman: University of Oklahoma Press, 1962.

Costo, Rupert, and Jeannette Henry. *Indian Treaties: Two Centuries of Dishonor.* San Francisco: Indian Historian Press, 1977.

Council on Interracial Books for Children, comp. *Chronicles of American Indian Protest.* 1971. New York: Council on Interracial Books for Children, 1979.

Dahl, Dick. "Law Practice: The Casino Boom Is Forging New Relationships between American Indians and the Law." *American Bar Association Journal* (May 1995): 86.

Davis, Leicester Knickerbocker. "Thomas L. Sloan—American Indian." *American Indian Magazine* 7 (August 1920): 39–40.

Debo, Angie. *And Still the Waters Run.* Princeton: Princeton University Press, 1940.

———. *A History of the Indians of the United States.* Norman: University of Oklahoma Press, 1970.

———. *The Rise and Fall of the Choctaw Republic.* Norman: University of Oklahoma Press, 1961.

Deloria, Vine, Jr. *Behind the Trail of Broken Treaties.* 1st ed. New York: Delacourte, 1974. Austin: University of Texas Press, 1985.

———, ed. *American Indian Policy in the Twentieth Century.* Norman: University of Oklahoma Press, 1985.

Deloria, Vine, Jr., and Clifford Lytle. *American Indians, American Justice.* Austin: University of Texas Press, 1983.

———. *The Nations Within.* New York: Pantheon, 1984.

DeMallie, Raymond J. "American Indian Treaty Making: Motives and Meanings." *American Indian Journal* 3 (January 1977): 2–10.

Deskaheh: Iroquois Statesman and Patriot. Onchiota, NY: Six Nations Indian Museum, n.d.

Dorsey, J. O. "Omaha Sociology." *Bureau of American Ethnology Bulletin* 3 (1884): 211–370.

Drinnon, Richard. *Facing West: The Metaphysics of Indian-Hating and Empire-Building.* New York: New American Library, 1980.

Driver, Harold E. *Indians of North America.* Chicago: University of Chicago Press, 1961.

Drucker, Philip. *Cultures of the North Pacific Coast.* San Francisco: Chandler, 1965.

———. *The Northern and Central Nootkan Tribes.* Bureau of American Ethnology Bulletin no. 144. Washington, DC: Smithsonian Institution, 1951.

Echo Hawk, Walter. "Loopholes in Religious Liberty." *Cultural Survival Quarterly* 17:4 (1994): 62–65.

———. "Native American Religious Liberty: Five Hundred Years after Columbus." *American Indian Culture and Research Journal* 17:3 (1993): 33–52.

———. "Who Owns the Past? How Native American Indian Lawyers Fight for Their Ancestors' Remains and Memories." *Human Rights* 16:3 (1989): 24–29, 53–55.

———, guest editor. "Repatriation of Native American Remains" (special issue). *American Indian Culture and Research Journal* 16:2 (1992).

Echo Hawk, Walter, and C. Echo Hawk. *Battlefields and Burial Grounds: The Indian Struggle to Protect Ancestral Graves in the United States.* Minneapolis: Lerner Publications, 1994.

Echo Hawk, Walter, and Jack F. Trope. "The Native American Graves Protection and Repatriation Act: Background and Legislative History." *Arizona State Law Journal* 24:1 (Spring 1992): 35–77.

Ewen, Alex. "A Supreme Court Question of Power: High Court Paves Legal Road to States' Supremacy." *Native Americas* 13:2 (Summer 1996): 26–29.

Fairchild, Hoxie Neale. *The Noble Savage: A Study in Romantic Naturalism.* New York: Russell & Russell, 1961.

Fay, George Emory, ed. *Charters, Constitutions, and By-laws of the Indian Tribes of North America.* Museum of Anthropology, Occasional Publications, University of Northern Colorado. 1967–1981.

Fixico, Donald. *Termination and Relocation: Federal Indian Policy, 1945–1960.* Albuquerque: University of New Mexico Press, 1986.

Fletcher, Alice, and Francis La Flesche. *The Omaha Tribe.* Bureau of American Ethnology Bulletin 27 (1911). Reprint. New York: Johnson Reprint Corp., 1970.

French, Laurence A. *The Winds of Injustice: American Indians and the U.S. Government.* New York: Garland, 1994.

———, ed. *Indians and Criminal Justice.* Totowa, NJ: Allanheld, Osmun, 1982.

Fritz, Henry E. *The Movement for Indian Assimilation, 1860–1890.* Philadelphia: University of Pennsylvania Press, 1963.

Gage, Matilda Joslyn. *Woman, Church, and State.* 1893. Watertown, MA: Persephone Press, 1980.

Gearing, Fred. *Priests and Warriors: Social Structures for Cherokee Politics in the Eighteenth Century.* Memoir 93, American Anthropological Association, Vol. 64, No. 5, Part 2, October 1962.

Getches, David H., Daniel M. Rosenfeld, and Charles F. Wilkinson. *Cases and Materials on Federal Indian Law.* St. Paul, MN: West Publishing, 1979, 1993.

Gibson, Arrell Morgan. *The American Indian; Prehistory to the Present.* Lexington, MA: D. C. Heath, 1980.

———. *The Oklahoma Story.* Norman: University of Oklahoma Press, 1978.

Goldberg, Carole E. "Public Law 280: The Limits of State Jurisdiction over Reservation Indians." *UCLA Law Review* 22 (1975): 535–594.

———. *Public Law 280: State Jurisdiction over Reservation Indians.* Los Angeles: UCLA American Indian Studies Center, 1975.

The Great Law of Peace of the Longhouse People. Rooseveltown, NY: Akwesasne Notes/White Roots of Peace, 1971.

Green, J., and S. Work. "Comment: Inherent Indian Sovereignty." *American Indian Law Review* 4 (1976): 311–342.

Grinde, Donald A., Jr. *The Iroquois and the Founding of the American Nation.* San Francisco: Indian Historian Press, 1977.

———. "The Reburial of American Indian Remains and Funerary Objects." *Northeast Indian Quarterly* (Summer 1991): 35–38.

Grinde, Donald A., Jr., and Bruce E. Johansen. *Ecocide of Native America.* Santa Fe, NM: Clear Light, 1995.

———. *Exemplar of Liberty: Native America and the Evolution of Democracy.* Los Angeles: UCLA American Indian Studies Center, 1991.

Grinnell, George Bird. *The Cheyenne Indians: Their History and Ways of Life.* 1923. New York: Cooper Square Publishers, 1962.

Hanke, Lewis. *Aristotle and the American Indians.* Chicago: Henry Regnery Company, 1959.

Harmon, George D. *Sixty Years of Indian Affairs: Political, Economic, and Diplomatic, 1789–1850.* Chapel Hill: University of North Carolina Press, 1941.

Harring, Sidney L. *Crow Dog's Case: American Indian Sovereignty, Tribal Law, and United States Law in the Nineteenth Century.* New York: Cambridge University Press, 1994.

Hasse, Larry J. "Termination and Assimilation: Federal Indian Policy, 1943 to 1961." Ph.D. dissertation, Washington State University, 1974. Ann Arbor, MI: University Microfilms, 1974.

Hauptman, Laurence M. "Big Deal?" *Journal of Ethnic Studies* 9 (Summer 1981): 119–124.

———. *The Iroquois and the New Deal.* Syracuse, NY: Syracuse University Press, 1981.

Hertzberg, Hazel W. *The Search for an American Indian Identity: Modern Pan-Indian Movements.* Syracuse, NY: Syracuse University Press, 1971.

Higgins, F. "International Law Considerations of the American Indian Nations by the United States." *Arizona Law Review* 3 (1961): 74–85.

Hoebel, E. Adamson. *The Law of Primitive Man.* Cambridge, MA: Harvard University Press, 1954.

———. *The Political Organization and Law-ways of the Comanche Indians.* 1940. Memoirs of the American Anthropological Association, no. 54. Menasha, WI: AAA, 1976.

Hoffman, Walter James. *The Menomini Indians.* 1896. New York: Johnson Reprint Corp., 1970.

Holt, H. Barry, and Gary Forrester. *Digest of American Indian Law: Cases and Chronology.* Littleton, CO: Fred B. Rothman & Co., 1990.

Horsman, Reginald. *Expansion and American Indian Policy, 1783–1812.* East Lansing: Michigan State University Press, 1967.

Hosen, Frederick E., comp. *Rifle, Blanket, and Kettle: Selected Indian Treaties and Laws.* Jefferson, NC: McFarland, 1985.

Hoxie, Frederick. *Parading through History: The Making of the Crow Nation in America, 1805–1935.* New York: Cambridge University Press, 1995.

———. "Towards a 'New' North American Indian Legal History." *American Journal of Legal History* 30 (1986): 351–357.

Iverson, Peter. *Carlos Montezuma and the Changing World of American Indians.* Albuquerque: University of New Mexico Press, 1982.

Jackson, Helen Hunt. *A Century of Dishonor.* 1881. New York: Harper & Row, 1965.

Jacobs, Wilbur. *Dispossessing the American Indian: Indians and Whites on the Colonial Frontier.* New York: Charles Scribner's Sons, 1972.

———. "Wampum: The Protocol of Indian Diplomacy." *William and Mary Quarterly*, 3rd ser., 4:3 (October 1949): 596–604.

Jaimes, M. Annette. "Nationalism and Racism: The Theological Roots of Racism and American Indian Identity." In *Historical Reflections: Cross Cultural Contact*, ed. Joel Martin and M. Annette Jaimes. Alfred, NY: Alfred University, 1993.

———, ed. *The State of Native America.* Boston: South End Press, 1992.

Jemison, G. Peter. "Sovereignty and Treaty Rights: We Remember." *St. Thomas Law Review* 7 (1995).

Johansen, Bruce E. *Forgotten Founders: Benjamin Franklin, the Iroquois, and the Rationale for the American Revolution.* Ipswich, MA: Gambit, 1982.

———. *Life and Death in Mohawk Country.* Golden, CO: North American Press/Fulcrum, 1993.

———. *Native American Political Systems and the Evolution of Democracy: An Annotated Bibliography.* Westport, CT: Greenwood Press, 1996.

Johansen, Bruce E., and Donald A. Grinde, Jr. *The Encyclopedia of Native American Biography.* New York: Henry Holt, 1997.

Johansen, Bruce E., Donald A. Grinde, Jr., and Barbara Mann. *Debating Democracy: The Iroquois Legacy of Freedom.* Santa Fe, NM: Clear Light, 1996.

Johansen, Bruce E., and Roberto F. Maestas. *Wasi'chu: The Continuing Indian Wars.* New York: Monthly Review Press, 1979.

Johnson, Ralph W. "The State versus Indian Off-Reservation Fishing: A United States Supreme Court Error." *Washington Law Review* 47 (1972): 207–208.

Josephy, Alvin, ed. *America in 1492: The World of the Indian Peoples before the Arrival of Columbus.* New York: Afred A. Knopf, 1992.

Josephy, Alvin, Jr. *Red Power.* New York: McGraw-Hill, 1979.

Kappler, Charles J., ed. *Indian Affairs: Laws and Treaties.* 2 vols. Washington: U.S. Government Printing Office, 1904–1941.

———. *Kappler's Indian Affairs: Laws and Treaties.* Washington, DC: U.S. Government Printing Office, 1979– .

Kavanagh, Thomas W. *Comanche Political History: An Ethnohistorical Perspective, 1706–1875.* Lincoln: University of Nebraska Press, 1996.

Kelly, Lawrence C. *The Assault on Assimilation: John Collier and the Origins of Indian Policy Reform.* Albuquerque: University of New Mexico Press, 1983.

————. "The Indian Reorganization Act: The Dream and the Reality." *Pacific Historical Review* 44 (August 1975): 291–312.

Kickingbird, Kirke, Alexander Tallchief Skibine, and Lynn Kickingbird. *Indian Sovereignty*. Washington, DC: Institute for the Development of Indian Law, 1983.

Kickingbird, Kirke, and Karen Ducheneaux. *One Hundred Million Acres*. New York: Macmillan, 1973.

Kickingbird, Kirke, and Lynn Shelby Kickingbird. *Indians and the U.S. Constitution: A Forgotten Legacy*. Washington, DC: Institute for the Development of Indian Law, 1987.

Kinney, J. P. *A Continent Lost—A Civilization Won: Indian Land Tenure in America*. Baltimore: Johns Hopkins Press, 1937.

Koch, Adrienne, and William Peden, eds. *The Life and Selected Writings of Thomas Jefferson*. New York: Modern Library, 1944.

Kroeber, A. L. *Handbook of the Indians of California*. Washington, DC: Interior Department, 1925.

Kupferer, Harriet J. *Ancient Drums, Other Moccasins: Native North American Cultural Adaptation*. Englewood Cliffs, NJ: Prentice-Hall, 1988.

Labaree, Leonard W., and Whitfield J. Bell, Jr., eds. *The Papers of Benjamin Franklin*. New Haven, CT: Yale University Press, 1950–.

Lacey, L. "The White Man's Law and the American Indian Family in the Assimilation Era." *Arkansas Law Review* 40 (1986): 327–379.

Las Casas, Bartolomé de. *Brevísima Relación de la Destrucción de las Indias*. Madrid: Ediciones Catedra, 1982.

————. *The Tears of the Indians*. Ed. Colin Steele. New York: Oriole Editions, 1972.

Lazarus, Edward. *Black Hills, White Justice: The Sioux Nation versus the United States, 1775 to the Present*. New York: HarperCollins, 1991.

Levitan, Sar A. and Barbara Hetrick. *Big Brother's Indian Programs—with Reservations*. New York: McGraw-Hill, 1971.

Lewis, David Rich. "Native Americans and the Environment: A Survey of Twentieth-Century Issues." *American Indian Quarterly* 19:3 (Summer 1995): 423–450.

Llewellyn, Karl N., and E. Adamson Hoebel. *The Cheyenne Way: Conflict and Case Law in Primitive Jurisprudence*. Norman: University of Oklahoma Press, 1941.

Lowie, Robert H. *The Crow Indians*. 1935. New York: Holt, Rinehart, and Winston, 1966.

————. *Primitive Society*. New York: Boni and Liveright, 1920.

Lowman, Bill. *220 Million Custers*. Anacortes, WA: Anacortes Printing, 1978.

Lurie, Nancy O. "The Indian Claims Commission Act." *Annals of the American Academy of Political and Social Science* 311 (May 1957): 56–70.

Lyons, Oren, John Mohawk, Vine Deloria, Jr., et al. *Exiled in the Land of the Free: Democracy, Indian Nations, and the U.S. Constitution*. Santa Fe, NM: Clear Light, 1992.

Mann, Barbara. "The Fire at Onondaga: Wampum as Proto-writing." *Akwesasne Notes* n.s. 1:1 (Spring 1995): 40–48.

Manypenny, George W. *Our Indian Wards*. New York: Da Capo Press, 1972.

Mardock, Robert W. *The Reformers and the American Indian*. Columbia: University of Missouri Press, 1971.

Matthiessen, Peter. *In the Spirit of Crazy Horse*. New York: Viking, 1983.

McKee, Jesse O., and Jon A. Schlenker. *The Choctaws: Cultural Evolution of a Native American Tribe*. Jackson: University Press of Mississippi, 1980.

McLaughlin, Michael R. "The Dawes Act, or Indian General Allotment Act of 1887: The Continuing Burden of Allotment." *American Indian Culture and Research Journal* 20:2 (1996): 59–105.

McNickle, D'Arcy. *Native American Tribalism: Indian Survivals and Renewals*. New York: Oxford University Press, 1973.

———. *The Surrounded*. 1936. Albuquerque: University of New Mexico Press, 1964. Reprint, 1978.

Mead, Margaret, ed. *Cooperation and Competition among Primitive Peoples*. New York: McGraw-Hill, 1937.

Meriam, Lewis. *The Problem of Indian Administration*. Baltimore: Johns Hopkins Press, 1928.

Mooney, James. "Myths of the Cherokee." In J. W. Powell, *Nineteenth Annual Report, Bureau of American Ethnology*. Washington, DC: Smithsonian Institution, 1897–1898, part 1.

Moquin, W., and C. Van Doren, eds. *Great Documents in American Indian History*. New York: Praeger, 1973.

Morgan, Lewis Henry. *League of the Ho-De-No-Sau-Nee, or Iroquois*. Rochester, NY: Sage & Bros., 1851.

Nabokov, Peter, ed. *Native American Testimony*. New York: Viking, 1991.

Nietfield, P. *Determinants of Aboriginal Micmac Political Structure*. Ann Arbor, MI: University Microfilms, 1981.

Oberg, K. "Crime and Punishment in Tlingit Society." *American Anthropologist* 36 (1934): 145–156.

O'Brien, Sharon. *American Indian Tribal Governments*. Norman: University of Oklahoma Press, 1989.

———. "Federal Indian Policy and Human Rights." In *American Indian Policy in the Twentieth Century*, ed. Vine Deloria, Jr. Norman: University of Oklahoma Press, 1985.

Otis, D. S. *The Dawes Act and the Allotment of Indian Lands*. Norman: University of Oklahoma Press, 1973.

Parker, Arthur C. "The Role of the Iroquois in the Science of Government." Arthur C. Parker Papers, Box 11–15, Special Collections, Rush Rhees Library, University of Rochester, Rochester, New York.

Parman, Donald L. *The Navajos and the New Deal*. New Haven, CT: Yale University Press, 1976.

Perdue, Theda. *Slavery and the Evolution of Cherokee Society: 1540–1866*. Knoxville: University of Tennessee Press, 1979.

Pevar, Stephan L. *The Rights of Indians and Tribes: The Basic ACLU Guide to Indian and Tribal Rights*. Carbondale: Southern Illinois University Press, 1992.

Philp, Kenneth R. *John Collier's Crusade for Indian Reform, 1920–1954*. Tucson: University of Arizona Press, 1977.

———, ed. *Indian Self-Rule*. Salt Lake City: Howe Brothers, 1986.

Pommersheim, Frank. *Braid of Feathers: American Indian Law and Contemporary Tribal Life*. Berkeley: University of California Press, 1995.

———. *Broken Ground and Flowing Waters: An Introductory Text*. Rosebud, SD: Sinte Gleska College, 1979.

Price, Monroe. *Law and the American Indian: Readings, Notes, and Cases*. Indianapolis: Bobbs-Merrill, 1973.

Prucha, Francis Paul. *American Indian Policy in the Formative Years*. Cambridge, MA: Harvard University Press, 1962.

———. *American Indian Treaties: The History of a Political Anomaly*. Berkeley: University of California Press, 1994.

———. *The Great Father: The United States Government and the American Indians*. 2 vols. Lincoln: University of Nebraska Press, 1984.

———, ed. *Documents of United States Indian Policy*. Lincoln: University of Nebraska Press, 1975.

Quain, B. H. "The Iroquois." In *Cooperation and Competition among Primitive Peoples*, ed. Margaret Mead. New York: McGraw-Hill, 1937.

Reid, John Phillip. *A Better Kind of Hatchet: Law, Trade, and Diplomacy in the Cherokee Nation during the Early Years of European Contact*. University Park: Pennsylvania State University Press, 1976.

———. "The European Perspective and the Cherokee Law." *Appalachian Journal* 2 (Summer 1975): 286–293.

———. *A Law of Blood: The Primitive Law of the Cherokee Nation*. New York: New York University Press, 1970.

Rodnick, David. "Political Structure and Status among the Assiniboine Indians." *American Anthropologist* 39 (1937): 408–416.

Rountree, Helen C. *The Powhatan Indians of Virginia: Their Traditional Culture*. Norman: University of Oklahoma Press, 1989.

Royce, Charles C., comp. *Indian Land Cessions in the United States*. Eighteenth Annual Report of the Bureau of American Ethnology. Washington, DC: Bureau of American Ethnology, 1899.

Rushforth, Scott, and Steadman Upham. *A Hopi Social History*. Austin: University of Texas Press, 1992.

Russell Tribunal. *Report of the Fourth Russell Tribunal on the Rights of the Indians of the Americas*. Nottingham, England: Russell Tribunal, 1980.

Sabatini, J., ed. *American Indian Law: A Bibliography of Books, Law Review Articles, and Indian Periodicals*. Albuquerque: American Indian Law Center, University of New Mexico, 1973.

Sando, Joe S. *Pueblo Nations: Eight Centuries of Pueblo Indian History*. Santa Fe, NM: Clear Light, 1992.

Schusky, Ernest L. *The Right to Be Indian*. San Francisco: American Indian Educational Publishers, 1970.

Scott, J. "Zoning: Controlling Land Use on the Checkerboard: The Zoning Powers of Indian Tribes After *Montana v. United States*." *American Indian Law Review* 10 (1982): 187–209.

Shattuck, Petra, and Jill Norgren. *Partial Justice: Federal Indian Law in a Liberal Constitutional System*. New York: Berg, 1991.

Shepardson, Mary. *Navajo Ways in Government: A Study in Political Process*.

Memoir 96, American Anthropological Association, Vol. 65, Part 2, June 1963.

Skogen, Larry C. *Indian Depredation Claims, 1796–1920*. Norman: University of Oklahoma Press, 1996.

Sloan, Thomas L. "Law and the American Indians." *American Indian Magazine* 2 (April–June 1913): 166–182.

Slotkin, Richard. *The Fatal Environment*. New York: Atheneum, 1985.

Smith, Jean Edward. *John Marshall: Definer of a Nation*. New York: Henry Holt, 1996.

Society of American Indians. *The Papers of the Society of American Indians*. Ed. John William Larner, Jr. Microfilm. Wilmington, DE: Scholarly Resources, 1986.

Spaeth, Nicholas J., Julie Wrend, and Clay Smith, eds. *American Indian Law Deskbook*. Niwot: University Press of Colorado, 1993.

Stannard, David E. *American Holocaust: Columbus and the Conquest of the New World*. New York: Oxford University Press, 1992.

Strickland, Rennard. *Fire and the Spirits: Cherokee Law from Clan to Court*. Norman: University of Oklahoma Press, 1975.

Swanton, John R. *Early History of the Creek Indians and Their Neighbors*. Bulletin no. 73 of the Bureau of American Ethnology. Washington, DC: Bureau of American Ethnology, 1922.

————. "The Social Significance of the Creek Confederacy." *Proceedings of the International Congress of Americanists* 19 (1915).

Tate, Michael. *The Upstream People: An Annotated Research Bibliography of the Omaha Tribe*. Metuchen, NJ: Scarecrow Press, 1991.

Taylor, Graham D. *The New Deal and American Indian Tribalism: The Administration of the Indian Reorganization Act, 1934–45*. Lincoln: University of Nebraska Press, 1980.

Thorpe, Dagmar. "The Ceremony of Making Peace: The Navajo Peacemakers Court." *Native Americas* 13:3 (Fall 1996): 54–57.

Tibbles, Thomas Henry. *The Ponca Chiefs: An Account of the Trial of Standing Bear*. Lincoln: University of Nebraska Press, 1972.

Tooker, Elisabeth, ed. *The Development of Political Organization in Native North America: 1979 Proceedings of the American Ethnological Society*. Washington, DC: American Ethnological Society, 1983.

Tyler, S. Lyman. *A History of Indian Policy*. Washington, DC: Bureau of Indian Affairs, 1973.

Utley, Robert M. *The Last Days of the Sioux Nation*. New Haven, CT: Yale University Press, 1963.

Van Doren, Carl, and Julian P. Boyd, eds. *Indian Treaties Printed by Benjamin Franklin, 1736–1762*. Philadelphia: Historical Society of Pennsylvania, 1938.

Vecsey, Christopher, ed. *Handbook of American Indian Religious Freedom*. New York: Crossroad, 1991.

Venables, Robert. "Revisiting 1984" (review essay). *Native Americas* 13:1 (Spring 1996): 60–62.

Vestal, Stanley. *Warpath and Council Fire: The Plains Indians' Struggle for Sur-*

vival in War and in Diplomacy, 1851–1891. New York: Random House, 1948.

Vitoria, Francisco de. *Francisci de Victoria de Indis et de Jure Belli Relectiones*. Trans. John Pawley Bate; ed. Ernest Nys. Washington, DC: Carnegie Institution, 1917. Reprint. Dobbs Ferry, NY: Oceana Press, 1964.

Wagner, Sally Roesch. "The Iroquois Confederacy: A Native American Model for Non-sexist Men." *Changing Men* (Spring–Summer 1988): 32–33.

———. *The Untold Story of the Iroquois Influence on Early Feminists*. Aberdeen, SD: Sky Carrier Press, 1996.

Wallace, Anthony F. C. *The Death and Rebirth of the Seneca*. New York: Vintage, 1972.

Wallace, Paul A. W. *The White Roots of Peace*. Philadelphia: University of Pennsylvania Press, 1946.

Washburn, Wilcomb E. *Red Man's Land, White Man's Law*. New York: Scribner, 1971.

———, comp. *The American Indian and the United States: A Documentary History*. 4 vols. New York: Random House, 1973.

Watkins, Arthur V. "Termination of Federal Supervision: The Removal of Restrictions over Indian Property and Person." *Annals of the American Academy of Political and Social Science* 311 (May 1957).

Watkins, Arthur. "Termination of Federal Supervision: The Removal of Restrictions over Indian Property and Person." In *The Rape of Indian Lands*, ed. Paul W. Gates. New York: Arno Press, 1979.

Weeks, Philip. *Farewell, My Nation: The American Indian and the United States, 1820–1890*. Arlington Heights, IL: Harlan Davidson, 1990.

Weinberg, Bill. "Land and Sovereignty in Hawai'i: A Native Nation Re-emerges." *Native Americas* 13:2 (Summer 1996): 30–41.

Wheaton, Henry. *Elements of International Law*. Boston: Dana, 1866.

Whiteley, Peter M. *Deliberate Acts: Changing Hopi Culture through the Oraibi Split*. Tucson: University of Arizona Press, 1988.

Wilkinson, Charles F. *American Indians, Time, and the Law: Native Societies in a Modern Constitutional Democracy*. New Haven, CT: Yale University Press, 1987.

Wilkinson, Charles F., and Eric R. Biggs. "Evolution of the Termination Policy." *American Indian Law Review* 5:1 (1977): 139–184.

Wilkinson, Charles F., and Christine L. Miklas, eds. *Indian Tribes as Sovereign Governments: A Sourcebook on Federal-Tribal History, Law, and Policy*. Oakland, CA: AIRI Press, 1988.

Williams, C. Herb, and Walt Neubrech. *Indian Treaties: American Nightmare*. Seattle: Outdoor Empire Publishing, 1976.

Williams, Paul, and Curtis Nelson. *The Tree and the Great Law of Peace*. Ottawa: Royal Commission on Aboriginal Peoples, in press.

Williams, Robert A., Jr. *The American Indian in Western Legal Thought: The Discourses of Conquest*. New York: Oxford University Press, 1990.

———. "Linking Arms Together: Multicultural Constitutionalism in a North American Indigenous Vision of Law and Peace." *California Law Review* 82 (1994).

Woodbury, Hanni, ed. and trans. *Concerning the League: The Iroquois League*

Tradition as Dictated in Onondaga by John Arthur Gibson. Winnipeg: University Press of Manitoba, 1992.

Worcester, Donald, ed. *Forked Tongues and Broken Treaties.* Caldwell, ID: Caxton, 1975.

Wright, J. Leitch. *The Only Land They Knew: The Tragic Story of the American Indians in the Old South.* New York: Free Press, 1981.

Wright, Ronald. *Stolen Continents: The Americas through Indian Eyes since 1492.* Boston: Houghton Mifflin, 1992.

Wunder, John R. *"Retained by the People": A History of American Indians and the Bill of Rights.* New York: Oxford University Press, 1994.

Wunder, John R., series editor. *Native Americans and the Law: Contemporary and Historical Perspectives on American Indian Rights, Freedoms, and Sovereignty.* New York: Garland Publishing, 1996.

Vol. 1: *Native American Law and Colonialism, before 1776 to 1903.*

Vol. 2: *Constitutionalism and Native Americans, 1903–1968.*

Vol. 3: *The Indian Bill of Rights, 1968.*

Vol. 4: *Recent Legal Issues for American Indians, 1968 to the Present.*

Vol. 5: *Native American Cultural and Religious Freedoms.*

Vol. 6: *Native American Sovereignty.*

Index

About the Editor and Contributors

RUSSEL LAWRENCE BARSH is associate professor of Native American Studies at the University of Lethbridge, Alberta.

TIMOTHY BRAATZ is a doctoral candidate in history at Arizona State University.

BRUCE A. BURTON was professor of English literature at Castleton State College, where he taught writing, poetry, the novel, Greek tragic drama, and native studies for twenty-six years.

DUANE CHAMPAGNE is associate professor of sociology and director of the American Indian Studies Center at the University of California, Los Angeles.

CHARLES RILEY CLOUD is a member of the Cherokee Nation of Oklahoma with the mixed blood of the Cherokee, Scotch, and Irish. He is the first and only member of a federally recognized Indian tribe to serve as a state judge in Virginia.

DONALD A. GRINDE, JR., is professor of history and director of ethnic studies at the University of Vermont.

BRUCE E. JOHANSEN is Robert T. Reilly Professor of Communication and Native American Studies at the University of Nebraska at Omaha.

He is the author/editor of numerous books including *Native American Political Systems and The Evolution of Democracy: An Annotated Bibliography* (Greenwood, 1996).

BARBARA A. MANN is a doctoral candidate in English at the University of Toledo.

JOE B. MARSHALL is a Mi'kmaw (Micmaq) elder and president of the Union of Nova Scotia Indians.

FRANK POMMERSHEIM is professor of law at the University of South Dakota.

DALE STOVER is professor of philosophy and religion at the University of Nebraska at Omaha.

JERRY STUBBEN is an associate professor in the Center for Family Research in Rural Mental Health, Iowa State University, Ames.

MICHAEL L. TATE is professor of history at the University of Nebraska at Omaha.

ISBN 0-313-30167-0

9 780313 301674

HARDCOVER BAR CODE